Comparative Kadai

The Tai Branch

**Summer Institute of Linguistics and
The University of Texas at Arlington
Publications in Linguistics**

Publication 124

Publications in Linguistics is a series published jointly by the Summer Institute of Linguistics and the University of Texas at Arlington. The series is a venue for works covering a broad range of topics in linguistics, especially the analytical treatment of minority languages from all parts of the world. While most volumes are authored by members of the Institute, suitable works by others will also form part of the series.

Series Editor

Donald A. Burquest
University of Texas at Arlington

Volume Editor

Mary Huttar

Production Staff

Laurie Nelson, Managing Editor
Karoline Fisher, Compositor
Hazel Shorey, Graphics Arts

Comparative Kadai

The Tai Branch

Jerold A. Edmondson
and
David B. Solnit
Editors

A Publication of
The Summer Institute of Linguistics
and
The University of Texas at Arlington
1997

© 1997 by the Summer Institute of Linguistics, Inc.
Library of Congress Catalog No: 96-60289
ISBN: 1-55671-005-4
ISSN: 1040-0850

Printed in the United States of America
All Rights Reserved

No part of this publication may be reproduced, stored in a retrieval system, or transmitted in any form or by any means—electronic, mechanical, photocopy, recording, or otherwise—without the express permission of the Summer Institute of Linguistics, with the exception of brief excerpts in journal articles or reviews.

Copies of this and other publications of the Summer Institute of Linguistics may be obtained from

International Academic Bookstore
Summer Institute of Linguistics
7500 W. Camp Wisdom Rd.
Dallas, TX 75236-5699

Voice: 972-708-7404
Fax: 972-708-7433
Email: academic_books@sil.org
Internet: http://www.sil.org

Contents

Introduction 1
  Jerold A. Edmondson and David B. Solnit

Maps 27

I. Zhuang

The Tonal Cylinder in Sanfang Zhuang 35
  Wei Feng and Jerold A. Edmondson

The Interaction between Zhuang and the Yue (Cantonese)
Dialects 57
  Huang Yuanwei

Regional Variants and Vernaculars in Zhuang 77
  Zhang Yuansheng and Wei Xingyun

Village Names in Guangxi Province and Northeastern Thailand 97
  Pranee Kullavanijaya

Wuming Zhuang Tone Sandhi: A Phonological, Syntactic,
and Lexical Investigation 107
  Wil C. Snyder and Lu Tianqiao

II. Other Northern Tai

Front /a/ and Back /ɑ/ in Biandan Mountain Bouyei 141
Ni Dabai

The Sound System of the Bouyei Language and Its
Special Features 147
Wang Wei

Linguistic Prediction: The Case of Saek 161
Paul K. Benedict

III. Central Tai

Implications of the Retention of Proto-Voiced Plosives and
Fricatives in the Dai Tho Language of Yunnan Province for a
Theory of Tonal Development and Tai Language Classification 191
Theraphan L-Thongkum

The Sound System of the Tày language of Cao Bằng
Province, Vietnam 221
Hoàng Văn Ma

IV. Southwestern Tai Languages and General Tai

A Preliminary Examination of Tay Tac 235
by Jean Donaldson and Jerold A. Edmondson

'Near' and 'Far' in Tai 267
William J. Gedney

Tai-Kadai Arthropods: A Preliminary Biolinguistic Investigation 291
James R. Chamberlain

The Emergence of the Length Distinction in the Mid-front
Vowels *e-ee* in Thai 327
Puttachart Dhananjayananda

Comparative Shan 337
Jerold A. Edmondson and David B. Solnit

Cited Forms Index 361
Authors, Languages, and Subjects 375

Introduction

Jerold A. Edmondson and David B. Solnit

The Tai Branch. The Tai languages of East and Southeast Asia are found as far north as Guizhou Province in China and extend more than half way down the Malay Peninsula. In the west there are remnants of Shan settlers from Myanmar (formerly Burma) still found in Assam and the surrounding areas of India. In the east some Zhuang remain in Lianshan Zhuang-Yao Autonomous County, Guangdong Province of southern China, which, according to Chinese historians may have been the *Urheimat* of the Tai. The most numerous group of Tai speakers, of course, are the Thai of Thailand with a population of 55 million (Hoffman 1992). After that follow the Zhuang of Guangxi and Yunnan Provinces in China with 15 million, the Shan of Myanmar with 2.8 million (Hoffman 1992), the Bouyei of Guizhou Province in China, Vietnam, and Laos with 2.5 million, the Lao and Tai tribal groups of Laos with 2.1 million (Lao Peoples Democratic Republic Populations), the Tày (formerly known as Thổ) and Nùng of northern Vietnam with 1.9 million (Vietnam statistics), the Thái Dam and Thái Don (Black and White Tai) of northwestern Vietnam and China with about 1.1 million, and the Khamti and others living in Myanmar, Assam, and nearby areas of India. The total number of Tai speakers is greater than 80 million.

The majority of linguistic work done on Tai has focused on Thai. The Thai language is taught at many universities and institutions around the world. It can also be understood by many in Southeast Asia outside of Thailand. The economy of Thailand is characterized as 'fast rising' and 'an emerging market'. This prosperity as well as mere geography have brought a large number of other languages and cultures of Southeast Asia to its midst. Moreover, this part of the world has been a major theater of political and military activity this century, which has also contributed to greater ethnic and linguistic diversity.

Kadai and Tai-Kadai. We have entitled this book *Comparative Kadai: The Tai Branch*; this name obliges us to justify such a choice: what is Kadai and how is Tai a branch of it. In *Comparative Kadai: Linguistic Studies beyond Tai* (1988), we suggested that the genetic relationship among Thai and its relatives looks as follows:

(1) The Kadai hypothesis

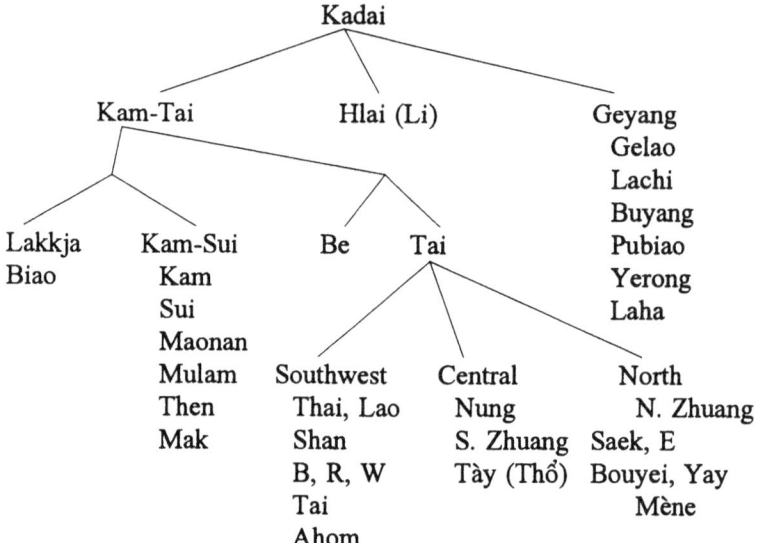

This proposal resembles closely that found in Paul K. Benedict's *Austro-Thai: Language and Culture* (1975). Geyang, a group including Gelao, Lachi, Buyang, Pubiao, and Yerong, is proposed by Liang Min (1990) based largely on cognate percentages. We use it here provisionally as a cover term for these lesser-known outlier languages (see also comments immediately below). In *Linguistic Studies beyond Tai* we wanted, among other things, to examine the place of some of the smaller languages, Lakkja and Be, in the grand scheme of the stock. David Solnit's paper argued that Lakkja lies outside of Kam-Sui and Mark Hansell's paper suggested that Be must be

Introduction 3

regarded as outside of Tai but closer to it than to Kam-Sui (KS) or others. It turned out that it was not these matters that were the center of interest. The controversial aspects in the Kadai Hypothesis of (1) above, as we found out, were our placing Tai and Kam-Sui in a subgroup and our refusal to place the outliers Hlai, Gelao, Lachi, in a similar subgroup. A tripartite or possibly quadripartite division of the stock is the position of those using the name Tai-Kadai, where Kadai presumably refers to the outliers just referred to. A variant of this view, expressed by Chamberlain (this volume), can be represented as follows:

(2)   The Tai-Kadai Hypothesis

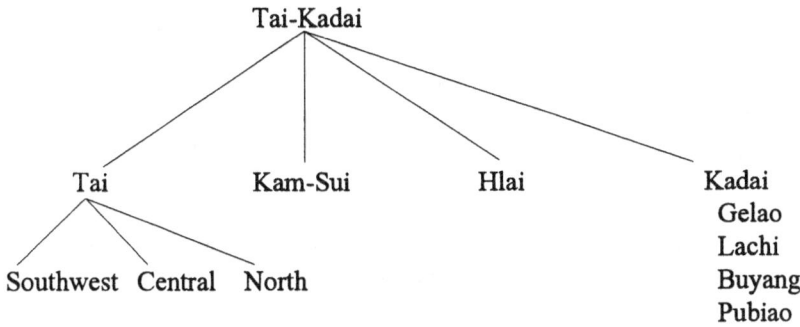

As is evident by the names of some of our contributions, this issue is as yet unresolved. As a result, some of the papers gathered here refer to the family as Tai-Kadai and others as Kadai. This issue will probably require more information and much more discussion before one of the two hypotheses sketched above wins general acceptance. We, nevertheless, would like at this point to mention some recent work that argues for the Kadai view in (1), namely Liang's 1990 study referred to above.

Liang investigates basic vocabulary items from Gelao, Pubiao, Buyang, and Lachi and compares them to that of Zhuang (Tai), Kam (KS), Hlai, and Miao (just to prove Geyang languages are not in the Miao-Yao stock).[1] Since he neither states his criteria for cognacy nor identifies which words in his lists are considered cognate, his findings must be considered provisional. His method also does not provide a means of separating true cognates from loanwords. Nevertheless, we find his results noteworthy, especially since

---

[1] The locations used for comparison are as follows: Zhuang (Wuming), Kam (Rongjiang), Tai Lɯ (Sipsong Panna), Miao (Guizhou Bijie), Yao (Guangxi Longsheng), Gelao (Guizhou Anshun, Guangxi Sanchong, Guangxi Moji), Lachi (Yunnan Maguan), Pubiao (Yunnan Malipo), Buyang (Yunnan Funing), Hlai (Hainan Baoding).

they concentrate on these small and until now understudied languages. Liang states that his Geyang group shares about 25% cognates equally with both Zhuang and Kam; there are about 8–10% cognates or closely related forms with Miao; and there are about 32–40% shared cognates among the Geyang group. Interestingly, within Gelao itself he found only about 54% common roots, even though the Gelao have stories and legends that allow us to regard them as a single group. We may infer that Gelao has been cloven into small groups of speakers isolated from their brethren at other locations and that isolation has promoted diversity. Liang also notices that Geyang languages have their own numeral systems and states that they have split their tones in ways unlike that in Kam-Tai languages.

As for Hlai (Li), Liang finds its genetic links to be no closer to Geyang than to Kam-Tai. In his statistics, Hlai shares about 25% in common with Geyang, about 30% in common with Zhuang, and about 25% cognates with Kam. He also remarks on its possessing its own numeral system and principles of tone splitting. Moving on to Tai, Liang rates the vocabulary shared by Zhuang of Wuming in Guangxi (Northern Tai) and the Dai (Tai Lɯ) of Sipsong Panna, Yunnan Province (Southwestern Tai), at the level of 64%. In other studies of Southwestern Tai, Luo Meizhen (1988) and Fan (1993) conclude that Central Thai (Siamese) of Thailand, though today geographically distant, is rated closer to Zhuang and Kam than it is to Hlai or Gelao. One way of interpreting these statistics is as follows: Kam-Sui and the Tai branch spent a longer time together and divided later. Hlai and Geyang left the parent language at an earlier date, but these two groups did not necessarily leave at the same time. Hlai may have diverged from the others early, at the time speakers of this language left for Hainan Island. An early but gradual separation would account for it sharing slightly more with Zhuang than with Kam. The Geyang group separated from Kam-Tai later but preserved many features of the parent language lost by all others.

Nomen est omen. As we stated above, there remains considerable controversy as to how many of these sisters and cousins of the Thai are really a part of the family. One of the reasons for the lack of clarity has been the autonyms used by the various Tai groups. Over the course of history there has been a waxing and waning in the focus on linguistic unity versus linguistic divergence in regard to names. As a result, there is a pattern of some COMMON FEATURES as well as CONSIDERABLE DIVERSITY running through the self-designations of these peoples.

One example of a pattern is the term 獠 *Liao* or *Lao*, common to many groups in China and Southeast Asia, for example the Gelao, Lao, Mulao, and Tulao. *Liao* itself apparently stems from the name of an ancient people, the Luo Yue or Western Yue 骆越, said by Chinese historians to be the precursors of the Tai and related groups in the period about 500 B.C.[2] For instance, Zhang Yinliang says the Liao and the Luoyue are the same people. There are many kinds of Liao (more than nine); each division took its name from the location where they lived, e.g., Dong Liao (Eastern Liao) and Shan Liao (Mountain Liao).

As for the designation *T(h)ai*, according to Dodd (1923), it is attested historically only quite late. Dodd and other older sources further interpret the term as meaning 'the freed', and link it with theory of the Nanzhao kingdom as a point of origin for all or many Tai movements. The breakup of Nanzhao in A.D. 1253 would then lend itself to a scenario of an emancipated population moving south and dubbing itself 'free'. However Nanzhao is not now considered to have been primarily Tai (cf. Luce 1985:100)—although it may well have been a multiethnic state including a Tai component—and the current consensus is that the point of dispersal for the Southwestern Tai at least is to be sought farther east, in the China-Vietnam border region (Gedney 1965, Chamberlain 1975, Fan 1993). Moreover, Condominas (1980) suggests that the term *T(h)ai* began as a self-designation and only later acquired the connotation of free, citing a parallel evolution in the etymon *franc* (Frank (n.), frank (adj.), franchise, etc.) Another view is that of Enriques (1933:71) who says facilely that T(h)ai is the Chinese Tai 太 or Da 大 meaning 'the great'.

An example of a fractional name is Nùng/Nong of the Zhuang/Nùng on the Sino-Vietnam borderlands, of whom it is said that they chose the family name of a defeated rebel hero, the famous and infamous Nong Zhigao, 農智高 as their group designation. In still another account of the name Nùng, W. Eberhard (1942a:187) points out that *nung* is the word 'I' (and we would add sometimes also 'you' or 'they') in the language of the Wu and Ou (Yue), suggesting a possible linkage to a location in the northeast of Yue territory near Shanghai and the territory around the mouth of the Yangtze. Beyond these are the names taken from the words or classifiers for person or people: *pu, k(h)un,* or *jai*, which often enter into designations such as, for example, Puthai, Puyai (Bouyei), and Khunthai.

---

[2]For *luo* 駱 Karlgren (1957:203) GSR766s gives Old/Middle Chinese forms *glâk/lâk* respectively. The character 獠 *Liao* is *liog/lieu* in Old and Middle Chinese GSR 1151n.

The Chinese character 駱 means, according to Karlgren, 'white horse with black mane' and therefore is probably an attempt in this compound to record the sound of a non-Chinese word with a similar sounding Chinese character. While much work in the field of the ethnic groups of ancient south China is yet to be done, lak^{10} is a common way of referring to one's own ethnic group even today, i.e., the Kam call themselves lak^{10} nin^2 $kəm^1$ literally 'the offspring or sons of the Kam'. lak^{10} is cognate with Siamese $luuk^{D4}$ 'son, child'.

Another term, the etymon represented by *Siam, Shan, Assam, Ahom*, has been associated historically with groups on the southern and western edges of the Tai-speaking world, usually as a name given by outsiders to Tai-speakers. The term first appears as <syām> in an inscription of Champa dated A.D. 1050 (Luce 1958), and in Myanmar in Pagan inscriptions in the year A.D. 1120 (Luce 1958, 1985:100). Of similar date is Khmer <syām> in a caption to an Angkor Wat relief.[3] The same etymon is assumed to be also represented in the names Assam and Ahom. One of the problems in the names of these groups is that names are often 'recycled' or used again when the original significance has been lost and this property leads to a rich inventory of folk etymologies. For example, some have stated that the term *Shan* comes from the Chinese 山 *shan* 'mountain' meaning 'mountain people', (Pfannmüller and Klein 1982:126). But, the Chinese character representing the Shan 撣 is read [ṣan⁴ tan³] today.

The kinship between the designations *Shan* for the Tai of Myanmar and *Siam* for the Tai of modern Thailand was noticed by older authors such as Grierson (1928) and Enriques: "The word *Siam* is indeed only another form of *Shan*." (Enriques 1933:70). The Burmese spelling ရှမ်း can be transliterated as <hram:>, with a modern pronunciation /hyan/. In this transcription of modern Burmese, /-n/ represents a feature of nasalization, which may be realized as nasalization of the vowel, or as a nasal consonant homorganic with a following consonant. Hence the English *Shan*. The graphic unit ရှ is ရ <r> with the subscribed hook ္ , indicating voicelessness. We may presume that a voiceless nonlateral liquid was the closest Burmese equivalent to a voiceless palatal or retroflex fricative, so the Burmese spelling would have been an attempt at representing a non-Burmese syllable of the form [çam], [ʃam], or [ṣam]. As for the history of the designation *Siam*, opinion remains divided; some say it should be pronounced [siyam] 'Western hills', whereas others say its meaning is obscure (Carthew 1952). Terrien de Lacouperie (1885:1) opines:

> As to the racial name which underlies the cognate appellatives of Shan and Siam, we have no hesitation whatever in dismissing, as inadequate to the exigencies of the case, the proposed etymology of *Siam* from the Sanscrit *çyâma*, "brown, or dark." The name is certainly older than this supposed origin would permit; and from its various appearances in the earlier seats of the race, where Sanscrit influences were not in activity, we cannot resist the conclusion that it is contemporaneous with the race itself. I am not indisposed to say that the *Shang* [Dynasty] (i.e., traders) who overthrew the Hia [Xia]

---

[3]Angkor Wat was built during the reign of Suryavarman II, 1113–?1150 according to Coedès (1962).

Introduction 7

dynasty and give their name to the following one, were connected with the Shan race, and that their very name (or a form of it) is perhaps the antecedent of that of Shan or Siam.

Terrien's equation of the *Shang* 商 of the Shang Dynasty (sixteenth to eleventh centuries B.C.) with *Siam* is hardly tenable, in view of the discrepancy between the final ŋ of Shang and the final m of Siam. He may be correct, however, in the pronouncement that Siam/Shan is an older designation than indicated by the previously mentioned inscriptions from Southeast Asia. There may be some relation to the state called *Dan* 撣 in the *Xinan Yizhuan [Account of the Southwestern Yi]* section of the *Hou Hanshu [Book of the Later Han]* (A.D. 25–220). This character had various readings [tan dan dzan źan], all with *shang* tone in Middle Chinese; it also occurs in the *Shuowen* with the reading *tan*, and the gloss *tí chí* 'lift'. Again the final consonant fails to correspond. The *Cihai* defines it either as Thailand (presumably the modern state) or as the name of an ethnicity *(zhongzu)*, with the *Hanshu* cited for the latter meaning. We do not know how far back the identification of 撣 with Tai-speaking groups can be dated. Certainly its association with the Burmese/English form *shan* cannot predate the loss in spoken Burmese of final nasal contrasts, which can be no earlier than the oldest Burmese inscriptions (A.D. 1112 according to Bradley 1978).

Kadai traits. We now undertake the task of listing some of the traits that can be used to divide the Kadai languages as shown above. Common Kadai traits include (1) Every syllable possesses a tone, there is relatively little change of tone (sandhi) in context; (2) Clusters of stop (oral and nasal) plus liquid must be assumed for the proto language; (3) Modifiers are postposed, and clause structure is verb-medial; (4) Morphemes are largely monosyllabic; (5) A common core vocabulary can be described, for example:

(3)		Gelao1	Gelao2	Hlai	Kam	Zhuang	Thai
'pig'		m̥au↓	mau˩	pou˥	ŋu$^{5'}$	mou^1	mu$^{1'}$
'bird'		m̩˧naŋ√	ma√no↙	tat˩	nok^8	nok^8	nok^8
'blood'		pla˥	pla↙	ta:t˩	pha:t$^{9'}$	lɯːt^9	lɯət^9
'intestine'		sai˧	ta˩se˥	ra:i↙	sa:i$^{3'}$	sa:i^3	sai^3
'rain'		n̩√mən√	mæ√	fun˥	pjən^1	fun^1	fon$^{1'}$
'teeth'		m̩˧pje√	pjan√	fan˥	pjan^1	fen^1	fan^1
'dream'		——	la˩pjan√	fan˥	pjan^1	phan^1	fan$^{1'}$

Here Gelao 1 and 2 represent the vernaculars of Sanchong and Moji Gelao both found in Longlin Various Nationalities Autonomous County, Guangxi

Province, (from Edmondson's field notes) and the remainder from Wang (1984). Notice especially the last pair of words for 'teeth' and 'dream'. These two roots are virtually homophonous from Gelao to Thai, differing only very slightly, and must have been very similar all the way back to the proto-language. The invariable regularity among these and similar examples of core vocabulary constitutes very strong evidence of genetic relation.

It is also not difficult to demonstrate a common heritage between Tai and Kam-Sui that is closer than that between Hlai or Geyang. One obvious area of common vocabulary concerns wet paddy rice farming terminology.

(4)

	Thai	Zhuang	Bouyei	Dai	Kam
'rice plant'	$khau^3$	hau^4	hau^4	xau^3	$qəu^4$
'rice sdlng'	kla^3	kja^3	$tɕa^3$	ka^3	ka^3
'rice strw'	$faaŋ^2$	$fɯːŋ^2$	$fɯːŋ^2$	$fəŋ^2$	$paŋ^1$
'plow'	$thai^{1'}$	$kwai^1$	$ɕai^1$	$thai^1$	$khəi^{1'}$
'c pole'	$khaan^2$	$haːn^2$	$haːn^2$	$kaːn^2$	$laːn^2$
'rice mortar'	———	rum^1	zum^1	$kəm^1$	$kəm^1$
'w buf'	$khwaːi^2$	$vaːi^2$	$vaːi^2$	$xvaːi^2$	kwe^2

	Mulam	Sui	Lakkja	Gelao	Hlai
'rice plant'	hu^3	$ʔau^4$	kou^3	$moŋ^ɣ$	$muːn^3$
'rice sdlg'	kra^3	ka^3	$kjie^3$	———	fan^1
'rice strw'	$m̥aːŋ^1$	$waːŋ^1$	$waːŋ^2$	———	$ɲiŋ^3$
'plow'	$khrai^1$	$kwai^1$	lai^2	$ndav$	$ɬei^6$
'c pole'	$qhaːn^1$	$ʁaːn^1$	$ʔaːn^2$	———	$tshai^1fia^{?7}$
'r mortar'	$kəm^1$	$kəm^1$	$kjuən^3$	———	———
'w buf'	hwi^2	$kɯ^2$	sui^3nou^2	$ntai\text{?}lu\text{?}$	tui^3

Note especially the first two, the most basic terms, showing the cleavage between Gelao-Hlai and all others.

Features of Tai versus Kam-Sui. What then are some of the distinctive features of Tai as opposed to Kam-Sui? These fall basically into two groups, phonological structure and lexical structure. The phonological differences between Tai and Kam-Sui are as follows:
  1. Kam-Sui largely lacks the back nonrounded vowels /ɯ ɤ/ so common in Tai. /ɯ/ occurs only in Maonan (e.g., $hɯ^1$ 'embankment'). A vowel transcribed /ə/ is slightly more common in Kam-Sui but is generally limited to closed syllables and Chinese borrowings (except in Mulam).

Introduction

2. There is a class of forms that originally come from dyadic roots (those that may once have consisted of two syllables), in which Kam-Sui tends generally to weaken the medial consonant to form a cluster with appropriate consequences on tonal development; often the cluster degrades in secondary development to a palatalized consonant /pj mj kj/. Tai languages tend by contrast to truncate the first syllable, sometimes preserving traces of the original in the tonal developments, e.g., 'blood' Kam $ph(j)a:t^{D1L}$ versus Thai $lu:t^{D1L}$; 'wine' Kam $khwa:u^{C1}$ versus Thai $la:u^{C1}$; 'dog' Lakkja $khwɔ^{A1}$ versus Thai ma^{A1}. There are other forms that work differently, as in (5).

(5)   moon   Tai *bluan   KS ɲaan
      flower   Tai *blook   KS nuk
      eye   Tai *pra (FKL *tra)   KS *thla (Thurgood 1988:179–218)

In this type, Tai preserves a labial-liquid cluster which in Kam-Sui has undergone various degrees of assimilation.

3. Kam-Sui has tone splitting that follows the voiced-low principle to the letter. Northern Tai languages generally do as well, but Central and Southwestern Tai evidence a wide range of developments other than voiced-low. Moreover, there is a consistent difference in three-way splitting: in those languages with evidence of tripartition, Tai always puts glottalized initials in the 'mid' category (whether middle phonetically or structurally), usually joined by voiceless unaspirated obstruents. Kam-Sui languages without exception assign aspirates (including voiceless sonorants) to the mid category.

4. Although dead syllables (with final stops) differ from live syllables (with final sonorants)[4] in tonal development, the pitch shapes of dead-syllable tones can nearly always be equated with the pitch shapes of some subset of live-syllable tones. In Kam-Sui these equations are generally A=DS and C=DL; whereas in Tai B=DL or C=DL are common, and reflexes of proto-tone A seldom enter the picture.

5. There is systematic variation of diphthong and monophthong (e.g., ai ~ i, the 'Gedney puzzle' phenomenon also found between Northern Tai and Southwestern-Central Tai) between Tai and Kam-Sui, as in fai^{A2} versus fi^{A1} 'fire' (cf. Strecker 1988).

6. There are a number of diagnostic vocabulary items or tone categories. Some items are cognate but differ in proto-tone. For example, 'pig' and 'dog' in Kam-Sui are in B1 and A1 respectively, whereas in Tai and Geyang they are both in the same category; 'rat' is C1 in Kam-Sui but

---

[4]The terms are from traditional Siamese grammar.

A1 in Tai. For further examples of these and the following type see Li (1965). Other items are unrelated morphemes in the two groups; 'ricefield' in Kam-Sui is ja^{B1}, whereas in Tai it is na^{A2}; 'tongue' in Kam-Sui is ma^{A2}, whereas in Tai it is lin^{A2}, using Siamese to represent Tai and Kam to represent Kam-Sui.

The divisions of Tai. There are basically two positions on the question of the divisions within Tai, the tripartite division espoused by Li Fang-Kuei (1977) and the two plus one taxonomy of Haudricourt (1956).

Li Fang-Kuei, on the basis of vocabulary and phonology, decided that there were three divisions in Tai and that presumably they were about equal distance apart. These he called Northern (NT), Central (CT), and Southwestern (SWT). In the area of phonology, he noted that NT fails to have a stable aspiration contrast in its sound system, whereas CT and SWT possess this feature. NT also fails to have the tightness of voice in the C (or sometimes B) tone category found in CT and SWT, even though this distinction has almost disappeared in Bangkok Thai. CT has characteristic reflexes of certain proto-Tai clusters, such as *thr and *tr with many CT languages showing /th/ or /h/.

Some diagnostic vocabulary items seem to be found in only one of Li's three subgroups. These include:

(6)   Sanfang (NT) Bo-ai (NT)   Longzhou (CT) Siamese (SWT)

'tiger'	kuk^{55}	kuk^{DIS}	(tii^{C1})	(sia^{C1})
'cloudy'	———	(pum^{A2})	$kham^{A1}$	$(kham^{B2})$
'mat. y. brother'	(na^{C2})	(na^{C2})	$khau^{C1}$	(na^{C2})
'cold'	———	(nit^{DIS})	$(da:\eta^{C1})$	$naau^{A1}$

Li, however, cites vocabulary items shared by all three possible pairings, including NT and SWT to the exclusion of CT. These patterns he takes to be evidence of the equal status of the three divisions. Especially significant in this connection are items shared by NT and SWT to the exclusion of CT, such as the following:

(7)   Bo-ai (NT)   Longzhou (CT)   Siamese (SWT)

	Bo-ai (NT)	Longzhou (CT)	Siamese (SWT)
'knife'	mit^{D2}	$(pja?^{C2})$	$miit^{D2}$
'to warn'	$tiin^{A1}$	——	$tuan^{A1}$
'road'	$hɔn^{A1}$	(lo^{B2})	$hɔn^{A1}$

(Longzhou forms from Li 1940)

Haudricourt and others see a greater divide between SWT and CT on one hand, and NT (sometimes called Dioi or Yai in this context) on the other (see Haudricourt 1948, 1956).

Here we should remark on how this linguistic classification corresponds to the ethnolinguistic classification presently official in China. The overall division follows political boundaries for the most part; thus Dai in Yunnan, Bouyei in Guizhou, and Zhuang in Guangxi with some extension into Yunnan. As it happens, the languages of the Dai nationality are almost exclusively SWT, but things are less simple in the other two provinces. Zhuang of Guangxi includes both NT and CT languages, this distinction being recognized in the form of a divide between northern (NT) and southern (CT) dialects *(fangyan)* of the Zhuang language (Zhuangyu). Bouyei of Guizhou is largely NT, although the Western division of Bouyei exhibits unusual features, some of which resemble CT (see Wang's article in this volume).

As for subgrouping within the branches, Li (1957) remarks on divisions within NT. Currently Chinese linguists recognize seven divisions within Northern Zhuang (cf. Edmondson 1993) and three within Bouyei.

In SWT, Chamberlain (1975) has extended Gedney's landmarks of genetic affiliation in the form of a hierarchy, (1) p/ph; (2) tone *A column split/merger pattern; (3) tone *BCD columns split/merger patterns; and (4) B-DL coalescence.

(8) Hierarchy of historical features of Southwestern Tai

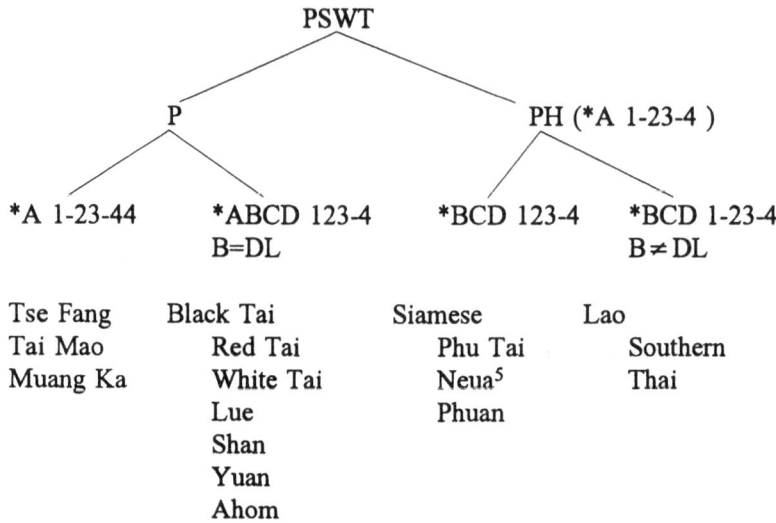

Tse Fang	Black Tai	Siamese	Lao
Tai Mao	Red Tai	Phu Tai	Southern
Muang Ka	White Tai	Neua[5]	Thai
	Lue	Phuan	
	Shan		
	Yuan		
	Ahom		

For the notations ABCD 1234 see the discussion below. Subgrouping proposals have also been made by Li (1977:49) and Brown (1975) for that portion of SWT represented in Thailand and Laos (but excluding Black/White/Red Tai). Li's proposal is based on patterns of tone split and merger; Brown does not state the rationale behind his detailed *Stammbaum*, but one could probably be extracted from his extensive charts and formulae.

A brief history of comparative historical studies of the Tai Branch

In the past it has generally been assumed that Tai is a part of a grand Sino-Tibetan family. The support for that idea comes from some obvious similarity found between Chinese and Thai: monosyllabicity, tones, similar syntax and construction, and shared vocabulary (possibly loaned).

The history of the Tai people is a complex and controversial affair. Nearly all authorities agree that the Tai *Urheimat* lies in southern China. In a recent paper Vallibhotama (1993) has suggested that there were two migrations from Guangxi to Southeast Asia; one from the coastal area and later a second migration from the inland areas of Guangxi. The more traditional view (as portrayed in, e.g., de Beauclair 1986:482, but see also Fan 1993) has it that

---

[5]Chamberlain's placement of Neua in the PH branch in this chart is probably an error, since Neua is a P language, as he states in the text on the same page.

Introduction 13

three groups among the Tai diverged. They first followed the course of the Xijiang (West River) through Guangxi into Northeast Vietnam becoming the Zhuang, Tày, and the Nùng. A second turned to the west first contacting the Yi 彝 (formerly called Lolo) and then veering south along the course of the Red River into Vietnam to become the White/Black/Red Thai. And finally, a third group went furthest west or was settled early in Yunnan and then advanced into upper Burma and then south along the rivers into northern Thailand. This view accounts for the current locations of the Central and Southwestern groups; presumably those who stayed behind in south-central China became the Northern Tai.

Chamberlain (1975) has argued that the location of the Tai peoples before descending into Southeast Asia was in Cao Bằng Province of northern Vietnam near the ancient city of Ba Thục (reputedly just to the north of today's Cao Bằng City) "[a] hotbed of military and political upheavals in the eighth century which we suggest may have been the instigating factor in the westward and southwestward migrations" (Chamberlain 1975:60).

We would like to point out that speaking of 'Tai peoples' and 'their history' glosses over several important distinctions: those between language, culture, and biological descent (Vallibhotama 1993). If we can ascertain that speakers of Tai languages entered what is now Thailand in, say, the 11th century A.D., that is certainly an important and useful finding. But if one's goal is to understand the history and culture of Thailand, one would certainly not wish to stop with the linguistic history. It is the interaction between these Tai speakers and the Mon, Khmer, Lawa, and other cultures that held sway in the area at the time of the Tai arrival that began the process resulting in the modern Thai nationality and culture. In another area, Condominas (1980) has explored ways in which Tai immigrants into Southeast Asia have incorporated indigenous people (and so presumably their cultural and linguistic influence) into their social system.

Probably the first modern linguistic treatment of Tai as a genetic linguistic group is found in the works of Henri Maspero. In 1911 he described regular correspondences among Siamese, Ahom, Shan, Black Tai, White Tai, Thô, and Dioi. In the following year, in the course of a historical study of Vietnamese, he concluded that Tai and Vietnamese were genetically related, largely because of their shared tonal system (Maspero 1912).

Lunet de Lajonquière (1906) also has much valuable information about the locations, customs, practices, and languages of the Tai groups in northern Vietnam at the turn of the century. He also provides word lists in Quốc Ngữ script.

Another early survey of Tai that may be called comparative, if only in the form of a travelogue, was that of William Clifton Dodd (1923), an early American missionary to northern Thailand and Laos. Dodd wandered over much of Southeast Burma, Thailand, Laos, Southern China, and Vietnam remarking on the cultural and linguistic state of the peoples he encountered. He distinguished the literate and nonliterate Tai, a grouping that includes the Thai, Lao, Shan, and Dai of Yunnan as opposed to the Zhuang, Tày, and Nùng of Guangxi and Vietnam.

Somewhat later Wulff (1934), as part of a comparative study of Chinese and Tai, described the regular correspondences, including those of tone, holding in lexical items shared by the two language families. (These items may, of course, be interpreted either as evidence of genetic relation or of ancient contact.)

J. Marvin Brown (1965) used linguistic data to argue for a certain kind of linguistic prehistory. His 'Ancient Thai' is reconstructed on the basis of data entirely from languages of Thailand and Laos (including one displaced Shan village in Chiangrai Province of northern Thailand).

At the same time considerable fieldwork was being undertaken by Li Fang-Kuei. He worked on the Zhuang languages of southern China and confirmed a definite relation between them and the Thai. The pinnacle of this research was achieved in his *Handbook of Comparative Tai* (1977).

Also active from the 1940s onward has been André-Georges Haudricourt. His work has been especially significant in linking the data from the Tai groups of Vietnam and China into the overall picture of Tai studies.

Finally, there are the contributions of William J. Gedney of University of Michigan. Gedney is a consumate field worker and cautious investigator of a great many forms of Thai and Lao. He has also made significant investigations of several Tai groups in depth in Thailand and Laos (Saek) as well as Vietnam (Yay, Western Nung) and China (Lungming, Sz Lok). His voluminous data is now being made available in the series published by University of Michigan Center for South and Southeast Asian Studies.

As far as unexplored territory among Tai languages goes, it can be said that only in northern Vietnam are there languages which today remain relatively unstudied. Grierson (1928) gives a comprehensive introduction to the Tai languages of India and Burma, including Ahom, Shan, Khamti, Tairong, and Nora. Diller (1993) provides an update on this area. Lunet de Lajonquière (1906) describes the locations, customs, and practices of groups in Vietnam, but his language data is less satisfactory and there exists as yet no update to this research. Remarkable features in these two areas are: (1) SOV word order in some Khamti sentences thought to be the result of language contact with Tibeto-Burman speakers and (2) voiced stop initials in low tones in some kinds of Tày of Cao Bằng and Zhuang/Nung of Wenshan in China (see L-Thongkum as well as Hoàng, this volume). According to Professor Hoàng Văn Ma, Linguistics Institute, Social Sciences Institute of Vietnam, a Tày himself, the following Cao Bằng Province locations have voiced stop and voiced fricative reflexes of proto-Tai voiced stops and fricative consonants (Box 4 in a Gedney chart; see Wei and Edmondson, this volume): Trùng Khánh, Hòa An, Hà Quang, Thông Nông, Nguyễn Bính, Trà Lĩnh, Quàng Hòa, and Hạ Lang.

Notation of tones, initials, and finals

Tai studies have been confusing because of variations in the notation stemming from differences in the frame of reference used by different investigators. First, we address the question of the syllable-final semivowels. Gedney and others in what may be called the American tradition treat them as consonants and write them with consonantal symbols such as [-y -w -ɰ]. They point out that in Tai there are no possible syllable shapes aiC/auC/aɯC (where C stands for an arbitrary consonant). By assuming that -Vi/-Vu/-Vɯ are in fact phonologically -Vy/-Vw/-Vɰ, then no further apparatus is necessary; double consonant codas are simply forbidden as a syllable type in Tai. A second point is that in many Tai languages vowel length is contrastive only in syllables with codas, i.e., syllables ending in /m n ŋ p t k/ as well as the semivowels. Treating these semivowels as consonants allows us to state simply that length is contrastive in closed syllables but not in open syllables, which are always phonetically long[6]. It is perhaps also relevant that the Siamese script writes most final semivowels with consonant symbols.

F.-K. Li and other Chinese scholars, by contrast, use vocalic forms for the codas of diphthongs. So /-i -u -ɯ/ correspond to /-y -w -ɰ/.

A further complicating factor to consider is the Vietnamese script. Some of the Tai branch languages use the Quốc Ngữ script. For that reason long and short diphthongs are indicated by the orthographic sequences *-ai -ao* (long) and *-ay -au* (short). Authors notating Tai languages in Quốc Ngữ often make no mention of how closely the Tai sounds being written correspond to the Vietnamese sounds ordinarily written with the Quốc Ngữ script. This problem is perhaps most acute for tones, since it seems especially unlikely that all the Tai tones being notated really are phonetically identical in pitch and voice quality to the Vietnamese tones ordinarily notated with the same diacritics. Beyond that, there is the problem of transcribing *f* and *ph* in Quốc

---

[6]In Siamese and a few other SWT languages, syllables may be written with final short vowels, but they are always pronounced with final glottal stop. One may then choose either to regard the glottal stop as a phoneme, making these closed syllables; or to regard length as contrastive in all syllable types and analyze the glottal stop as an automatic consequence of short vowels in (underlyingly) open syllables. Note that virtually none of these words with orthographic final short vowels are inherited from proto-Tai; see Putthachart in this volume for some discussion of [e] in this regard.

Ngữ script. Since <ph> in Vietnamese is [f], then how is one to transcribe [ph]?

Notation of tones is perhaps the most vexing of these problems and not only in Quốc Ngữ. Tonal notation comes in two types, DIACRITIC and ALPHANUMERIC. Notations that are truly arbitrary in their designation of tones are not common, but one type that does qualify as arbitrary is the current official Zhuang orthography. This uses syllable-final letters to mark tones, e.g., *naz* /na^{31}/ 'ricefield'; *naj* /na^{55}/ 'face'. The same method has been used by various other romanizations for Hmong-Mien languages (see Purnell 1987 for details on some Mien Yao scripts).

Besides simply designating one member of the tonal inventory, the notation usually contains information of two kinds, phonetic and etymological. Nonarbitrary notations containing phonetic information include the two Chao methods, i.e., the tone letters (diacritic) and the 1-through-5 numeric notation. Diacritics like those used in the Haas Siamese transcription (*á* high, *à* low) may also be placed in this category although their representation of pitch contour is more impressionistic.

Notations containing etymological information must refer either explicitly or implicitly to the proto-Tai tones A B C D. Essentially all such systems use the four proto-Tai tones as horizontal coordinates on a grid, with the tone-splitting laryngeal features of initial consonants providing the vertical coordinates. There are, then, several variables effecting the actual system generated: the ordering given to the proto-tone categories, the degree of explicitness of reference to the proto-tones, and the degree of etymological transparency.

The ordering variable involves two decisions. First is a choice between the Chinese and the Thai traditions, which determines the relative ordering of the two categories called B and C in Tai and *shang* 'rising' and *qu* 'departing' in Chinese. There is no variation in the A and D categories, which are always ordered first and last respectively.

Thai scholars and those strongly influencing and influenced by this tradition, including both F.-K. Li and William J. Gedney, arrange tone categories as they are taught in traditional Thai textbooks and according to Thai dictionary order. That is, one begins with proto-tone A, which has no orthographic tone mark, and then examines those written with the diacritics *mai eek* 'primary mark' and *mai thoo* 'secondary mark', in that order. Note that this procedure is made possible by the fact that Thai orthography is highly etymological, essentially representing the pre-tone split phonological system.

Work by Chinese scholars and those focusing on the loan relationship between Thai and Chinese, such as Paul K. Benedict, use a system similar to that assumed for Middle Chinese and based on the regular correspon-

Introduction

dences between the Tai and the Middle Chinese tones, namely *shang* = *mai thoo*, *qu* = *mai eek*, in that order.

Having determined as it were the left-to-right order of the proto-tones, and having combined that notion with the tone-splitting features to generate a two-dimensional matrix, there is a subsidiary ordering variable, namely the choice of priority between verticality and horizontality in counting the boxes of the matrix. Chinese scholars and F.-K. Li agree in choosing vertical priority, meaning that the A boxes are counted first, top to bottom, then the B boxes, and so on:

(9) 1   3   5   7
     2   4   6   8

When vowel length conditions different reflexes of the D tone, Chinese scholars write 7 and 8 for the tones conditioned by short vowels, and 9 and 10 for those conditioned by long.

Gedney and many of his students choose horizontal priority, counting across the top first, then the bottom, although other considerations can and do alter this basic pattern.

(10) 1   2   3
     4   5   6

It may be noted that horizontal priority has been used occasionally by Chinese scholars as well, such as Fu et al. (1956) on Tai Lɯ.

Regarding the variable of degree of etymological transparency, firstly, notation may directly refer to the proto-tones, usually as A B C D (Egerod uses 0 1 2 in reflection of Siamese orthography). Here the first ordering variable wreaks havoc: the Siamese-based ordering used by Li, Gedney, and others corresponds to the Chinese-based ordering as follows:

(11) Siamese-based B = Chinese-based C
      Siamese-based C = Chinese-based B

Secondly, there is the matter of split and merger patterns. Li assumes that since voicing-conditioned tone splits are found in virtually all Tai dialects, any other tone-splitting conditioning is secondary (perhaps later chronologically, or perhaps in a more abstract sense). Voicing-conditioned splits may be referred to as the 'standard' type. He therefore uses A1, A2, B1, B2, etc., in which 1 indicates tones conditioned by nonvoiced initials and 2 indicates those conditioned by voiced (note that here the nonvoiced category includes the glottalized initials, whose glottalization feature was operant in conditioning tone splits even though they were also phonetically voiced). But when nonstandard splits and cross-proto-tone mergers are in evidence, this practice can obscure etymological information. For example, the modern Siamese falling tone is a merger of proto-Tai B tone as conditioned by voiced intials and proto-Tai C tone as conditioned by non-voiced initials. If our concern is simply to identify the tone, we can call it 3 in the Gedney system, and either 3 or 6 in the Chinese system. But if we want to indicate the etymological origin, we ought to call it B2-C1 or the like. For another example, the common NT pattern of splitting the C tone between voiceless initials on one hand versus glottalized and voiced on the other is, in Chinese sources, put as a change from tone 3 to 4 conditioned by voiced (glottalized) initials. Implicit in such a formulation is the view that the C tone first underwent a 'standard' split between voiced and non-voiced initials, and subsequently the glottalized members of the non-voiced category split off and merged tonally with the voiced category. But that is only one possible scenario.

The most explicit notation in current use is found in the publications of Chamberlain, who uses numerals 1234 for Gedney's four classes of proto-initials. 1 is voiceless friction sounds (voiceless aspirated obstruents, voiceless fricatives, voiceless sonorants), 2 is voiceless unaspirated obstruents, 3 is glottalized consonants, and 4 is voiced consonants. As an example, the Siamese falling tone in this notation is B4–C123; the two NT reflexes of the C tone are C12 and C34.

However, the search for full etymological transparency sooner or later encounters an obstacle. Although Gedney's 'spectrum' observation—that the same laryngeal features of consonants condition tones in a principled way in all Tai languages—is very largely true, it has exceptions. One such exception is represented by the Tho languages described by L-Thongkum (this volume), in which row 2 includes voiceless sonorants and fricatives as well as voiceless unaspirated obstruents, leaving only voiceless aspirated obstruents in row 1. A similar but not identical pattern is reported by Li (1977:49–50) for Tianbao in the same geographic area. This means that a 1234 notation cannot be universal.

Reconstructions. The initials, finals or vowels, and tones of the Tai protolanguage have been reconstructed with varying degrees of comprehensiveness by Li (1977), Haudricourt (1956), and by Sarawit (1973). In *Linguistic Studies beyond Tai* (1988) Thurgood proposes a reconstruction for KS. There are also general remarks about proto-Tai reconstruction in the introduction to that volume.

Introduction

The syllabic iron curtain. In remarks at the 25th anniversary meeting of the International Conference on Sino-Tibetan Languages and Linguistics (1992), Professor William J. Gedney used the metaphor of a syllabic curtain to express one of the central issues in comparative Tai studies. He said that Professor Li Fang-Kuei and he had for years assumed that the historical development of Tai could be accounted for solely in terms of single integral syllables with initial consonants, rhymes with nuclear vowel and possibly vocalic or consonant codas, and tones. Each syllable was separated from surrounding ones by means of a curtain of a type that hindered a syllable from influencing its neighbors. The structure of most words in contemporary languages throughout the Tai branch is, moreover, resolutely monosyllabic. He went on to say that some investigators such as Professor Paul K. Benedict had for years been slipping in front and behind this curtain at will. In Gedney's opinion most of the initials can be accounted for in terms of single syllables. But he noted that the rhymes and tones were a problem for those espousing the syllabic curtain in Tai.

Gedney was expressing the view that in the last few years more and more evidence has emerged to suggest that the curtain around Tai syllables is transparent to at least some historical processes. In fact, there is now considerable reason to believe that even the initial consonants cannot be accounted for solely in terms of syllables surrounded by sealed and opaque curtains.

The situation becomes even more difficult if one wishes to relate Tai to its sister branch Kam-Sui—as numerous articles in *Comparative Kadai: Linguistic Studies beyond Tai* (1988) demonstrated, and as suggested in Edmondson and Yang (1994), disyllabic forms seem inevitable. Consider for example, the word lup^7 'centipede' in Yongning, a location in southern Zhuang speaking territory. At most locations this word is $klup^7$ or $kjup^7$, which may indicate an original source $*kVlup$ (V= some unknown vowel).

Nonlinear processes in the history of Tai branch languages. Gedney's syllabic curtain and the growing sense of its inadequacy can be expressed in the contemporary idea that phonological analysis must be nonlinear. There are processes that are unaccommodated in a theory requiring sounds to be in a single line like beads on a string. Instead sounds interact as if some processes were on different planes (tiers) of phonological representation. There is considerable evidence emerging that such nonlinear processes have a role to play in historical comparative work just as in nondevelopmental accounts. Some of these nonlinear processes figure prominently in Benedict's (this volume) reconstruction, e.g., his 'vocalic transfer' and 'canonical reduction on the left (or right)'. In Benedict's view the tools need to fit the object; since the history of Kadai languages is extraordinarily tortuous and swampy, 'industrial strength' analytical techniques are in order.

Spelling conventions. We have endeavored to standardize the spelling of foreign words in this volume except as noted. Generally, Hanyu Pinyin is used for all transcription of Chinese.

Comparative Kadai: The Tai Branch contains examples of several types of comparison. There are worthy examples of reconstructive linguistics seeking the parent we glimpse only indistinctly in offspring languages (Gedney, Ni, Benedict); there are examples of onomastic comparisons in the domain of the living world and of social organization (Chamberlain, Kullavanijaya); and there are examples of description and placement of lesser known languages (Donaldson and Edmondson, Wei and Edmondson). There are examples of comparison of sounds over time and work on how these arose. Regrettably, Southwestern Tai is over represented and Central Tai under represented. Much is left to do, but we hope this work points in the right direction.

References

Bản Đô các dân tộc ở Việtnam. 1979. [Map of the ethnic groups of Vietnam].

Benedict, Paul K. 1975. Austro-Thai: Language and culture. New Haven: Human Relations Area Files Press.

———. 1989. KD clusters/dyads: PT *pl/*p-l/*phl. Kadai 1:10–14.

Bradley, David. 1978. Proto-Loloish. London: Curzon Press.

Brown, J. Marvin. 1965. From ancient Thai to modern dialects. Reprinted 1985 From ancient Tai to modern dialects and other writings on historical Thai linguistics. Bangkok: White Lotus Press.

———. 1975. The great tone split: Did it work in two opposite ways? In J. G. Harris and J. R. Chamberlain (eds.), Studies in Tai linguistics in honor of William J. Gedney, 33–48. Bangkok: Central Institute of English Language. Reprinted in From ancient Thai to modern dialects and other writings on historical Thai linguistics. Bangkok: White Lotus Co., Ltd.

Buyiyu Diaocha Baogao. 1958. [Field report on the Bouyei language.] Beijing: Kexue Chubanshe.

Các thành phần dân tộc Việtnam. 1983. [Ethnic groups of Vietnam (as recognized by the Bureau of Census of Vietnam)].

Carthew, M. 1952. The history of the Thai in Yunnan, 2205 B.C.–A.D. 1253 Journal of the Siam Society 40(1):1–38.

Chamberlain, James R. 1975. A new look at the history and classification of the Tai languages. In J. G. Harris and J. R. Chamberlain (eds.), Studies in Tai linguistics in honor of William J. Gedney, 49–66. Bangkok: Central Institute of English Language.

———. 1991. Tay Mène. Paper presented at the 24th ICSTLL, Bangkok and Chiangmai, Thailand.
Coedès, George. 1962. Les peuples de la peninsule Indochinoise. Paris: Dunod.
Condominas, Georges. 1980. L'espace social à propos de l'Asie du Sud-Est. Paris: Flammarion.
Day, Arthur Colin. 1966. The syntax of Thổ [Tày], a Tai language of Vietnam. Ph.D. dissertation. University of London.
De Beauclair, Inez. 1986. Ethnic groups of South China. In Ethnographic studies: The collected papers of Inez de Beauclair. Taipei: Southern Materials, Inc.
Diller, Anthony. 1993. Tai languages in Assam: Daughters or ghosts? In C. J. Compton and J. F. Hartmann (eds.), Papers on Tai languages, linguistics, and literatures, Occasional Paper 16, 5–43. De Kalb: Northern Illinois University Center for Southeast Asian Studies.
Dodd, William Clifton. 1923. The Tai race: Elder brother of the Chinese. Cedar Rapids, Iowa: The Torch Press.
Eberhard, Wolfram. 1942a. Kultur und Siedlung der Randvölker Chinas. Leiden: E. J. Brill.
———. 1942b. Lokalkulturen im alten China. Leiden: E. J. Brill.
Edmondson, Jerold A. 1991. Some Kadai languages of northern Guangxi, China. In Sudaporn Luksaneeyanawin (ed.), Pan-Asiatic Linguistics 1, 28–43. Bangkok: Chulalongkorn University Printing House.
———. 1992. Fusion and diffusion in E. Guangxi Province, China. In T. Dutton, M. Ross, and D. Tryon (eds.), Memorial volume for Don C. Laycock, 131–41 Pacific Linguistic Series. Department of Linguistics, Australian National University, Canberra.
———. 1994. Change and variation in Zhuang. In K. Adams and T. Hudak (eds.), Papers from the Second Annual Meeting of the Southeast Asian Linguistics Society 1992, 147–85. Tempe Program for Southeast Asian Studies, Arizona State University.
——— and David B. Solnit, eds. 1988. Comparative Kadai: Linguistic studies beyond Tai. Summer Institute of Linguistics and the University of Texas at Arlington Publications in Linguistics 86. Dallas.
——— and Yang Quan. 1994. Tone geometry in Kam-Sui: Contours, edges and dimorphism. Minzu Yuwen 2:50–62.
Egerod, Søren. 1961. Studies in Thai dialectology. Acta Orientalia 26(1–2):43–91.
Enriques, C. M. 1933. Races of Burma. (Handbooks for the Indian Army.) Delhi: Manager of Publication.

Fan Honggui. To appear. Tonggensheng de minzu: Zhuang-Tai gezu yuanyuan yu qianxi. [Ethnicities sprung of one root: Origins and migrations of the Zhuang and Thai.] Nanning: Guangxi Minzu Xueyuan. ms.

———, Meng Weiren, Xu Quanyin, and Gu Shaosong, tr. 1986. Yuenan beifang shaoshu minzu. Nanning: Guangxi Minzu Xueyuan Minzu Yanjiusuo. [Vietnam's northern minorities]. Chinese translation and adaptation of Vietnam Social Sciences Committee (ed.) 1978. Các dân tộc ít người ở Việt Nam (các tinh phía bắc). Hanoi: Social Sciences Committee Publishing House.

Ferlus, Michel. 1993. Phonétique et écriture du Tai de Qui Châu (Vietnam). Cahiers de linguistique-Asie Orientale 22:87–106.

Freiberger, Nancy and Vy Thị Bé. 1976. Nùng Fan Slihng vocabulary. Manila: Summer Institute of Linguistics.

Fu Maoji, Dao Shixun, Tong Wei, and Dao Zhongqiang. 1956. Phonemic system of Chiang Rong. Yuyan Yanjiu 1:223–64.

Gedney, William J. 1965. Review of J. Marvin Brown. From ancient Thai to modern dialects. Social Science Review 3(2):107–12.

———. 1972. A check list for determining tones in Tai dialects. In M. Estellie Smith, (ed.), Studies in linguistics in honor of George L. Trager, 423–37. The Hague: Mouton.

———. 1989. Selected papers on comparative Tai studies. R. Bickner, J. Hartmann, T. Hudak, and P. Peyasantin (eds.), Michigan Papers on South and Southeast Asia 29. Ann Arbor: University of Michigan Center for South and Southeast Asian Studies.

Gohain, Aimya Khang. 1991. The Tai language as spoken by the Tai-Phakaes. In Sudaporn Luksaneeyanawin (ed.), Pan-Asiatic linguistics 1:44–59. Bangkok: Chulalongkorn University Printing House.

Grierson, G. A. 1928. Linguistic survey of India 2. Mon Khmer and Siamese-Chinese families (including Khassi and Tai). Delhi, Varanasi, and Patna: Motilal Bariarsidas.

Guo Xiliang. 1986. Hanzi guyin shouce. [Handbook of Ancient Chinese characters]. Beijing: Beijing Daxue Chubanshe.

Haudricourt, André-Georges. 1948. Les phonèmes et le vocabulaire du thai commun. Journal Asiatique 236:197–238

———. 1956. De la restitution des initiales dans les langues monosyllabiques: le problème du thai commun. Bulletin de la Société de Linguistique de Paris 52(1):307–22.

———. 1960. Note sur les dialectes de la région de Moncay. Bulletin de l'École Française d'Extrême-Orient 50:167–77.

———. 1961. Bipartition et tripartition des systèmes de tons dans quelques langues d'Extrême-Orient. Bulletin de la Société de linguistique de Paris 56:163–80.

Hoffman, Mark S., ed. 1992. The world almanac and book of facts. New York: Pharos Books.
Hou Hanshu [Book of the later Han]. A.D. 25–220.
Hudak, Thomas J., ed. 1991. William J. Gedney's The Yay language: Glossary, texts, and translations. Michigan Papers on South and Southeast Asia 38. Ann Arbor: University of Michigan Center for South and Southeast Asian Studies.
———. 1992. William J. Gedney's The Tai dialect of Lungming: Glossary, texts, and translations. Thomas J. Hudak (ed.), Michigan papers on South and Southeast Asia 39. Ann Arbor: University of Michigan Center for South and Southeast Asian Studies.
Karlgren, Bernhard. 1957. Grammata serica recensa. Stockholm: The Museum of Far Eastern Antiquities.
Lao Peoples' Democratic Republic Population by Ethnic Group. 1985. Vientiane: Institute of Ethnology.
LeBar, Frank M., Gerald C. Hickey, and John K. Musgrave. 1964. Ethnic groups of Mainland Southeast Asia. New Haven: Human Relations Area Files Press.
Li Fang-Kuei. 1940. The Tai dialect of Lungchow: Texts, translation and glossary. Institute of History and Philology Monograph Series A 16. Taipei: Academia Sinica.
———. 1943. The hypothesis of a preglottalized series of consonants in Primitive Tai. Bulletin of the Institute of History and Philology 11:177–88.
———. 1944. The influence of the Primitive Tai glottal stop and preglottalized consonants on the tone system of Po-ai. Bulletin of Chinese Studies 4:59–68.
———. 1947. Phonology of the Tai dialect of Wu-Ming. Bulletin of the Institute of History and Philology 12:293–303.
———. 1956. The Tai dialect of Wu-Ming (texts, translation and glossary). Shanghai: Academia Sinica. The Institute of History and Philology. Monograph Series A 19.
———. 1957. The Jui dialect of Po-ai: Phonology. Bulletin of the Institute of History and Philology 28:551–66.
———. 1960. A tentative classification of Tai dialects. In S. Diamond (ed.), Culture in history: Essays in honor of Paul Radin, 951–59. New York: Published for Brandeis University by Columbia University Press.
———. 1965. The Tai and Kam-Sui languages. Lingua 14:148–79.
———. 1977. A handbook of comparative Tai. Honolulu: The University of Hawaii Press.
Liang Min. 1990. The Lachi language. Kadai 2:35–44.

Liang Tingwang. 1987. Zhuangzu Fengsu Zhi. [Zhuang customs]. Beijing: Zhongyang Minzu Xueyuan Chubanshe.
Lowis, C. C. 1919. The tribes of Burma. Rangoon: Office of the Superintendent, Government Printing.
Luce, Gordon Hannington. 1958. The early Syam in Burma's history. Journal of the Siam Society 46:2.
———. 1985. Phases of pre-pagan Burma, 2 vols. Oxford University Press.
Lunet de Lajonquiere, Etienne. 1906. Ethnographie du Tonkin septentrional. Paris: E. Leroux.
Luo Meizhen. 1988. Dai Tai cihui bijiao. [A comparison of Tai and Thai]. Minzu Yuwen 2:26–34.
Manich, M. L. 1967. History of Laos (including the history of Lannathai, Chiengmai). Bangkok: Chalermnit.
Maspero, Henri. 1911. Contribution à l'étude du système phonétique des langues Thai. Bulletin de l'École Française d'Extrême-Orient. 11:153–69.
———. 1912. Étude sur la phonétique historique de la langue annamite les initiales. Bulletin de l'École Française d'Extrême-Orient. 112(1):1–127.
Morev, L. N. 1988. Yazik Sek. (Yaziki narodov Asii i Afriki.) Moskva: Akademiya Naik SSSR.
Naing, Min. 1960. Races of Burma (in Burmese). Rangoon: Ministry of Union Culture.
Pfannmüller, Günter and Wilhelm Klein. 1982. Burma the Golden. Bangkok: Apa Productions (hk) Ltd. for The Bookseller Co., Ltd.
Purnell, Herbert. 1965. Phonology of a Yao dialect spoken in the province of Chiengrai, Thailand. Hartford Studies in Linguistics 15. Hartford Seminary Foundation.
———. 1987. Developing practical orthographies for the Iu Mien (Yao), 1932–1986: A case study. Linguistics of the Tibeto-Burman Area 10 (2):128–41.
Qin Xiaohang. 1991. Evolution of the clusters *pl*, *kl*, and *ml* in the local vernacular of Hongshuihe Zhuang. Guangxi Zhuangzu Zizhi Qu Shaoshu Minzu Yuyan Wenzi Gongzuo Weiyuanhui. [Committee on language and literacy, Guangxi-Zhuang Autonomous Region]. Unpublished paper.
Sarawit, Mary. 1973. The Proto-Tai vowel system. Ph.D. dissertation. University of Michigan.
Saul, Janice E. and Nancy Freiberger Wilson. 1980. Nung grammar. Summer Institute of Linguistics and the University of Texas at Arlington Publications in Linguistics 62. Dallas.
Savina, F. M. 1910. Dictionnaire tay-annamite-français precede d'un précis de grammaire tay et suivi d'un vocabulaire français-tay. Hanoi: Imprimerie d' Extrême-Orient.

———. 1924. Dictionnaire étymologique français-nùng-chinois. Hong Kong: Imprèmerie de la Société des Missions Etrangères.
Solntseva, N. V. and Hoàng Văn Ma. 1986. Materalii sovetsko-vietnamskoe lingvisticheskoe ekspeditsii 1979 goda: Yazik Laxa. Moskva: Nauka.
Strecker, David. 1985. The classification of the Caolan languages. In S. Ratanakul, David Thomas and S. Premsirat (eds.), Southeast Asian linguistic studies presented to André-G. Haudricourt. Bangkok: Mahidol University.
———. 1988. Gedney's puzzle in Kam-Sui. In Edmondson and Solnit (eds.), Comparative Kadai: Linguistic studies beyond Tai, 107–27.
Tanakorn, Sungkep. 1983. A phonological study of Lao Ngaeo with comparisons to five Tai dialects. M.A. thesis. Mahidol University, Bangkok, Thailand.
Terrien de Lacouperie, Albert Etienne Jean Baptiste. 1885. Cradle of the Shan race. In Archibald Ross Colquhoun, Amongst the Shans. London: Field and Tuer; Simpkin, Marshall and Co.; Hamilton, Adams and Co. and New York: Scribner and Welford.
Thongphiew, Urairat. 1989. A phonological comparison of Roi-et Thai and Vientiane Lao. M.A. thesis. Mahidol University, Bangkok, Thailand.
Thurgood, Graham. 1988. Notes on the reconstruction of proto-Kam-Sui. In Edmondson and Solnit, 179–218.
Vallibhotama, Srisakra. 1993. Zhuang: The oldest Tai. Silpakorn University, Bangkok, Thailand. ms.
Vietnamese Statistics. 1989. Tóm tắc kết quả tổng điều tra dân số. Hà Nội: Nhà Xuất Bản Thống Kê.
Vy Thị Bé, Janice E. Saul, and Nancy Frieberger Wilson. 1982. Nùng Fan Slihng-English dictionary. Manila: Summer Institute of Linguistics.
Wang Jun, ed. 1984. Zhuang-Dong yuzu yuwan jianzhi. Beijing: Minzu Chubanshe.
Wei Feng and Jerold A. Edmondson. 1990. Rongshui Sanfang Zhuangyu. Fieldnotes. 150 p. glossary with instrumental analysis.
Wei Qingwen and Qin Guosheng. 1984. Zhuangyu jianzhi. In Wang Jun ed., Zhuang-Dong yuzu yuyan jianzhi. Beijing: Minzu Chubanshe.
Wulff, Kurt. 1934. Chinesich und Tai. Sprachvergleichende Untersuchungen (Danske Vedenskabernes Selskab, Historisk-Filiologiske. Meddelelser 20.3). Copenhagen: Levin and Munksgaard.
Xie Zhimin. 1983. The vocalic alternation of the Zhuang language in Longzhou, Guangxi. Yuyan Yanjiu 2:212–18.
Zhang Junru. 1982. An etymological study of the ancient loan words in Zhuang language (in Central South Guangxi) borrowed from ancient Ping dialect of Han language. Yuyan Yanjiu 1:197–219.

———. 1986a. The trend, state and gradual change of sound change in Tai languages. Minzu Yuwen 1:27–37.
———. 1986b. The development and changes of three finals ɯ, əɯ, aɯ in Zhuang languages. Minzu Yuwen 6:20–24.
———. 1987. Loan words in the Zhuang language in the Ping dialect of Guangxi Province. Yuyan Yanjiu 1:185–89.
Zhang Shengqun, ed. 1988. Guangxi-Zhuangyu dimin xinji. [Glossary of Guangxi Zhuang place names]. Nanning: Guangxi-Zhuang Minorities Publishing House.
Zheng Yiqing. 1987. The reflexion of the initial consonants of Proto-Tai in Jinxi speech of the Zhuang language. Minzu Yuwen 6:35–45.
Zhongguo Da Baike Quanshu, Minzu. 1986. [Great Chinese Encyclopedia, Ethnic Groups]. Beijing and Shanghai: Zhongguo Da Baike Quanshu Chubanshe.
Zhuangyu yinxi [Zhuang phonology]. 1959. Beijing: Chinese Academy of Social Sciences.

Introduction

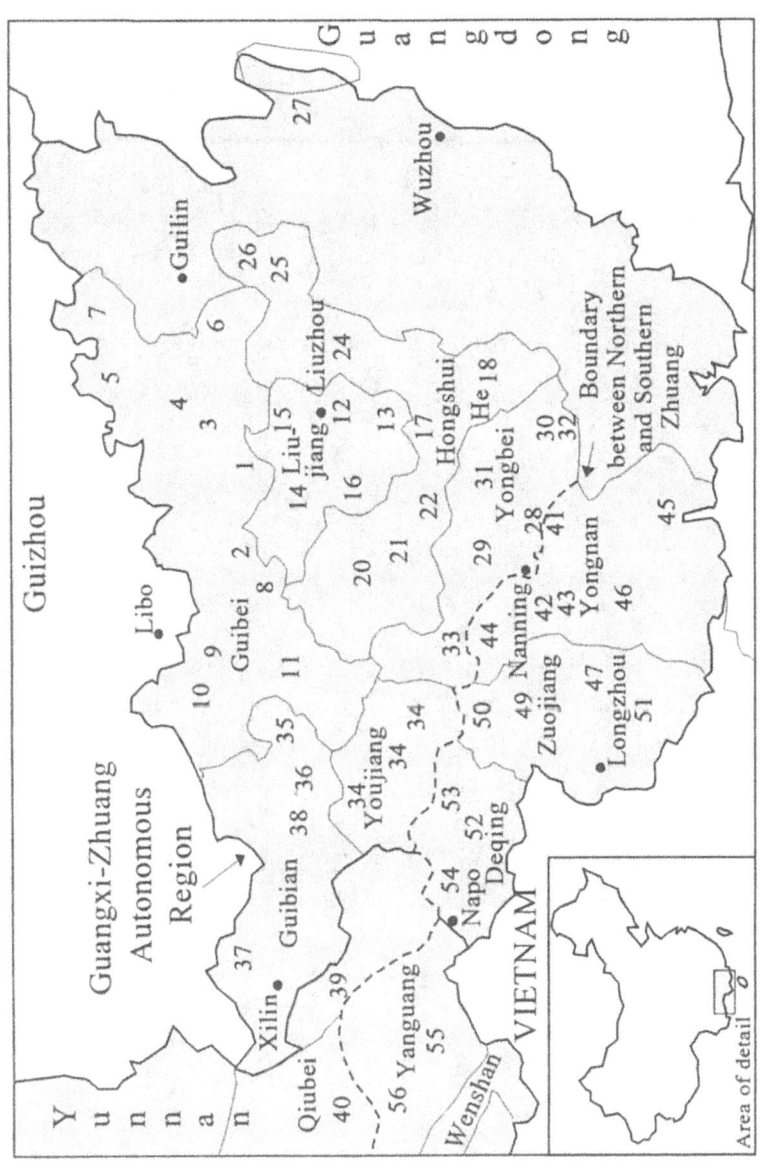

Map 1. Northern and Southern Zhuang areas

Jerold A. Edmondson and David B. Solnit

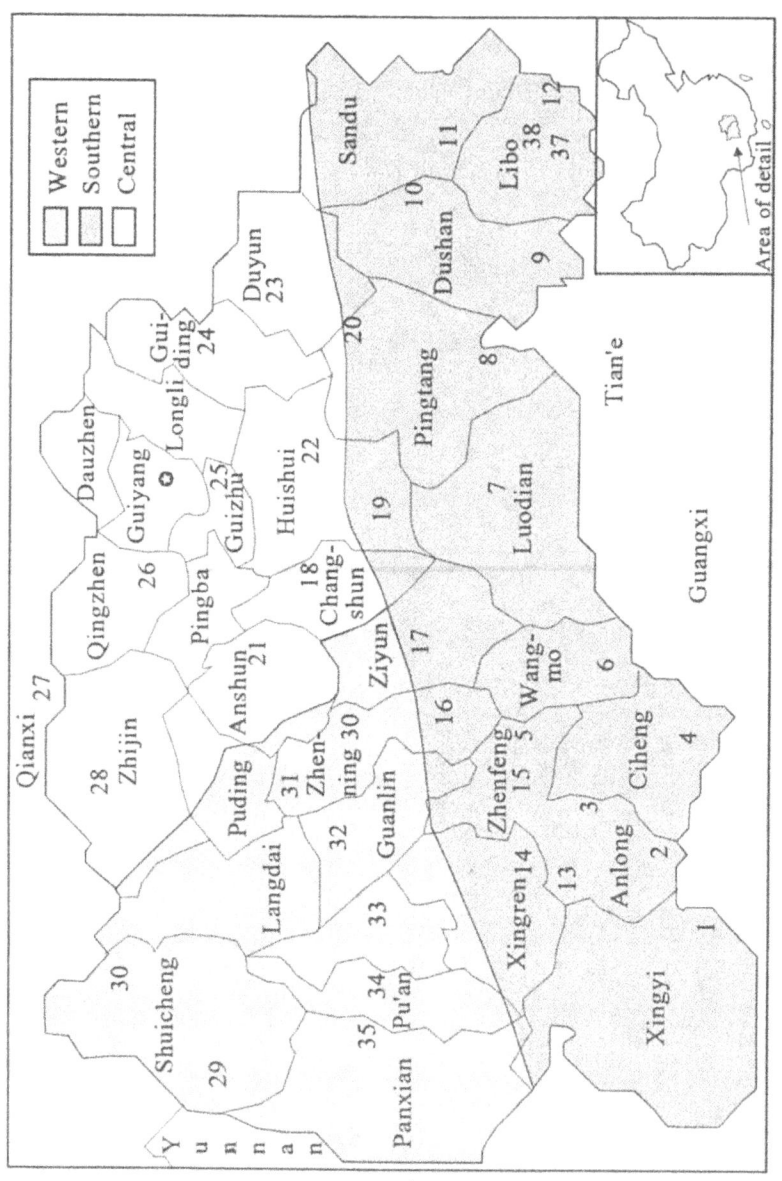

Map 2. Bouyei Areas

Introduction

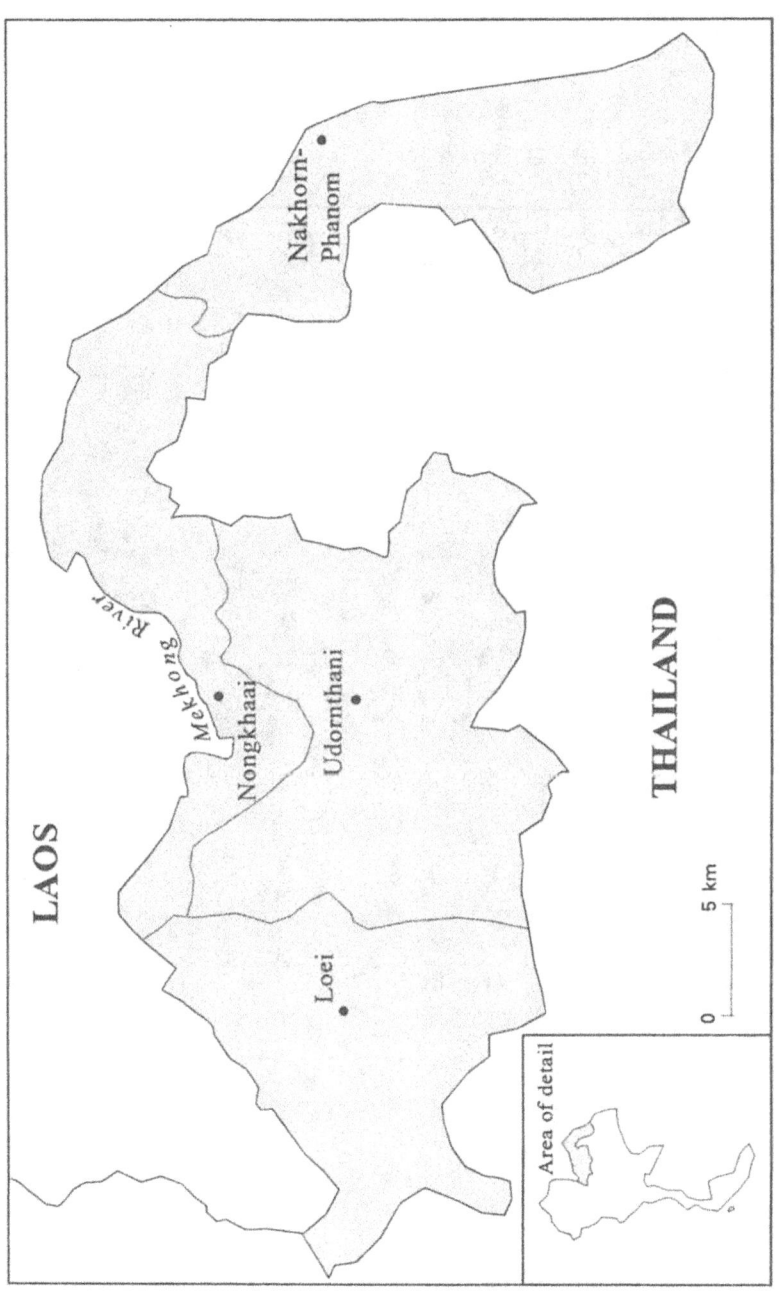

Map 3. Northeast Thailand

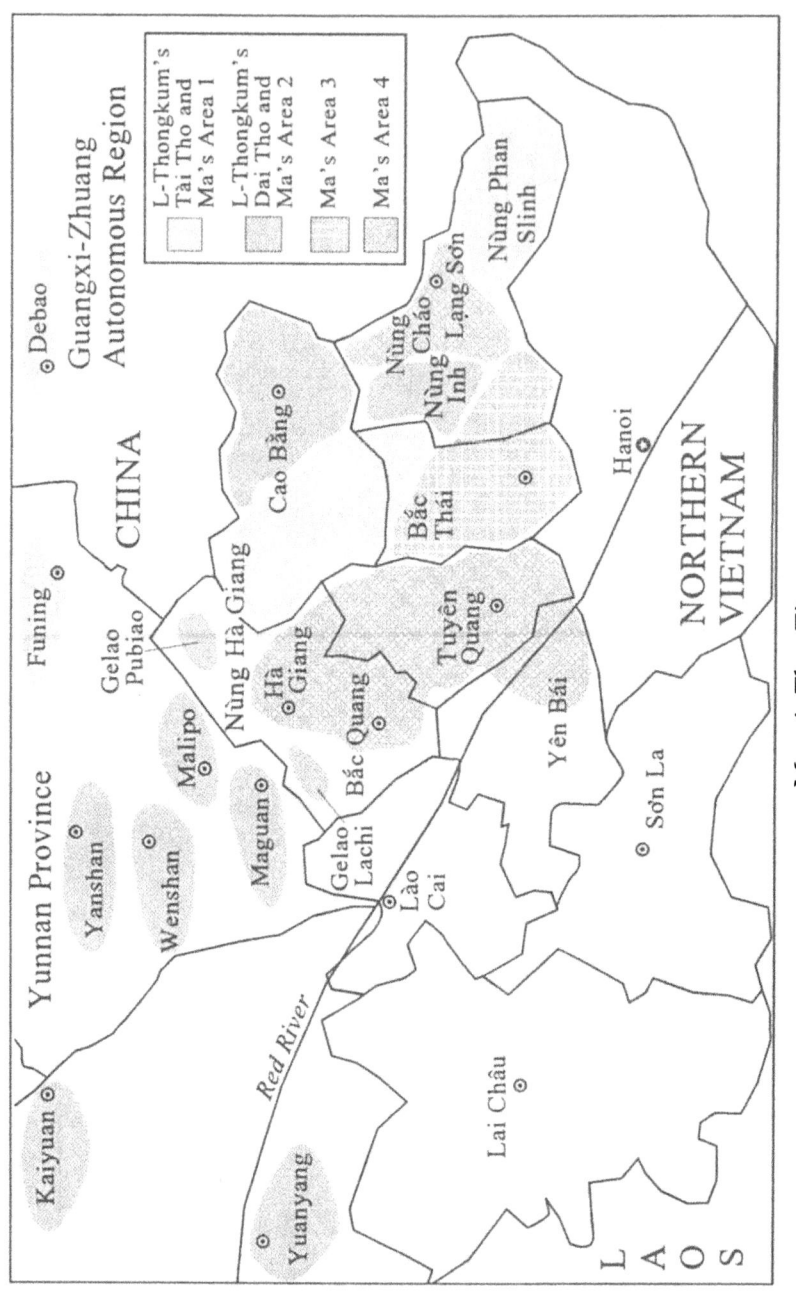

Map 4. Tho~Tày areas

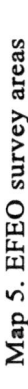

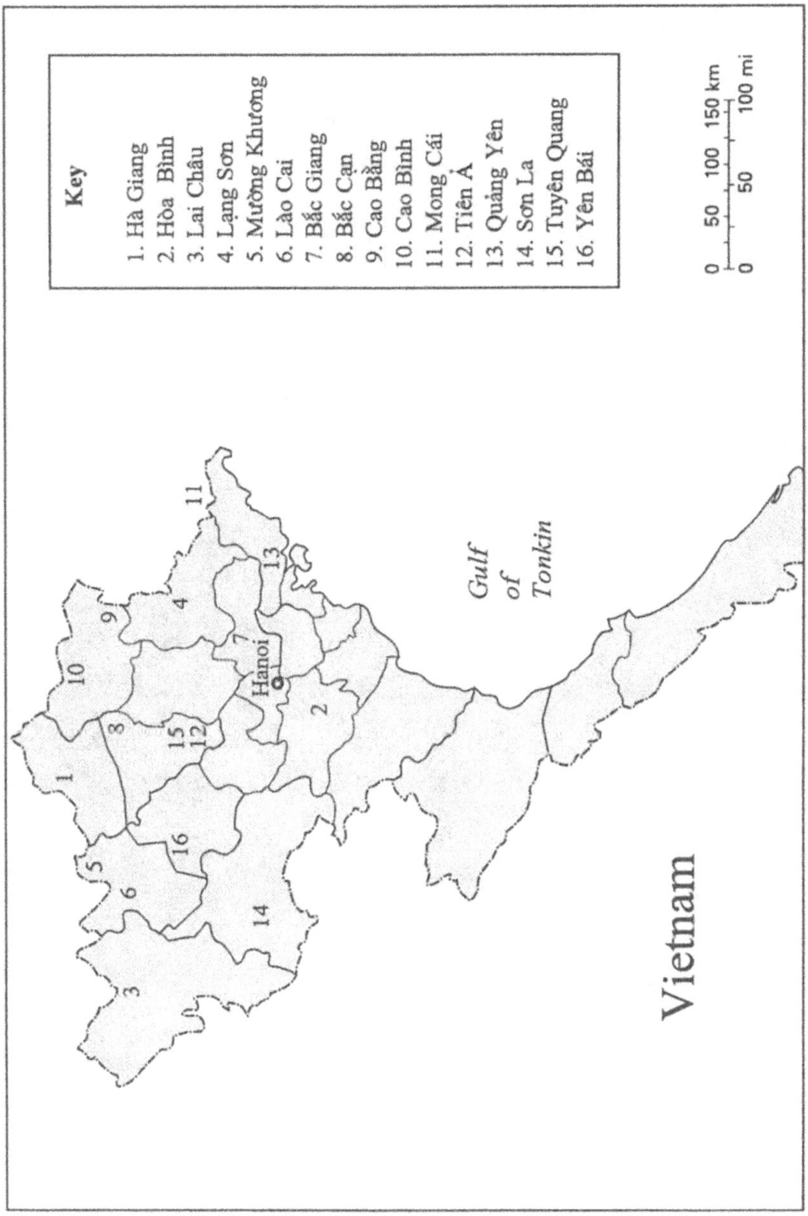
Key
1. Hà Giang
2. Hòa Bình
3. Lai Châu
4. Lạng Sơn
5. Mường Khương
6. Lào Cai
7. Bắc Giang
8. Bắc Cạn
9. Cao Bằng
10. Cao Bình
11. Mong Cái
12. Tiên Ả
13. Quảng Yên
14. Sơn La
15. Tuyên Quang
16. Yên Bái
0 50 100 150 km
0 50 100 mi
Hanoi
Gulf of Tonkin
Vietnam

Map 5. EFEO survey areas

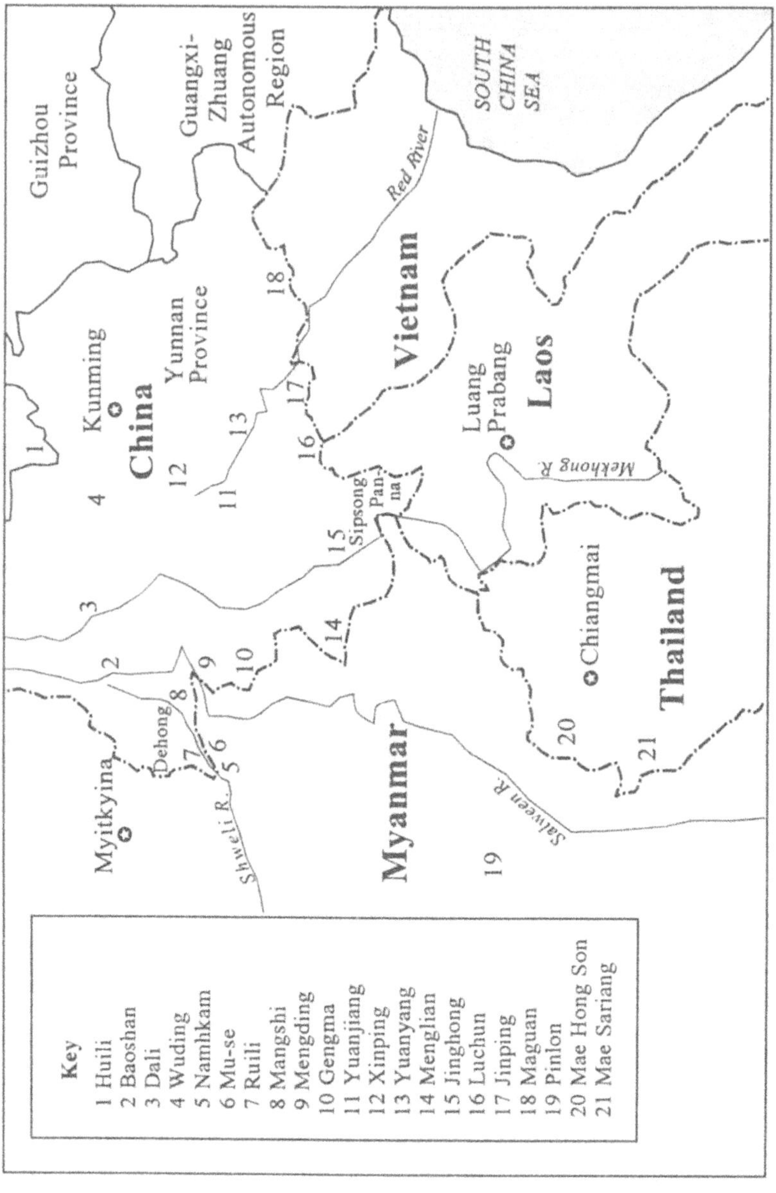

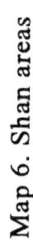

Map 6. Shan areas

I. Zhuang

The Tonal Cylinder in Sanfang Zhuang

Wei Feng and Jerold A. Edmondson

> ... if we can get these special Northern consonants moved to the very top of the chart, this would make them contiguous to the voiced initials of the bottom row of boxes—if we roll the chart into a cylinder with the top row joining the bottom, making our spectrum continuous, as in a color spectrum, with "violet" at one extreme found to be adjacent to "red" at the other. Gedney (1970)

Introduction

Professors Li Fang-Kuei, André-Georges Haudricourt, William J. Gedney, and J. Marvin Brown have shown in much of their work that there is a

---

A part of this research was supported by a grant to Jerold A. Edmondson from the Committee for Scholarly Communication with China and the National Endowment for the Humanities. In February 1990 Edmondson visited Rongshui Miao Autonomous County of Guangxi-Zhuang Autonomous Region to collect data on Kadai languages of that area. Ms. Wei Feng, native-speaker linguist, about 35 years of age, produced large samples of Sanfang Zhuang, which were studied instrumentally for pitch contours, the nature of the 'preglottalized' initials, and other features. She also wrote down over the next months an exhaustive inventory of her personal Zhuang vocabulary using Zhuang script as she has enlarged it to encompass her local vernacular, a total of 2,500 words. These were entered into a database and subsequently analyzed by Edmondson, who is responsible for the write-up that appears here. Many thanks to Professors David Solnit and William J. Gedney of the University of Michigan, and Dr. Luo Yongxian of Australian National University for comments on a draft of this paper.

powerful principle underlying the relationship between the initials and tones in languages of the Tai branch that was active in the proto-language. While this relationship has been formulated in many ways, perhaps the most popular account is found in Gedney (1972). It requires a division of the old initial consonants and tones into a grid of five columns and four rows. This kind of figure we call a Gedney diagram. (See figure 2, p. 4.) The columns Gedney labeled A, B, C, DL, and DS (A, B, and C being open syllables, and DS and DL being short closed and long closed syllables, respectively). The first three columns, A, B, and C, correspond to the tones in the Tai parent language and the last two, DL and DS, are thought to have been toneless originally. The rows represent properties of the consonant initials in the proto-language; the first row Gedney labeled '1-voiceless friction', including voiceless aspirated stops such as *ph, voiceless fricatives such as *f, and voiceless sonorants such as *hn. The second row was called '2-voiceless unaspirated stops' such as *p. The third was called '3-glottal stop', *ʔ and 'preglottalized consonants'[1] *ʔb, and the fourth was called '4-voiced consonants' such as *b. At various places and times then, new tonal categories developed by splitting between rows in a way that kept contiguous boxes in the same category. For example, A1, A2, and A3 as a group are distinct from the tone found in vocabulary with original A4 initials, but, according to the *principle of contiguity in splitting*, A1 and A3 could not ally to contrast to A2 and A4. The rule for the Northern Tai languages (and in many places elsewhere as well) was generally to divide between rows 3 and 4 so that 1, 2, and 3 consonant initials yielded the High or Series 1 set of contrastive tones, one each for the columns A, B, C, DL, and DS on the one hand, whereas on the other, Row 4 voiced initials engendered the Low or Series 2 set of contrastive pitches.[2] Usually there was a concomitant loss of voicing of the original stops and fricatives in Row 4. The result was a language with five tones in Series 1 and five tones in Series 2; in each series there are three tone categories on open syllables, one on the short closed syllable, and one on the long closed syllable. Furthermore, the pitch trajectories of closed syllable tone categories resemble those of the open syllable tone categories, whereby the categories that correspond vary in different genetic subdivisions of the branch.

While the tonal principles in Tai generally follow the rules sketched above, there are nevertheless a number of violations. Gedney in his 'spec-

---

[1] We write 'preglottalized' in quotation marks because some have found the term phonetically questionable.

[2] This splitting of tones does not hold for many kinds of Bouyei, especially those sorts found in Western Guizhou Province in which the split in the C tone groups is between Rows 2 and 3. This pattern is also found in the Yay studied by Gedney (1991).

trum' paper (1989:187) suggests a way of eliminating this apparent Northern Tai wild contrariety. The Northern subbranch of Tai has several virtually definitive characteristics that involve the Rows 1 and 4 of a Gedney diagram: (1) in Northern Tai few if any aspirated voiceless stops have survived in daughter languages; these have all merged with the corresponding voiceless unaspirated stops, and (2) the vocabulary with certain original voiced initials found in Row 4 and vocabulary with original voiceless friction initials found in Row 1 show a minor but unmistakable tendency to demonstrate the opposite tone from that predicted. So, for example, Row 4 words usually have the Series 2 or low tones (predicted pattern) but also in many cases show a Series 1 or high tone category (unpredicted pattern). Moreover, Row 1 words usually have the Series 1 tone category but in some cases show a Series 2 tone category. This tonal reversal—lows for highs or highs for lows—has been noticed by Li (1977) as well. One can see the effects of this tendency by plotting as a function of initial the number of instances of tonal reversals in Li's Bo-ai vocabulary (1977), which he used to represent the northern Tai subbranch.[3]

(1)   Tonal reversals as a function of initial consonant (data from Li 1977)

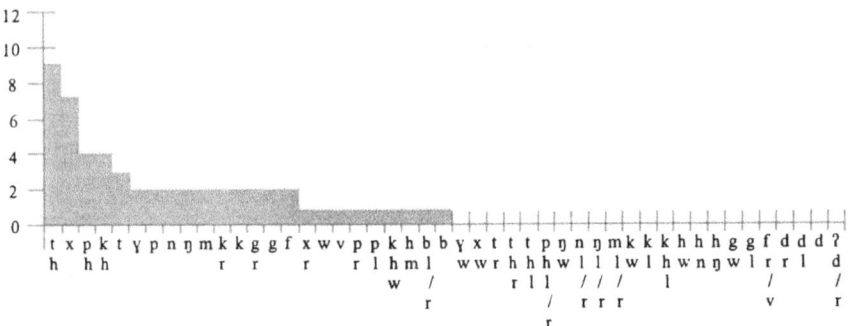

As (1) displays, tonal reversals occur most with voiceless friction initials, aspirates, and velar fricatives, according to the order /th x ph kh t/.

Rows 1 and 4 seem to share some tonogenetic properties but they are, obviously, not contiguous in a Gedney diagram and should not, on the standard view, show any affinities. Nonetheless, they seem to. Noting this

---

[3]We have counted all examples of unexpected highs or lows in the representative points, Siamese, Longzhou, and Bo-ai, without regard for differences in the columns; thus a correspondence between Siamese $phaa^{C1}$ 'cloth, clothing' and Bo-ai (Po-ai) $puuu^{B2}$ counts as tonal reversal, but Siamese $leen^{A1}$ 'grandchild' and Bo-ai lan, len^{C1} does not. For the initial *th, which has the largest number of reversals, 11 of 21 examples, about 50%, show this pattern.

puzzle, Gedney suggests that the principle of contiguity in tonogenesis can be preserved if one assumes that the Gedney diagram can be rolled into a cylinder that joins Rows 1 and 4. By abutting the top and bottom rows, as in (2), some Row 1 items can ally with Row 4 and some Row 4 items can behave like Row 1 items.

(2)   The rolling of the tonal cylinder

	A	B	C	DL	DS
1					
2			SERIES 1 TONES		
3					
4			SERIES 2 TONES		

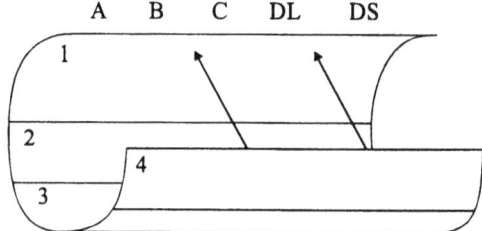

In this paper we discuss the occurrence of unexpected tones of this type in Sanfang Zhuang of Rongshui Miao Autonomous County, Guangxi, which possesses an extraordinarily large number of lexical items with unpredicted reversed tones. In most cases, Sanfang has all the instances of tonal reversal Li documents for Bo-ai and many more besides; especially it has prominent cases of items from Row 4 possessing Series 1 tones.

Sanfang Zhuang Autonomous Township is located in the western part of Rongshui Miao Autonomous County of Northeast Guangxi-Zhuang Autonomous Region. It belongs to the Guibei Vernacular Area of Zhuang, which has not been studied by foreign scholars before to the best of our knowledge. In 1989 of the 22,374 people living in Sanfang Township 14,388 were Zhuang.[4]

---

[4]Rongshui County had a total population of 438,012 distributed as follows: Miao 165,364; Han 133,279; Zhuang 60,425; Kam 47,074; Yao 27,307; Sui 2,244; Mulam 1,145; Tujia 1,073; Hui 69; Maonan 16; Yi 10; and Manzhu 6.

The sounds of Sanfang Zhuang

Initials

Sanfang has 46 initial consonants: /p t k pj tj kj pw tw kw kjw mb nd ŋg mbj ŋgj ndw ŋgw ŋgjw ts tsj tsw f ɕ s h ʐ hj sw hw ʐw m n̪ n ŋ mj nj mw nw n̪w ŋw l lj lw j jw w/. This number is about twice as large as the number of initials found in Wuming Zhuang, namely 23 (Wang 1984).
Examples of Sanfang Zhuang initials are:

(3)
C		Cj		Cw		Cjw	
pa^2	'father'	pja^1	'eye'	pwa^2	'to even'		
ta^1	'mother's father'	$tjiːu^1$	'sly'	twa^2	'steelyard'		
ka^3	'to kill'	kja^3	'to wait'	kwa^1	'pot'	$kjwaːu^1$	'spider'
mba^1	'harrow'	$mbjaːi^1$	'to wilt'				
nda^1	'back bag'			$ndwaːu^1$	'to pry open'		
$ŋgau^4$	'rice'	$ŋgjam^4$	'to bathe'	$ŋgwaːi^1$	'buffalo'	$ŋgjwan^1$	'sentence'
tsa^1	'to lack a vehicle'	$tsjaːu^3$	'suppress'	$tswy^2$	'hammer'		
fa^1	'iron'						
$ɕa^1$	'to owe'						
sa^1	'paper'			swa^2	'to flush, rinse'		
ha^3	'five'	hjo^6	'to study'	hwa^5	'flower'		
$ʐo^3$	'to know'			$ʐwa^4$	'to grasp'		
ma^1	'dog'	mja^3	'press flat'	mwa^6	'grindstone'		
na^1	'thick'	nja^1	'to glue'	nwa^6	'glut. rice'		
$n̪u^6$	'urine'			$n̪wy^6$	'fruit pit'		
$ŋa^2$	'to sprout'			$ŋwa^4$	'roof tile'		
la^2	'basket'	$ljaːu^3$	'scar'	lwa^2	'gong'		
ja^1	'search'			jwe^1	'comb'		
wa^1	'flower'						

Rhymes

There are 73 rhymes in Sanfang including seven simple vowel rhymes /i ɯ u e o a ɤ/ (the remainder are complex). Simple vowels are assumed to count phonologically as long. The unusual vowel is /ɤ/, which, on the basis of comparative evidence, turns out to be the monophthongized reflex of the proto-Tai diphthong *əɯ. Otherwise, in closed syllables the Tai high vowel nuclei occur in long and short variants. Of the nonhigh vowel nuclei a and *o* occur long and short (with some gaps), while *e* occurs only long; generally contrasts of length are not common. Li (1977) avers long high vowels were not originally long but instead came from diphthongs; length today in nonhigh vowels was originally from a quality difference, mid vowels generally yielding short reflexes and original low vowels yielding long reflexes. Li completes the system by saying that there were two types of diphthongs: those having a first element high and those having a first element nonhigh.

Sanfang Zhuang supports Li's model fairly well. High vowels mostly do not exhibit a direct long-short contrast; instead there is a short vowel versus vowel plus schwa contrast. Among nonhigh vowels there is length contrast for /a/, but Li would assume short *a* comes from *ə. As for the others, /e/ occurs only long; the back vowels /oː o/ may come from *ɔɔ and *o. Examples of these rhymes are given here.

(4) Front   Central   Back

i iəm iən iəŋ iəp iət   ɯ ɯːn ɯəŋ ɯət ɯək   u uːn uəŋ uət uək
iək   ɯn ɯŋ ɯt ɯk   um un uŋ up ut uk
im in iŋ ip it ik

e eːm eːn eːŋ   a aːm aːn aːŋ aːp aːt   o oːm oːn oːŋ   ɤ
eːp eːt eːk   aːk   oːp oːt oːk
                                am an aŋ ap at ak   om on oŋ op ok

In Sanfang there are also two types of diphthongs as predicted; two of the high first element type /iːu ɯːi/ (but not /ia ɯːa ua/ which were all monophthongized) and six of the nonhigh first element type /eːu oːi aːu aːi au ai/, whereby the short diphthongs /au ai/ are presumably from *əu and *əi.

(5) Diphthongs

iːu   ɯːi
eːu   oːi
            aːu au   aːi ai

Tones

Sanfang has six tones on CVV syllables and four tones on CV(V)C$_2$ syllables (C$_2$=/p t k/). The pitch trajectories have been determined instrumentally but we do not present the pitch plots here. The tone categories may be illustrated as follows:

(6) | Tone Category | Tone value | Example | |
| --- | --- | --- | --- |
| A1 | 41 | tsa^1 | 'vehicle, cart' |
| A2 | 3231 | tsa^2 | 'tea' |
| C1 | 452 | tsa^3 | 'to tear' |
| C2 | 312 | tsa^4 | 'thin (not dense)' |
| B1 | 44 | tsa^5 | 'to borrow' |
| B2 | 21 | wa^6 | 'talk' |
| D1L | 45 | $ta{:}p^{7L}$ | 'to carry on a pole' |
| D1S | 55 | tap^{7S} | 'liver' |
| D2L | 23 | $ta{:}p^{8L}$ | 'to change' |
| D2S | 22 | tap^8 | 'to pile' |

The most remarkable feature of the tones of Sanfang is the especially complex contouring of Tone 2. It begins at mid level, drops slightly before rising again to mid level, and then falls to the lowest level. Also, it is difficult to see an easy correspondence of the pitch trajectory of the dead tones with that of live tones, as is usually assumed for the Tai branch.

One other dramatic novelty of Sanfang is the existence of tone doublets. A goodly number of items may appear with either the Series 1 or with the Series 2 tone. Both forms are used in the speech community. So, for example, 'hand' can be said $fuŋ^1$ or $fuŋ^2$; both are understood and employed.

From ancient Tai to Sanfang

In treating the historical changes that have led to Sanfang (SF), we begin with the rhymes as these developments are less complex. The basis of our discussion are the reconstructions in Li (1977). At times we suspect these forms might better be analyzed as loans, but we note also that they seem to behave parallel to native vocabulary.

Sources of the Sanfang rhymes

/i/ comes from *i in CVV syllables and in closed syllables from PT *iə → NT *iː → i and PT *iɛ → NT *iː → i, as illustrated respectively by pi¹ 'year'; mit⁷ˢ 'classifier for knives'; and ndiŋ¹ 'red'. The Sanfang rhymes -iəC come mostly from Han loans of comparatively recent date.

/ɯ/ is from PT *ɯ in CVV syllables as in tsɯ⁴ 'to buy' and in closed syllables from *ɯɯ as in fɯŋ¹ 'hand' and fɯn¹ 'rain'.

/u/ is from *u in CV(C) syllables as in mu¹ 'pig'; tu¹ 'door'; tsuk⁸ˢ 'ripe'; puk⁸ˢ 'pomelo', from PT *uə → NT *uu → u as in muk⁸ˢ 'mucus'; also PT *uu → NT *uu → u as in lum² 'to forget'.

/e/ comes from PT *ɛ; it is always long, as in ẕeːŋ¹ᐟ² 'force, strength'; kjeːn¹ 'arm'; kje⁵ 'old'; NT tends to raise this vowel nucleus to e.⁵

/a/ is from PT *a in CVV syllables as in ma¹ 'dog'; pja¹ 'eye'; pa³ 'father's older sister'; maːk⁷ᴸ 'fruit'; the PT *e, which always occurs in closed syllables, is changed to Sanfang a as in kjat⁷ˢ 'fish scale'; nan² 'louse'; ŋgam¹ 'bitter'; tap⁸ 'to fold'. Also the instances of PT *uk/ŋ become /a/ in Sanfang as in mak⁸ˢ 'ink'; taŋ² 'to arrive'; and tak⁸ˢ 'male', with lowering of the vowel caused by the following velar consonant. From PT *ə are the examples man² 'tuber'; pjak⁷ˢ 'vegetable'; and tap⁷ˢ 'liver'.

/o/ comes from PT *ɔ as in ŋgo¹ 'neck'; mbo⁵ 'well, spring', and also from PT *uo as in ẕo³ 'to know'; ndoːk⁷ᴸ 'bone'; from PT *uu → NT *o → SF o, as in mot⁸ˢ 'ant'. Some also come from the original diphthong PT *ou → NT *ɔɔ → Sanfang o, as in po⁵ 'blow, to'; and from the diphthong PT *ou, as in mo⁵ 'new'.

/ɤ/ comes exclusively from PT *əɯ. We list here all examples of the rhyme in our corpus, many of which have established Tai cognates in other languages and some of which have uncertain sources: ẕɤ¹ 'what'; hɤ³ 'to give'; jɤ¹ 'long'; jɤ² 'exclamation'; jɤ⁶ 'to stretch'; kjɤ¹ 'bamboo container for grasshoppers'; kjɤ² 'where'; kjɤ³ 'near'; kjɤ⁴ 'overweight'; kwɤ⁴ 'to do'; lɤ² 'where, which'; lɤ⁴ 'arrogant'; lɤ⁶ 'rotten'; mbɤ¹ 'leaf'; mbɤ⁴ 'daughter-in-law'; mɤ³ 'large'; mɤ⁵ 'to threaten'; ndɤ¹ 'inside'; n̥ɤ¹ 'have a speech impediment'; nɤ² 'crown of skull'; ŋgjɤ⁴ 'reluctant'; pɤ¹ 'bib'; pjɤ² 'how many, which one'; sɤ¹ 'clear'; sɤ³ 'to serve'; tɤ¹ 'gizzard'; tɤ³ 'to fight to eat'; and tsɤ² 'local fabric, hemp'.

/ɯə/ comes from PT *ɯa → *ɯə ~ *ɯa as in hɯəŋ¹ 'tail'.

---

⁵The notation 1/2 as a tone category means that this lexical item occurs in Sanfang sometimes with tone category 1 and sometimes with tone category 2.

/ɯːi/ from PT *uːi as in kɯːi² 'husband'; kɯːi⁶ 'to ride on horseback'; pɯːi² 'to scare'.
/oːi/ is from PT *u̯i → oːi as in mvoːi¹ 'bear', probably also labializing the initial. The others in the category are mostly from Han loans with rhyme -ei, as in poːi¹ 'to accompany'; loːi² 'tired'; and tsoːi¹ 'to blow'.
/iə/ from PT *ia is preserved as in piən⁵ 'to change'.

Sanfang also has the following reflexes for the proto-Tai diphthongs *ɛi, as in fi¹/² 'fire' and zui² 'chicken louse'; *uo as in kju¹ 'salt' and zu¹ 'boat'; and *ue as in nuk⁷ˢ 'deaf' and tu⁶ 'bean'.

Initials and tones

In many ways Sanfang displays its heritage by exhibiting many NT traits. As is the rule in NT, original aspirated voiceless stops, found in Row 1 of the Gedney chart, have merged with their corresponding voiceless unaspirated counterparts of Row 2, i.e., /ph th tsh kh/ become respectively /p t ts k/. Moreover, as in all branches of Tai, the voiceless sonorant series (except for /hr/) /hm hn hɲ hŋ hl hw/ merge with the plain voiced series /m n ɲ ŋ l w/.

Sanfang is decidedly atypical in the development of its Row 3 and Row 4 consonant initials. Vocabulary having initials in the 'preglottalized' series, reconstructed by Li Fang-Kuei as *ʔb *ʔd, and some, but not all items having proto voiced stop initials (Row 4), reconstructed by Li as *b *d *g, have merged, yielding reflexes in Sanfang that are the fully voiced (pre-nasalized) consonants /mb nd ŋg/; also *ʔj becomes j. In parallel fashion, the original Row 3 glottal stop initial /ʔ/ with abrupt onset of voicing has become nonabrupt, taking the place of articulation of the following vowel sometimes with accompanying nasal murmur; e.g., ʔoːi³ 'sugarcane' in Wuming is Sanfang woːi³. Compare also ʔaːm⁵ 'mouthful' and the related ŋgaːm¹. For Wuming ʔen¹ 'tendon, sinew' Sanfang has ɲin². This change is generally characterizable as hard onset becoming soft onset.

Two of the voiced fricatives have merged with their voiceless counterparts, i.e., v → f and z → s. The voiced velar fricative /ɣ/ has not combined with x, however, but has undergone an independent development. In yet another change that runs exactly counter to the trend of voiced fricatives becoming devoiced, the original voiceless fricative *f has become voiced /w/; this change is also characteristic of NT at many locations.

Proto-Tai vocabulary descended from *r are found predominantly in high tones today: zu¹ 'what'; zo³ 'to know'; zaːn¹ 'house'; zau¹ 'we'; zeŋ¹/² 'force, strength'; zoːŋ¹ 'nest'; zui¹ 'chicken louse'; and zam¹ 'rice husk; bran'.

Perversely and unpredictably, exactly those lexical items that are descended from ancient voiced stops /b d dz g/, later become /mb nd ŋgj ŋg/, show a significant number of high tone reflexes or dual tone reflexes, whereas those that develop into voiceless stops have low tones. For example, vocabulary from original voiced stops and affricates: pau^6 < $*bau^{B2}$ 'plane'; pa^2 < $*ba^{A2}$ 'father'; pi^2 < $*bi^{A2}$ 'fat'; tai^6 < $*dai^{B2}$ 'bag'; and tum^2 < $*dum^{A2}$ 'wet' should be contrasted with nda^5 < $*da^6$ 'river, ford, wharf'.

Incidentally, Sanfang Zhuang is not unique in demonstrating fully voiced reflexes of the original voiced consonants. Haudricourt (1950) notes their presence in Cao Bằng as found in the EFEO survey data collected in 1937. Professor Hoàng Văn Ma, Linguistics Institute, Social Sciences Institute of Vietnam, a Tày (Central Tai) himself from Trùng Khánh, indicated that the following Cao Bằng Province locations in Vietnam have voiced stop and voiced fricative reflexes of proto-Tai voiced stops and fricative consonants (Row 4 in a Gedney chart): Trùng Khánh, Hòa An, Hà Quang, Thông Nông, Nguyên Bình, Trà Lĩnh, Quảng Hòa, and Hạ Lang. He produced some examples of his own pronunciation of vocabulary with this feature for Jerold A. Edmondson during a visit in August 1993 (cf. also his treatment of this question in Hoàng this volume).[6] $*\gamma$ is preserved in the word γa^2 'thatch grass, cogongrass'. The word da^5 'river' also retains the original voiced stop $*d$, which is in the high B tone only because B doesn't split.

The phonological rules of Sanfang Zhuang: Segmental. There are a number of generalizations that can be made about the possible shapes of words in Sanfang Zhuang.

(7)   Mergers of aspirated stops with unaspirated voiceless stops

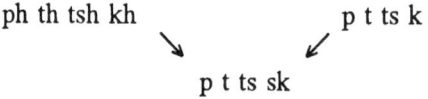

p t ts sk

(all in high tones, except where aspirated in NT, have low tones generally)

*aspirated   *unaspirated

*ph pu^4 'male'; pun^1 'hair,   *p po^5 'blow'; pau^5 'to
       feathers'; pa^5 'to split, to cut   report'; put^{7S} 'lung'; pit^{7S}
       open'   'duck'

---

[6]We were first made aware of this feature by Peter Ross of Australian National University, who has recently done fieldwork in some of these locations.

The Tonal Cylinder in Sanfang Zhuang 45

*aspirated   *unaspirated

*th tem^1 'in addition'; tu^6 *t tap^{7S} 'liver'; tu^1 'door'; tu^1
       'chopsticks'; ti^6 'dense (not   'we'; $tɤ^1$ 'gizzard'
       thin)'; tam^2 'pond'

*tsh sik^{7S} 'to tear up'   *ts $tsat^{7S}$ 'seven'; $tsim^5$ 'to
                                                                          marinate, dip into'; sak^{7S} 'to
                                                                          stop up'

*kh ka^1 'leg'; ka^3 'to kill'; $ka{:}i^1$ *k kai^5 'chicken'; kju^3 'nine';
       'to sell'; kau^1 'horn' kau^5 'old' kat^{7S} 'to cut with
                                                                scissors, to bite'; $ku{:}n^{1,}$ 'to
                                                                       eat'

(8)   Mergers of friction consonants with a variation

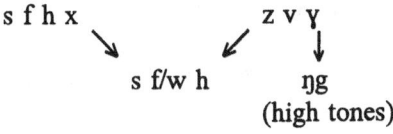

(high tones)

*s si^5 'four'; sai^3 'intestine';   *z sak^{8S} 'to wash clothes'; $so{:}i^4$
      $sɤ^1$ 'clear'; sip^{7S} 'ten'; $sa{:}m^1$ 'left'; $so{:}i^2$ 'pillow'; $so{:}ŋ^2$
      'to weave'; $so{:}ŋ^1$ 'two';   'loosely woven basket'; $tsɯ^4$
      $sa{:}m^1$ 'three'   'to buy'

*f fun^1 'rain'; wa^1 'cover';   *v $fun^{1/2}$ 'firewood'; $fi^{1/2}$ 'fire';
      $wa{:}i^5$ 'cotton'; $wueŋ^3$ fak^{8S} 'hatch'; $wuaŋ^5$ 'side,
      'millet'; $wa{:}i^1$ 'dam'; $wo{:}n^1$ half'; wat^{D2L} 'to pound, whip'
      'song'; $wuəŋ^1$ 'to mend
      clothes'

*h ha^2 'five'; $hɤ^3$ 'to give';
      hat^{7S} 'morning'; hap^{7S} 'to
      shut, dam'; $huət^{7L}$ 'waist,
      hips';

*x	hui⁵ 'dry'; ha⁵ 'to give in marriage'; heːŋ¹ 'chopping block'; heːu³ 'tooth'; heːu¹ 'green'; ŋgam¹ 'bitter'; ŋgau⁴ 'rice'; ŋg(j)ai⁴ 'excrement'; ŋgo⁵ 'joint'	*γ	ŋgaːi¹ 'to spit out, to gag'; ŋgam⁵/⁶ 'evening'; ŋgan¹ 'to itch'; ŋgan⁵ 'to praise, flatter'; ŋgaːŋ¹ 'chin'; ŋgo¹ 'neck'; ŋgaːn¹/² 'carrying pole'; ŋgwun¹/² 'person'
*xw	va⁵ 'trousers'; van¹ 'axe'	*γw	ŋgjwan¹ 'sentence'; ŋgwaːi¹/² 'buffalo'; ŋgon¹ 'smoke'; kjwau¹ 'spider'

(9) Mergers of 'preglottalized' stops with original voiced stops with a variation

ʔb ʔd ʔbl/r   b d g gl gr
ʔdl/r
         ↘   ↙   ↓
       mb nd ŋg ŋgj ʐ   p t k kj ʐ

*ʔb	mbo⁵ 'well'; mba⁵ 'shoulder'; mbɤ¹ 'leaf'; mbak⁷ˢ 'to chop'; mbaːn³ 'village'; mbaŋ¹ 'thin (not thick)'; mbau¹ 'light (not heavy)'	*b	mbɤ⁴ 'daughter-in-law'; pau⁶ 'to plane'; puk⁸ˢ 'pomelo'
*ʔd	nda⁵ 'to scold'; nda¹ 'cloth for carrying a baby'; ndaːi³ 'hemp, thread'; ndaːŋ⁵ 'lye, potash, lime'; ndi¹ 'good'; ndiŋ⁵ 'to pour'; nduk⁷ˢ 'rotten'	*d	nda⁵ 'river, ford'; nda⁴ 'to bet, dare'; ndau¹ 'moss, aquatic'; tum² 'wet'
*ʔbl/r	ndiən¹ 'moon, month'; mbj; mbi¹ 'gall'; pjat⁷ˢ 'to pick'; ndaːŋ⁵ 'pattern, whitish spot'	*bl	
		*br	mbjoŋ⁵ 'half, deficient'; mbaːŋ¹ 'lie, untruth'
*ʔdl/r	ndok⁷ˢ 'bone'; ndaːŋ¹ 'body'; ndau¹ 'star'; ndiŋ¹ 'red'; ndɤ¹ 'inside'	*dl	ʐak⁸ˢ 'to steal'; ʐaːk⁸ᴸ 'to pull'; ʐum¹/² 'wind'; ʐuk⁸ˢ 'room'; ʐup⁸ˢ 'to touch, rub'; ʐoːt⁸ᴸ 'to slide down, slip'

The Tonal Cylinder in Sanfang Zhuang

*dr $z̩u^1$ 'boat'; $z̩a:k^{8L}$ 'root'; $z̩uk^{8S}$ 'room'

*g $kuun^2$ 'above'; $ngje:p^8$ 'narrow'; kap^{8S} 'to seize, catch'; $ka:p^{8L}$ 'to pinch, hold with beak'; kam^6 'to press tight'; kon^5 'tree stump'; kon^5 'to break, cut'; $kuŋ^3$ 'arched, bent'; nga^5 'price'

*gl $ne:ŋ^2$ 'insect'; $kjap^8$ 'just now, right'

*gr $kjum^6$ 'cover'

Another provocative feature of Sanfang Zhuang is the large number of tone doublet items. Many identical lexical items appear in either the high or low tone category. While we have not undertaken a sociolinguistic study of the usage here, we have the impression that both manifestations are common. These seem to be in exactly the same places that Bouyei has voiced original but now voiceless fricatives in odd numbered tones, i.e., $f \rightarrow v$; $h \rightarrow \gamma$; and $s \rightarrow z$.

(10) Sanfang tone doublets   Proto form

Sanfang	Proto	Gloss
$z̩a:ŋ^{1/2}$	*$nl/ra:ŋ^A$	'bamboo shoot'
$z̩e:ŋ^{1/2}$	*$rɛŋ^A$	'strength'
$z̩au^{1/2}$		'we (incl.)'
$z̩aŋ^{5/6}$	*$nəŋ^B$	'to sit'
$z̩o:ŋ^{5/6}$		'bright'
$z̩um^{1/2}$	*$dlu̯om^A$	'wind'
$faŋ^{1/2}$	*$mwaŋ^A$	'demon, spirit'
$fi^{1/2}$	*$vɛi^A$	'fire'
$fun^{1/2}$	*$vɯ:n^A$	'firewood'
$fuŋ^{1/2}$	*$mwɯ:ŋ^A$	'hand'
$ŋgam^{1/2}$		'carrying pole'
$ŋgam^{5/6}$	*γam^A	'evening'
$ŋgje:u^{1/2}$		'scissors'
$ŋgje:u^{5/6}$		'to shout'
$ŋgwa:i^{1/2}$	*γwai^A	'water buffalo'
$ŋgwun^{1/2}$	*$\gamma u̯un^A$	'person'

Sanfang tone doublets   Proto form
$kwa^{1/2}$ 'what'
$lau^{1/2}$ 'story of a building'

It is of some interest that only three initials are involved in this set, /z̩ f ŋg/ (as well as two unpredicted initials as in the final two words). It is also noteworthy that the A tone is most apt to show this two-height ambiguity. While we were not able to find reliable proto-Tai cognates for all these items, most of the examples that were in Li (1977) have initial consonants that are voiced, both sonorants and obstruents.

Sanfang Zhuang is one of the places that has voiced velar stops. Examples with this feature are presented here.

(11) /ŋg-/

$ŋge^4$	'fish gig'	$ŋge^5$	'to multiply, sprout'				
$ŋga^4$	'to hesitate'	$ŋga^1$	'crack'	$ŋga^5$	'to occupy; price'	$ŋga^4$	'to block; straw'
$ŋgo^4$	'later'	$ŋgo^5$	'joint' < *x	$ŋgo^1$	'neck' < *ɣɔ		
$ŋgu^5$	'to pair up'	$ŋgu^4$	'to tangle'				
$ŋgɯ^1$	'ditch'	$ŋgɯ^5$	'to expand, enlarge'				
$ŋgeːu^1$	'scissors'	$ŋgeːu^4$	'unravel'	$ŋgeːu^5$	'to scream'		
$ŋgaːu^4$	'kind of fish'	$ŋgaːu^5$	'kind of fish'	$ŋgaːu^4$	'rice, cooked; grain' < *xəu		
$ŋgaːi^1$	'shoe; to gag'	$ŋgaːi^5$	'to stack'	$ŋgai^4$	'excrement'		
$ŋgam^1$	'bitter; moss'	$ŋgam^{5/6}$	'evening' < *ɣam				
$ŋgaːm^1$	'to suck'	$ŋgaːm^5$	'ceramic pot'				
$ŋgan^1$	'itch'	$ŋgan^4$	'diligent; to press'	$ŋgan^5$	'to admire, envy'	$ŋgaŋ^1$	'fat'
$ŋgaːn^{1/2}$	'carrying pole'	$ŋgaːn^5$	'toward; to patch; sweat'	$ŋgaːŋ^1$	'chin'		
$ŋgoːm^4$	'nausea'	$ŋgom^4$	'to turn'	$ŋgoːm^1$	'to become arched'		
$ŋgon^1$	'smoke'	$ŋgon^5$	'bracelet'	$ŋgoŋ^1$	'deep water'		

The Tonal Cylinder in Sanfang Zhuang

ŋgoːn^1	'carrying pole'	ŋgoːn^4	'to dishevel, squander'	ŋgoːn^5	'to splash on'	ŋgoːŋ^4	'necklace; handle'
ŋgɯən^1	'to sprinkle'	ŋgun^4	'to pull out'	ŋguŋ^4	'river bend'		
ŋgap^8	'to itch'	ŋgut^8	'to curl'	ŋgoːk^8	'corner'	ŋguɯk^8	'thick'

(12) /ŋgw-/

ŋgwa^1	'to shut'	ŋgwa^1	'picture'
ŋgwaːi$^{1/2}$	'buffalo'	ŋgwaːi^5	'bad'
ŋgwaːn^5	'to exchange'	ŋgwun$^{1/2}$	'person'
ŋgwap^8	'quilt, padded clothes'	ŋgwat^8	'to stir; throw a fit'	ŋgwɯt^8	'to scribble'

(13) /ŋgj-/

ŋgji^1	'to solidify'	ŋgji^4	'bitter'	ŋgja^1	'non-slick, tight'
ŋgjo^5	'female name; envy'	ŋgju^1	'to swim'	ŋgjɯ^4	'be reluctant to go'
ŋgjau^1	'sunset'	ŋgjau^4	'to fall off'	ŋgjaːu^4	'to declare a fast friendship'
ŋgjai^1	'to love dearly'	ŋgjai^4	'excrement'	ŋgjeːu$^{1/2}$	'scissors'
ŋgjim^1	'fire tongs'	ŋgjeːm^4	'valley'	ŋgjum^4	'to gulp'
ŋgjam^1	'to repeat'	ŋgjam^4	'to bathe'	ŋgjam^5	'together'
ŋgjin^4	'to be fed up with'	ŋgjin^5	'to wake up'		
ŋgjeːn^4	'sticking food'	ŋgjeːn^1	'side'		
ŋgjan^1	'range of mountains'	ŋgjan^5	'scar'	ŋgjoːn^5	'to expose'
ŋgjeːŋ^4	'cannot stand to see'				
ŋgjaŋ^1	'to glare'	ŋgjaŋ^5	'to weigh'	ŋgjaːŋ^1	'to groan'
ŋgjeːp^8	'narrow'	ŋgjap^8	'just now'	ŋgjaːp^8	'to cut with shears'
ŋgjit^8	'kindling'	ŋgjeːt^8	'stingy'	ŋgjat^8	'sand in food'
ŋgjak^8	'to stop up a leak'	ŋgjaːk^8	'rope'		

(14) /ŋgjw-/

ŋgjwi¹	'to skew'	ŋgjwe⁴	'askew, crooked'	ŋgjwe⁵	'to scold'
ŋgjwa⁴	'unsteady'	ŋgjwaːu⁴	'to swallow'	ŋgjwaːu⁵	'astringent'
ŋgjwaːɨ⁵	'to pull out with roots'	ŋgjwaːɨ⁵	'to forget gradually'		
ŋgjwam⁵	'accompany'	ŋgjwam¹	'to peel in a circle'	ŋgjwom⁵	'to burn'
ŋgjweːn¹	'reed organ'	ŋgjwan¹	'sentence'	ŋgjwaːn¹	'to eat ravenously'
ŋgjwaŋ¹	'to fall apart'				
ŋgjwoːt⁸	'to jump over'				

Tonal cylinder

What is evident from examining the initials and tones in Sanfang Zhuang is that there is unexpected voicing in initials /mb nd ŋg/ and there is unexpected high tone (in some cases it is apparently free variation of high and low tones) for vocabulary with these initials. This result seems paradoxical, since voiced initials, according to the usual analysis, result only in low tones. In fact, the majority pattern in other locations in Tai demonstrates low tones in these vocables. Moreover, it is noteworthy that the high-low tone categories and the voiced-voiceless initials for a considerable number of cases seem reversed.

We can think of two accounts of these data. The first or *VOICE = BREATHY HYPOTHESIS is a phonetic solution that would assume that at least some of the fully voiced obstruents of the Tai parent language (Row 4) were not only voiced, but that they possessed strong breath which is associated with a spread glottis. Many investigators have noted that contemporary Siamese realizes ancient /b d g/ as aspirated stops. It has also been noticed that the proto-Tai *r must have had this characteristic. As Li (1977:142) says

> This consonant was probably a Proto-Tai tongue-tip vibrant or trill, which probably required strong breath to achieve ... Among the SW dialects, it is preserved as r- in Ahom and Siamese, but L has a literary pronunciation hr-, a voiceless r, for the common h- in ordinary speech ... That this *r- was accompanied by strong breath (voiced?) can be shown not only by its development into h- in many SW dialects, but also by the development of the Proto-Tai *pr- and *tr- into Proto-CT *phr- and *thr-.

Exactly as predicted by this hypothesis, the Sanfang reflexes of the Proto-Tai *r- develop high tones, while at the same time preserving today a voiced initial consonant /z/. That vocabulary which developed from an initial *r- are found today in high tones, suggests that Sanfang Zhuang was especially prone to develop high tones whenever the initial had spread glottis with other initials. However, there remains the question of how to account for the tone doublets, i.e., the appearance of high and low tones in syllables with initial /f ŋg/. Since Sanfang is the only reported case of this phenomenon, it is unlikely that we should rethink the proto-Tai sources from which these forms derive.

The second account is a phonological solution, the MULTIPLE TONE SPLIT HYPOTHESIS, which would not be guided by the phonetic properties of reflexes of *r. Instead, it would require that tones in Sanfang split by two different processes: (1) tone splitting in connection with the loss of *voicing* and (2) tone splitting in connection with the loss of *preglottalization*. The first process is the most well known and well attested in Southeast Asian languages. It is found in all Tai languages. The second type is mentioned by L-Thongkum (this volume) who notes that tone splitting—as suggested by Haudricourt 1961—could begin with the loss of voicelessness of sonorants [Row 1] or possibly with the loss of 'preglottalization' [Row 3]. We would like to propose that Sanfang is, in fact, a case of the latter. On the basis of the current sound and lexical inventories of Sanfang Zhuang we assume that the original 'preglottalized' stops lost the feature *abrupt onset* in unconditioned sound change; as a consequence, many lexical items with initials /ʔb ʔd ʔj ʔ/ develop *soft onsets* in /mb nd j/ and C_h, a consonant homorganic in place of articulation with the following vowel. These two processes can be illustrated as follows:

(15) Voicing tone splitting   Preglottalization tone splitting

                                     *ʔb → mb (unconditioned change)
*p → p   mb → mb
*b → p + (low tone)   *b → mb + (low tone)

While the exact nature of the voicing in proto voiced consonants is not known with certainty, the Sanfang data suggest that the new prenasalized series /mb nd/ and the original voiced series /b d/ still contrasted. Meanwhile, another innovation began in the voiced velar fricative /ɣ/, changing it into a prenasalized velar stop /ŋg/. It is likely that /ɣ/ → /g/ → /ŋg/ aided or was aided by the change /ʔb ʔd ʔj ʔ/ → /mb nd j/ and C_h. But even if it was not, the development of a stop from /ɣ/ is widespread throughout the Tai branch, as Li 1977 reports. The tone splitting moment arrived when the contrast between prenasalized consonants and plain voiced consonants collapsed leaving the nasalized form as the survivor, but assigning to original plain voiced initial syllables low tone and to derived prenasalized initial syllables high tone. Thus, as the figure above makes clear, original voiced consonants, i.e., *b, could develop in two ways, to p or to mb. That is why there exist still today some items from *b with mb- and some with p-. But, the phonological contrast between prenasalized and plain voiced consonants is simply a matter of timing, and it is likely that the initials of some lexical items from the original voiced set could cross over to the prenasalized set without there being a conditioning environment. We know from the study of sound change in general that it happens gradually and not all lexical items undergo change simultaneously. Thus, it is possible that many or most of the lexical items losing the segmental contrast /g/ → /ŋg/ would do so with concomitant low tone. However, a few of them might have mutated earlier from /g/ to /ŋg/ in unconditioned change without tonal consequences, joining the models established by the prenasalized voiced stops /mb nd ɟ/ and C_h; when the /mb/ versus /b/ contrast was displaced by pitch, they would be assigned to the high tone set. Note that high tones are apparently a common consequence of prenasalized voiced stops, as the data in Sui demonstrates (Li 1948). The result was the seemingly paradoxical situation that some items from Row 4 have high tones with prenasalized initials and others have low tones with voiceless initials. What this account provides is the resolution to such a paradox; there was another tone splitting process that intervened to aid in transporting items, destined to develop into the low series, into the high series. One good example of the effect of this process is the word nda^5 'river', which at all other locations is found in tone 6. There were also others that changed first to prenasalized initials and they would no longer feed the *b → p rule; these would have /mb nd ŋg/ initials and later low tones.

Finally, there are the doublets with initial f-. At the moment we can only speculate that original *v may also have allied with the newly created prenasal series. The mechanism for this innovation is unclear. This second account basically assumes that our current reconstructions of the Tai proto language are essentially correct and that the Sanfang developments are idiosyncratic.

References

Brown, J. Marvin. 1965. From ancient Thai to modern dialects. (Original Ph.D. dissertation submitted to Cornell University, 1962.) Reprinted 1985

From ancient Thai to modern dialects and other writings on historical Thai linguistics. Bangkok: White Lotus Co., Ltd.
Buyiyu Diaocha Baogao. 1958. [Field report on the Bouyei language.] Beijing: Kexue Chubanshe.
Edmondson, Jerold A. 1991. Some Kadai languages of northern Guangxi, China. In Sudaporn Luksaneeyanawin (ed.), Pan-Asiatic linguistics 1 28–43. Bangkok: Chulalongkorn University Printing House.
———. 1992. Fusion and diffusion in E Guangxi Province, China. In Thomas Dutton, Malcom Ross, and Darrel Tryon (eds.), Memorial volume for Don C. Laycock (Pacific Linguistic Series) 131–41. Canberra: Department of Linguistics, Australian National University.
———. 1994. Change and variation in Zhuang. In Karen Adams and Thomas Hudak (eds.), Papers from the Second Annual Meeting of the Southeast Asian Linguistics Society 1992, 147–185. Tempe: Program for Southeast Asian Studies, Arizona State University.
——— and David B. Solnit, eds. 1988. Comparative Kadai: Linguistic studies beyond Tai, Summer Institute of Linguistics and the University of Texas at Arlington Publications in Linguistics 86. Dallas.
——— and Yang Quan. 1994. Tone geometry in Kam-Sui: Contours, edges and dimorphism. Minzu Yuwen 2:50–62.
Fan Honggui, Meng Weiren, Xu Quanyin, and Gu Shaosong, tr. 1986. Yuenan beifang shaoshu minzu. Nanning: Guangxi Minzu Xueyuan Minzu Yanjiusuo [Vietnam's northern minorities]. Chinese translation and adaptation of Vietnam Social Sciences Committee (ed.) 1978. Các dân tộc ít người ở Việt Nam (các tỉnh phía bắc). Hanoi: Social Sciences Committee Publishing House.
Gedney, William J. 1970. A spectrum of phonological features in Tai. Paper presented at the Third International Conference on Sino-Tibetan Language and Linguistics, Cornel University, Ithaca.
———. 1972. A check list for determining tones in Tai dialects. In M. Estelle Smith (ed.), Studies in linguistics in honor of George L. Trager, 423–37. The Hague: Mouton.
———. 1989. Selected papers on comparative Tai studies. In R. J. Bickner, J. Hartmann, T. J. Hudak, and P. Peyasantiwong (eds.), Michigan papers on South and Southeast Asia 29. Ann Arbor: Center for South and Southeast Asian Studies, University of Michigan.
Haudricourt, André-Georges. 1950. Les consonnes preglottaliées in Indochine. Bulletin de la Société de Linguistique de Paris 46:172–82.
———. 1961. Bipartition et tripartition des systèmes de tons dans quelques langues d'Extrême-Orient. Bulletin de la Société de Linguistique de Paris 56:163–80.

Hudak, Thomas J., ed. 1991. William J. Gedney's The Yay language: Glossary, texts, and translations. In Michigan papers on South and Southeast Asia 38. Ann Arbor: Center for South and Southeast Asian Studies, The University of Michigan.

———. 1992. William J. Gedney's The Tai dialect of Lungming: Glossary, texts, and translations. Michigan papers on South and Southeast Asia 39. Ann Arbor: Center for South and Southeast Asian Studies, The University of Michigan.

Li Fang-Kuei. 1940. The Tai dialect of Lungchow: Texts, translations and glossary. Institute of History and Philology. Monograph Series A 16. Taipei: Academia Sinica,

———. 1943. The hypothesis of a preglottalized series of consonants in Primitive Tai. Bulletin of the Institute of History and Philology 11:177–88.

———. 1944. The influence of the Primitive Tai glottal stop and preglottalized consonants on the tone system of Po-ai. Bulletin of Chinese Studies 4:59–68.

———. 1947. Phonology of the Tai dialect of Wu-Ming. Bulletin of the Institute of History and Philology 12:293–303.

———. 1948. The distribution of initials and tones in the Sui language. Language 24:160–67.

———. 1956 The Tai dialect of Wu-Ming (Texts, translation and glossary). Institute of History and Philology Monograph Series A 19. Shanghai: Academia Sinica.

———. 1957. The Jui dialect of Po-ai: Phonology. Bulletin of the Institute of History and Philology 28:551–66.

———. 1960. A tentative classification of Tai dialects. In S. Diamond (ed.), Culture in history: Essays in honor of Paul Radin, 951–59. New York: Published for Brandeis University by Columbia University.

———. 1977. A handbook of comparative Tai. Honolulu: University of Hawaii Press.

Wang Jun, ed. 1984. Zhuang-Dong yuzu yuyan jianzhi. Beijing: Minzu Chubanshe.

Wei Feng and Jerold A. Edmondson. 1990. Rongshui Sanfang Zhuangyu. Fieldnotes. 150 pp. glossary with instrumental analysis.

Zhang Junru. 1982. An etymological study of the ancient loan words in Zhuang language (in Central South Guangxi) borrowed from ancient Ping dialect of Han language. Yuyan Yanjiu 1:197–219.

———. 1986a. The trend, state and gradual change of sound change in Tai languages. Minzu Yuwen 1:27–37.

———. 1986b. The development and changes of three finals ɯ, əɯ, aɯ in Zhuang languages. Minzu Yuwen 6:20–24.

———. 1987. Phonological changes in the Zhuang vernacular of Wenma. Minzu Yuwen 5:10–18.

Zhuangyu yinxi. 1959. [Zhuang phonology]. Beijing: Chinese Academy of Social Sciences.

The Interaction between Zhuang and the Yue (Cantonese) Dialects

Huang Yuanwei
Central University of Nationalities
Beijing, China

Yue, or Cantonese, is one dialect group of the Han language. Varieties are traditionally called *Guangdong Hua* 'Guangdong speech', or in Guangxi Province, *Bai Hua* 'ordinary speech, vernacular'. Yue dialects are widely spoken in Guangdong and Guangxi as well as in Hong Kong, Southeast Asia, and other places around the world. The distinctive phonological characteristics of the Yue dialects are well known; they preserve fairly well the phonological appearance of Middle Chinese. For example, "there is a full inventory of nasal codas /-m -n -ŋ/ as well as consonantal stop codas /-p -t -k/. There are eight or nine tones, and as many as ten tones in Yulin and Bobai of Guangxi Province" (Zhan 1981:166) (counting the entering tone, i.e., those with consonantal stop codas as tones). Therefore, its phonology is richer than that of Modern Standard Chinese (MSC), the standard language of China, also known as Mandarin or Putonghua.

Wuming Mandarin or Wuming Guanhua belongs to the Northern Guangxi (Guibei) area of Southwestern Mandarin; it is spoken in urban Wuming. According to the census of 1988, the population of Wuming County was 602,955. Of these 522,211 were Zhuang, making up 86.6% of the whole, and 80,153 were Han, making up 13.3%; other groups numbered 591, making up 0.1%. Wuming County can therefore be called an area of concentrated

Zhuang settlement. The county seat area of Wuming has a population of 31,865, of which 26,276 are Zhuang, making up 82.5% of the total; 5,423 of which are Han, making up 17%; the population of other nationalities is 166, making up 0.5%.

Wuming Mandarin possesses some special characteristics. For example, a small number of final stops are preserved, with /-p/ merging to /-t/, while /-k/ codas are retained. For example, 'ten' is not the expected *ςip^{42} but ςit^{42}. There are five tones and two derived tones, i.e., Yinping with tone value 33, Yangping with tone value 31, Shang with tone value 55, Qu with tone value 24, Yangru with tone value 42, as well as derived Qusheng with tone value 35 and derived Yinru with tone value 55. The derived tones are mainly used in Zhuang loan words.

Living in the midst of a great sea of Zhuang, the Han people all are able to speak Zhuang for purposes of communication. But since the town of Wuming is the center of political, economic, and cultural activities, Wuming Mandarin is the main means of communication. When the Zhuang people speak Wuming Mandarin, they cannot avoid mixing in some elements of Zhuang phonology, lexicon, and grammar. The Han residents also understand Zhuang, so that they unconsciously receive influence from the Zhuang language too. Wuming Mandarin is therefore a mixture of Chinese and Zhuang. For example, in (1) $\eta a^{24}\ \eta a\colon\eta^{35}$ 'domineering' is a Zhuang word.

(1) $ni^{55}\ \varsigma e^{24}\ ko^{24}\ jin^{31}\quad han^{55}\ \eta a^{24}\qquad \eta a\colon\eta^{35}$
     you this CLF person very   perverse unreasonable
     You are very domineering.

In the following example, the words $m\partial^{55}$ 'not', $kap^{55}kep^{55}$ 'to cover', and $lo^{33}po^{33}$ (a particle with exclamatory meaning, resembling Mandarin *la*) are Zhuang.

(2) $ni^{55}\ \varsigma it^{42}\ m\partial^{55}\ \varsigma it^{42}\ m\partial^{55}\ \varsigma it^{42}\ kap^{55}kep^{55}\ khi^{55}la\colon i^{31}\ lo^{33}po^{33}$
     you eat not eat not eat cover   up   PTC
     Are you going to eat it or not? If you aren't, I am going to cover it up.

The Han people accept this expression subconsciously and have gradually become accustomed to it. In short, Wuming dialect is a kind of special Chinese which can be understood only by the Zhuang intellectuals and is unintelligible to the people from other places than the town of Wuming.

Wuming Zhuang is a Northern Tai language and Han belongs to the Sino-Tibetan family. They share common characteristics of phonology, lexicon, and grammar. Because of close contact over many centuries, Wuming

Zhuang has been deeply influenced by Han. Many loans came into Zhuang and a large part of these were borrowed at an early time from the Yue Branch of Chinese. Recent loans, by contrast, have come into Zhuang mostly from Southwest Mandarin which has been encroaching on the local Yue dialects for some time. In narrating everyday occurrences there are about 10% Han loans present in most people's speech; in speaking about affairs of government and political terms the number of Han lexical items would reach about half the total number of words. But the influence has not gone in only one direction; it is bidirectional. Yue and Wuming Mandarin, having been in contact with Zhuang for many centuries, have received substantial influence from Zhuang. This article analyzes the nature of that interaction among Zhuang, Yue, and Wuming Mandarin and draws tentative conclusions about the influence of Zhuang on Yue dialects in general, and on Wuming Mandarin in particular.

Aspects of the phonology, lexicon, and grammar of Yue and Wuming Mandarin have all been affected by the Zhuang language.

Phonology

/s/. "About one half of the locations in the Yue-speaking area have the lateral fricative initial [ɬ]" (Zhan 1981), or the interdental fricative [θ] stemming from the Middle Chinese initial consonant *s 心.[1] "In Guangdong, Gaozhou; the Four Counties (Sei Yap) of Taishan, Xinhui, Enping, Kaiping; as well as the 'Two Yangs', Yangjiang and Yangchun; and in Guangxi, the Guinan region, all have [ɬ] or [θ]" (Zhan 1981).

For example: 'Three' is $ɬaːm^{55}$ in Guangdong Taishan, $θaːm^{53}$ in Guangxi Mengshan, $ɬaːm^{33}$ in Longzhou Zhuang, and $θaːm^{24}$ in Wuming Zhuang. The /ɬ/ and /θ/ in Zhuang are changes from an original /s/. The /θ/ is found at 26 (46%) of the 56 geographic locations from which data on Zhuang was gathered in the 1950s (cf. Zhuangyu Yinxi 1959); the sound /ɬ/ is found at 14 (25%) of the data points; and the /s/ is found at 28% of the data points. The majority of the /θ/ points are in the north of Zhuang territory whereas the /ɬ/

---

[1] Editor's note. Middle Chinese initial consonants were listed in Chinese sources such as the Yunjing or Mirror of Rhymes of the thirteenth century, by means of the Thirty-Six Initials. The Thirty-Six Initials are a set of Chinese characters organized by place of articulation, from velar to labial, and by manner, from voiceless stop to glides. Tones of Middle Chinese are traditionally called ping 'level', shang 'rising', qu 'departing', and ru 'entering'. Each of these had a high and a low register variant, the yin and the yang. In the discussion below the author uses the established terms yinping or high level tone, yanping or low level tone, etc.

points are found mostly in the south of Zhuang territory (cf. Edmondson 1994). The sounds /ɬ θ/ are another characteristic of Zhuang-influenced Yue dialects and are otherwise unattested in varieties of Chinese.

Palatal nasal. In Hepu, Qinzhou, Mengshan, etc., there is a palatal nasal /ɲ/, which comes from the Middle Chinese initial *ri 日. For example, $ɲan^{31}$ 'person' in the Yue of Guangxi Mengshan as compared to $ɲuŋ^{31}$ 'mosquito' for the Zhuang of Guixian. Both these initials are reflexes of palatal nasals: Middle Chinese *ń (Karlgren's *ńź) for the former, and proto-Tai (Li Fang-Kuei 1977) *ñ for the latter.

/auɯ/. In Wuming Mandarin there is a final /auɯ/. For example, the nickname *Xiǎo èr hēi* 'Young Blacky' ('small' + 'two' + 'black'), in Wuming Mandarin is $siau^{55}$ $auɯ^{24}$ $hauɯ^{31}$. Note that the rhyme /auɯ/ only arises in Kadai languages, e.g., Wuming Zhuang $sauɯ^{24}$ 'book'. It is virtually nonexistent in Han. Its occurrence in Wuming Mandarin is a further indication of influence from Zhuang.

Tones in Wuming Mandarin. The derived *qusheng* 35 and *yinru* 55 in Wuming Mandarin are mainly used in loan words from Zhuang. For example, $ŋa^{24}ŋaːŋ^{35}$ 'domineering' and $juk^{55}jaːk^{55}$ 'untidy', as in (3).

(3) ta^{33} $coːn^{33}$ ti^{33} $i^{33}fu^{31}$ $juk^{55}juk^{55}jaːk^{55}jaːk^{55}$
     s/he wear POSS clothes untidy
     The clothes s/he is wearing are untidy.

/m n/. In Yue dialects, the sonorant initials /m n/ can occur in *yin* (upper) series tones. This is quite rare in modern Mandarin. Examples are: mit^{55} 'to tear' (*yinru* category), $niŋ^{55}$ 'hold, take' (*yinping* category), nam^{35} 'believe' (*yishang* category). This is clear evidence of influence from Zhuang.

Lexicon

According to the materials currently in the writer's possession, Yue has received relatively more lexical influence from Zhuang, while Wuming Mandarin has received relatively less.

(4)   'happy'

Wuming Mandarin aːŋ³⁵

tʰa³³ aːŋ³⁵ ho³³
s/he happy PFT
S/he is happy.

Wuming Zhuang aːŋ³⁵

kau²⁴ aːŋ³⁵ ya⁴² saːi⁴²
I   happy very
I am very happy.

(5)   'to cover'

Wuming Mandarin kap⁵⁵kep⁵⁵

ni⁵⁵ ɕit⁴² mə⁵⁵ ɕit⁴² mə⁵⁵ ɕit⁴² kap⁵⁵kep⁵⁵ khi⁵⁵laːi³¹ lo³³po³³
you eat   NEG eat   NEG eat   cover   up   PTC
Are you going to eat it or not? If you aren't I am going to cover it up.

Wuming Zhuang kop³³

kop³³ ki⁵⁵plak⁵⁵ kɯn³¹ taːi³¹ yeːt³⁵ tuik⁵⁵
cover vegetable   ascend table   tight   impinge
Cover up the vegetables on the table.

(6)   'anxious'

Wuming Mandarin mə³⁵

ŋo⁵⁵ mə³⁵   mə³⁵   hi³³
I   anxious anxious PTC
I am very anxious!

Wuming Zhuang ʔbɯ³⁵

kau²⁴ ʔbɯ³⁵   ʔbaːt⁵⁵ ʔbaːt⁵⁵
I   anxious very
I am really anxious.

(7) 'not'

Wuming Mandarin *mə⁵⁵*

ni⁵⁵ ɕit⁴² mə⁵⁵ ɕit⁴²
you eat   NEG eat
Are you going to eat it or not?

Wuming Zhuang *ʔbɯ⁵⁵*

kau²⁴ ʔbɯ⁵⁵ pai²⁴ lo³³
I   NEG   go   PFT
I am not going.

(8) 'concave'

Nanning Yue *map⁵⁵*

ni⁵⁵ tʰiu³¹ lu³¹ map⁵⁵map⁵⁵ tat⁴²tat⁴²
this CLF   road concave   convex
This road is bumpy.

Wuming Mandarin *map⁵⁵*

ɕe²⁴ kʼaːi⁵⁵ ti²⁴ map⁵⁵ hia²⁴ kʼə²⁴ lo³³
this piece land depressed down go   PFT
This piece of land is sunken.

Wuming Zhuang *ʔbop⁵⁵*

tuŋ⁴² waːi³¹ ʔbop⁵⁵ ʔbaːŋ⁵⁵ ʔbaːŋ⁵⁵
belly buffalo concave much   much
The water buffalo's belly is really hanging down.

(9) 'stingy'

Wuming Mandarin *keːt⁴² ɕi⁵⁵*

tha³³ ɕi²⁴ keːt⁴² ɕi⁵⁵ laːu⁵⁵
s/he be   stingy   fellow
He is a skinflint.

Wuming Zhuang *ke:t³³*

ʔdak⁵⁵ nai⁴² ke:t³³ hu⁴²
CLF this stingy PTC
This person is very stingy.

(10) 'to decay'

Wuming Mandarin *nuk⁵⁵*

ɕe³⁵ tui³³ za:i³¹ ho⁵⁵ nuk⁵⁵ lo³³
this pile fuel fire rotten PFT
This pile of firewood is rotten.

Wuming Zhuang *ʔduk⁵⁵*

ko²⁴ fai⁴² nai⁴² ʔduk⁵⁵ lo³³
CLF tree this rotten PFT
This tree is rotten.

Wuming Mandarin lacks the glottalized [ʔd] and uses [n] as a substitute.

(11) 'look for'

Guangzhou Yue *la³³*

hai³⁵ tʃɛk²² kwai²² t'uŋ³⁵ la³³ tʃœ⁵⁵ tʃi⁵⁵ pat⁵⁵
at CLF cabinet bucket look^for emerge CLF pen
to look for a pen in the drawer

Tianyang Zhuang *la¹³*

ku¹³ la¹³ muŋ³¹
I look^for you
I'm looking for you.

(12) 'pullet (young hen)'

Guangzhou Yue *kai⁵⁵ hɔːŋ³⁵*

ŋo¹³ maːi²⁴ tʃɛk⁴² kai⁵⁵ hɔːŋ³⁵
I   buy   CLF   pullet
I have bought a pullet.

Wuming Zhuang *kai³⁵ haːŋ³³*

tu³¹ kai³⁵ haːŋ³³ oːk   ɣai³⁵ lo³³
CLF pullet   discharge egg   PFT
The pullet laid an egg.

Guangzhou Yue *kai⁵⁵ hɔːŋ³⁵* and Wuming Zhuang *kai³⁵ haːŋ³³* have exactly the same meaning and agree in structure, i.e., the general term precedes and the modifier follows, the opposite of modern Chinese.

(13) 'all, entirely'

Guangzhou Yue *haːm²¹ paːŋ²¹ laːŋ²¹*

ni⁵⁵ ti⁵⁵ je¹³ haːm²¹ paːŋ²¹ laːŋ²¹ kwai⁵⁵ ŋo¹³
this several things entirely   belong me
These things all belong to me.

Wuming Zhuang *ham³¹ paŋ³¹ laŋ³¹*

kjoŋ³⁵ ɣau³¹ ham³¹ paŋ³¹ laŋ³¹ pai²⁴ liu⁴²
PL   we   entirely   go   finish
We all go.

(14) 'just now, good, correct'

Guangzhou Yue *ŋaːm⁵⁵*

khy¹³ ŋaːm⁵⁵ tʃœt⁵⁵ hy³³
s/he just   emerge go
S/he has just now gone out.

ŋo¹³ thuɲ³¹ khy¹³ hu³⁵ ŋaːm⁵⁵
I together s/he very good
I get on very well with him/her.

ni¹³ kam³⁵ ɕu³³ mau¹³ ŋaːm⁵⁵ po³⁵
you that^way do NEG correct PTC
It's not right if you do it like that.

Wuming Zhuang ŋaːm³⁵

te²⁴ ŋaːm³⁵ ma²⁴
s/he just return
S/he has just returned.

kau²⁴ ɕau³⁵ te²⁴ ʔbau⁵⁵ ŋaːm⁵ 5D kai⁵⁵   aːi²⁴
I with s/he NEG good how^much much
I don't get on too well with him/her.

(15) 'revolve, turn'

Guangzhou Yue pan³³

khy¹³ pan³³ lɔːi²¹ pan³³ hy³³
s/he turn come turn go
S/he turns back and forth.

Wuming Zhuang pan³⁵

an²⁴ lok⁵⁵ pan³⁵ luːt⁵⁵ luːt⁵⁵
CLF wheel turn roll roll
The wheel keeps on turning.

(16) 'tread, trample'

Guangzhou Yue tam²²

tʃɛk²² kai⁵⁵ tʃei³⁵ pi³⁵   jan²¹ti²¹ tam³³ ʃi³⁵ tʃo³⁵
CLF chicken ? undergo people trample die PFT
The chick was trampled to death by somebody.

Wuming Zhuang *tam³³*

tam³³   ta:k⁴²   tu³¹ nau²⁴ nuŋ³⁵ ya:i²⁴ pai²⁴
trample fast   CLF   rat   that   die   go
Hurry and stomp that rat to death.

(17) 'tender, softened, sodden'

Guangzhou Yue *nam²¹*

ŋau²¹ juk⁴² pau⁵⁵ tak⁵⁵ hu³⁵   nam²¹
ox   flesh stew   get   good   tender
The beef is stewed to tenderness.

Wuming Zhuang *nam³¹*

no³³ wa:i³¹ wa³⁵   au³⁵   tuk⁵⁵ nam³¹   nut³³
flesh ox   tendon stew   get   tender very
The beef tendon is stewed to tenderness.

(18) 'shiver'

Guangxi Yue *ɬan³¹*

ŋo¹³ la:ŋ¹³ tak⁵⁵ ɬan³¹   hy³³
I   cold   get   shiver very
I'm so cold I'm shivering.

Tianyang Zhuang *ɬan³¹*

ku²⁴ nit⁵⁵ tuk⁵⁵ lan³¹   pai²⁴
I   cold   get   shiver go
I'm so cold I'm shivering.

(19) 'itch'

Guangzhou Yue *han²¹*

ŋo¹³ tʃɛk³³ tʃau³⁵ jou³³ han²¹ jou³³ thuŋ³³
I   CLF   hand   also   itch   also   ache
My hand itches and aches.

Wuming Zhuang *han³¹*

kɯ²⁴ pɯək³⁵ ha:m⁴²haɯ³¹ ho²¹ han³¹ ja:k⁴²ja:k⁴²
eat taro half-cooked throat itch very
If you eat half-cooked taro, your throat becomes very itchy.

(20) 'frog'

Guangzhou Yue *kap⁵⁵*

lo³³ tʃek³³ kap⁵⁵ na¹³ hu³⁵ fi³¹
that CLF frog female good fat
That female frog is very fat.

Wuming Zhuang *kop⁵⁵*

no³³ kop⁵⁵ ti:m³¹ θiŋ⁵⁵ ya:ɨ⁴²ɕa:ɨ⁴²
flesh frog sweet clear very
The frog meat tastes quite fresh.

(21) 'vexed'

Nanning Yue *sam⁵⁵ ja:p⁵⁵*

ŋo²⁴ haɯ³⁵ sam⁵⁵ ja:p⁵⁵ ke³³
I good heart vexed PTC
I am quite vexed.

Wuming Zhuang *θim²⁴ ja:p³⁵*

te²⁴ θim²⁴ ja:p³⁵ θi³¹θi³¹
s/he heart vexed very
S/he is unusually vexed.

(22) 'flash, flicker'

Guangzhou Yue *ja:p⁵⁵*

ko³³ tʃek³³ taŋ⁵⁵ ja:p⁵⁵ ha¹³ tʃou²² tʃik⁵⁵ tʃo³⁵
that CLF lamp flicker descend then extinguish
That lamp flickered once and went out.

Wuming Zhuang *jap⁵⁵*

ʔdaːu⁴²ʔdai³⁵ *jap⁵⁵* tep⁴²tep⁴²
star   flash flash
The stars are twinkling.

(23) 'slip off, take off (clothing), slip and fall'

Yue dialects *lat⁵⁵*

ni⁵⁵ kin³¹ tʃaːm⁵⁵ lat⁵⁵ tʃik⁵⁵ tʃo³⁵
that   CLF   shirt   shed   color   PFT
That piece of clothing has faded.

jat⁵⁵ lat⁵⁵ tʃau³⁵ tʃek³³ ʔuːn³⁵ thiːt³³lok⁴² ti³¹
one   slip   hand   CLF   bowl   fall   earth
As soon as it slipped from his/her hand, the bowl fell to the ground.

Wuming Zhuang *luɯt⁵⁵*

pai³¹ luɯt⁵⁵ faɯ³¹ an²⁴ waːn⁵⁵ ɕou³³ tuɯk⁴² waːi³³
one   slip   hand   CLF   bowl   then   undergo   ruined
As soon as it slipped from his/her hand, the bowl was broken.

(24) 'don't' (negative imperative)

Guangzhou Yue *mi¹³*

mi¹³   kɔːŋ¹³ pi¹³   a⁵⁵   saːm⁵⁵ tɛŋ⁵⁵
doˆnot speak   give   A   San   listen
Don't tell A San.

Wuming Zhuang *mi⁵⁵*

kau²⁴ mi⁵⁵ yo⁴² laɯ²⁴
I   not   know   PTC
I don't know.

(25) 'this'

Guangzhou Yue ni^{55}

ni^{55} ti^{55} hai^{21} mat^{55} je^{24}
this CLF be   what   thing
What are these things?

Tianyang Zhuang ni^{33}

$ka{:}i^{35}$ ni^{33} $ka{:}i^{35}$ ma^{31}
CLF   this   CLF   what
What are these?

(26) 'some, a little'

Guangzhou Yue ti^{55} (tit^{55})

pi^{13} ti^{55} ηo^{13}
give a^little me
Give me a little.

Wuming Zhuang ti^{24}

hau^{55} kau^{24} ti^{24} he^{24}
give   me   a^little one
Give me a little.

(27) 'not, have not'

Guangzhou Yue mau^{13}

mau^{13} $m\varepsilon^{55}$ $t\int i^{21}$
not^have any   affair
It doesn't matter.

Wuming Zhuang $\text{ʔ}bau^{55}$

kau^{24} $\text{ʔ}bau^{55}$ $ha\eta^{55} lau^{24}$
I   not   like
I don't like it.

(28)   'foolish, slow-witted, stupid'

Guangzhou Yue ŋɔːŋ²¹

khy¹³ jou¹³ ti⁵⁵   ŋɔːŋ²¹
s/he have a⌃little foolish
S/he is a bit foolish.

Wuming Zhuang ŋoŋ³⁵

te²⁴ ŋoŋ³⁵ ŋut
s/he foolish very
S/he is very foolish.

For the above words and expressions no source can be found in Chinese, but the source can be found in Zhuang; moreover, the sources are living words, showing that they are the result of influence from Zhuang.

Grammar

Postposed modifiers. Postposed modifiers are one of the distinguishing characteristics of Tai and Kadai languages. In MSC, modifiers generally appear in front of their head nouns. However, in Yue dialects some modifiers have the opposite ordering, agreeing with Zhuang. For example:

(29)   'hen'

Nanning Yue kai⁵⁵ na²⁴

kai⁵⁵   na¹³   o⁵⁵   taːn²¹
chicken female discharge egg
The hen lays eggs.

Wuming Zhuang kai³⁵ me³³

kai³⁵   me³³   ok³⁵   yai³⁵ lo³³
chicken female descend egg PFT
The hen laid eggs.

(30) 'guest'

   Nanning Yue *jan³¹ haːk³³*

   ŋo¹³ uk⁵⁵ jou¹³ jan²¹ haːk³³ loːi²¹
   I   house have person guest come
   Guests have come to my house.

   Wuming Zhuang *pau⁴² heːk⁵⁵*

   pau⁴² heːk⁵⁵ tau⁵⁵ lo³³
   people guest arrive PFT
   The guests arrived.

Postposed adverbials. Postposed adverbial expressions are also a distinguishing characteristic of Tai and Kadai languages. In MSC adverbials usually appear in front of the predicate, whereas in Yue dialects and in Wuming Mandarin some adverbials are postposed, just as in Zhuang. For example in adverbials of time, all of the following mean 'You go first, I'll go afterwards.'

(31) MSC

   nĭ   xiàn   zŏu wŏ hòu   zŏu
   you beforehand go   I   afterwards go

   Yue

   ni²⁴ haːŋ³¹ ʃin⁵⁵   ŋo²⁴ haːŋ³ kan⁵⁵ mi²⁴
   you go   beforehand I   go   follow tail

   Wuming Mandarin

   ni⁵⁵ zou⁵⁵ seːn³³   ŋo⁵⁵ zou⁵⁵ hou²⁴
   you go   beforehand I   go   afterwards

   Wuming Zhuang

   muŋ³¹ plaːi⁵⁵ koːn³⁵   kau²⁴ plaːi⁵⁵ kan²⁴ laŋ²⁴
   you   go   beforehand I   go   follow back

With adverbials of frequency, all of the following mean 'Buy another two jin [half kilo] of bananas'.

(32) MSC

    zài   mǎi liǎng jīn xiāngjiāo
    again buy two jin banana

    Yue

    maːi^{13} lɔːŋ^{13} kan^{55} hɔːŋ^{55}tʃiu^{55} tim^{55}
    buy two jin banana increase

    Wuming Mandarin

    maːi^{55} ljaːŋ^{55} kin^{33} hjaːŋ^{33}ɕiu^{33} seːn^{33}
    buy two jin banana beforehand

    Wuming Zhuang

    ɕau^{42} soːŋ^{24} kan^{24} jaːŋ^{33}ɕiu^{33} tem^{24}
    buy two jin banana increase

Position of double objects. As to the position of double objects in MSC, indirect object is usually put first after the verb, and direct object put next. However Yue dialects and Zhuang have the order verb-direct object-indirect object (except when the direct object includes a numeral-classifier expression). For example (all mean 'give you the money'):

(33) MSC

    gěi nǐ qiǎn
    give you money

    Yue

    pi^{13} tʃhin^{31} ni^{13}
    give money you

Wuming Zhuang

hau^{55} ɕi:n^{31} muŋ^{31}
give money you

Comparative sentence. In MSC, the structure of a comparative sentence is A + *bǐ* 'compared with' + B + adjective. Yue, Wuming Mandarin, and Zhuang use this pattern, but they also allow another structure: A + adjective + ['more than'] + B.
The following four sentences all mean 'I am taller than you'.

(34)   MSC

wǒ bǐ   nǐ   gāo
I   compared⌢with you high

Yue

ŋo^{13} kau^{55} ko^{33} ni^{13}
I   high more⌢than you

Wuming Mandarin

ŋo^{55} ka:u^{33} ko^{24} ni^{55}
I   high more⌢than you

Wuming Zhuang:

kau^{24} sa:ŋ^{24} kwa^{35} muŋ^{31}
I   high more⌢than you

Final emphatic particle. In Wuming Mandarin and Zhuang, a sentence including direct object and complement may add a final particle expressing emphasis. MSC does not have this kind of construction. For example:

(35)   Wuming Mandarin

ta^{55} zʅ^{55} ca:ŋ^{33}jiŋ^{33} khə^{24}
beat die fly   PTC
Kill the fly!

Wuming Zhuang

to³³ tu³¹ nau²⁴ ya:i²⁴ pai²⁴
beat CLF rat   die   PTC
Kill the rat!

Note: In both examples the final particle may also be glossed 'go, away'.

Interrogative sentence. In MSC there are three ways to form a yes-no question. The first is the use of intonation, the second is to add a final particle, and the third is the use of an affirmative and a negative simultaneously. The following three examples mean 'Are you going to Nanning?'

(36) a. *nǐ   qù   nánníng*
        you go   Nanning

  b. *nǐ   qù   nánníng   ma*
     you go   Nanning   PTC

  c. *nǐ   qù   bù   qù   nánníng*
     you go   not go   Nanning

Yue, Wuming Mandarin, and Zhuang use the third structure in the majority of cases. If there is an object, it is put between the affirmative and the negative. The following three examples mean 'Are you going to Nanning?'

(37)   Yue

       ni²⁴ hy³³ na:m³¹niŋ³¹ mau²⁴ hy³³
       you go   Nanning   NEG   go

       Wuming Mandarin

       ni⁵⁵ khə²⁴ na:n³¹ niŋ³¹ mə⁵⁵ khə²⁴
       you go   Nanning   NEG   go

Zhuang:

muɯŋ³¹ pai²⁴ naːm³¹ niŋ³¹ ʔbau⁵⁵ pai²⁴
you   go   Nanning   NEG   go

Manner of action. The following is not used in MSC but often found in Wuming Mandarin and Zhuang. This meaning is expressed by adding the verb 'to get, want'. Contrast the MSC example with the three examples following, all four meaning 'a crying child is not a good child'.

(38)   MSC

ài   kū-de   háizi   bù   guāi
fond^of weep-PTC child NEG good

Yue

sai³³ lau¹³ huk⁵⁵ lo¹³ mau¹³ kwaːi⁵⁵
small child weep want NEG good

Wuming Mandarin

hua³¹caːi⁵⁵ khuk⁴² jaːu²⁴ mə⁵⁵ kuaːi³³
child   weep   want NEG good

Wuming Zhuang

luk⁴²ŋe³¹ tai⁵⁵ au²⁴ ʔbɯ⁵⁵ kwaːi²⁴
child   weep get NEG   good

To sum up, Han and Zhuang have for a long period of time lived mixed together, with frequent interchange and close contact, making it natural that the languages should influence and permeate each other. In this article we have described some of the phonological, lexical, and grammatical influences that Yue and Wuming Mandarin have received from Zhuang.

References

Edmondson, Jerold A. 1994. Change and variation in Zhuang. In Karen Adams and Thomas Hudak (eds.), Papers from the Second Annual Meeting of the Southeast Asian Linguistics Society 1992, 147–85. Tempe: Program for Southeast Asian Studies, Arizona State University.

Karlgren, Bernhard. 1957. Grammatia Serica Recensa. Stockholm: The Museum of Far Eastern Antiquities, Bulletin 29. Reprinted by Elanders Boktryckeri Aktiebolag, Göteborg, 1964.

Li Fang-Kuei. 1977. A handbook of comparative Tai. Honolulu: The University Press of Hawaii.

Zhan Bohui. 1981. Modern Chinese dialects. Hubei People's Publication House.

Zhuangyu yinxi. 1959. [Zhuang phonology]. Beijing: Chinese Academy of Social Sciences.

Abbreviations

CLF	classifier	POSS	possessive
NEG	negative	PTC	particle
PFT	perfective		

Regional Variants and Vernaculars in Zhuang

Zhang Yuansheng and Wei Xingyun
Central University for Nationalities
Beijing, China

Editors' Introduction. In addition to the value of the data and analysis, Professors Zhang and Wei in this article provide for those unable to read Chinese an excellent example of the approach taken by many contemporary Chinese investigators of minority languages. Two characteristics of this approach are worth mentioning. The emphasis is first of all on description and comparison of different varieties of a language. This survey character reflects the motivation for the original studies that underlie this paper and the *Zhuangzu jianzhi* (Wei and Qin 1980), namely the practical need to choose a standard, to which all other varieties can be related by statements of regular correspondences. Readers with diachronic interests may wish to 'transform' some of these correspondence statements into rules of historical split and merger patterns. For example, Zhang and Wei state that the /ɣ/ of Wuming has in the Zuojiang Local Variety merged with /t h/ in odd-numbered tones and with /l/ in even-numbered tones. This can be restated, with some simplification, as: Northern Tai *hr corresponds to Central Tai *thr and *hr, the reflexes being /ɣ/ in Wuming and /t/ or /h/ in Zuojiang (examples cited from Longzhou), all reflexes having odd-numbered tones; and proto-Northern Tai *r corresponds to Central Tai *r, the reflexes being Wuming /ɣ/ and Longzhou /l/, with even-numbered tonal reflexes.

The Zhuang and the general situation of the Zhuang language

The Zhuang [tṣuaŋˇ] (which the Chinese represent today with the character 壮) have the largest population of all minority people in China. In the census of 1990 the numbers of Zhuang exceeded 15,400,000. Their principal area of settlement is located in Guangxi-Zhuang Autonomous Region, where more than 13 million live (see map 1). In Guangxi the Zhuang are found not only in the countryside, but they also comprise a sizable component of the urban population in such places as Nanning, Baise, Hechi, and Liuzhou. In Yunnan Province there are Zhuang at Wenshan Zhuang-Miao Autonomous Prefecture and a few other counties with a total population numbering more than 1,000,000. In Guangdong Province there are Zhuang at Lianshan Zhuang-Yao Autonomous County and surroundings, numbering more than 100,000. In Guizhou at Southeast Miao-Kam Autonomous Prefecture and in Hunan Province at Jianghua Yao Autonomous County there are 20,000. The Zhuang are usually settled in concentrations uninterrupted by other groups; still in some places they are mixed with Han, Yao, Miao, Kam, Mulam, Maonan, and Sui peoples.

In terms of geographic range, the Zhuang inhabit areas stretching from 99°57' to 112° east longitude and 21°31' to 26°45' north latitude—in the east from Guangdong Province at Lianshan Yao Autonomous County to Yunnan Province Wenshan Zhuang-Miao Autonomous Prefecture, and in the south from the South China Sea coast to Guizhou Province Congjiang County in the north.

Zhuang areas are mountainous and water rich. More than 2,000 years ago there were outposts of the Qin and Han Emperors of China established in this territory. These officials had been dispatched to govern this frontier zone. Zhuang prehistory may stretch back much further. Archeological materials indicate that precursors of the Zhuang more than 5,000 years ago knew how to cultivate rice in wet paddies. In the Spring and Autumn Period (770–476 B.C.) they wrought very high quality bronze drums in southern Guangxi in territory along the cliffs of the Zuojiang River. Also, there are fifty places with cliff painting reflecting ancient Zhuang customs and practices. The most well-known site is at Huashan in Ningming County.

The Zhuang have their own language, which in China is said to belong to the Sino-Tibetan family of languages, Tai Branch (called Zhuang-Dai Branch in Chinese). In this branch are also Bouyei, Dai of Yunnan, Lao, Thai, Shan, Nùng, and Tày. Consider the following examples of cognates among some of these:

(1) | Zhuang (Wuming) | Dai (Sip) | Lao | Thai | |
|---|---|---|---|---|
| taŋ¹ŋon² | ta¹van² | ta¹wen² | duaŋ²ta²wan² | 'sun' |
| γum² | lum² | lum² | lom² | 'wind' |
| fun¹ | fun¹ | fon¹ | fon¹ | 'rain' |
| γam⁴ | nam⁴ | nam⁴ | nam⁴ | 'water' |
| fei² | fai² | fai⁴ | fai² | 'fire' |
| fai⁴ (nam⁴) | kɔ¹mai⁴ | mai⁴ | ton³mai⁴ | 'tree' |
| na³ | na³ | na³ | na³ | 'face' |
| ta¹ | ta¹ | ta¹ | ta² | 'eye' |
| naŋ¹ | naŋ¹ | naŋ¹ | phiu¹naŋ¹ | 'skin' |
| tap⁷ | tap⁷ | tap⁷ | tap⁷ | 'liver' |
| mou¹ | mu¹ | mu¹ | mu¹ | 'pig' |
| saːŋ¹ | suŋ¹ | suŋ¹ | suːŋ¹ | 'tall' |
| tam⁵ | tɛm⁵ | tam⁵ | tam⁵ | 'short' |
| na¹ | na¹ | na¹ | na¹ | 'thick' |
| baːŋ¹ | baːŋ¹ | baːŋ¹ | maːŋ¹ | 'thin' |
| laːi¹ | laːi¹ | laːi¹ | laːi¹ | 'much' |
| dei¹ | di¹ | di¹ | di¹ | 'good' |

Zhuang is thought to have evolved from one of the ancient Yue languages (Luo Yue); the other Yue languages, all of which were originally not Chinese, over the centuries were very strongly influenced by Han, so that today the people in these areas speak languages regarded as Han, e.g., Cantonese and Min. Zhuang and Han do show a great many common features, and, according to some, these resemblances today are the result of common origins, whereas others see in such likenesses the result of language contact. One point of shared features is the tone and coda system of Zhuang and Chinese. Except where these have changed (as in the case of Mandarin) the two are remarkably similar, e.g., each has a system of tone splitting into high and low registers and possesses syllable codas /-m -n -ŋ -p -t -k/.

Zhuang varieties

Zhuang is divided into 'northern' and 'southern' varieties by a line running along the Yongjiang and the Zuojiang Rivers (see map 1). The southern varieties stretch from Yunnan Province, Guangnan Prefecture, Wenshan County across southern Guangxi. The northern varieties encompass about two-thirds of the Zhuang population and stretch from

Nanning northward to Longsheng and Sanjiang Counties in the northeast, to Guiping and Guixian in the southeast. In the West northern Zhuang extends to Longlin County and northern Yunnan in the northern sectors of Guangnan Prefecture and links up with the Bouyei of Guizhou Province, whose language closely resembles northern Zhuang. The southern varieties of Zhuang make up only one-third of the total population.

Within the southern forms there are numerous subdivisions. Major groups are: Yongning South, Liaofu, Longzhou, Long'an, Jingxi, Debao, Ningming, Tiandeng, and in Yunnan Wenshan, Jianshan, Guangnan South. In northern Vietnam the Nùng and the Tày (formerly called Thô 土) are also closely related to the Zhuang.

The two major variants—northern and southern—are thus divided on the basis of vocabulary and phonology. Within each of these major variants, local vernaculars can be further separated, seven in the north and five in the south (see map 1). The basic areas and distinguishing characteristics are presented below.

Northern vernacular areas

Guibei vernacular. Luocheng, Huanjiang, Rongshui, Rong'an, Sanjiang, Yongfu, Longsheng, Hechi, Nandan, Tian'e, Donglan.[1]

The phonological features distinguishing this area are: the initial /ɣ/ < *hr in odd numbered tones is realized as /j/, and in even numbered tones /ɣ/ < *r as /s l/. Moreover, in many places there are numerous palatalized or labialized initials.

(2) /ɣ/ → /j/
      Luocheng ja^1 'to search'
      Rong'an jou^1 'head louse'
                      $juːi^1$ 'comb'
                      $jaːp^7$ 'carrying pole'

     /ɣ/ → /l/
      Sanjiang lai^2 'long'
      Donglan lei^6 'uncultivated land'

     /ɣ/ → /s/
      Rong'an $saːn^2$ 'house'
                      sam^4 'water'

---

[1]Some data have been collected from areas other than those listed on map 1.

Regional Variants and Vernaculars in Zhuang   81

In Rong'an there are also the following palatalized and labialized initials /lj tj nj sj mw lw ɲw/ beyond those found elsewhere.

Liujiang vernacular. Liujiang, Laibin North, Yishan, Liucheng, Xincheng.

The phonological features distinguishing this area include a greater than normal number of palatalized and labialized sounds. These categories of initials occur in Han loans. Aside from the usual initials with secondary articulation one finds /pw bw tw dw nw sw ɕw lw jw ɣw pj bj tj dj lj sj ɕj hj/. These initials are not found in most Zhuang locations. Except for /b/ none of these carry 'preglottalization'. For example:

(3)   Liucheng
      $twa:n^2$ 'riddle' sju^5 'drill'
      $nwai^1$ 'snow' $ɕwa:i^3$ 'to step on'
      lwa^2 'gong' $tja:u^5$ 'to jump'
      $swa:n^5$ 'to calculate' $ɕja:u^5$ 'banana'
      $ɣwan^4$ 'to overflow' ljo^2 'to invade'
      $jwa:ŋ^2$ 'emperor' $nja:n^2$ 'bride'

Moreover, rhymes /ei ou/ are realized as /i u/ in all eight tones; for example, di^1 'good', fi^2 'fire', pi^2 'fan', tu^1 'door', ju^2 'oil'.

Hongshuin He (River) vernacular. Laibin South, Du'an, Mashan, Shilong, Guixian, Luzhai, Lipu, and Yangshuo. This area is located mostly along the drainage of the Hongshui He.

The phonological features distinguishing this area are (except for Du'an and Yangshuo) 'preglottalized' nasals /ʔm ʔn/ instead of stops /ʔb ʔd/, and /ʔŋ ʔŋw/ instead /ŋ/ or /w/. Also there are two categories of rhymes /ei ou/, and tone categories are very regular and as expected.

(4)   Shilong
      $ʔma^5$ 'to carry on the $ʔnan^1$ (general classifier)
                     back'
      $ʔma:ŋ^5$ 'scar' $ʔŋa:i^1$ 'to lean'
      $ʔnam^1$ 'black' $ʔŋa^1fai^4$ 'tree branch'
      $ʔnaŋ^1$ 'nose'   (cf. Wuming
                                         $ŋa^1fai^4$)

Guixian
ʔŋwet⁷   'to dig'
(cf. Wuming vaːt⁷)
ʔŋwa¹   'to scratch'
ʔŋwaːn³   'bowl'
(cf. Wuming vaːn³)

Yongbei vernacular. Yongning North, Wuming, Binyang, Hengxian, Pingguo.

Only in this area does one find the initial /ɣ/; also clusters /pl ml kl/ are preserved (however, there are instances of /pj p/ and /kj/, which are sometimes realized as /ƫ/). For example:

(5) Wuming
    pla¹   'fish'   mla²   'a kind of pineapple'
    plaːi³   'to walk'   mlaːi²   'saliva'
    plak⁷   'taro'   mlaːk⁸   'slippery'

    Hengxian
    kla³   'rice seedling'   ploːm¹   'skinny'
    klai¹   'far'

The long high vowels in this area are ingliding diphthongs, i.e., /iː- uː- ɯː-/ are /iə uə ɯə/. Moreover, at Yongning North in some places there are no voiced stop initials /b d/, since these have merged with /m n/, as in bau¹ → mau¹ 'light weight' and dei¹ → nui¹ 'good'. The initial /ɣ/ becomes /l/ as in ɣei⁶ → lui⁶ 'uncultivated or incultivatable land'. Some of the palatalized initials become plain: /pj kj/ become /p k/.

Youjiang vernacular. Tiandong, Tianyang, Baise, and generally the area of the basin of the Youjiang River.

In these locations Zhuang initials have been simplified to twelve through mergers; for instance /pj kj/ are /tɕ/, /mj/ has become /n/, and /ɣ/ has become /l/. 'Preglottalized' initials in tone 3 in this location are found in tone 4. Examples are:

(6) Zhuang   Youjiang
      pja:i³   *tɕa:i³*   'walk'
      pjom¹   *tɕom¹*   'hair'
      pja¹   *tɕa¹*   'fish'
      mja:i²   *na:i²*   'saliva'
      ɣam⁴   *lam⁴*   'water'

Also /ei ou/ are realized as /i u/. As for the rhymes:

(7) Zhuang   Youjiang
      dei¹   *di¹*   'good'
      fei²   *fi²*   'fire'
      ɕi⁵   *ɕia⁵*   'to borrow'
      tu²   *tua²*   (classifier for animals)

Guibian vernacular. Includes Fengshan, Lingyun, Tianlin, Longlin, and Yunnan Guangnan North.

There is generally merger of /e ɛ/ and /o ɔ/. For example:

(8) Fengshan
      /ɛu/
      mɛu¹   'cat'
      vɛu⁵   'chipped rim'

      /ɛ:m/
      nɛ:m¹   'to stick'
      lwɛ:m¹ 'spear'

      /ɛ:ŋ/
      bɛ:ŋ¹   'thin'
      ŋɛ:ŋ⁵   'crooked'
      nɛ:p⁷   'to pick up food'

There are also the labialized rhymes /tw nw lw sw ɕw jw kjw/. The tone categories are also altered in significant and characteristic ways. For example, those items with the initials /ʔ b d/ are found in even numbered tones:

(9) $ba^5 \to ba^6$ 'shoulder'
    $ba:t^7 \to ba:t^8$ 'times'
    $da^5 \to da^6$ 'to abuse verbally'
    $dai^3 \to dai^4$ 'must'

Lingyun and Longlin
$ba:n^3 \to ba:n^4$ 'village'

These roots undergo identical changes in the vast majority of Bouyei locations (cf. Buyiyu Diaocha Baogao 1959).

Qiubei vernacular. Yunnan Qiubei area.

The initial /f/ only occurs in Han loan words; nonloans have the initial /v/, for instance $fa:i^1$ 'dam' is here $va:i^1$. In most locations /pj mj/ become /p m/. The long vowels with coda -a:k simplify to -a, -o:k to -uə. Also the rhymes /e:k u:k ɯ:ik/ become /iə u ɯ/ respectively. Moreover, in most locations there is a diphthongization of /e o/.

(10) -a:k → -a
    $pa:k^7$ pa^5 'to keep one's mouth shut'
    $ta:k^7$ ta^5 'to expose to the sun'
    $\gamma a:k^8$ $\gamma uə^6$ 'tree root'

-o:k → -uə
    $do:k^7$ $duə^5$ 'bone'
    $ʔo:k^7$ $ʔuə^5$ 'to come out'

/e:k u:k ɯ:k/ → /iə u ɯ/
    $he:k^7$ $jiə^5$ 'guest'
    $\gamma u:k^8$ γu^6 'to vomit'
    $kɯ:k^8$ $kɯ^6$ 'scaly dragon or dragon of ill fortune'

diphthongization of /e o/
    me^6 $miə^6$ 'mother'
    no^6 $nuə^6$ 'meat'

Southern varieties of Zhuang

Yongnan vernacular. Yongning South, Fusui Central and North, Long'an, Jinzhou, Shangse, and Chongzuo areas.

The particular traits of this lectal area are that it is very prone to developing new tone splits, and also that /b d/, which occur on odd-numbered tones only, merge with /m n/ (except for Shangse and Chongzuo). For instance:

(11) Wuming   Fusui Central
      bin^1 min^1 'to fly'
      bo^5 mo^5 'water spring or well'
      $doŋ^1$ $noŋ^1$ 'woods'

      Wuming   Fusui
      $baːn^3$ $maːn^3$ 'village'
      bau^1 mau^1 'thin (not thick)'
      da^5 na^5 'to scold'
      $daŋ^1$ $naŋ^1$ 'nose'

There are many sound mutations among initials. Initial /ɣ/ of Wuming Zhuang becomes /tʰ/ in odd-numbered tones, and in even-numbered tones it becomes /l/ at times, or in some places in odd and even tones /hl/. For example:

(12) Wuming   Long'an
      *thr-
      $ɣin^1$ $tʰin^1$ 'stone'
      $ɣaːp^7$ $tʰaːp^7$ 'to carry on a pole'
      *dl-
      $ɣum^2$ lum^2 'wind'
      $ɣeːŋ^2$ $leːŋ^2$ 'knife'

      Wuming   Shangse
      $ɣaːu^1$ $laːu^1$ 'quantity'

In voiced initials of even-numbered tones in some places there is a breathy voice element with these syllables, $dvai^2$ 'table' or $bvan^4$ 'village'. Furthermore, except for Long'an and Chongzuo, there are no palatalized initials.

Zuojiang River vernacular. Longzhou (Longjin), Daxin, Tiandeng, Ningming, and generally in the basin of the Zuojiang River.

The features of this vernacular are that in odd numbered tone vocabulary the /ɣ/ of Wuming is realized as /t h/, whereas even numbered tone vocabulary with initial /ɣ/ in Wuming correspondingly show /l ɬ n/. Note that this kind of phenomenon is also found in Shangse and Chongzuo. For example:

(13) Wuming   Longzhou
    ɣin¹   hin¹   'stone'
    ɣaːp⁷   haːp⁷   'to carry on a pole'
    ɣan¹   han¹   'to perceive'
    ɣeːk⁷   heːk⁷   'pot'
    ɣeːŋ²   ɬeːŋ²   'strength'
    ɣo⁴   ɬu⁴   'to know'
    ɣoːk⁸   noːk⁸   'outside'
    ɣam²   lam²   'husk'
    ɣot⁷   that⁷   'fart'

Rhymes in southern Zhuang are somewhat simplified.

Deqing vernacular. Jingxi, Debao, Mubian, and Napo.

In this area there is a voiced reflex of /ɣ/. For example in Debao ɣau² 'we (inclusive)', ɣaːn² 'house'; at Mubian ɣa¹ 'to search for', ɣai⁶ 'wasteland, uncultivated land'. There are, generally speaking, some examples of lexical items, that in northern Zhuang possess initial /ɣ/, which in this vernacular area develop in different ways. For example:

(14) northern Zhuang   Dejing
    ɣaːm¹   t'aːm¹   'to carry on the shoulder'
    ɣiːŋ¹   taːŋ¹   'tail'
    ɣaːp⁷   t'aːp⁸   'to carry on a pole'
    ɣam⁴   noːm⁴   'water'
    ɣoːk⁸   noːk⁸   'outside'
    ɣum²   lɔːm²   'wind'

At Jingxi ɣa¹ is k'ja¹ 'to search for'. Although some places have the initials /tj sj lj/ or other palatalized initials, mostly these occur in Han loans. Except for Mubian, rhyme /ɯː/ becomes /yː/ and /i/ is /ə/.

Yanguang vernacular. The most important areas are in Yunnan at Guangnan South and the Yanshan area.

There is considerable merger of initials; elsewhere in southern Zhuang there are initials /ts kj/ but here there is a merger of /tʃ tsʰ kʰj/ to /tʃʰ/. For example, Tiandeng tsa², Jingxi kja², and Yanshan tʃa² 'tea'; at Jingxi kʰja¹ is Yanshan tʃʰa¹ 'to search', kʰjai⁵ at Debao is tʃʰai⁵ 'egg'. In Yanshan there is a reflex of /ɣ/ corresponding to that found at Debao. There is no length contrast found in dead syllables, e.g., Yanshan /it ip ik/.

(15) southern Zhuang   Yanshan
dip⁷   *dip⁷*   'raw'
diːp⁷   *dip⁷*   'love'

mat⁷   *mat⁷*   'flea'
kaːt⁷   *kat⁷*   'to break'

nak⁷   *nak⁷*   'heavy'
paːk⁷   *pak⁷*   'hundred'

There are no rhymes /ei ou/. For instance, *fei²* is *fai²* 'fire' and *dei¹* is *dai¹* 'good'.

Wenshan vernacular. The most important areas are in Yunnan Wenshan, Malipo, and Guibian.

Some original voiceless consonants are voiced (or perhaps original voiced stops with concomitant low tones have not devoiced, cf. Zhang Junru 1987 and L-Thongkum this volume). Even numbered tones with initial /p t k ts s/ in this location become /b d dz z/. As a result in some places, the 'preglottalized' voiced stops and the plain voiced stops merge to a plain voiced stop but are kept separate by their tones: *bẽ¹* 'thin (not thick)' versus *bi²* 'fat' and *dã¹* 'black' versus *do⁶* 'river'. There are examples of palatalized or labialized initials. In this place, vocabulary with rhyme *a* + stop loses this consonant, and nasal codas disappear leaving a nasalized vowel. For example:

(16) *tap⁷*   *ta⁴*   'liver'
     pat⁷   *pa⁴*   'to sweep'
     sam¹ *sã¹*   'three'

Common features of northern and southern Zhuang

1. Every syllable has an initial, a rhyme, and a tone. In closed syllables there is strong evidence of a long vowel/short vowel contrast. Generally, there are six tones in syllables with vocalic or nasal codas and two to four tones in syllables with voiceless stop codas. Initials have influenced the development of tones in similar and usual ways, and there is also tonal correspondence in common vocabulary between the northern and southern varieties.
2. Zhuang at every location has six vowel contrasts /a e o i u ɯ/; all distinguish for length except for /e/. Short vowels occur in syllables

with codas. Codas can be formed by the vowels /i u ɯ/ (as well as by consonants).
3. There are about twenty consonant contrasts in each location. There is variation in the number of contrastive consonants with secondary articulations, i.e., palatalizations and labializations /pj kj mj kw ŋw/. /m n ŋ p t k/ can form the initial as well as the coda of a syllable.

Differences between northern and southern Zhuang

1. Southern Zhuang has a set of aspirated voiceless stop initials, which northern Zhuang (except for Sanjiang) doesn't have:

(17)

	'kill'	'near'	'walk'	'vegetable'	'kick'	'arrive'
Northern						
Wuming	ka^3	$klaɯ^3$	$pla:i^3$	$plak^7$	tik^7	$taŋ^2$
Laibin	ka^3	$kjaɯ^3$	$pja:i^3$	$pjak^7$	tik^7	$taŋ^2$
Tianyang	ka^3	$tɕai^3$	$tɕa:i^3$	$tɕak^7$	tik^7	$taŋ^2$
Guangnan	ka^3	$kjaɯ^3$	$pja:i^3$	$pjak^7$	tek^7	$taŋ^2$
Southern						
Chongzuo	k^ha^3	$k^hjə^3$	$p^hja:i^3$	$p^hjɯk^7$	$t^hɯk^7$	$t^hɯŋ^1$
Yongning	k^ha^3	$k^haɯ^3$	$p^ha:i^3$	p^hak^7	t^hek^7	$t^haŋ^1$
Longzhou	k^ha^3	$k^hjaɯ^3$	$p^hja:i^3$	p^hjak^7	t^hik^7	$t^hɯŋ^1$
Guangnan	k^ha^3	$k^hjaɯ^3$	p^hai^5	p^hek^7	t^hek^7	$t^haŋ^1$

2. Although southern Zhuang has an aspirated set of initials, these do not always correspond one-to-one with unaspirated initials in northern Zhuang. Often there are two initials with the same place of articulation or same manner of articulation. One finds southern:northern alternations of the type, for instance, ph:f(v); pʰj:p~t; h:t; tʰ~h:ɣ~j; kʰ:h; kʰj~hj:ɣ~j; kʰw:w.

(18)

	'cloud'	'rain'	'soft shell turtle'	'dry in sun'	'crack open'	'laugh'	'louse'
Southern							
Longzhou	p^hu^3	p^hon^1	p^ha^1	$p^hja:k^7$	$pje:k^7$	hai^3	hau^1
Shangse	p^hy^3	p^hon^1	p^hy^1	$ta:k^7$	t^hek^7	hai^3	t^hou^1
Long'an	$p^hɯ^3$	p^hun^1	$p^hɯ^1$	$ta:k^8$	tek^8	tai^3	$hjiu^2$

Regional Variants and Vernaculars in Zhuang   89

	'cloud'	'rain'	'soft shell turtle'	'dry in sun'	'crack open'	'laugh'	'louse'
Northern							
Wuming	$fɯ^3$	$fɯn^1$	$fɯ^1$	$ta{:}k^7$	tek^7	tai^3	yau^1
Yishan	—	$vɯn^1$	—	$ta{:}k^7$	tek^7	tai^3	jau^1

	'carry on shoulder'	'excrement'	'rice'	'sieve'	'tung tree'	'trousers'	'horizon'
Southern							
Longzhou	$ha{:}m^1$	k^hi^2	k^hau^3	$k^hjɔŋ^1$	k^hjau^1	$khwa^5$	$khwa{:}ŋ^1$
Shangse	$ta{:}m^1$	k^hoy^2	hau^4	$laŋ^1$	lou^1	—	$wa{:}ŋ^1$
Long'an	$ta{:}m^1$	hai^4	hau^4	$hjaŋ^1$	$hjau^1$	wa^5	$wa{:}ŋ^1$
Northern							
Wuming	$ya{:}m^1$	hai^4	hau^4	$yaŋ^1$	yau^1	wa^5	$wa{:}ŋ^1$
Yishan	$ja{:}m^1$	hai^4	hau^4	$jaŋ^1$	jau^1	wa^5	$wa{:}ŋ^1$

3. Zhuang /ɣ/ is the initial that varies at virtually every location. In northern varieties it is manifested sometimes as /l/. But, where in odd numbered tones it does not merge with /j/, there is generally a separate contrastive segment /ɣ/. In southern Zhuang there is generally no segment /ɣ/ (some places it is realized as /hl/ or /hɺ/); in both odd and even numbered tones there are three or more reflexes of /ɣ/. In Longzhou, for instance, there is no segment /ɣ/, but those items appear mostly with initials /h s l/. A small number of items even have /ŋ n t th kh khj/, but only in odd numbered tones; /s l n ɲ/ occur only in even numbered tones.

(19)

	North			South			
Wuming	Huanjiang	Tianyang	Longzhou	Long'an	Jingxi		
$ɣa{:}u^1$	$ja{:}u^1$	$la{:}u^1$	$ha{:}u^1$	$hla{:}u^1$	$k^hja{:}u^1$	'quantity'
$ɣin^1$	jin^1	lin^1	hin^1	t^hin^1	$t^hən^1$	'stone'
$ɣau^3$	jau^3	lau^3	hau^3	t^hau^3	t^hau^3	'warm'
$ɣim^1$	jim^1	lim^1	tim^1	t^him^1	t^him^1	'full'
$ɣau^5$	jiu^5	lau^5	hau^5	$hlau^5$	hau^5	'to bark'
$ɣo{:}i^1$	$jo{:}i^1$	$lo{:}i^1$	wi^1	$hlo{:}i^1$	wei^1	'comb'
$ɣam^2$	$ɣam^2$	lam^2	$ɬam^2$	$hlam^2$	$hjam^2$	'husk'
$ɣu^2$	you^2	lua^2	$lɯ^2$	hlu^2	ly^2	'boat'
$ɣum^2$	$ɣom^2$	lum^2	lum^2	lum^2	lam^2	'wind'
$ɣam^4$	$ɣam^3$	lam^4	ham^4	ham^4	ham^4	'water'

	North			South			
Wuming	Huanjiang	Tianyang	Longzhou	Long'an	Jingxi		
ɣoːk⁸	ɣoːk⁸	noːk⁸	noːk⁸	loːk⁸	noːk⁸	'outside'
-a²	-na²	-la²	-ŋa²	-ŋa²	-ŋa²	'sesame'

4. The 'preglottalized' initial /ʔj/ of northern Zhuang is lost in southern Zhuang.

(20)

	North			South		
Wuming	Shilong	Laibin	Chongzuo	Longzhou	Ningming	
ʔjoːm⁵	—	—	jo²	joːm⁵	—	'perceive'
ʔjau⁵	ʔjɯ⁵	ʔjɯ⁵	jou⁵	ju⁵	jou⁵	'live'
ʔjɯ¹	ʔjɯ¹	ʔjɯ¹	—	ja¹	ja¹	'medicine'
ʔjɯːk⁷	ʔjɯːk⁷	—	—	jaːk⁷	—	'hungry'

5. There are systematic differences between northern and southern initials.

(21)

	Wuming (N)	Southern	
f ~ m	fau²	mɯ²	'hand'
	fai⁴	mai⁴	'tree'
	fɯ²	mɯ²	'uncultivated area'
n ~ m	nan²	man²	'body louse'
	nai¹	mɯːi¹	'snow, frost'
	neːŋ²	meːŋ²	'fly, insect'
l ~ d	lak⁸	dak⁷	'deep'
	lai¹	dai¹	'ladder'

6. There are north-south differences in regard to vowel length.

(22)

Wuming (N)	Southern Zhuang	
nuk⁷	nuːk⁷	'deaf'
nin²	noːn²	'sleep'
ɣuk⁸	luːk⁸	'tadpole'
ɣoːŋ⁶	ɬuŋ⁶	'dawn'
nuːŋ⁴	noːŋ⁴	'y. sibling'
ŋɯ²	ŋu²	'snake'
ɣaːn²	ɬaːn²	'home, house'
ɣaːk⁸	tsɯːk⁸	'rope'

Regional Variants and Vernaculars in Zhuang 91

7. Tonal differences are as follows:

(23) Wuming (N)   Southern Zhuang
      ma^1 ma^2 'come back'
      man^3 man^4 'plum'
      man^6 man^5 'solid'
      $ma:i^5$ $ma:i^3$ 'widow'
      na^4 na^5 'mother's brother'
      nei^4 nai^3 'this'
      $no:i^4$ $no:i^6$ 'small'
      no^6 nu^4 'meat'
      tam^3 tam^5 'weave'
      hau^4 k^hau^3 'rice'
      $ŋo^4$ $ʔo^3$ 'reed'

8. The Zhuang tonal system shares many common features with the Han system. There are six open syllable tones and tone 7 and 8 are found in closed syllables. There is considerable variation of tone value from place to place, but the tone categories are quite similar.

(24) | | 'thick' | 'paddy' | 'face' | 'horse' | 'cross' | 'river' |
|---|---|---|---|---|---|---|
| Wuming (N) | na^{24} | na^{21} | na^{55} | ma^{42} | kwa^{35} | ta^{33} |
| Laibin (N) | na^{24} | na^{231} | na^{33} | ma^{24} | kwa^{53} | ta^{21} |
| Shilong (N) | na^{53} | na^{33} | na^{44} | ma^{13} | kwa^{35} | ta^{31} |
| Liujiang (S) | na^{42} | na^{231} | na^{53} | ma^{24} | kwa^{33} | ta^{22} |
| Baise (S) | na^{13} | na^{31} | na^{45} | ma^{33} | kwa^{24} | ta^{22} |
| Longzhou (S) | na^{33} | na^{21} | na^{24} | ma^{32} | kwa^{55} | ta^{11} |

The tone values of northern Zhuang locations are more similar to each other; for instance the tone values of areas in the basins of the Hongshui River drainage and the Liujiang River drainage show strong resemblance. Wuming and the Youjiang River drainage locations are also similar.

Comparison of northern and southern Zhuang vocabulary

The vocabulary of northern Zhuang is mostly alike with a small number of differences. There are four basic kinds of lexical differences.

1. The lexical variation is much smaller than the phonological variation.
2. Southern Zhuang and northern Zhuang have a number of systematic lexical differences:

(25)   'louse'   'comb'   'he'   'flower'   'cloth'   'clothing'

1 nan^2 $sɯ:i^2$ te^1 wa^1 $paŋ^2$ pu^6
2 nan^2 $sɯ:i^2$ te^1 va^1 $paŋ^2$ pu^6
3 nan^2 $ɬɯ:i^2$ te^1 wa^1 $paŋ^2$ pia^6

4 min^2 $mo:n^2$ min^2 $pjo:k^7$ $pa:i^3$ $ɬɯə^3$
5 min^2 $mo:n^2$ $mən^2$ $jo:k^8$ $pʰa:i^3$ $ɬɯə^2$
6 $mən^2$ $mo:n^2$ $mən^2$ $pjo:k^7$ $pʰa:i^3$ $ɬi^3$

       'sheep'   'sky'   'sweat'   'skinny'   'do'

1 $ji:ŋ^2$ $bɯn^1$ $ha:n^6$ $plo:m^1$ $ku:k^8$
2 $ju:ŋ^2$ bun^1 $ha:n^6$ $po:m^1$ ku^6
3 $juɐŋ^2$ $bɯn^1$ $ha:n^6$ lo^2 $kuɐk^8$

4 be^3 fa^4 $hɯ^5$ heu^5 hit^7
5 be^3 fa^4 $hə^5$ $he:u^5$ $he:t^7$
6 be^3 fa^4 ti^6 $he:u^5$ $he:t^7$

N 1 = Wuming, 2 = Laibing, 3 = Tiandong
S 4 = Longzhou, 5 = Daxin, 6 = Chongzuo

3. Between northern and southern Zhuang there are a considerable number of lexical litmus tests. For instance, in the northern Zhuang centered along the Hongshui River the most prototypical northern vocabulary is found. In northern Zhuang there is generally common vocabulary whereas in the south there are independent developments at many locations.

(26)   'head'   'yesterday'   'heaven'   'slippery'   'horn'
     North $kjau^3$ $lɯ:n^2$ $bɯn^1$ $ɣau^2/mja:k^8$ kau^1

1   N   N   N   N $ko:k^7$
2    $tʰu^1$ $-wa^2$ fa^4 N kok^7
3    $tʰu^1$ $-wa^2$ fa^4 $ma:k^8$ N
4   hu^1 $-wa^2$ fa^4 N kok^7

	'flower'	'goose'	'yellow'	's/he'
North	wa^1	$ha{:}n^5$	$he{:}n^3$	te^1
1	N	$pu{:}n^6$	$N/luŋ^1$	man^2
2	N	N	N	N
3	$dɔk^7$	N	N	N
4	$pjo{:}k^7$	$pɯn^6$	$lɯ{:}ŋ^1$	min^2

N = northern form, 1 = Yongnan, 2 = Dejing, 3 = Yanguang, 4 = Zuojiang

(27)
South	'table'	'mud'	'bowl'
1	$tso{:}ŋ^2$	tom^1	t^hui^3
2	$ta{:}i^2$	$S/na{:}m^6$	$ʔwa{:}n^3$
3	S	$na{:}m^6$	S
4	S	$na{:}m^6$	S
5	$ta{:}i^2$	$na{:}m^6$	$wa{:}n^3$
6	$ta{:}i^2$	$na{:}m^6$	$wa{:}n^3$
7	S	$na{:}m^6$	S

S = southern form, 1 = Yongbei, 2 = Youjiang, 3 = Guibian, 4 = Hongshui He, 5 = Liujiang, 6 = Guibei, 7 = Qiubei

4. The place-to-place lexical variations in northern Zhuang are smaller than in the southern area.

In 1955 a study was carried out by the Chinese Academy of Social Sciences and linguistic researchers from Guangxi on the northern and southern varieties of Zhuang in Guangxi Province. 2,350 commonly used lexical items were compared. Of these, 1,592 were the same or similar in the two varieties. Specifically, some of the point-to-point comparisons are:

(28)
	same	different
Wuming:Tiandong	1,155 (73.3%)	437 (26.7%)
Wuming:Laibin	1,851 (86.4%)	211 (13.6%)
Wuming:Liujiang	1,206 (75.8%)	386 (24.2%)
Laibin:Tiandong	1,197 (75.3%)	395 (24.7%)
Binyang:Huanjiang	1,243 (78.1%)	349 (21.9%)

The mean value for common vocabulary in northern Zhuang areas was 77.9%.

(29)	same	different
Fusui:Debao	1,115 (70.1%)	477 (29.9%)
Jinzhou:Debao	996 (63.3%)	596 (36.7%)
Chongzuo:Debao	1,135 (71.3%)	457 (28.7%)

The mean value for common vocabulary in southern Zhuang areas was only 68.3%.

These numbers show that common cognate vocabulary across the two major varieties is not small. It usually numbers about 65%.

(30)	same		different
Wuming:Chongzuo	1,084 of 1,587	(68.2%)	508 (31.8%)
Laibin:Longzhou	966 of 1,592	(67.7%)	406 (32.3%)
Liujiang:Longzhou	864 of 1,426	(60.6%)	562 (39.4%)

There are a number of vocabulary items found very widely in Zhuang. Most are items that express things found in everyday life. Wuming sound values are used here to illustrate:

(31)
bin^1	'to fly'	$kɯn^1$	'eat'	pau^1	'crab'
$ba{:}ŋ^1$	'thin'	lau^3	'wine'	pi^2	'fat'
bau^1	'leaf'	$lɯk^8$	'children'	pit^7	'duck'
ba^5	'shoulder'	lin^4	'tongue'	pla^1	'mountain'
$ba{:}n^3$	'village'	lap^7	'dark'	$plak^7$	'vegetable'
$ʔak^7$	'chest'	mou^1	'pig'	$pla{:}i^3$	'walk'
$ʔo{:}k^7$	'to come out'	ma^1	'dog'	$ɣam^4$	'water'
$ɕai^1$	'to plow'	not^8	'ant'	$ɣa{:}n^2$	'house'
$ɕaɯ^4$	'to buy'	mo^5	'new'	$ɣu^2$	'boat'
$da{:}ŋ^1$	'body'	na^3	'face'	$ɣok^8$	'bird'
$daŋ^1$	'nose'	$naŋ^1$	'skin'	$ɣiu^1$	'smile'
dam^1	'to plant'	na^2	'paddy'	$ɣa{:}p^7$	'carry on a pole'
hau^4	'rice'	nou^1	'rat'	sai^3	'intestine'
$ha{:}u^1$	'white'	nak^7	'heavy'	$sa{:}ŋ^1$	'tall'
ha^3	'five'	nin^2	'to sleep'	so^6	'straight'

ke:n¹ 'arm'   *na¹* 'thick'
kai⁵ 'chicken'   *pa:k⁷* 'mouth'

These items are obviously a part of the early vocabulary shared by both northern and southern Zhuang.

The Zhuang language has had its own writing system since 1954. It is a romanization and is modeled on the sound inventory of Wuming.

References

Buyiyu Diaocha Baogao. 1959. [Field report on the Bouyei language]. Beijing: Kexue Chubanshe.

Li Fang-Kuei. 1940. The Tai dialect of Lungchow: Texts, translations and glossary. Institute of History and Philology Monograph Series A 16. Taipei: Academia Sinica.

Wei Qingwen and Qin Guosheng. 1980. Zhuangyu jianzi. Beijing: Minzu Chubanshe.

Zhang Junru. 1987. Zhuangyu Wenma Tuyu de Yinlei Yanbian. [Phonological changes in Wenma Patois of Zhuang]. Minzu Yuwen 5:10–18.

Zhuangyu yinxi. 1959. [Zhuang phonology]. Beijing: Chinese Academy of Social Sciences.

1 Guibei Vernacular
1 罗城 Luocheng
2 环江 Huanjiang
3 融水 Rongshui
4 融安 Rong'an
5 三江 Sanjiang
6 永福 Yongfu
7 龙胜 Longsheng
8 河池 Hechi
9 南丹 Nandan
10 天峨 Tian'e
11 东兰 Donglan

2 Liujiang Vernacular
12 柳江 Liujiang
13 来宾北 Laibin (N)
14 宜山 Yishan
15 柳城 Liucheng
16 忻城 Xincheng

3 Hongshui He Vernacular
17 来宾南 Laibin (S)
18 贵县 Guixian
19 石龙武 Shilong (Wu)
20 都安 Du'an
21 马山 Mashan
22 上林 Shanglin
23 石龙象 Shilong (Xiang)
24 鹿寨 Luzhai
25 荔浦 Lipu
26 阳朔 Yangshuo
27 贺县 Hexian

4 Yongbei Vernacular
28 邕宁北 Yongning (N)
29 武鸣 Wuming
30 横县北 Hengxian (N)
31 宾阳 Binyang
32 横县南 Hengxian (S)
33 平果 Pingguo

5 Youjiang Vernacular
34 田东 Tiandong
35 田阳 Tianyang
36 百色 Baise

6 Guibian Vernacular
37 凤山 Fengshan
38 凌乐 Lingle
39 隆林 Longlin
40 田林 Tianlin
41 云南广南北 Yunnan Guangnan (N)

7 Qiubei Vernacular
42 云南丘北 Yunnan Qiubei

8 Yongnan Vernacular
43 邕宁南 Yongning (S)
44 扶绥中 Fusui (Central)
45 扶绥北 Fusui (N)
46 隆安 Long'an
47 钦县 Qinxian
48 上思 Shangsi
49 崇左 Chongzuo

9 Zuojiang Vernacular
50 龙津 Longjin
51 大新 Daxin
52 天等 Tiandeng
53 宁明 Ningming

10 Deqing Vernacular
54 靖西 Jingxi
55 德保 Debao
56 睦边 Mubian

11 Yangguang Vernacular
57 云南广南南 Yunnan Guangnan (S)
58 砚山 Yanshan

12 Wenshan Vernacular
59 文山 Wenshan

Village Names in Guangxi Province and Northeastern Thailand

Pranee Kullavanijaya
Department of Linguistics
Chulalongkorn University, Bangkok, Thailand

Editors' Introduction. In this article the names of villages are cited according to the official language of their respective political units, namely Guangxi-Zhuang Autonomous Province and the Kingdom of Thailand. In the case of Thailand, the language is Standard Thai, which is cited in a phonetic transcription. The Zhuang standard language is based on the Northern Zhuang dialect of Wuming, and is cited in the official romanization, occasionally with Southern Zhuang (Longzhou) equivalents added, also in official romanization. To the Zhuang romanization we have added a phonetic transcription in slanted brackets. It should be understood that, in both Guangxi and northeastern Thailand, the village names would be pronounced by local speakers according to the local vernacular, which in many cases differs from the standard. Since this article deals with the structural makeup and the semantics of the names, rather than their phonology, the official-language equivalents are used for simplicity's sake.

This article is based on a research report of the same name. The research, done in 1992, was financially supported by the Toyota Foundation.

Introduction

Place names such as the names of the rivers, hills, and villages not only serve as location references, but provide, in fact, a wealth of information about an ethnic group of people. Village names may reveal the history of the group—their ways of living, their migrations, their contact with other ethnic groups. Many English place names ending in *-by, -thorp, -beck, -dale,* for example, tell us about the Scandinavian invaders to the British Isles. The present article studies the village names in six counties of the Guangxi-Zhuang Autonomous Region in China in comparison with the village names in four *changwats*[1] in the northeastern part of Thailand (see map 3). The main purpose of the study is to see whether there is any difference in the way the Zhuang and the Thai name their villages. It is hypothesized that basically, there should be similarities rather than differences. Also, it is hoped that the study will reveal the ways of living of these two Tai ethnic groups. Finally, it is expected that the study of the Zhuang village names will tell whether the northern Zhuang and the southern Zhuang, living close to each other, differ or not in the way they name their villages.

The reason for selecting four changwats in the northeastern part of Thailand should be given here. Geographically, these four changwats are closest to the Guangxi-Zhuang Autonomous Region. Moreover, data for these four changwats in Thailand were available to the researcher at the time she studied them. Finally, if further research can be done for the Tai village names in northern Laos and northern Vietnam, the picture of the Tai villages will be complete, and some information about Tai migration might be revealed. At the moment, data on village names in Laos and Vietnam are not yet available.

Data on the Zhuang village names are taken from *Guangjsih vahcuengh diegmengz senjciz* published by Guangxi Nationalities Publishing House in 1988. However, data from local documents, collected with the help of Fang Ying, a professor from the Guangxi Institute of Nationalities, are also used where published data are scarce or when some results of the study need to be confirmed.

The Zhuang village names are from the following seven counties which were selected to cover the northern Zhuang and the southern Zhuang groups, in the areas from the north to the south of the province (see map 1).

---

[1]*changwat* is a Thai term used to refer to a unit in the Thai administrative system. It is lower than *phaak* but higher than *amphoe* in the following hierachy: *pratheet* 'country'; *phaak* 'region'; *changwat* 'province or provincial city'; *amphoe, tambon, baan* 'village'.

(1)   1. Tian'e county   with 85 village names
      2. Xilin county   with 32 village names
      3. Donglan county   with 312 village names
      4. Napo county   with 119 village names
      5. Longzhou county   with 100 village names
      6. Ningming county   with 89 village names
      7. Long'an county   with 107 village names

Counties 1–3 are northern Zhuang, 4–7 are southern Zhuang. Altogether the Zhuang data contain 844 names: 429 are northern Zhuang and 415 are southern Zhuang.

Data on the Thai village names are from a list prepared by the Ministry of the Interior in 1989 and 1991. These are village names in the four provinces Loei, Nongkhaai, Nakornphanom, and Udornthani, all of which are in the northernmost part of northeast Thailand (see map 3).

(2)   1. Changwat Loei   with 501 village names
      2. Changwat Nongkhaai   with 761 village names
      3. Changwat Nakhornphanom   with 596 village names
      4. Changwat Udornthani   with 2,119 village names

Altogether the Thai data contain 3,977 village names.

Zhuang village names

Structure of the village names. From the Zhuang data of 844 village names, it is found that almost all names are made up of two words. Only about 45 names are composed of three words. Words in the village names are monosyllabic, some of which are borrowings from Cantonese and other Chinese dialects. For example,[2] in *lajgeng* /la^3 keŋ^1/, the element *geng* /keŋ^1/ 'small hill' is borrowed from Cantonese; in *nazbohyen*, /na^2 po^6 jen^1/ *yen* is a borrowed form of the Chinese *xian* 'county' Of the two-word village names, 90% are noun-noun or noun-adjective constructions. There are also adjective-noun and preposition-noun constructions, but these are very few in number. The following are some examples of Zhuang two-word village names.

---

[2]Examples from the Zhuang data are given first in the Zhuang writing system, followed by phonetic transcription in slanted brackets. The Zhuang script indicates tones with final letters as follows: no symbol = 1, z = 2, q = 5, j = 3, x = 4, and h = 6.

(3) N-N   *nazrin* /na² rin¹/ (*naz* /na²/ 'field' + *rin* /rin¹/ 'stone')
            luegmboq /luːk⁸ bɔ⁵/ (*lueg* /luːk⁸/ 'valley' + *mboq* /bɔ⁵/ 'well')
      N-Adj *mbanjmoq* /baːn¹ mɔ⁵/ (*mbanj* /baːn¹/ 'village' + *moq* /mɔ⁵/ 'new')
            nazgvangq /na² kwaːŋ⁵/ (*naz* /na²/ 'field' + *gvangq* /kwaːŋ⁵/ 'wide')

Zhuang favorite village names. When the 844 village names were examined, it was seen that a large number of them shared the same first words. There are 133 words which are used as the first word of more than one village name, out of which 33 appear at a frequency rate of 3 to 152 occurrences. The village names which begin with one of these 33 words will be called 'favorite village names'. Out of the 33 words, only four words are found in village names in all seven counties under study. They are *naz* /na²/ 'field', *mbanj* /baːn³/ 'village', *rungh* /ruŋ⁶/ ~ *lungh* /luŋ⁶/ 'plain in the valley', and *bak* /paːk⁷/ 'mouth, opening'. The frequency of occurrences of these four words in 844 names is 365 names or 43.25% of the total. We may call village names with these four words the 'most favorite Zhuang village names'. The following table shows the distribution of each in the northern and southern Zhuang village names.

(4) Northern and Southern Zhuang village names

	N. Zhuang 429 villages	S. Zhuang 415 villages
naz /na²/	24.0%	16.38%
mbanj /baːn³/	14.21%	11.56%
rungh /ruŋ⁶/ ~ *lungh* /luŋ⁶/	3.03%	10.12%
bak /paːk⁷/	3.49%	3.85%

The above table shows that while village names with *naz* /na²/, *mbanj* /baːn³/, and *bak* /paːk⁷/ are more or less equally frequent in the northern and southern Zhuang village names, *rungh* /ruŋ⁶/ ~ *lungh* /luŋ⁶/ is much more preferred in southern Zhuang. Moreover, village names with *naz* /na²/ as the first word show a constant distribution in all areas.

The data on the less favorite village names (names beginning with the 29 words that are second in frequency to *naz* /na²/, *mbanj* /baːn³/, *rungh* /ruŋ⁶/ ~ *lungh* /luŋ⁶/ and *bak* /paːk⁸/) reveal that some words occur only or mostly in the northern Zhuang village names, while some occur only in the southern ones. *rij* /ri³/ 'canal', for example, occurs as the first word almost exclusively in the northern Zhuang area, whereas *go* /kɔ¹/ 'tree', *goek* /kɔk⁷/ 'tree trunk', and *naemx* /nam⁴/ 'water' are found mostly in the southern Zhuang area.

These words may be used to predict whether a village name belongs to the southern or northern Zhuang area.

Role of the second word in the Zhuang village names. Study of the second words in the most favorite Zhuang village names yields a result which deserves some comment. In a village name construction, the second word modifies the first word, or the head noun. In *nazrin* /na² rin¹/, *nazrungz* /na² ruŋ²/, the second words *rin* /rin¹/ 'stone' and *rungz* /ruŋ²/ 'banyan tree' indicate the physical characteristics of the area: whether the area is stony or whether there is a banyan tree in the area. In many cases, the second word makes the village name become metaphoric, for example, *naznou* /na² nou¹/ 'field' + 'mouse' indicates that there must be a rock or a hill in the area that looks like a mouse. In *mbanjdoeng* /baːn³ tɔŋ¹/ 'village' + 'forest', *mbanjdaiz* /baːn³ taːi²/ 'village' + 'plateau', and *mbanjdoemq* /baːn³ tɔm⁵/ 'village' + 'basin', the second words inform us about the location of the villages. In *mbanjlaj* /baːn³ la³/ 'village-below', *mbanjgwnz* /baːn³ kɯn²/ 'village-above', and *mbanjgyang* /baːn³ kjaːŋ³/ 'village' + 'central, middle', the second words illustrate the points where the villages are located. The latter examples give the picture of a group of villages where one village is located north or south of another village or among the villages. Such a picture helps explain a development of a small community or a small village into a bigger community.

The study of the village names in seven counties has shown that there is no significant difference in the construction of village names between Northern and Southern Zhuang. Both Northern and Southern Zhuang name their villages according to the physical characteristics of the location: *rungh* /ruŋ⁶/ ~ *lungh* /luŋ⁶/ 'plain surrounded by hills', *lueg* /luːk⁸/ 'plain in the valley', *bya* /pja¹/ 'rocky mountain', *boh* /bɔ⁶/ ~ *bo* /bɔ¹/ 'hills', *ndoi* /dɔːi⁴/ 'earthen hill', *luengq* /luːŋ⁵/ 'ridge', *rij* /ri³/ 'stream in the mountain'. It is suggested from the village names that the areas where the Zhuang live are mountainous, but that they live on the plains or valleys. Also, it is clear that the Zhuang are rice growers. Other kinds of plants often found in the village names are bamboo and banyan trees. As for bamboo there must be many kinds: *faiz* /faːi²/, *baenz* /ban²/, *goeng* /kɔŋ¹/, and *dan* /taːn¹/. These words show that bamboo must be an important plant in the life of the Zhuang.

Thai village names

Structure of the village names. The Thai village names are taken from four *changwats* in the uppermost part of northeastern Thailand: Loei, Nongkhaai, Nakhornphanom, and Udornthani, as mentioned above. From the data of 3,977 village names, it is found that the names can consist of two, three, or even four words. However, similar to the Zhuang data, the two-word names comprise the majority. The words in the Thai village names are not only monosyllabic but can be disyllabic or polysyllabic. These multisyllabic words are usually loans from Pali or Sanskrit. The following are examples of two- and three-word village names; each word can be monosyllabic or polysyllabic.

(5) Two-word village names

    naa ʔɔ̌ɔ   'field' + 'a kind of grass'
    pàak phuu   'mouth' + 'mountain'
    noon sǒmbuun 'mound, hill' + 'perfect'

(6) Three-word village names

    nɔ̌ɔŋ dɔ̀ɔk bua   'swamp' + 'flower' + 'lotus'
    khôok klaaŋ sǎamákkhii 'mound' + 'middle' + 'unity'

Again, similar to the Zhuang data, the Thai village names show repetition of the first words. Out of the 3,977 names, 2,674 names or 67% of the total show the repetition of 22 words occurring as the first word.[3] Although these 22 words are found in village names in all four changwats, the rate of their occurrences varies greatly, that is, from 15 times to 520 times.

The three words that show constant distribution and highest rate of frequency in all four changwats are *nɔ̌ɔŋ* 'swamp', *naa* 'field', and *noon* 'small hill'. The table below shows their occurrences in the four changwats.

(7) Distribution and frequency of three words in Thai village names

	Loei	Nongkhaai	Nakhorn-phanom	Udorn	Total	
Number of Villages	501	761	596	2,119	3,977	
nɔ̌ɔŋ 'swamp'	44	98	79	299	520	13.07%
naa 'field'	77	77	116	176	446	11.21%
noon 'small hill'	15	92	18	248	373	9.37%

We call village names with one of these three words in the first position the 'most favorite Thai village names' in the northeastern part of Thailand.

---

[3] It should be observed that there are a large number of words which occur as first word in the village names. About 400 words occur only in one name and the rest occur in more names but are not found in all four changwats.

Role of the second word in Thai village names. The second words can be grouped according to their grammatical categories into groups of nouns and adjectives. When the second words are nouns, they usually signify plants, animals, or physical characteristics and accordingly add more information to the names. For example:

(8) nɔ̌ɔŋ dɔ̀ɔk bua   'swamp' + 'flower' + 'lotus'
     phoon sai   'ridge' + 'banyan tree'
     nɔ̌ɔŋ plaa dùk   'swamp' + 'catfish'
     nɔ̌ɔŋ sǔa khraaŋ   'swamp' + 'tiger' + 'moan'
     naa khôok   'field' + 'mound'

It is observed that there are certain co-occurrence preferences. The second words signifying plant names and animal names usually occur with *nɔ̌ɔŋ* and *naa* and rarely with *noon*.

When the second words are adjectives, they usually signify fertility, size, shape, and other qualities; for example:

(9) noon saʔàat   'small hill' + 'clean'
     noon sìwílai   'small hill' + 'civilized'
     phoon sǔuŋ   'ridge' + 'tall'

Such qualifications can be assumed to be the qualifications of the villages or the locations. Sometimes the names tell what the villagers wish their village to be. This usually occurs when the second words signify fertility. These words are observed to be borrowed from Pali, Sanskrit, Cambodian, and even English:

(10) noon sǒmbuun   'small hill' + 'perfect'   (Sanskrit borrowing)
     noon sawǎn   'small hill' + 'heaven'   (Sanskrit borrowing)
     noon sǎmraan   'small hill' + 'happiness'   (Khmer borrowing)
     noon ʔudom   'small hill' + 'fertile'   (Pali/Sanskrit borrowing)
     noon sìwílai   'small hill' + 'civilized'   (English borrowing)

As has been mentioned, the Thai village names may contain three words; if they do, the third word usually signifies the point of location or direction, for example:

(11) naa yaaŋ tâi   'field' + 'a kind of tree' + 'south'
     naa yaaŋ nǔa   'field' + 'a kind of tree' + 'north'

mài 'new' is also found in this position signifying the more recent establishment of a village of the same name; for example, *naa hêεw mài* suggests that there is already a village named *naa hêεw*.

What has been mentioned above for the second and third words in the most favorite Thai village names applies also to the less favorite village names.

When considering the favorite village names altogether, that is, both most favorite and less favorite names as mentioned above, it is seen that the first names suggest four groups of physical locations:

1. rice fields and other fields
   - *naa* 'ricefield'
   - *thûŋ* 'field, plain'

2. water resources
   - *hûai* 'stream'
   - *paak* 'mouth of a river or stream'
   - *nɔ̌ɔŋ* 'swamp'
   - *kùt* 'a kind of swamp'
   - *thâa* 'river'
   - *bùŋ* 'a type of low land near water'
   - *nám* 'water'

3. hilly land
   - *khôok* 'mound'
   - *phuu* 'mountain'
   - *noon* 'mound'
   - *dɔɔn* 'high land, mound'
   - *phoon* 'knoll'

4. woods
   - *pàa* 'forest'
   - *doŋ* 'forest'
   - *lâu* 'deserted land'

It can be deduced from the groups above that the land where the four changwats are located is hilly, has different types of water resources, and is a rice-growing area. These inferences are found to be physically correct. The area is called the Sakonnakhorn basin, where to the north lies the Phuu Phaan mountain chain and the Maekhong River. Several streams flow into the Maekhong River and the basin is scattered with swamps.

Conclusion

A comparison of the Zhuang and Thai favorite village names gives the following results.

Similarity in the construction of the village names. Both the Zhuang and Thai village names show that the majority of the village names are two-word structures, containing two nouns or a noun and an adjective. When the village names contain three words, the third word in both languages is usually a word indicating a point of location, direction, or time of settlement. Such use of the third word gives us a picture of a small village expanded into a group of villages. Also, it suggests a means for villagers to keep their identity when they move to a new location.

Similarity in the first word. Both the Zhuang and Thai favorite village names show a way the Zhuang and the Thai name their villages according to physical characteristics of the location. This is usually seen in the first word of the names. We can learn through these first words that the Zhuang live in mountainous areas with different kinds of mountains or on plains of different heights; while the Thai live on low land with swamps or other kinds of water resources and small hills. The use of *naa* or *naz* /na^2/ 'rice field' in both languages indicates that both the Zhuang and the Thai are rice farmers.

Differences in sources of borrowing. The Zhuang village names show some Cantonese and Mandarin loanwords whereas the Thai names show borrowed words from Pali, Sanskrit, Cambodian, and even English. Pali and Sanskrit words in the Thai village names are found most frequently and often they are synonymous with the Thai words. Probably for the villagers, the use of Pali and Sanskrit gives the names higher prestige. Therefore, instead of saying *naa phii* 'fertile rice field', using a Thai word /phii/, one uses *naa sŏmbuun* (Sanskrit) or *naa ʔudom* (Pali /Sanskrit).

Finally, there are some Thai village names which show a different way to name a village. These village names do not tell about the physical characteristics of the land; for example:

(12)　　*sĭi sùwan*　　　　'good' + 'gold'
　　　　níkhom sìwílai　'settlement' + 'civilized'

These names do not express anything in connection with the physical features of the land. Here, all the words are Pali and Sanskrit, and the names show the wish for a perfect village.

References

Guangxi Institute of Nationalities. 1988. Guangjsih vahcuengh diegmingz senjciz [Dictionary of Zhuang place names]. Nanning: Guangxi Nationalities Publishing House.

Jespersen, Otto. 1955. Growth and structure of the English language. New York: Doubleday and Company.

Kullavanijaya, Pranee. 1992. Chue mubaan nai monthon Kwangsi laephaak tawanork chiang nuea khong pratheet Thai [Village names in Guangxi Province and the northeastern part of Thailand]. Bangkok: Chulalongkorn University Press.

Wuming Zhuang Tone Sandhi: A Phonological, Syntactic, and Lexical Investigation

Wil C. Snyder, Summer Institute of Linguistics
and
Lu Tianqiao, Central University of Nationalities, Beijing, China

1 Introduction

The Zhuang language of Southern China extends over most of Guangxi Province, and is also found in Yunnan, Guizhou, and Guangdong Provinces, as well as in Vietnam. The Zhuang language actually consists of two major varieties, Northern Zhuang and Southern Zhuang. According to the classic divisions in Li (1977), Northern Zhuang belong to the Northern Tai subbranch and Southern Zhuang belongs to the Central Tai subbranch. These two major varieties are then divided by Chinese scholars in turn into seven northern vernacular areas and five southern vernacular areas (see map 1). It must be stated, however, that even within these divisions, many

---

We would like to thank Jerry Edmondson for his help and encouragement in researching this topic, and Prof. Zhang Yuansheng for sharing his insight into the Zhuang language with us. Responsibility for errors is ours alone. Finally, we would like to express our thanks to the people at the Central University of Nationalities, Beijing, China for their cooperation and help in researching the Zhuang language.

subdivisions exist that differ in tones, lexicon, and in initials and rhymes. The linguistic situation in Zhuang is, needless to say, complex (cf. Zhang and Wei, this volume).

The Zhuang people comprise the largest minority group in China; recent statistics show the ethnic Zhuang population to be around 15,000,000. Of this 15,000,000, there are among the Zhuang many whose first language is not Zhuang; some speak Han or other minority languages. Nonetheless, those ethnic Zhuang that actively use the Zhuang language make up the larger portion of the population. There are no reliable statistics concerning the number of speakers, however.

The official Zhuang language and the basis of the writing system is Wuming County, Shuangqiao Village (Northern Zhuang). Since this kind of Zhuang plays such an important role, we have chosen to discuss it as a point of reference to which two other varieties can be compared (see Li 1990). This geographic sector is clearly linguistically active in Zhuang. Long'an is, for example, west of Wuming and belongs to Southern Zhuang, whereas Pingguo is just north of Long'an but belongs to Northern Zhuang. Wuming County is 42 kilometers north of Nanning, the capital of Guangxi. All three of these counties are located within a 50 kilometer radius approximately, but their tonal systems, as will be shown, are very different.

In this paper we investigate Shuangqiao Zhuang tone sandhi from an autosegmental and syntactic perspective. We attempt to explain the sandhi phenomena in Shuangqiao in depth, covering phonological, syntactic, and lexical factors, in addition to positing a method for analyzing the peculiarities of Zhuang tone sandhi.

One of the characteristics of Kadai languages is an abundance of tones. We will posit an autosegmental sandhi mechanism for the Zhuang varieties, which we hope will prove useful in analyzing other Kadai languages with tone sandhi.

2 Zhuang tone system and possible sandhi changes

2.1 Data. Shuangqiao Zhuang has a total of six tone values. Open syllables (all syllables except for those with oral stops as coda) can take any of the six.

Wuming Zhuang Tone Sandhi

(1) tone   value

1	24	*pai¹*	'to go'
2	21	*muŋ²*	'you'
3	55	*ha³*	'five'
4	42	*ɣam⁴*	'water'
5	35	*suɪ⁵*	'to wash'
6	33	*taɯ⁶*	'chopsticks'

Closed syllables have long/short vowel contrast, and can take the following tone values:

(2) tone   value

7	55	*ti:t⁷*	'iron'
7'	55	*nap⁷'*	'insert'
8	35	*na:p⁸*	'to clamp'
9	33	*ka:p⁹*	'to press'
9'	33	*nat⁹'*	'classifier for grain'
10	42	*la:p¹⁰*	'wax'

2.2 Sandhi. Tones 1, 2, 5, 6, 8, 9, 9' undergo change in context. Specifically, tones 1, 5, 8 can change to 55. Tones 2, 6, 9 can change to 42. Notice that tones 7 and 7' do not undergo sandhi changes, even though they have the same tone values as 9 and 9'. What is the mechanism that causes Wuming tones to undergo sandhi in this way? First, we will discuss how to represent this kind of complex tone system geometrically and then show how the sandhi changes can be accounted for.

As discussed in Yip (1989),[1] tones of East Asian languages seem to have a different structure than those of African languages. The East Asian tone is thought to consist of a melodic unit (sequence of highs and lows) under a higher node. African languages involve clusters of highs and lows.

(3)

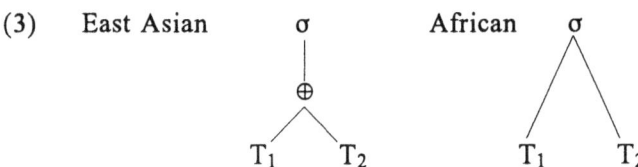

---

[1] Also see Edmondson and Yang (1994).

The East Asian tone consists of a TONE ROOT TIER, symbolized by ⊕, along with the geometric branching structure. The tone root adds a new level beyond that found in previous representations, thus simultaneously accounting for Asian contours as (a) being made up of high tones and low tones as well as (b) acting together as a unit, since East Asian tones can occur on any syllable. On the other hand, African tones act as clusters, only building up into contours at the end of a polysyllabic sequence by spreading. As discussed in Yip (1989), the root tone can take values of H or L, and the root tone's value is held constant over the syllable (unlike T_1, T_2 above, which can branch to form rises or falls).

Now, in complex tonal languages such as Kadai languages, the question is what sort of geometry is involved? In Wuming Zhuang, there are two level, two rising, and two falling tones. The two rising tones both can have a branching structure such as:

(4)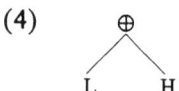

Yip has suggested that such systems can be better described by having the tone root tier be a high and a low register. The difference between the two rising tones, and for that matter the two falling and two level tones, is simply that one is higher overall (register) and the other is lower overall (register). This can be represented in a geometrical fashion:

(5)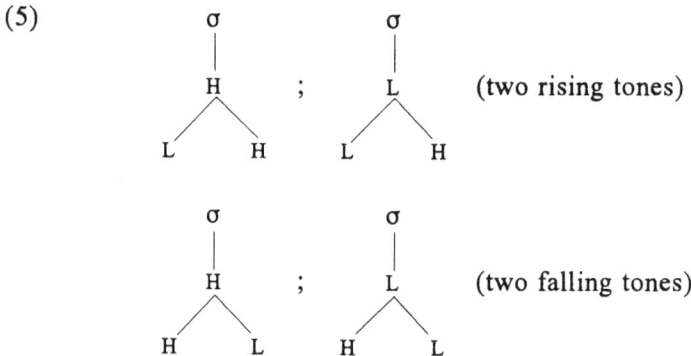

The structures in (5) represent the Wuming tones 5 (35), 1 (24), 4 (42), and 2 (21).[2] There is, however, a further and necessary refinement to representing level tones. A 55 tone value would clearly be (with the Obligatory Contour Principle):

(6)   ⊕
       |
       H
       |
       H

But a 33 tone is structurally ambiguous, being either:

(7)   ⊕   ⊕
       | |
       H or L
       | |
       L   H

We believe that if the tone is truly mid (33), and not 44 or 22 (see below for discussion of other Zhuang varieties with these tone values), its representation might be determinable by its behavior within the system, by its sandhi properties. For Wuming Zhuang we have chosen the 33 tone to be represented as:

(8)   ⊕
       |
       H
       |
       L

As a consequence of the preceding discussion, we will represent the tone structure of languages such as Zhuang as

---

[2]In these representations, there is a case of identical pitch values being assigned different features, and a case of identical feature specifications representing different pitch values. For the former: tones 1 (24) and 4 (42) cover an identical pitch range, yet one is assigned to the Low register and the other to the High. For the latter: both the coda of tone 1 and the onset of tone 4 are Low register dominating H tone, yet the former is 4 on the pitch scale while the latter is 2. It may be that the 4 and the 2 in these cases have the value 3, as the analyses of the internal contouring correctly predict Wuming sandhi phenomena.

(9)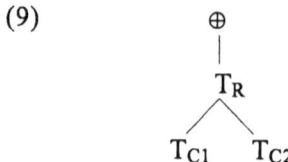

where T_R is the Register (root) tone (H or L), and T_{C1} and T_{C2} are the Contour tones.

Wuming tone sandhi involves changes from tone values 24 and 35 to 55, and from tone values 21 and 33 to 42. The structures of the changed tones 3 (55) and 4 (42) are, respectively:

(10)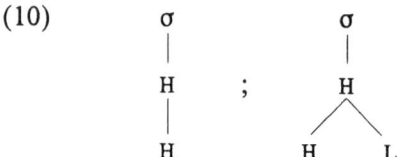

Both sandhi forms begin high, then either continue high or fall. Tones 1 (24) and 5 (35) are represented as follows, the right edge of the tone contour ending high.

(11)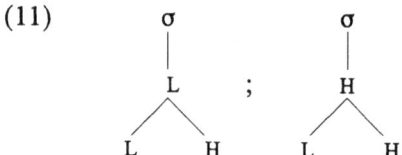

Tones 2 (21) and 6 (33) are represented as follows, with the right edge ending low.

(12)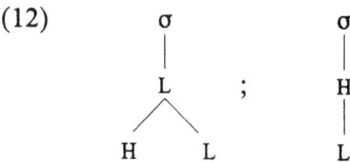

It can be seen by this that the tonal structure of the sandhi tone is

(13)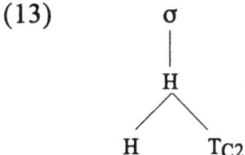

where T_{C2} is the right edge of the original tone. So the change /1/ → [3] geometrically looks like

(14)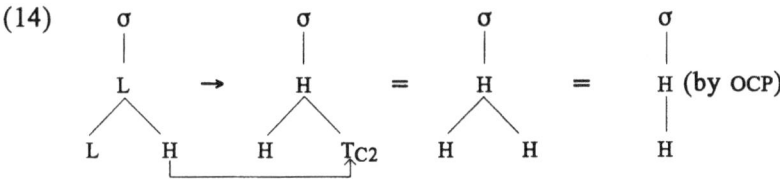

It can be seen that the value of the right edge of the contour remains unchanged. Tones 1, 2, 5, 6, 8, 9 and 9' all change to the structure of (13).

It should be stressed that for this language, the sandhi rule is, in effect, 'context free', or more properly, that this alternation cannot be analyzed as an assimilation. That is, the rule does not take into account the environment for its form. A tone undergoing sandhi always, regardless of environment—as long as there is one—changes to the form (13). In §3.1 we discuss the fact that for tones which can undergo sandhi, only certain following tones 'trigger' sandhi on that syllable. However, this does not mean that the form (13) depends on the melody of the following tone for its form; it only depends on the existence of a following tone to trigger it. The restriction on which following tones can trigger sandhi is more of a restriction on tonal combinations, and does not affect form (13). So the sandhi form (13) is rather a 'preferred' or default tonal geometry into which any tone that undergoes sandhi will change.

As is seen in the following section, the other two varieties under consideration have no restriction on sandhi with regard to following tones. This sort of sandhi phenomenon is a result, we believe, of the 'rigid' nature of East Asian tone contours, especially in this case of Kadai tonal structure. The edges of the tonal geometry seem to be less affected by environment. As should be noted, there are Kadai languages which do not have tonal sandhi at all. For example, Kam has a total of nine distinctive contours, yet has absolutely no tone sandhi. This testifies as to the rigidity of tones in these kinds of languages. Edmondson and Yang (1994:54) state:

From the data thus far it appears as if contours in Africa have amorphousness of powdered charcoal that can be whisked along in the wind, those of the Han language the large lattice structure of coal breakable into smaller pieces, and in Kadai and Hmongic-Mienic they may have the internal structure of more compact and dense crystals.

2.3 Comparison of sandhi systems. We now compare the sandhi systems of the three Zhuang varieties studied in this article. It is noteworthy that the sandhi mechanisms are different for each variety.

The Long'an variety has the following tones:

(15) Tone   Value

Tone	Value		
1	25	na^1	'thick'
2	24	na^2	'wet field'
3	44	na^3	'face'
4	22	ma^4	'horse'
5	55	ma^5	'mother'
6	21	ma^6	'shoulder'
7	55	tap^7	'liver'
7'	44	$tha{:}p^{7'}$	'tower'
8	21	$na{:}p^8$	'to pay'
8'	22	$la{:}p^{8'}$	'wax'

The geometry for these tones is

(16)

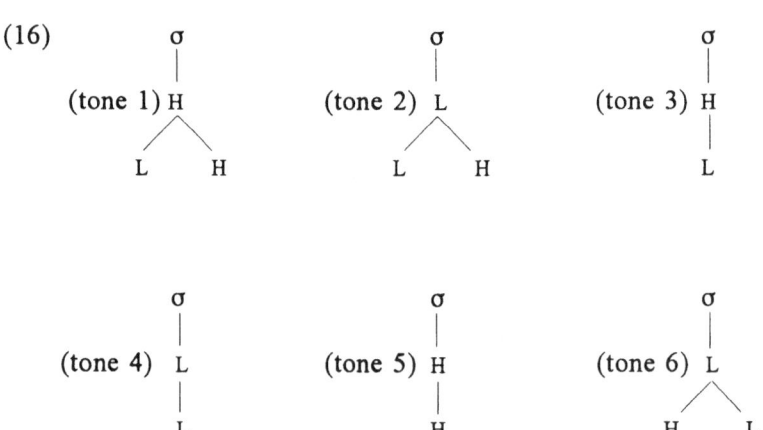

The sandhi changes in Long'an are 1 → 3, and 2, 6 → 4. The sandhi tone values 44 and 22 are of high register and low register, respectively, and both have a low level contour.

We posit a sandhi rule of the form where the contour tones are either rising or falling.

(17)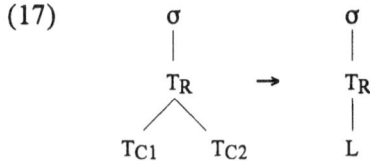

When a rising or falling tone is in the high register and it undergoes sandhi, it changes to a level low tone within the high register (becoming 44). When a rising or falling tone is in the low register, it changes to a level low tone in the low register (becoming 22).[3] This sandhi process is illustrated in (18) and (19).

(18) $phja^{25} + hu\eta^{25} \rightarrow phja^{44} + hu\eta^{25}$ 'big mountain'
        mountain big

(19)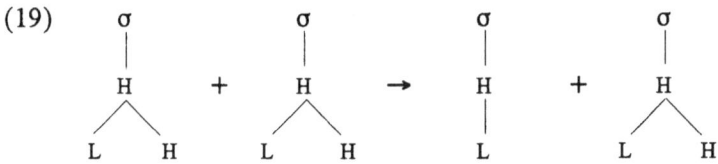

---

[3]It must be noted that in Long'an Zhuang there is a class of words which undergo a tone sandhi change of /6/ → [3]. The Wuming cognates of these words have high rising tone and implosive stops as initials, whereas in Long'an the words have 21 pitch value and nasal initials. It is unknown exactly why this particular class of words undergoes sandhi in this manner. This sandhi process contradicts the general sandhi rule (17) for Long'an tone sandhi, but will not be considered further in this paper.

The Pingguo variety has the following tones:

(20) Tone   Value

1	24	pi^1	'year'
2	21	$ŋon^2$	'day'
3	55	hen^3	'yellow'
4	33	hau^4	'rice'
5	35	$faːi^5$	'cotton'
6	11	ta^6	'river'
7	55	$ɣat^7$	'fungus'
7'	55	$taːp^{7'}$	'tower'
8	35	$maːk^8$	'fruit'
9	11	$ɣaːk^9$	'root'
10	33	$laːp^{10}$	'wax'
10'	33	$luk^{10'}$	'child'

Tones 1, 5 change to 55, and tones 2, 6 change to 33. The sandhi forms are both in the high register, differing only in the relative height of the tones. We propose a sandhi rule of the following form:

(21)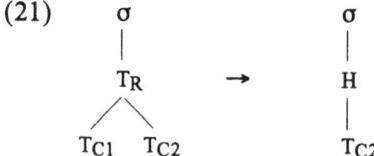

The tones that change are either rising or falling, and are raised to the high register. If the right hand edge of the original tone is low (T_{C2} = L), then the resulting sandhi tone is the 33. If the right hand edge of the original tone is high (T_{C2} = H), then the resulting sandhi tone is 55.

It can be seen from comparing these three varieties that the tone sandhi mechanisms, even for relatively close varieties, can be very different.

3 Factors affecting sandhi

3.1 Tonal combinations. In Wuming Zhuang, unlike the other two varieties under consideration, tone sandhi depends on the tone that follows (as well as the syllable shape of that following tone (see §3.2)). For example:

(22) a. *wun²\⁴ huŋ¹ ku⁶\⁴ hoŋ¹*
person big do   work
Adults work.

b. *wun² ʔi⁵ ku⁶\⁴ ŋam²*
person small do game
Children play.

(23) a. *soŋ¹ pau⁴ pai¹ ra:m¹\³ ta:i²*
two CLF go carry table
Two persons go to carry the table.

b. *sai⁵ pau⁴ pai¹ ra:m¹ hau⁴*
four CLF go carry rice
Four persons go to carry the rice.

In the above examples, the (a) sentence has a word which undergoes tone sandhi that does not undergo tone sandhi in the (b) sentence (*wun²* and *ra:m¹*), the difference being the tone value of the following word (the words occur in the exact same syntactic environment). Each tone that can undergo sandhi is affected by the following tone; with some following tones it can change, with others it cannot. Below is a chart of the various tonal combinations, with the combinations producing sandhi marked (x). The spaces marked 'L' indicate that only if the second tone is of the Light syllable type can sandhi occur on the first syllable (see §3.2 below). (See appendix for examples of all combinations.)

(24)

		second syllable					
		24	21	55	42	35	33
first	24	x	x	L			L
syllable	21	x	x	L			L
	55						
	42						
	35					x	
	33	x	x	x		x	x

Of the many different Zhuang varieties, Wuming is by far the most complex with regard to tonal change in context (Zhang Yuansheng, pc). The other two varieties studied in this article, Long'an and Pingguo, have no restrictions on sandhi with regard to the following syllable. In other words, for Long'an and Pingguo, the above chart would be completely filled with x's. Long'an and Pingguo sandhi depends only on syntactic and speech rate factors.

We now discuss why Wuming sandhi occurs only with certain tonal combinations, and attempt to formulate rules governing the sandhi system.

In many tonal languages, the mechanism involved when sandhi is influenced by the following tone is one of association of the following tone (or the left edge of the following tone) with the preceding one. Goldsmith (1976:25) gives an example from Igbo:

(25) ekwe ci akhwa   →   ekwe ci akhwa
       │ │   │   │   │ \ │ │   │
       H H   L   L H   H H L L H

Ekwe was carrying eggs.

The high (H) tone on *we*, becomes falling HL due to the influence of the following L on *ci*. In Mandarin Chinese, however, a different sort of process seems to take place. Two third tones together give rise to sandhi of the preceding third tone to a second tone (third is 214, second is 35).

(26)   hen³ + hao³ → hen² + hao³
       very   good
       very good

The tonal structure can be viewed as

(27)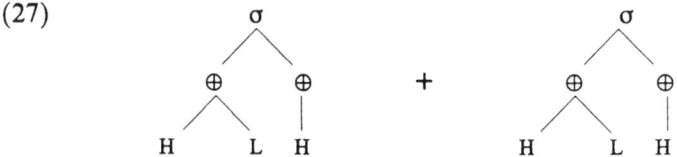

What seems to cause sandhi here is not an influence of the left edge of the following tone on the right edge of the preceding one, but simply a deletion of the left edge of the preceding tone.

(28)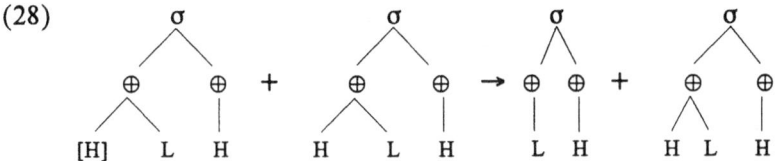

The two third tones, both being falling-rising, are physiologically difficult to produce in normal or rapid speech, and therefore the first H is omitted, making the tones of the two words fit together in a 'smoother' manner. The third tone followed by any other tone (except another third) also undergoes a similar deletion process.

(29) $hen^{214} + man^{41} \rightarrow hen^{21} + man^{41}$
    ADV   slow
    very slow

The third tone in this case changes from 214 to 21, in a process such as

(30)

where the H-L of σ_1 is lower overall than the H-L of σ_2 (inadequately captured here still).

We believe that some of the sandhi processes in Zhuang relate to the following tones with a similar principle, that is, physiological ease of speech. The tonal contours simply change their structure to be physiologically more economical.

Three rules can be posited to account for the influence of the following tone in Wuming Zhuang. These rules hold for all Wuming (see §3.2 on the influence of light syllables).

(31) RULE 1 If two syllables occur together (σ_1, σ_2), each having T_R = L, then σ_1 can change.

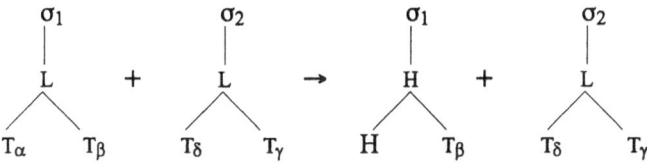

RULE 2 If two syllables occur together (σ_1, σ_2) and have the same T_R and the same contour, tone sandhi can occur.[4]

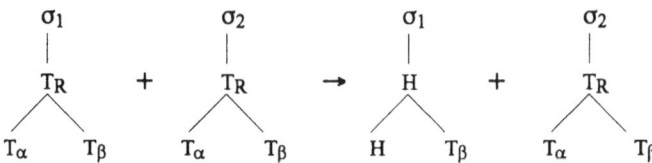

RULE 3 The mid-level even tone seems to be very 'unstable' and can change with any following tone except tone 4 (42).

3.2 The CVC influence. The 'dead' or checked tones in Kadai languages seem to have a special status. The checked syllables are thought to have had no tone originally, but later borrowed the tones of other syllable types. The original CV syllables had three tones which split into high and low reflexes under influence of the voicing state of the initial consonant. In Zhuang, and possibly in other Kadai languages, we can posit that (C)(C)V(V)C_s syllables (where C_s is a stop), although having branching structure, count as light, while the other syllable types CVV, CVG (VG = glide), CVC_n (C_n = nasal), act as heavy syllables.[5] In Zhuang, the CVC syllable (with both long and short vowels) has a special status in regard to tone change in context. A following word of syllable type[6] (C)V(V)C_s, irrespective of tone, can cause tone sandhi on the previous word, if the previous word has $T_R = L$ (i.e., tones 1, 2). For example:

(32) a. ən$^{l\backslash 3}$ kjɔp$^{7'}$ nai^4 kai^3-la:i^1 ŋan^2
 CLF bamboo^hat this how-much money
 How much is this bamboo hat?

---

[4]This does not apply, of course, to two 42 or 55 tones, since both 55 and 42 tones do not change. They are already in the sandhi form.

[5]The rationale in calling syllables with final stops 'light', lies in the timing of these syllables. In Zhuang, no other syllable is spoken with a shorter time span than the checked syllable. The checked syllables are of two types, having 'long' and 'short' vowels. However, even the checked syllables with long vowels occupy a very short time span. In this paper we follow the standard Chinese practice of writing v: for the 'long vowel' and v for the 'short vowel'.

[6]It has been reported by Zhang Yuansheng (1983) that for some speakers in Wuming county, only if the following syllable is (C)VC_s (a checked syllable with a short vowel) can sandhi occur.

b. *ən¹ piu³ nai⁴ ti³ ha³ pa:k⁸ man²\⁴ ŋan²*
CLF watch this worth 5 100 yuan money
This watch is worth 500 yuan.

(33) a. *kau¹ si:ŋ³ ʃi:ŋ⁴ ji:ŋ²\⁴ luk⁹'*
I want raise sheep child
I want to raise some lambs.

b. *tau² dat⁷' rɯ² ʃaŋ⁶*
hold tight ear scale
Hold tight the handle of the steel-scale!

In (32a) and (33a), tone sandhi occurs on *ən¹* and on *ji:ŋ²*. In (32b) and (33b), sandhi does not occur on *ən¹* or on *rɯ²*, even though the tonal environment is the same as in the (a) sentence. As a result, a final rule must be posited dealing with this phenomenon.

(34) RULE 4 If two syllables occur together (σ_1, σ_2) where σ_1 is a syllable with $T_R = L$ and σ_2 is a light syllable $(C)(C)V(V)C_s$, then σ_1 can undergo tone sandhi.

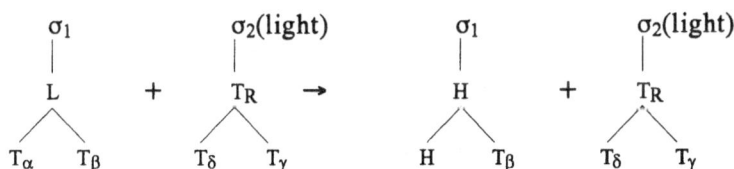

3.3 Syntactic factors. The phonological factors discussed above can be viewed as necessary but not sufficient conditions for sandhi to occur. Another factor involved in the sandhi process is the syntactic structure. The syntactic structure influences which words are paired closely with other words. For example, a noun and modifying adjective are both within the same syntactic constituent, the Noun Phrase, and are closely bound semantically. As a result, a pair of words of this sort constitute a phonological phrase. The timing between syllables (whether the syllables are linked rapidly or slowly) greatly influences the occurrence of sandhi. For example, in Mandarin, two third tones occurring together produce sandhi on the first (see (26) above). The rate of speech threshold which will produce sandhi in different syntactic positions differs for each speaker and in different circumstances. In Wuming Zhuang, we believe the rate of speech between two syllables is definitely a factor. In Mandarin, however, in a string of third tones, all the preceding third tones can change, leaving only the last tone unchanged. Mandarin sandhi can occur across syntactic boundaries. In very rapid speech the following can occur:

(35)　$ba^{3\backslash 2}$　$shui^{3\backslash 2}\text{-}guo^{3\backslash 2}$　$gei^{3\backslash 2}$　wo^3
　　　PTC　fruit　　　　　　give　me
　　　Give me the fruit.

[s[NP[OBJ MRKR ba][N $shui\text{-}guo$]][VP[V gei][N wo]]]

In Wuming Zhuang, the syntactic conditions for sandhi are somewhat stricter. Using the notation of X-bar syntax, the syntactic condition for sandhi can be stated as:

(36)　If two syllables occur together under an X constituent (where X can be Noun, Verb, Preposition, etc. . .) with the structure

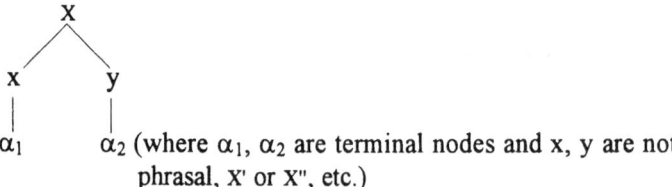

α_2 (where α_1, α_2 are terminal nodes and x, y are not phrasal, X' or X", etc.)

　　　Then α_1 can undergo sandhi.

In no other syntactic configurations can sandhi take place. The following two sentences are examples:

(37) a. te^1　pai^1　$ya^{1\backslash 3}$　saw^1
　　　　he　go　read　book
　　　　He goes to look for books.

　　b. te^1　pai^1　ya^1　$saw^{1\backslash 3}$　kun^1
　　　　he　go　read　book　Chinese
　　　　He goes to look for Chinese books.

1\3 indicates a sandhi change from tone 1 to 3. According to the rules posited in the phonological section, in each sentence any of the words except the last could change. However, the syntactic structure restricts sandhi. Only when both the syntactic and phonological conditions are met, does sandhi occur. The structures of these two sentences are:

(38) a.

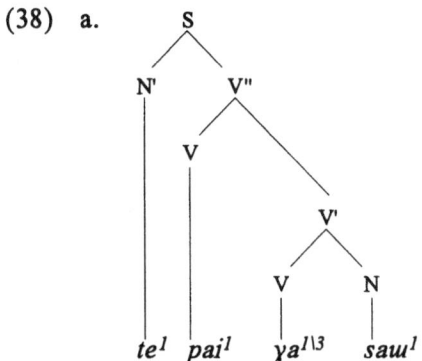

b.

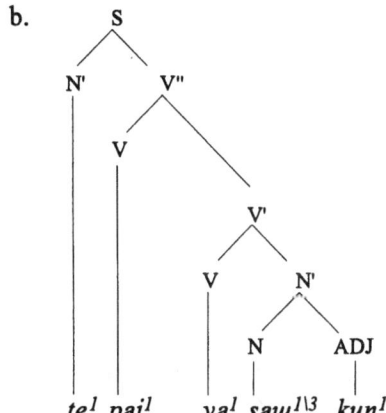

In each sentence, the sandhi takes place whenever the constituents are related in the manner demonstrated in (36). In (37a) it is under V'; in (37b) it is under N'. As another example, take the following two sentences with verb combinations:

(39) a. *wun²\⁴ sa:i¹ pai¹ ʃai¹\³ na²*
person male go plough field
The men go to plough the field.

b. *te¹ ma¹ kɯ¹*
he come^back eat
He comes back to eat.

In (39a) the first verb in the verb combination ʃai¹\³ na² changes, but the first verb in the combination ma¹ kɯ¹ of sentence (39b) does not. We can see why in the following diagrams.

(40) a.

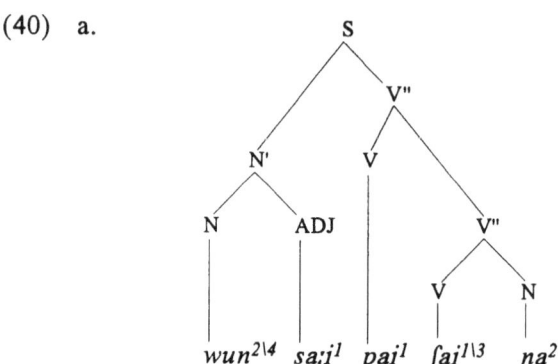

b.

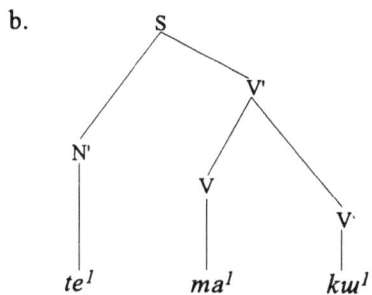

In (40a), ʃai¹ takes an object, and so is under the structure (36). In (40b), the verb kɯ¹ 'plough' is intransitive, and so does not occur under the structure (35). When, however, the verbs pai¹ 'go' or ma¹ 'come back' occur as directionals in combination with other verbs, they act as verbal modifiers.

(41) a. muŋ² roŋ²\⁴   pai¹ kau¹ pai¹\³ ma¹
       you descend go I   go   back
       You go down, I go back.

Each conjunctive part of (41) has the structure

(42)

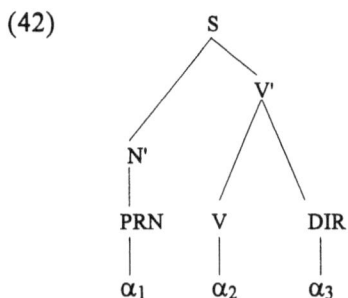

α_2 in (42) changes because it occurs under the structure (36).

Another interesting phenomenon in Zhuang can be seen in the following examples:

(43) a. *te¹ tok⁹\¹⁰ sauɯ¹ ʔdai¹*
 he read book good
 It's good that he goes to school.

b. *te¹ tok⁹ sauɯ¹\³ ʔdai¹*
 he read book good
 He reads good books.

Although the lexical items and word order are the same, the meaning is quite different. The difference is signaled on the surface by sandhi. Consider the syntactic structures of (44ab):

(44) a.

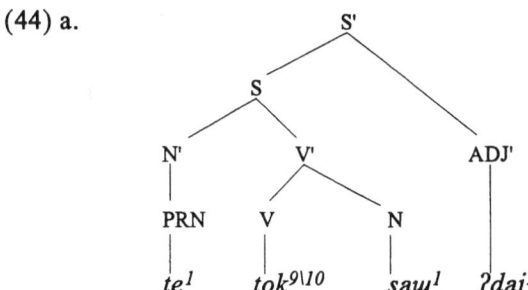

b.

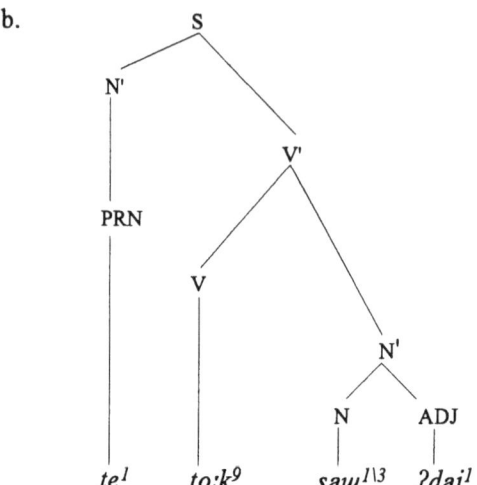

As can be seen, the syntactic structure is different, which, in turn, triggers the respective sandhi. In (44b) the phonological conditions for sandhi of *saɯ¹* are met. It is simply a sequence of tones which can, by Rule 1, undergo sandhi. However, because *saɯ¹* in (44a) does not occur under the syntactic rule (36) no sandhi occurs. In (44a) *tok⁹* does undergo sandhi since both phonological and syntactic conditions are met. In (44b) *saɯ¹* undergoes sandhi while *tok⁹* does not. Zhang (1983) gives other examples of this nature.

Whether or not other Zhuang varieties have a similar syntactic sandhi constraint as (36) has not yet been researched in sufficient detail to report on. Also, as is noted in §4, exceptions to (36) do occur. We would like to mention one exception in this section, in that it concerns sandhi outside the syntactic boundary of rule (36). In the following example,

(45) *te¹\⁶ ma¹\⁶ ʔau¹\³ ʃiːn²*
  he   come want money
  He comes to get money.

the tones that fit the phonological criteria for change all undergo sandhi, regardless of the syntactic structure. Also, the first two tones change to mid tone 6 instead of tone 3. This occurs only in very rapid speech, and is simply a phonetic effect of fast speech. The tones tend to be 'smoothed out' to mid. Whether there are other criteria for sandhi of this sort has not been fully investigated.

4 Exceptions

4.1 Lexical factors. In Wuming Zhuang there are certain words that can undergo sandhi in combination with any tone. These particular words are ones that are very frequently used, or are used as a sort of prefix with other words. For example, ta^6 is a word meaning 'young female'.

(46) $ta^{6\backslash 4}$ $la{:}u^1$ 'granddaughter'
    $ta^{6\backslash 4}$ hai^2 'maternal aunt'
    $ta^{6\backslash 4}$ pa^3 'paternal aunt'
    $ta^{6\backslash 4}$ kim^4 'aunt (wife of mother's brother)'
    $ta^{6\backslash 4}$ ni^5 'little girl'
    $ta^{6\backslash 4}$ $ŋai^6$ 'second daughter'
    $ta^{6\backslash 4}$ $ʔia{:}k^8$ 'horrid girl'
    $ta^{6\backslash 4}$ $he{:}k^7$ 'girl guest'
    $ta^{6\backslash 4}$ $ʃat^{7'}$ 'seventh daughter'
    $ta^{6\backslash 4}$ $lu{:}k^9$ 'girl from the mountains'
    $ta^{6\backslash 4}$ $me{:}k^{10}$ 'the wheat girl'
    $ta^{6\backslash 4}$ $ʃak^{9'}$ 'the girl pickpocket'

In Zhang (1983), other words are cited which undergo sandhi in combinations with any other tone.

(47) me^6 'mother'
    po^6 'father'
    $luk^{9'}$ 'small child'
    $ta{:}i^6$ 'number ...' (as in 'number 1', etc.)

An obvious reason for sandhi of this sort is close cognitive association. This particular class of words is used often, closely associated with many other words, forming word groups of sorts. An interesting fact about this class of words, though, is that they are all of tone value 33 (6, 9, 9') or tone value 21 (2). Why this is so is not clear at present.

4.2 Syntactic factors. Consider the following two examples.

(48) a. $ŋan^{2\backslash 4}$ $ʃan^1$ $ŋan^{2\backslash 4}$ kja^3 $ʃuŋ^3$ mi^2
    money real money false all have
    There is both real and false money.

b. *raːn²\⁴ kim¹ nau² raːn²\⁴ tiːt⁷*
   house gold or house iron
   gold house or iron house

In each of these examples, the first word undergoing sandhi does so according to the above-mentioned phonological and syntactic rules, but the second word undergoing sandhi does so in violation of the phonological conditions. In (48a) and (48b) *ŋan²* and *raːn²* change before tone 1 according to Rule 1. But they also change before tones 3 and 7, respectively. This is because these sentences are of the form

(49) $\sigma_1 + \sigma_2 \ldots + \sigma_1 + \sigma_n$

where $\sigma_1 + \sigma_2$ fit the phonological conditions for change, but $\sigma_1 + \sigma_n$ do not. The $\sigma_1 + \sigma_n$ change occurs presumably to match the change in the beginning. In addition to form (49), the following form also causes sandhi on both σ_1's:

(50) $\sigma_1 + \sigma_n \ldots + \sigma_1 + \sigma_2$

where the conditions of (49) are the same for (50).

In the syntactic structure (36) if σ_2 is a pronoun, σ_1 does not change. Take, for example, the following two phrases:

(51)   *ra¹ kau¹*
      look for me

      ra¹\³ kau¹
      look for vine

kau¹ has two meanings, 'I/me' and 'vine'. When *kau¹* 'I/me' is used, no change occurs, when *kau¹* 'vine' is used, change occurs.

A final exception to be noted is the sandhi occurring on the verb *tuk⁹'* 'to be'. In most sentences, *tuk⁹'*, even under the proper phonological and syntactic conditions, does not undergo sandhi. However, in passive sentences, sandhi does occur.

(52) a. *tu² nai⁴ tuk⁹' mau¹*
      CLF this is   pig
      This is a pig.

b. ŋon²\⁴luːn² te¹ tuk⁹\¹⁰ faːt⁹ lo⁶
yesterday   he is   whip PTC
Yesterday he was whipped.

The non-passive sentence (52a) has no change, whereas the passive (52b) does.

5 Conclusion

Although there is much research yet to be done on Zhuang tone sandhi, especially with regard to the many varieties of Zhuang, we have found from initial research that the geometrical structure of Zhuang tones is hard-and-fast, being little affected by the edges of neighboring tones. In addition, the syntactic structure plays an important role in determining tone sandhi. In Shuangqiao Zhuang the syntax (in addition to the phonological component) seems to determine almost completely the occurrence of sandhi. However, as mentioned above, the other two varieties discussed may be influenced less directly by the syntax, and more by the mapping of the syntactic component onto the metrical structure of the language. Much more work needs to be done in this area.

In comparing the three varieties of Zhuang it is interesting to note the differences in tone sandhi. The sandhi structure for each as represented in (13), (17), and (21) is different. Shuangqiao Zhuang, unlike the other two, depends on the following tones with regard to sandhi. The relationship between the historical development of these varieties and the differences in sandhi may be an interesting topic to pursue.

Appendix: Examples of tonal combinations

(Tone 1 + tone n)

kau¹ tau³ nai³ ya¹\³ kim¹
I   come here look gold
I came to look for gold.

kau¹ pet⁸ tiːm³ ʃuŋ¹ tau³ ʃuŋ³ ʔbau³ yan¹\³ wun²
I   eight point clock come even not   see   person
I didn't see anybody even though I came as early as eight.

luk⁹\¹⁰ ŋe² te¹ han³ kɯ¹ piŋ³
child   his likes eat cakes
His child likes to eat cakes.

ʔdɯːn¹ nai⁴ ʔdɯːn¹\³ ʃiːt⁷
month this month festival
This month is a festival month.

te¹ hat⁷' naŋ² kɯ¹\³ ʃuk⁷'
he every morning eat porridge
He eats porridge every morning.

hɯn³ pla¹ ʔdam¹ fai⁴
go^up hill plant tree
Go up the hill to plant trees!

au¹ laːp¹⁰ ma¹ tiːm³ taŋ¹
get wax return ignite lamp
Get some wax as a light.

hau⁴ ʃuŋ³ teŋ¹ fɯn¹ ɣa⁵ toŋ³ teu² lo⁶
rice all suffer rain sudden flush away PTC
The rice has been washed away by a shower.

kai³ kɯ¹ naŋ¹ maːk⁸
do^not eat skin fruit
Don't eat the rind.

te¹ ʔbau³ mi² ŋan² ʔjɯ¹ piŋ⁶
he not have money treat illness
He doesn't have money to treat his illness.

tu²\⁴ ma¹\³ kjaːt⁹ nai⁴ puːt³ ʔbau³ ʔdai³ lo⁶
CLF dog paralyzed this run not okay PTC
This paralyzed dog cannot run now.

ɣau² au¹ ɣin¹\³ mak⁹' ma¹ ku⁶\⁴ mak⁹'
we use stone ink to make ink
We make ink with an ink stick.

(Tone 2 + tone n)

ɣaːn² te¹ tɯk⁹' ɣaːn²\⁴ ɣin¹
house his is house stone
His house is a stone house.

ɣaːn² kau¹ tɯk⁹' ɣaːn²\⁴ ʃiːŋ²
house my is wall house
My house is an earthen wall house.

ʔbau¹ nai⁴ tɯk⁹' ʔbau³ tɯk⁹' ŋan² kja³
piece this is not is money false
Is this false money?

ki² nai⁴ taːi²\⁴ toŋ² taːi²\⁴ tiːt⁷ ʃuŋ³ mi²
place this table bronze table iron all have
There are both bronze tables and iron tables here.

wun²\⁴ kjik⁷' tuŋ⁴ ʔiːk⁸
person lazy stomach hungry
A lazybones is often hungry.

pai¹ ʔbau³ pai¹ jau² ɣam⁴
go not go swim water
Are you going swimming?

toi⁵ haːi² nei⁴ mu² faːt¹⁰
pair shoe this rub sock
This pair of shoes wears out socks.

ŋon² nai⁴ mi² ɣum² ʔi⁵
day this has wind small
There is a breeze today.

wun²\⁴ ʔjaːk⁸ ʃi³ jiːŋ⁶ nai⁴ kaːŋ³
person evil only manner this talk
Only an evil person talks this way.

jau² tu⁶ ham⁵   ɣaŋ¹
oil bean comparatively fragrant
Soy-bean oil smells more delicious.

te¹ mi² soŋ¹ toi⁵   ha:i²⁴ kji:k⁹
he has two pairs shoe   wood^shoe
He has two pairs of wooden shoes.

kau¹ mi² soŋ¹\³ tu² wa:i²¹⁴ tak⁹'
I   have two CLF buffalo male
I have two male buffaloes.

(Tone 3 + tone n)

ɣau² taŋ² ʃiŋ¹   ʃau⁶ ka³ mau¹
we   arrive spring^festival just kill pig
We'll kill the pig as soon as spring festival arrives.

sai² lauɯ² huɯn³ ta:ŋ² ha⁶
time which start class PTC
When does the class begin?

na³ tin³ ho³ ʔjauɯ³ ɣa:i⁴ʃa:i⁴
face short hard see   much
A short face looks very ugly.

an¹ nai⁴ tuɯk⁹' ʔwa:n³ ti:t⁷
CLF this is   bowl   iron
This is an iron bowl.

kai³   kuɯ¹ ʃuk⁷' ʃap⁷'
do^not eat porridge cold
Don't eat cold porridge!

au¹ bɔ:n³ ɣam⁴ ma¹ ʃau⁴
use pot water return contain
Get a water pitcher to hold it.

ɣau² ham⁶naŋ²   ti:m³ la:p¹⁰
we   every^evening ignite wax
We use wax as a source of light every evening.

muɯŋ² kuɯ¹ ʔbau³ kuɯ¹ ɣau³ kai⁵
you eat not   eat head chicken
Do you eat chicken heads?

au¹ fai² ma¹ ʃɯt⁷' sa:p⁸
use fire return burn roach
Burn the roaches with fire.

tu²ⁱ⁴ yo:k⁹ nai⁴ tat⁷' fɯ:t⁹ lo⁶
CLF bird this cut wing PTC
The wings of this bird have been cut off.

te¹ jau⁵ la³ fai⁴ taŋ³ lɯk⁹'
he at under tree wait child
He was waiting for his child under the tree.

(Tone 4 + tone n)

pi¹ nai⁴ mi² ɣam⁴ huŋ¹ pɯ⁶
year this have water big PTC
Mind you, there are floods this time of year.

kɯn²ⁱ⁴ jɯ³ ʃuŋ³ tɯk⁹' hai⁴ ji:ŋ²
above grass all is dung sheep
There is sheep dung all over the grass.

tu²ⁱ⁴ hoŋ² nai⁴ tɯk⁹' ma⁴ to³
CLF red one is horse local
This red one is a local horse.

kai³ au¹ ki³ ɣam⁴ kji:k⁷ lo⁶
do^not want CLF water sediment PTC
Don't keep this sedimentary water!

kai³ hau³ tu²ⁱ⁴ kai⁵ sai⁴ plak⁷'
do^not let CLF chicken peck vegetables
Don't let the chicken peck the vegetables.

kau¹ ʔbau³ mi²ⁱ⁴ ŋan² ʃau⁴ hau⁴ lo⁶
I not have money buy rice PTC
I've run out of money to buy rice.

wa:i⁵ au¹ⁱ³ tɔm¹ ma¹ lum⁴ me:k¹⁰
quick get earth return cover wheat
Be quick to cover the wheat with earth.

ma⁴ ʔi⁵ ʔbau³ mi²\⁴ yeŋ²
horse small not   have strength
A small horse is not powerful.

la³ ʃɔːŋ² ʃuŋ³ tɯkᵍ' hai⁴   saːp⁸
under bed   all   is   droppings roach
There are roach droppings all under the bed.

kau¹ siːŋ³ ʃau⁴ maːu⁶
I   want buy cap
I want to buy a cap.

ʃai⁴ kwaːkᵍ ku⁶\⁴ taːi² ʔbau³ ʔdai¹
tree crack make   table not   good
Cracked wood is not good for making tables.

ko¹ ʃai⁴ lɯkᵍ' nai⁴ ma³ ʔdai³ waːi⁵
CLF tree child this grow obtain fast
This tree shoot grows fast.

(Tone 5 + tone n)

te¹ taːi⁵ rɔ⁵   kjɔŋ¹ ʃuŋ³   tiŋ⁵ ʔbau³ yan¹
he even strike gong even   listen not   see
He can't even hear the striking of a gong!

pai¹ au¹ ʃai⁴ tɔ⁵ taːi²
go   get wood make table
Go get some wood to make a table!

kai⁵   tɔ³   ham⁵ ʔdai¹ kɯ¹
chicken local more good eat
Home bred chicken tastes better.

tiu² ʃai⁴ nai⁴ ku⁶ kan⁵   kwaːk⁷ tin³ laːi¹
CLF wood this make handle hoe   short too
This piece of wood is too short to make a hoe handle.

kau¹ ʔbau³ kɯ¹ mai⁵ ʃɯt⁷'
I   do^not eat vinegar weak
I don't eat weak vinegar.

tu^2 lau^2 $tuk^{9'}$ han^5 pau^4
CLF which is   goose male
Which is a gander?

te^1 wa^5 $le:k^{10}$ $\int un^3$ tan^3
he pants split even wear
He even wears split pants!

an^1 $\gamma ai^{5\backslash 3}$ kai^5 nai^4 $\textit{?}i^5$ $la:i^1$
CLF egg chicken this small much
This egg is too small.

$\int u:\eta^5$ an^1 $ka^{5\backslash 3}$ $ye:k^8$ $\int au^6$ $\textit{?}dai^3$
put CLF rack pan just okay
It'll be okay to just put up a pan rack.

γau^2 pai^1 $hen^{2\backslash 4}$ ta^6 sui^5 pu^6
we go side   river wash clothes
We go to the river to wash clothes.

$\textit{?}jau^5$ nai^4 sui^5 $wa:t^9$
at   here wash dipper
Wash the wooden dipper here.

kau^1 $pai^{1\backslash 3}$ $ka:i^1$ $\int au^4$ kai^5 $luk^{9'}$
I   go   street buy chicken child
I'm going downtown to buy some young chickens.

(Tone 6 + tone n)

$no^{6\backslash 4}$ mau^1 pi^2 $la:i^1$ $\textit{?}bau^3$ pan^2
meat pig fat much not good
Pork that's too fat is not good.

kai^3 $\textit{?}jau^5$ $\textit{?}dau^1$ yam^4 $\int a:p^{6\backslash 4}$ jau^2
do^not at   inside water put^in oil
Don't put oil into the water!

tan^3 $pu^{6\backslash 4}$ tin^3 $\int au^6$ $\textit{?}dai^3$ lo^6
wear clothes short just okay PTC
It'll be okay to just put on a short jacket.

kau¹ han³ kɯ¹ no⁶\⁴ ʔjiːp⁷
I   like eat meat   pickled
I like to eat salted meat.

ɣai⁶ plak⁷' hauɯ⁵ la⁵
plot vegetable dry PTC
Is the vegetable plot dry yet?

hɯn³ pla¹ kwut⁹' fai⁴
goˆup hill dig   tree
Go up to the hills to dig trees!

ʔdaɯ¹ hau⁴ mi² ʃe⁶ meːk¹⁰
inside rice have grain wheat
There are wheat grains in the rice.

waːi⁵ taɯ² pau⁴ ʃak⁹'\¹⁰ ke⁵ ha⁴
quick hold CLF thief   old PTC
Be quick to catch that hardened thief.

au¹ tiːt⁷ ma¹ ku⁶\⁴ reːk⁸ ʔdai¹
get iron return make pan   good
It's good to make cooking pans with iron.

au¹ ki³ma² tau³ mu⁶\⁴ miːn⁶
get what   come grind wheat
What shall I use to grind the wheat?

ɣau² au¹ jaːŋ³ ku⁶\⁴ ʃaːk⁹
we   use straw make rope
We make ropes with straw.

ʃaɯ⁴ ti¹ no⁶\⁴ ʃuk⁹' ma¹ kɯ¹\³ ʃaːi²
buy some meat cooked return eat lunch
Go buy some prepared meat for lunch.

References

Cai, Peikang. 1987. Wuming Zhuanghua de liandu biandiao [Wuming Zhuang tone sandhi]. Minzu Yuwen 1:20–26.

Cheng, Lisa S. 1987. Derived domains and Mandarin third tone sandhi. In Anna Bosch, Barbara Need, and Eric Schiller (eds.), Papers from the twenty-third Annual Regional Meeting of the Chicago Linguistic Society (Part Two: Parasession on Autosegmental and Metrical Phonology). Chicago Linguistic Society 23:16–28.

Edmondson, Jerold A. and David B. Solnit, eds. 1988. Comparative Kadai: Linguistic studies beyond Tai. Summer Institute of Linguistics and the University of Texas at Arlington Publications in Linguistics 86. Dallas.

—— and Yang Quan. 1994. Tone geometry in Kam-Sui: Contours, edges and dimorphism. Minzu Yuwen 2:50–62

Goldsmith, John. 1976. Autosegmental phonology. Bloomington: Indiana University Linguistics Club.

Li Fang-Kuei. 1977. A handbook of comparative Tai. Honolulu: The University Press of Hawaii.

Li, Risen. 1990. A tentative analysis of tone sandhi in Pingguo Zhuang. ms.

Radford, Andrew. 1981. Transformational syntax. Cambridge: Cambridge University Press.

Yip, Moira. 1989. Contour tones. Phonology 6:149–74.

Zhang, Yuansheng. 1983. Zhuangyu liandu biandiao guilu jiqi yu yufa de guanxi [Zhuang tone sandhi rules and their relation to grammar]. Minzu Yuwen Yanjiu. 93–113. Chengdu: Sichuan Minzu Chubanshe.

II. Other Northern Tai

Front /a/ and Back /ɑ/ in Biandan Mountain Bouyei

Ni Dabai
Central University for Nationalities
Beijing, China

In Bouyei, when /a/ functions as an open rhyme, it is always long; when it is followed by a coda, it has, in most (geographical) locations, contrastive length.

(1) Rhymes and examples of contrastive vowel length in Bouyei varieties

Rhyme	first local variety Wangmo Zhexiang		second local variety Huishui Danggu		third local variety Jinglong Zitang	
aːi	laːi^1	'many'	yaːi^2	'write'	saːi^1	'man'
ai	lai^1	'flow'	yai^2	'long'	sai^1	'snail'
aːu	haːu^1	'white'	saːu^1	'young woman'	jaːu^1	'measure (rice)'
au	hau^1	'stink'	sau^1	'post'	jau^1	'dog barks'
aːm	ɕaːm^1	'ask'	yaːm^1	'carry, two people'	taːm^6	'to infuse'
am	ɕam^1	'sink'	yam^1	'testicle'	tam^6	'trample, tread'
aːn	haːn^1	'assent, respond'	maːn^6	'chili pepper'	vaːn^2	'musk deer, muntjac'
an	han^1	'busy'	man^6	'steady'	van^2	'chop, behead'

	first local variety		second local variety		third local variety	
Rhyme	Wangmo Zhexiang		Huishui Danggu		Jinglong Zitang	
aːŋ	ʔdaːŋ¹	'body'	ʔbaːŋ¹	'thin'	jaːŋ¹	'stir fry'
aŋ	ʔdaŋ¹	'nose'	ʔbaŋ¹	'bamboo section'	jaŋ¹	'sieve'
aːp	kaːp⁸	'hold under arm'	taːp⁷	'to stick, glue'	jaːp⁷	'carry with pole'[1]
ap	kap⁸	'grasp'	tap⁷	'liver'	jap⁷	'piglet'
aːt	ʔdaːt⁷	'scald'	ʔbaːt⁷	'scar'	ʔdaːt⁷	'hot'
at	ʔdat⁷	'tight'	ʔbat⁷	'hunger'	ʔdat⁷	'tight'
aːk	—		taːʔ⁷	'dry in sun'	laːk⁷	'collapse'[2]
ak	tak⁷	'to ladle out'	—		lak⁷	'deep'

Bouyei, in the region of Biandan Mountain in Zhenning, does not have contrastive length for /a/. What corresponds to the long /a/ of other locations is front [a], and what corresponds to short /a/ is back [ɑ].

(2) Examples of [a] and [ɑ] in Bouyei of Biandan Mountain in Zhenning

[a]		[ɑ]	
ʔban⁴	'village'	ʔbɑn⁴	'jar'
fan¹	'generation'	fɑn¹	'seed'
ɬan¹	'weave, plait'	ɬɑn¹	'hand over, pay'
than¹	'blanket'	thɑn¹	'to wear'
han⁵	'goose'	hɑn⁵	'salty'
van²	'to play'	vɑn²	'tooth, day'
maŋ²	'busy'	mɑŋ²	'blunt'
faŋ¹	'horizontal'	fɑŋ¹	'work (n.)'
tsaŋ⁶	'skilled'	tsɑŋ⁶	'weigh'
zaŋ²	'chaff'	zɑŋ²	'strength'
ʔdaŋ¹	'body'	ʔdɑŋ¹	'make sound'
ɬaŋ¹	'high'	ɬɑŋ¹	'fathom'
laŋ⁵	'to play'	lɑŋ⁵	'pull'
kaŋ¹	'middle'	kɑŋ¹	'dress up, pretend, pack, load, install'

The above examples demonstrate clearly that Biandan Mountain front [a] corresponds to long /a/, and back [ɑ] to short /a/. But the Bouyei of this area also has the following type of words in which there is a contrast between front and back low vowels when they function as an open rhyme.

---

[1] jap⁷ 'piglet' and jaːp⁷ 'carry on a pole' are from the Zhenning Muyi lect.
[2] lak⁷ 'deep' and laːk⁷ 'collapse' are from the Zhenning Xinan lect.

(3) Examples of [a] and [ɑ] contrasting in an open rhyme

[a]		[ɑ]	
pa⁴	'touch'	pa⁴	'daughter-in-law'
pha³	'thunder'	pha³ (pa⁴)	'sister-in-law'
ma¹	'mother'	ma¹	'come'
ma²	'wild fruit'	ma²	'what'
tsa²	'mixed'	tsa²	'lean (of meat)'
ta²	'spin (thread)'	ta²	'to guard'
ta⁵	'older sister'	ta⁵	'dry in sun'
ʔda¹	'furnish'	ʔda¹	'inside'
ɬa¹	'paper'	ɬa¹	'clean'
ɬa⁴	'I, me'	ɬa⁴ (ʔo⁴)	'help'
la⁵	'collapse'	la⁵	'elephant'
ka²	'be stuck'	ka²	'want (to do)'
ka⁴	'oneself'	ka⁴	'engage in trade, commerce'
kha³	'kill'	kha³	'near'
ha⁴	'five'	ha⁴	'give'

As stated previously, front [a] corresponds to long /a/, and back [ɑ] to short /a/; but in Kadai languages when a vowel functions as an open rhyme it is long, virtually without exception. Biandan Mountain Bouyei open rhymes /a/ and /ɑ/ also follow this common rule and are both long. Consequently, it arises that the vowels /a/ and /ɑ/—when followed by a coda—are actually long /a/ and short /a/, and when there is no coda the contrast of long and short /a/ still exists (realized as front [a] and back [ɑ]) but both are pronounced long. This sort of subtle phenomenon is extremely rare in other languages of this family.

Analysis of the material in (3) shows that the words with front /a/ as rhyme have cognates in other languages and dialects with long vowels. For example:

(4) Cognates of Biandan words with front /a/ rhyme

Biandan	Wangmo	Zhuang	Dai	Kam	Sui	Mulam	Maonan	
pha³	pja³	pla³	fa³	pja³	ʔna³	pya³	va³	'thunder'
ta²	ta²	ta³	—	ɕa¹	—	—	sa³	'spin'
ka⁴	ka⁴	—	—	qa¹	—	ca¹	—	'oneself'
kha³	ka³	ka³	xa³	sa³	ha³	khya³	ha³	'kill'
ha³	ha³	ha³	ha³	—	—	—	—	'five'

The situation with cognates of words with the back /ɑ/ rhyme is somewhat more complicated. For example:

(5) Cognates of Biandan words with back /ɑ/ rhyme

Biandan	Wangmo	Zhuang	Dai	Kam	Sui	Mulam	Maonan	Hlai	
pa⁴	paɯ⁴	paɯ⁴	pai⁴ paɯ⁴	—	ça³	—	—	—	'daughter-in-law'
ta²	taɯ²	taɯ²	taɯ⁴	—	—	—	—	—	'guard'
ʔda¹	ʔdaɯ¹	ʔdaɯ¹	laɯ²	—	—	—	—	—	'inside'
ɬa¹	saɯ¹	(seɯ⁵)	—	—	—	(sjau⁵)	(sɛu⁵)	—	'clean'
kha³	tçaɯ³	kjaɯ³	kai³ kaɯ³	—	—	phyəi⁵	phjai⁵	plaɯ³	'near'
ha⁴	haɯ³	haɯ³	hɯ³ haɯ³	sai³'	ha:i¹	khye¹	—	—	'give'

Cognates of these words all have the diphthong /aɯ/ in standard Bouyei, and Northern Zhuang is basically the same. Sipsong Panna Dai has diphthong /ai/ and Dehong has /aɯ/; in Hlai the only cognate is 'near', also with /aɯ/; most Kam-Sui languages have /ai/. These data show that the Biandan Mountain back /ɑ/ rhyme corresponds to /aɯ/ or /ai/ in related languages. From the point of view of the Kam-Sui and Hlai materials, an earlier diphthong has tended towards monophthongization. However, the words in (5) do not have the same rhyme as 'thunder', 'spin', 'oneself', 'kill', 'five' of (4). The latter have a true long /a/ which has therefore evolved into Biandan Mountain [a], while the former have diphthongs /ai/ or /aɯ/ which have, therefore, in Biandan Mountain become back [ɑ].

ta⁵ 'dry in the sun' is *tak⁷* in standard Bouyei and Northern Zhuang. The loss of coda -*k* after long /a/ is not confined to the single location of Biandan Mountain; however, the rhyme ought to be /a/. It is not yet clear why it has become back [ɑ] in Biandan.

ka⁴ 'engage in trade' may be borrowed from ancient Han 賈, Old Chinese *ka (initial *jian*, rhyme *yu;* cf. Guo 1986:92) in the *shang* tone, with Biandan Mountain preserving the older pronunciation.

ma² 'what' is also a Han loan. 麼 has the Middle Chinese *he* rhyme, originally pronounced *mua*, later losing the onglide and becoming *ma* (Wang 1957 v.2, 452). Biandan Mountain Bouyei preserves the Middle Chinese pronunciation.

There remains one word with back /ɑ/ having identifiable cognates: *ma¹* 'come'. This word means 'come' as in 'come and go' in all Tai languages, but it has tone 2 in Be (Lingao) and Dai. In Kam-Sui the meaning is slightly different. Kam/Mulam/Maonan ma^1 and Sui $\underset{\circ}{m}a^1$ mean 'come back, return'. ma^1 and $\underset{\circ}{m}a^1$ in all these languages have long /a/ as rhyme; why does Biandan Mountain have back /ɑ/? We have examined data from various Kadai languages outside China, including Thai, Saek, White and Black Tai of Vietnam, Shan of Burma, and Ahom of India, and the situation basically agrees with that of the Tai and Kam-Sui languages of China. All have cognates with initial /m/ and long /a/ rhyme, with only occasional irregularities in the tone category. Thus, as long as our observations are confined to the Kadai languages, there is no way to discover why Biandan Mountain 'come' has back /ɑ/.

If we shift the point of view to the Austronesian languages, the situation is as follows: 'come' in Indonesian is *dataŋ*, in western Cham *mai;* in Bunun of Taiwan *minʃuma;* in Sanya Hui $zai?^{33}$. Indonesian *dataŋ* is cognate with $taŋ^2$ 'arrive' in various Kadai languages. Indonesian also has *mari* 'come back' from proto-Austronesian **mayi*, which can be compared to Kadai ma^1 'come'. The above-mentioned western Cham *mai*, the *m . . . ma* of Bunun *minʃuma*, and Sanya Hui $zai?^{33}$ all come from **mayi*. Biandan Mountain Bouyei 'come' has back /ɑ/, whose source may be short /a/, but no explanation can be found in the available Kadai data. Only the comparison with Austronesian makes it clear that ma^1 'come' is from the *ma-* of Austronesian **mayi*, and that since *ma-* is often unstressed in Indonesian syllable structure, the vowel /a/ does not have a dominant role in the syllable, and this is reflected in the back /ɑ/ of Biandan Mountain ma^1 (which may be a short vowel). Moreover, western Cham *mai* 'come' may substantiate the correspondence of Biandan Mountain back /ɑ/ with /ai/, as distinct from the cognates of front /a/.

References

Guo Xiliang. 1986. Hanzi guyin shouce [Handbook of Old Chinese pronunciations]. Beijing Daxue Chubanshe.

Wang Li. 1957. Hanyu Shigao [Outline of the history of Chinese]. Beijing Kexue Chubanshe.

The Sound System of the Bouyei Language and Its Special Features

Wang Wei
Central University for Nationalities
Beijing, China

Bouyei is the language of China's Bouyei minority nationality, which is classified as belonging to the Zhuang-Dong (or Kam-Tai) stock, the Zhuang-Tai (or Tai) Branch. The relationship of Bouyei to the Zhuang language is rather close. There are no major subvarieties of Bouyei, only a division into three vernacular groups: Southern Guizhou vernacular, Central Guizhou vernacular, and Western Guizhou vernacular, which are conventionally called first, second, and third vernaculars. The Bouyei number 2,540,000 according to 1990 estimates, and are located in the southern, central, western, and southwestern areas of Guizhou Province as well as in some places in Yunnan and Sichuan Provinces (see map 2).

Originally, the Bouyei had no orthography of their own. In 1956 a new romanized writing system was established, to which alterations were made in 1981 and 1985. It is currently being promoted in a portion of Bouyei territory. The Bouyei writing system is based on the Southern Guizhou variety of Bouyei as exhibited in the speech of Wangmo County Fuxing Township (referred to below as Wangmo Bouyei).

In this paper I provide a simplified introduction to Bouyei and its special features illustrating the sound system as it is manifested in Wangmo Bouyei.

Sound system

Bouyei is a tonal language; with few exceptions every syllable has an initial, a rhyme, and a tone. The initial is found at syllable onset with rhyme following. The tone is associated with the entire syllable. The initials occur voiceless and voiced, vowels are both short and long, and tones both live and dead. Initials, rhymes, and tones have all had influence on one another.

Initials. Wangmo Bouyei has a system of 37 initials; 20 are simple segments; three are palatalized segments; and fourteen are labialized segments. According to place and manner of articulation the initials can be charted as follows:

(1)

	stops	affricates	fricatives	nasals	laterals	palatalized	labialized
labial	p, ʔb		f, v	m		pj, mj	
alveolar	t, ʔd	ts	s, z	n	l		tw, ʔdw, sw, zw, nw, lw
prepalatal		tɕ	ɕ	ȵ		j	tɕw, ɕw, ȵw, jw
velar	k			ŋ			kw, ŋw
glottal	ʔ		h			ʔj	ʔw, ʔjw

1. /ʔb ʔd ʔdw/ are only slightly 'preglottalized'. In the following data for simplicity's sake these are rendered as /b d dw/.
2. Wangmo Bouyei does not have aspirated initials. /ts/ occurs only in contemporary Han loan words.
3. In Wangmo Bouyei the labialized initials occur in Han loans (except for /kw ŋw ʔw/).

(2) Initials with examples

p	pa^3	'pat. aunt'	h	ha^3	'five'
b	ba^5	'shoulder'	pj	pja^1	'fish'
f	fa^2	'iron'	mj	mja^6	'slick'
v	va^1	'flower'	ʔj	$ʔja^4$	'open (eyes)'
m	ma^1	'to come'	tw	twa^2	'sliding weight on steelyard'
t	ta^1	'eye'	dw	$dwaːt^7 dwa^4$	'to idle, loaf'
d	da^5	'to cry'	sw	swa^3	'spinning wheel'
(ts)	$tsɯn^1 tsʅ^1$	'politics'	zw	$zwaːm^1$	'carry on shoulder'
s	sa^1	'paper'	nw	$nɔk^8 nwa^2$	'to scour, erode'
z	za^1	'to search'	lw	lwa^2	'blurred, dim, vague'
n	na^1	'thick'	tɕw	$tɕwum^6 tɕwa^4$	'grope one's way'
l	la^3	'below'	ɕw	$ɕwai^1$	'plough'

tɕ	tɕa³	'rice seedling'	ɲw	ɲwau³	'pockmarked'
ɕ	ɕa³	'to wait'	jw	jwa⁴	'drive away'
ɲ	ɲa¹	'grass'	kw	kwa²	'right (side)'
j	ja⁶	'wife'	ŋw	ŋwa⁴	'roof tile'
k	ka¹	'to follow'	ʔw	ʔwa⁴	'stupid'
ŋ	ŋa²	'sprout'	ʔjw	ʔjwa⁴	'long (face)'
ʔ	ʔa⁴	'to open'			

Rhymes. In Wangmo Bouyei there are 98 rhymes (including nine rhymes found only in contemporary Han loan words). Rhymes can consist of a vowel or a vowel and a coda from the set /-i -u -ɯ -m -ŋ -n -p -t -k/. The rhymes are listed below by vowel length.

(3)
a		o	ɔ	e	ɛ	i		u	ɯ		ʅ
aːi	ai	oi								ɯi	
aːu	au			eu	ɛu	iu					
	aɯ					ie		uə		ɯə	
aːm	am	om	ɔm	em	ɛm	iːm	im	uːm	um	ɯːm	
aːn	an	on	ɔn	en	ɛn	iːn	in	uːn	un	ɯːn	ɯn
aːŋ	aŋ	oŋ	ɔŋ	eŋ	ɛŋ	iːŋ	iŋ	uːŋ	uŋ	ɯːŋ	ɯŋ
aːp	ap	op	ɔp	ep	ɛp	iːp	ip	uːp	up	ɯːp	ɯp
aːt	at	ot	ɔt	et	ɛt	iːt	it	uːt	ut	ɯːt	ɯt
	ak		ɔk		ɛk	iːk	ik		uk	ɯːk	ɯk

ua	ue	ui	əu	iau	uai	uan	uaŋ	ɚ

1. The nine rhymes in the last row occur only in contemporary Han loan words.
2. In rhymes without consonantal codas, all monophthongs are long, and all diphthongs are falling (except for the nine rhymes in the last row).
3. The vowel /a/ before consonantal codas is [aː] when long and [ɐ] when short.
4. In Wangmo Bouyei /o/ and /e/ have different heights depending on their length: when long they are [o] and [e], when short they are [ɔ] and [ɛ].
5. Before consonantal codas, the long vowels /i u ɯ/ have an offglide /ə/. Thus /iː- uː- ɯː-/ are [iə- uə- ɯə-].
6. /ʅ/ occurs only after the initials /ts s z/.

The rhymes are exemplified by the following lexical items.

(4)
a	ta^1	'eye'	ɛ	$hɛ^1$	'to neigh'
aːi	$taːi^1$	'to die'	ɛu	$vɛu^6$	'cracked rim'
aːu	$taːu^5$	'to turn around'	ɛm	$pɛm^3$	'flat'
aːm	$taːm^1$	'handle'	ɛn	$nɛn^1$	'wild cat'
aːn	$taːn^5$	'charcoal'	ɛŋ	$bɛŋ^1$	'thin (not thick)'
aːŋ	$taːŋ^5$	'each, respectively'	ɛp	$tɛp^7$	'to glue'
aːp	$taːp^8$	'plank'	ɛt	$ɕɛt^7$	'seven'
aːt	$taːt^7$	'to peel'	ɛk	$zɛk^8$	'thin (cloth)'
ai	tai^3	'to cry'	i	ti^2	'to hit'
au	tau^6	'grass ash'	iu	ziu^3	'carry in the hand'
aɯ	$taɯ^2$	'to guard'			
am	tam^5	'short, low'	ie	tie^5	'to put down'
an	tan^3	'to wear, put on (clothes)'	iːm	$tiːm^5$	'shop'
aŋ	$taŋ^2$	'to arrive'	iːn	$tiːn^1$	'to chat, talk'
ap	tap^7	'liver'	iːŋ	$tiːŋ^1$	'cucumber'
at	tat^7	'peel'	iːp	$tiːp^8$	'to trample'
ak	tak^7	'ladle out, dip out'	iːt	$diːt^7$	'be noisy, make trouble'
o	to^5	'horsefly'	iːk	$piːk^7$	'vegetable'
oi	toi^5	'bowl'			
om	tom^5	'heart'	im	tim^2	'to fill'
on	ton^5	'break off'	in	tin^1	'leg'
oŋ	$toŋ^6$	'stake, piling'	iŋ	$tiŋ^2$	'half'
op	kop^7	'to hold in the hands'	ip	dip^7	'raw'
ot	tot^7	'take off (clothes)'	it	tit^7	'to kick'
			ik	sik^7	'to tear'
ɔ	$tai^6tɔ^4$	'pocket'			
ɔm	$tɔm^5$	'collapse'	u	tu^1	'door'
ɔn	$tɔn^2$	'shack'	uə	$tuə^2$	'class. for animals'
ɔŋ	$tɔŋ^6$	'paddy wall'			
ɔp	$tɕɔp^7$	'straw hat'	uːm	$zuːm^4$	'warm, to roast'
ɔt	$dɔt^7$	'to drink'	uːn	$tuːn^5$	'to guess'
ɔk	$tɔk^7$	'to fall, drop'	uːŋ	$ɕuːŋ^5$	'to put'
			uːp	$tuːp^7$	'petal'
e	te^1	'earth'	uːt	$ʔuːt^7$	'to wipe'
eu	deu^1	'one'			
em	tem^3	'to light (lamp)'	um	tum^6	'to flood'
en	ten^6	'bed'	un	dun^4	'to swallow'
eŋ	$teŋ^1$	'nail'	uŋ	$tuŋ^4$	'belly'
ep	kep^7	'hoof'	up	tup^8	'to beat, pound'

et	pet^7	'eight'		ut	$\text{\textcent}ut^7$	'insipid, tasteless'
ɯ	$tɯ^6$	'chopsticks'		ɯk	$tɯk^7$	'bamboo strip'
ɯi	$mɯi^1$	'bear'				
ɯə	$pɯə^6$	'clothes'		ɯk	$tɯk^7$	'to catch (fish)'
ɯːm	$fɯːm^4$	'dusk'				
ɯːn	$vɯːn^1$	'folk song'		ן	$sן^1$	'book'
ɯːŋ	$fɯːŋ^2$	'rice straw'				
ɯːp	$bɯːp^7$	'forehead'		ua	hua^1fui^4	'chemical fertilizer'
ɯːt	$hɯːt^7$	'kidney'				
ɯːk	$ʔɯːk^7$	'to hiccup, burp'		ue	$kue^2tɯa^6$	'country'
				ui	$kui^1tsəu^6$	'Guizhou'
				əu	$məu^6$	'mǔ' (unit of area)
ɯn	$kɯn^1$	'to eat'		iau	$liau^1$	'Liao' (family)
ɯŋ	$tɯŋ^4$	'cane, walking stick'		uai	$suai^1$	'Suai' (family)
ɯp	$hɯp^8$	'handspan'		uan	$luan^4$	'Luan' (family)
ɯt	$pɯt^7$	'lungs'		uaŋ	$huaŋ^4$	'Huang' (family)
ui	$kui^1tsə$	'Guizhou'		ɚ	$ɚ^4$	'but'

Tones. Wangmo Bouyei has eight tones of which six are live tones (those syllables without a coda and those with codas /-m -n -ŋ/) and two are dead (those syllables with codas /-p -t -k/). Every tone category has its own tone value.

(5)

Proto tone	Tone	Tone value		
A1	1	24	na^1	'thick'
A2	2	11	na^2	'paddy'
C1	3	53	na^3	'face'
C2	4	31	na^4	'maternal uncle'
B1	5	35	na^5	'arrow'
B2	6	33	na^6	'otter'
DL1/DS1	7	35	$taːt^7/tat^7$	'to peel', 'poke'
DL2/DS2[1]	8	33	$kaːp^8/kap^8$	'hold under arm', 'grab'

---

[1]Editors' note: We have added the indicators of the tonal categories according to the system A1, A2, ... DL2, described by Li (1977). The Chinese system, with odd and even numbers for high and low registers respectively, is given in the next column.

In Wangmo Bouyei, the dead syllable tones 7 and 8 have the same tone values as the live syllables 5 and 6.

In Wangmo Bouyei, contemporary Han loan words have tones that match those found in Southwestern Mandarin as spoken in Guizhou Province; thus Han loans in the tone categories *yinping, yangping, shang, qu,* and *ru* are assigned to Bouyei tone categories 6, 4, 3, 1, and 2 respectively.[2] For example:

(6) | Tone categories | yinping | yangping | shang | qu | ru
| --- | --- | --- | --- | --- | --- |
| Loan word tones | $tsaŋ^6$ | $vaŋ^4$ | li^3 | $tsau^1$ | lu^2 |
| Family names | Zhang | Wang | Li | Zhao | Lu |

Structure of syllables

Wangmo Bouyei syllables can have several kinds of structures in regard to consonants and vowels:

(7) consonant + vowel + tone
    ku^1 'I'
    to^6 'to read'
    $sɿ^1$ 'book'
consonant + vowel + vowel + tone
    lau^3 'alcoholic beverage'
    sau^1 'clean'
    $laːi^1$ 'much'
consonant + vowel + consonant + tone
    $saːm^1$ 'three'
    $çik^7$ 'ruler'
    $paŋ^2$ 'cloth'
consonant + vowel + vowel + vowel + tone
    $huai^4piau^3$ 'appearance'
consonant + vowel + vowel + consonant + tone
    $lian^4huan^6$ 'celebration'
    $huan^4liaŋ^4$ 'millet'

---

[2]Editors' note: Professor Wang is referring to the names of the Middle Chinese tone categories: *ping* (level), *shang* (rising), *qu* (departing), and *ru* (entering). Each of these was known to have divided into two reflexes; a high register tone called *yin* (light), when the initial consonant was *qing* (voiceless), and *yang* (dark) when the initial consonant was *zhuo* (voiced).

vowel + tone (in contemporary Han loans)
ər⁴ 'but'
ər³ 'a sentence particle'

The relationship between initials, rhymes, and tones

The distribution of Bouyei initials, rhymes, and tones shows a definite interdependency. In Wangmo these are indicated below:

1. Of the vowels /a o ɔ e ɛ i u ɯ ɿ ɚ/, only /a/ can combine with any initial; /ɿ/ can combine only with /ts s z/; /i e ɛ/ cannot combine with palatalized initials; and /u ɯ o ɔ/ cannot combine with labialized initials.
2. The initials with a 'preglottal' element /ʔ ʔb ʔd ʔdw ʔj ʔw ʔjw/ appear only in syllables with tone categories 1, 4, 5, and 7 (with very few exceptions).
3. Codas /-p -t -k/ occur only in syllables having tones 7 and 8.

Special features of the three vernaculars of Bouyei

The grammar and lexicon of Bouyei at all locations are substantially the same. The phonologies exhibit the greatest differences. The Southern Guizhou vernacular is spoken in areas in the south and southwest of Guizhou at Wangmo, Dushan, and Libo as well as in Yunnan Luoping County and elsewhere. Central Guizhou is spoken in Guiyang City. The Western Guizhou vernacular is spoken in Pu'an as well as in Sichuan Dingnan County. The Southern and Central vernaculars are more alike in phonology, whereas the difference between Western and the others is somewhat greater. A comparison of differences may be portrayed as follows:

(8) Southern has aspirated initials, the majority of areas do not have the affricate /ts/ of Central and Western. Instead they have /ɕ/ or, in a smaller number of places, /s/.

Southern	Central	Western	
ɕo⁶/so⁶	tso⁶	tsuə⁶	'name'
ɕu⁴/su⁴	tsu⁴	tsə⁴	'to buy'
ɕam²/sam²	tsam²	tsaŋ²	'to play, amuse oneself'

(9) There are three palatalized initials /pj mj ʔj/ in Southern, whereas in Central at most locations and in Western there is only /ʔj/.

Southern	Central	Western	
pja¹	pa¹	pa¹	'fish'
pjau¹	pau¹	pau¹	'to burn'
mjai⁴	mai⁴	mai⁴	'rust'
mjaːn⁴	maːn⁴	maːn⁴	'to trample'
ʔjaːŋ⁴	ʔjaːŋ⁴	ʔjaːŋ⁴	'sabre'
ʔjap⁷	ʔjap⁷	ʔjaʔ⁷	'to flash (of lightning)'

(10) Southern has labialized initials /kw ŋw ʔw/ as well as /tw dw nw lw sw zw tɕw ȵw ɕw jw ʔjw/. Generally, Central and Western have only /kw ŋw ʔw/.

Southern	Central	Western	
kwa⁵	kwa⁵	kwa⁵	'to cross'
ŋwa⁴	ŋwa⁴	ŋwa⁵	'roof tile'
ʔwa⁴	ʔwa⁴	ʔwa⁴	'stupid'
twa²	to²	to²	'sliding weight on steelyard'
lwa²	la²	la²	'gong'
swa³	sa²	ɬa²	'bamboo raft'
zwaːm¹	zaːm¹	saŋ¹	'to carry on the shoulder'
ɕwaːŋ²	tsaːŋ²	tsaːŋ²	'bed'
jwa⁴	—	—	'to chase away'
ʔjwa⁴	—	—	'long (face)'

(11) Some Southern areas have the diphthong rhymes /ie uə ɯə/, which correspond to simple vowel rhymes in Central and Western.

Southern	Central	Western	
tie⁵	ti⁵	ti⁵	'to put down'
zie²	zɯ²	ji²	'ear'
tuə³	tu²	tu²	'classifier for animals'
zuə²	zu²	zu²	'boat'
ŋɯə²	ŋɯ²	ŋɯ²	'snake'
pɯə⁶	pu⁶	pu⁶	'clothes'

(12) Southern vowels generally have a length distinction when followed by a coda. Of these, the long /e o/ correspond to diphthongs /ia ua/ in Central and Western.

The Sound System of the Bouyei Language 155

Southern	Central	Western	
deu^1	diau^1	diau^1	'one'
zeŋ^2	ziaŋ^2	ziaŋ^2	'strength'
pet^7	piat^7	piat^7	'eight'
doi^1	duai^1	duai^1	'hill'
son^1	suan^1	ɬuan^1	'to teach'
tot^7	tuat^7	tuat^7	'to disrobe'

(13) In Southern the initial /tɕ/ can occur with vowels /a o e i/. In Central and Western /tɕ/ occurs only with vowels /e i/; elsewhere the corresponding initial is /k/.

Southern	Central	Western	
tɕai^1	kai^1	kai^1	'far'
tɕaːŋ^1	kaːŋ^1	kaːŋ^1	'drum'
tɕɔp^7	kap^7	kak^7	'straw hat'
tɕen^1	tɕian^1	tɕian^1	'arm'
tɕe^4	tɕe^4	tɕie^4	'grain drying area'
tɕim^1	tɕim^1	tɕiŋ^1	'needle'
tɕik^7	tɕik^7	tɕik^7	'lazy'

(14) Central, in native vocabulary has no aspirated initials or voiceless fricative initials /f ɕ h/, as Southern does. The cognate vocabulary in Central are realized with /v ts ɣ/ initials.

Southern	Central	
fan^1	van^1	'inch'
fan^2	van^2	'chop, hack'
ɕa^3	tsa^3	'to wait'
ɕa^4	tsa^4	'sparse'
ham^5	ɣaːm^5	'toward'
ham^6	ɣaːm^6	'evening'
hap^7	ɣap^7	'shut (door, gate)'

(15) Central, in most locations, has preserved both long and short vowel contrasts before a coda /-k/ (in some places it has become /-ʔ/), whereas this coda after long vowels has been lost in Southern and Western.

Southern	Central	Western	
ta⁵	ta:k⁷	ta⁵	'to expose to sun, dry in sun'
do⁵	duak⁷	duə⁵	'bone'
he⁵	jiak⁷	ɕie⁵	'guest'
ʔie⁵	ʔi:k⁷	ʔi⁵	'hungry'
zuə⁶	zu:k⁸	zu⁶	'to vomit'
ŋuə⁶	ŋu:k⁸	ŋu⁶	'horned dragon'
tak⁷	tak⁷	tak⁷	'ladle out, dip out'
tɔk⁷	tok⁷	tok⁷	'to fall, drop'
zɛk⁷	—	—	'side, beside'
tɕik⁷	tɕik⁷	tɕik⁷	'lazy'
tuk⁷	tuk⁷	tuk⁷	'bamboo strip'
tɯk⁷	tɯk⁷	tək⁷	'to catch (fish)'

(16) Western, in most places of native vocabulary, has aspirated /ph th kh tsh tɕh/ initials. Most of them occur in tone 3.

Southern	Central	Western	
pja³	pa³	pha³	'thunder and lightning'
pja:i³	pa:i³	phe³	'to go'
tan³	tan³	than³	'to wear, put on (clothes)'
tai³	tai³	thai³	'to cry'
ka³	ka³	kha³	'to kill'
ka:ŋ³	ka:ŋ³	kha:ŋ³	'to speak'
ɕa³	tsa³	tsha³	'to wait'
ɕam³	tsam³	tshaŋ³	'to wear (hat)'
tɕiu³	tsiu³	tɕhiu³	'heel, to follow'
ɕip⁸	tsip⁸	tɕhik⁸	'ten'

(17) Western, in most locations, has a voiceless lateral fricative /ɬ/ where Southern and Central have /s/.

Southern	Central	Western	
sa¹	sa¹	ɬa¹	'paper'
swa²	sa²	ɬa²	'boat'
sai³	sai³	ɬai³	'intestine'
sa:u⁴	sa:u⁴	ɬo⁴	'bamboo pole'
san⁵	san⁵	ɬan⁵	'to shiver'
so⁶	so⁶	ɬuə⁶	'straight'
sɛt⁷	siat⁷	ɬiat⁷	'fishing rod'
sak⁸	sak⁸	ɬaʔ⁸	'to wash clothes'

The Sound System of the Bouyei Language   157

(18) Western at most locations, has two sets of fricative initials /f s ç h v z j ɦ/; the voiceless fricatives generally occur only in odd-numbered tone categories, and voiced initials, only in even-numbered tone categories.

Southern	Central	Western	
vuɯn¹	vuɯn¹	fən¹	'rain'
vuɯn²	vuɯn²	vən²	'person'
hen³	jian³	çian³	'yellow'
hen⁴	jian⁴	jian⁴	'to gnaw'
ham⁵	ɣaːm⁵	haŋ⁵	'toward'
ham⁶	ɣaːm⁶	ɦaŋ⁶	'evening'
zak⁷	zak⁷	sak⁷	'to break off'
zak⁸	zak⁸	zak⁸	'to steal'

(19) Southern and Central simple vowel codas /i u e o/ correspond to diphthongs /ei əu ie uə/ in Western.

Southern	Central	Western	
di¹	di¹	dei¹	'good'
fi²	vi²	vei²	'fire'
ku³	ku³	khəu³	'nine'
pu⁴	pu⁴	pəu⁴	'male (chicken)'
se⁵	se⁵	ɬie⁵	'sour plum'
me⁶	me⁶	mie⁶	'mother'
to⁵	to⁵	tuə⁵	'wasp'
zo⁶	zo⁶	juə⁶	'to leak'

(20) Southern and Central diphthongs /aːi aːu/ correspond in Western to /e o/.

Southern	Central	Western	
laːi¹	vaːi¹	le¹	'much'
zaːi²	zaːi²	ze²	'to write'
pjaːi³	paːi³	phe³	'to go'
saːu⁴	saːu⁴	ɬo⁴	'bamboo pole'
taːu⁵	taːu⁵	to⁵	'to return'
paːu⁶	paːu⁶	po⁶	'full, satiated'

(21) Southern and Central diphthongs /aɯ/ correspond to /ɑ/ in Western, so that Western has two contrasting phonemes /a/ and /ɑ/.³

Southern	Central	Western	
sa¹	sa¹	ɬa¹	'paper'
saɯ¹	saɯ¹	ɬɑ¹	'be clean'
ta²	ta²	ta²	'to spin (yarn)'
taɯ²	taɯ²	tɑ²	'to guard'
ha³	ɣa³	ha³	'five'
haɯ³	ɣaɯ³	hɑ³	'to give'
na⁴	na⁴	na⁴	'maternal uncle'
paɯ⁴	paɯ⁴	pɑ⁴	'daughter-in-law'

(22) Western vowels before codas do not distinguish vowel length. Central merges long and short /a/ before codas.

Southern	Central	Western	
tɕen¹	tɕian¹	tɕian¹	'arm'
tɕen¹	tɕian¹	tɕian¹	'to snore'
doŋ⁴	duaŋ⁴	duaŋ⁴	'hard'
dɔŋ⁴	doŋ⁴	duaŋ⁴	'winnowing basket'
ʔiːt⁷	ʔiːt⁷	ʔit⁷	'to extend (one's arm, leg)'
ʔit⁷	ʔit⁷	ʔit⁷	'one'
luːŋ²	luːŋ²	luŋ²	'copper'
luŋ²	luŋ²	luŋ²	'older maternal uncle'
vɯːn¹	vɯːn¹	fən¹	'folk song'
vɯn¹	vɯn¹	fən¹	'rain'

(23) Western merges codas /-m/ and /-ŋ/ as well as /-p/ and /-k/ (or /-ʔ/). In some locations there are only /-n/ and /-ŋ/, as all the rest have disappeared.

Southern	Central	Western	
kɯn¹	kən¹	kən¹	'to eat'
jɯn²	kən²	kən²	'above'
saːm¹	ɬaːŋ¹	saːŋ¹	'three'
saːŋ¹	ɬaːŋ¹	saːŋ¹	'high, tall'
zaːm¹	saːŋ¹	saːŋ¹	'to carry'
zaːŋ¹	saːŋ¹	saːŋ¹	'to stir fry'

---

³Editors' note: See also the article by Professor Ni Dabai in this volume.

The Sound System of the Bouyei Language

Southern	Central	Western	
zat^7	sat^7	se^5	'fart'
zat^8	zat^8	ze^6	'to cut (with scissors)'
tap^7	ta$ʔ^7$	tɯ^5	'liver'
tak^7	ta$ʔ^7$	tɯ^5	'ladle out, dip out'
dap^7	da$ʔ^7$	dɯ^5	'to extinguish, go out'
dak^7	da$ʔ^7$	dɯ^5	'lump, piece'

(24) Western, in some locations, does not distinguish between voiceless and voiced fricatives. However, stops and affricates distinguish three sets: voiceless, fully voiced, and preglottalized voiced. The syllables with preglottalized initials occur only in odd numbered tones.

Southern	Central	Western	
pi^1	pi^1	pei^1	'year'
pi^2	pi^2	bei^2	'fertile'
ʔbi^5	ʔbi^5	ʔbei^5	'to shell (beans)'
ta^5	ta:$ʔ^7$	ta^5	'to expose to sun, dry in sun'
ta^6	ta^6	da^6	'river'
ʔda:t^7	ʔda:t^7	ʔda^5	'hot'
kau^1	kau^1	kəu^1	'rattan, vine'
kau^2	kau^2	gəu^2	'curved, bent'
ɕam^1	tsam^1	tsa:ŋ^1	'to sink'
ɕam^2	tsam^2	dzaŋ^2	'to play'
tɕim^1	tɕim^1	tɕiŋ^1	'needle'
tɕim^2	tɕim^2	dʑiŋ^2	'pincers, tongs'

(25) Western, in some places, only has five live syllable tones and two dead syllable tones. The tones of Southern and Central tone categories 3 and 4 have merged into one tone category. For example:

Southern	Central	Western	
na^1	na^1	na^1	'thick'
na^2	na^2	na^2	'paddy'
na^3	na$^{3(4)}$	na$^{3(4)}$	'face'
na^4	na$^{3(4)}$	na$^{3(4)}$	'maternal uncle'
na^5	na^5	na^5	'arrow'
ta^6	ta^6	ta^6	'river'
tak^7	ta$ʔ^7$	dɯ^6	'ladle out, dip out'

From the preceding examples it can be seen that, among the three vernaculars, Western has slightly more special features. The last three features especially are rare elsewhere in Tai or in Kadai. The interdialectal differences described above are not absolute; among all three vernaculars there are some instances of overlap. On the other hand even within a single vernacular area there are some differences. The present article simply describes the general state of affairs.

References

Li Fang-Kuei. 1977. A handbook of comparative Tai. Honolulu: The University Press of Hawaii.

Linguistic Prediction: The Case of Saek

Paul K. Benedict
Ormond Beach, Florida

Linguistic prediction comes in a variety of forms. In an early 1942 paper I fearlessly predicted as 'not unlikely' that other Kadai languages would be uncovered in the China-Vietnam border area (Benedict 1975:442), even at the very time that F.-K. Li had already begun his recording of the Kam-Sui languages.[1] Now, many years later, we have Lakkia (Guangxi, Jinxiu County) and recently Laha (North Vietnam, Sơn La and Lào Cai Provinces), as yet only in tantalizingly meager morsels.[2] It can now be further predicted, with an even greater margin of safety, that these newly uncovered linguistic treasure houses will in time contribute greatly to comparative Kadai and

---

Editors' note: This paper was presented at the 1976 meeting of the International Conference on Sino-Tibetan Languages and Linguistics held in Paris, France. It has been revised and an appendix has been written by Professor Benedict to reflect his current perspective.

[1] For another kind of linguistic prediction, see Goodenough 1981:55, which says, "A scientifically valid account of a language is one that enables us to predict whether or not any particular utterance will be accepted by the language's speakers as conforming to their standards for speaking."

[2] A lengthy study of Laha has in the meantime appeared (cf. Solntseva and Hoàng 1986).

Austro-Tai studies. Another prediction in the same paper, in implicit rather than explicit form, has not fared nearly so well.

> The above discussion does not exhaust the possibilities of the complex Thai-Indonesian field, and it is possible that a more searching analysis of Indonesian material will yield further comparison, yet it is believed that most of the important lexical correspondences have been uncovered.[!] (Benedict 1975:459)

This was much later (1966) described as an "unfortunate statement, which surely must be ranked with the most egregious overstatements of our times" (Benedict 1975:3). Predictions are always hazardous, and negative predictions doubly so, so that the linguist who indulges in them puts himself in a class with the physician who announces that a patient has only x months or x years to live, thereby exposing himself to the considerable risk of being outlived by the patient!

Another type of prediction, always perilous, is based on linguistic patterning or analogy. To cite from Southeast Asia material, Tamang (Nepal) has the following unusual set of reflexes: final *-a* < PTB **a* versus *-aa* < PTB **-ak;* also *-e* < PTB **-ey* (*me* 'fire' < PTB **mey*) versus *-ee* < PTB **-ay* (*mee* 'tail' < PTB **r-may*) (Tamang material from Taylor 1970; PTB forms from Benedict 1972b). Hence one can 'confidently' predict that Tamang will also, when material becomes available, be shown to have *-o* < PTB **-ow* versus *-oo* < PTB **-aw* (the returns are not yet in at this writing). Languages often fail to behave properly, however, and it is easy to go astray. In a set of Karen notes (Benedict forthcoming a; Benedict forthcoming c) I have attempted to show that a series of preglottalized surd stops must be set up for Proto-Karen, paralleling the preglottalized voiced stops (only **ʔb-* and **ʔd-*) reconstructed by Haudricourt (see the discussion in Benedict 1972b:fn. 367); and that loss of final stop *(*-ʔ)* can occur as a result of Matisoff's Rule (? + ? = ∅) in a form of this type. For example Pa-o (Taungthu) has *pì* 'skin' < PK **ʔpiʔ* (cognate of Jinghpo *phyiʔ*, Jili məphik) but *deʔ* 'wing' < PK **ʔdeʔ*, the rule not being operative after the voiced stop. Matisoff has pointed out to me (p.c. 5/28/79) that in Lahu, where this glottal dissimilation rule was initially described by him, the reverse situation holds, e.g., PBL **ʔbak* > Lh *pà* (with secondary high rising tone), but PBL **ʔpak* > Lh *pâʔ*. Perhaps we should now predict that it will eventually be shown that the glottalization feature is not the same in the two languages, e.g., that it is more 'implosive' in Karen (a resourceful linguist never runs out of predictions).

Yet another kind of prediction—and one with which this paper is primarily concerned—is involved in the linguistic undertaking which I have dignified with the term TELEO-RECONSTRUCTION: "reconstruction based on relatively isolated correspondences at a distance, without the step-by-step reconstruction of one or more intervening links." In Southeast Asia linguistics, by and large, and particularly in the past years, teleo-reconstruction of a sort was forced upon the linguist seeking to work in the broader 'macro-linguistic' or, above all, the 'megalolinguistic' field (Matisoff's terms). Thus as early as 1929 Simon made a systematic comparison of Tibetan and Chinese while much more recently Shorto (1973) has compared Mon directly with Khmer in an effort to set up a provisional Proto-Mon-Khmer vocalic system. The paper in which the term teleo-reconstruction was introduced (Benedict 1973) reviewed Tibeto-Burman tonal systems in the light of my earlier reconstruction (1972a) of a two-tone system for the parent Proto-Sino-Tibetan, based on the overall correspondence of the early Chinese tonal system with those of Proto-Burmese-Lolo and Proto-Karen. If Karen is indeed on the same taxonomic level as Proto-Tibeto-Burman—the point is arguable but the recent reconstruction of Proto-Karen final *-s (Benedict forthcoming b) would favor the arrangement in Benedict 1972b—one must perforce set up a two-tone system for the parent Proto-Tibeto-Karen, with a prediction that Proto-Tibeto-Burman also will eventually be shown to have had a two-tone system. Multiple data gaps still exist in Tibeto-Burman, as in Sino-Tibetan generally, so that a certain amount of teleo-reconstruction is forced upon the comparativist, unless he is content to refrain from playing the game at all, as some of our more conservative colleagues would have it.[3]

Austro-Tai is par excellence the field for teleo-reconstruction. It is sufficiently megalolinguistic for some eminent scholars still to doubt its very existence. It has gaps (vast areas of darkness, rather) especially on the mainland side, although new material has now become available on the Austronesian side for the key Formosan languages. The lacunae are particularly troublesome in the Kadai field, where only Tai itself and, to a lesser degree, the Kam-Sui languages are reasonably well known. The criticism of Benedict 1975 on this score by Gedney (1976a) is well taken, but at the present time we simply do not yet have adequate data for a satisfactory reconstruction of Proto-Kadai nor even for a firm reconstruction of one of

---

[3]Cf. the remark by Zide in "Introduction to Austroasiatic Number Systems"(Special issue of Linguistics 174:5):
> A usual difficulty in establishing Austroasiatic cognate relationships is the shakiness of the comparative phonology at longer distances. Smith's careful reconstructions for Proto-North-Bahnaric (PNB) are very useful, but for comparisons with, say, Munda—and for any work making use of Nicobarese data—much more close work needs to be done, and what follows here necessarily includes some more and less [sic] educated guesses.

the major Kadai components: Hlai of Hainan (formerly known as Li).[4] Rather we must for the present continue a modified teleo-reconstruction approach, combining Austronesian (and Formosan) reconstructions, on the one hand, with Tai and (less satisfactory) Kam-Sui and Miao-Yao reconstructions, on the other, in effect predicting what the gaps might hold. At times, the new material nicely confirms the suggested comparisons or reconstructions, e.g., Proto-Tai (Southwest Tai/Central Tai) *riak 'call' originally appeared to be cognate with Proto-Western-Austronesian (Dempwolff's 'Indonesian') *iyak 'cry out', reconstructed by Dempwolff on the basis of Malay ter/ia, Ngaja-Dayak kăr-iak and Tagalog iyak; but the initial presented a problem. Blust (1970) has now shown that the Tagalog form is irregular and that the root should be reconstructed *yiyak (he adds Kadazan gizak), thus confirming the correspondence; the recently recorded Pupeo (North Vietnam dialect of Pubiao or Laqua[5]) has riek 'weep', also from this Austro-Tai root, yielding the correct analysis of Pubiao dek < *rek, id. (with vocalic leveling, as found also in Saek $reek^5$ 'call' < *riak).

To cite an entirely different example, Benedict 1975 analyzes Proto-Western Austronesian *kaniŋ '(eye)brow' as an infixed form < *-n- or < *-l-) and compares it (via 'branching of the face') with Proto-Tai (Southwest Tai/Central Tai) *kiŋ^C '(small) branch' as well as with Ong-Be (Hainan) kiŋ 'finger' = 'branch of the hand' (Haudricourt's analysis), offering as a parallel Rukai (Formosa) *pilaka (> dialect palaka through assimilation) 'branch'; Proto-Tai *hna^B phraak 'forehead' = 'branching of the face' (*hna^B) (with vocalic assimilation and vocalic transfer); Dahl (1976) has added the following to Proto-Austronesian (=Proto-Western Austronesian), showing that the root was indeed part of the Proto-Austro-Tai corpus: *kiŋkiŋ 'finger' Maanjan kiŋkiŋ, Sakalava Malagasy kiŋki 'little finger', and Malay k-əl-iŋ kiŋ (<*-l-). On the mainland side, as shown below, Saek has played the major confirmatory and explanatory role, but the still poorly known Lakkia and Laha have also been of much help at times. Lakkia not only confirms the labial clusters in 'eye' and 'die' but also is unique in its retention of the labial stop in 'weep' (see below) and of the homologous labial cluster */ml/ in mlok 'bird' (< PAT *[ma]mlok, whence PWA *manuk), thus confirming an earlier reconstruction based on Kam-Sui forms: Sui, Mak nok, T'en nɔk, Kam mok, and even supplying a parallel form (!): mlet 'bee' < PAT *m[a]mlets 'sweet/bee' (PAN *manits ~ *mamits (*/m/ retained through

---

[4]Editor's note. While true at the time this paper was originally written, Ouyang and Zheng (1983) present data on Hlai spoken at ten locations. This information has been used by Matisoff (1988), Thurgood (1991), and Ostapirat (1993) to reconstruct the initials and vowels of this language.

[5]Laqua is more popularly known these days as Qabiaw or Pubiao from the paper by Zhang (1990).

assimilation) 'sweet') (cf. PAT *(q/)wal[u] 'bee/sweet' cited below). Laha, closely related to Pubiao and the 'newest' of the Kadai languages, generally maintains PAT/PKD *a and resembles Saek and White Sand Hlai in having final -l (see below). Hence Laha sa 'two' confirms (and clarifies) the cognation of Pubiao ðe, id. (-e < *-a) with PWA *duwa = *dəwha < PAN *dəwsa (Dyen 1965), id. Laha *(k-)zal 'rain': zal (Bản Bung) ~ kzen (Than-Uyên) (the latter dialect has *a > /e/ before the final dental, along with *-l > -n) supports in striking fashion what had hitherto been only an 'educated guess' about the likely relationship of a trio of badly eroded Kadai forms for 'rain' (Pubiao ðəu, Gelao diə, and Lachi a/ɲa */na[l]) with the widely distributed Proto-Austronesian root *qu(n)dzal, id.

Saek was the eye-opener, however, and its many surprises were soon to be confirmed in part by Lakkia.[6] Some of these features were rather of a confirmatory nature, as indicated below, but others were entirely unanticipated; we shall start by exploring the ramifications of one of these.

One can fairly say that Austro-Tai was founded on a pair of roots, extraordinary ones for 'eye' and 'die'. As noted in my 1942 paper (Benedict 1975:457): "The remarkable parallelism shown in the treatment of these two roots constitutes perhaps our most significant single piece of evidence for a Thai-Indonesian linkage."

One might have dispensed with the 'perhaps'. It occurred to me in 1940–41, while mucking about in the then existing gallimaufry of Southeast Asia languages, that any languages with a pair of correspondences for 'core' roots of this nature *must* be related, a prediction or (if you like) an 'educated guess'. The next four decades or so were to be spent, in large part, in an ever-widening attempt to understand just *how* these languages were related.

---

[6]The rich full-bodied materials on this language furnished by Gedney—a veritable linguist's 'case of sack'—have made this study possible, and I am greatly indebted to him for making these materials available to me. It is ironic that this outstanding skeptic of Austro-Tai should indirectly have contributed so much in support of the doctrine (if only we had more skeptics of this kind)! I have attempted to placate him, however, by indicating tones for Tai, Saek, and other forms cited, insofar as practicable (see his criticism (Gedney 1976) of the 'castrated' (toneless) forms cited in Benedict 1975); but I have stuck to my own system of tone designations (there are limits to placation). For the uninitiated, I designate these tones in accord with their correspondences in the Chinese tonal system, from which they were borrowed long ago (Benedict 1975:150–51), as in the works of Kun Chang and others. The system employed by Li and Gedney, based on Thai (Siamese) tone marks, transposes tones *B and *C, so that *B corresponds to Chinese *C, and *C to Chinese *B, to the utter confusion of newcomers to the field! Gedney has recorded the Saek language spoken in Thailand (see also Gedney 1970 and 1976 bis) while Haudricourt (1963) presents the somewhat different form of the language spoken in Laos. See also the valuable study of Lakkia by Haudricourt (1967).

I feel that the original prediction has been amply fulfilled. Nothing illustrates this more graphically (see below) than the pair of roots under discussion, where at the start (I) a simple reconstruction seemed inescapable, some of the deviant forms appearing to be quite unrelated. This was succeeded by an uncomfortable transitional stage (II) when the then new Proto-Tai reconstructions (by Li), based on Northern Tai (especially Wuming) forms, called for a (dental) consonant cluster in both roots. But the correspondences were in effect 'saved' by the emergence of key Formosan data (neglected by Dempwolff and others) showing special reflexes (now symbolized C = cluster) in both roots. The Saek and (later) Lakkia forms (III), with labial clusters, were totally unanticipated but served only to change the Proto-Austro-Tai reconstruction (from dental to labial cluster). Finally, (IV), a review of all the relevant Kadai data, including forms on hand from the beginning, revealed correspondences with other Kadai languages (especially in the root for 'die') and established the fact that two different clusters (such as */pr/ and */pl/) were to be reconstructed.

As if this were not enough, a final solution was achieved only by collation with a third root ('weep'), again with new Formosan data, with a special reflex in Lakkia, indicating that a */pl/ must be reserved for this root, leaving only */pr/ and */pl̥/ for the other two. A very complex history, to be sure, but it should be noted that the basic prediction remained undisturbed, whatever the forms might be. The following table supplies forms and notes.

(1) Austro-Tai 'eye'
     'die'

I. PWA *mata   SWT *taa^A CT *t(h)aa^A Dioi ta   Pb te   PAT *mata
       *matay   *taay^A *t(h)aay^A (NT) tai tie   *ma/tay

II. PLUS Paiwanic *maCa   Wuming ra   PAT *matra
          (Formosa) *maCay (NT) rai   *ma/tray

III. PLUS Saek praa^1 Lakkia pla   PAT *mapra
           (NT) praay^1 plei   *ma/pray

IV. PLUS Sui da^{11} Hlai sa/ça   Gelao   Lachi ?mcu?   PAT *mapra
              tai^{11} ?ple u?   pe   *ma/play
                                      [= plen]   pien

Notes: PAT *ma/ (stative prefix), versus *pa/ (causative prefix) (Paiwanic has *ma/Cay 'die' versus *pa/Cay 'kill'). Dahl (1977:120) reconstructs PAN *qat₂ay (= *qaCay) on the basis of Rukai wa'atsai, and Bunun is -'ataδ; but the Proto-Miao-Yao cognates (below) support the above type of reconstruction, indicating that the Formosan forms have been re-prefixed (not unusual in Paiwanic, and *qa/ is the ubiquitous prefix there).

In (I) above, to the Central Tai *thaa ~ haa* and *thaay ~ haay* doublets add Ong-Be (Hainan) *dá* 'eye' < **ta^A* and *dái* 'die' < **tay^A*. This is the 1942 line of the 'age of innocence' in Austro-Tai studies (Benedict 1975:407, 456–57) when the reconstruction seemed very simple. The Central Tai aspiration, along with the initial of Hlai *sa/ça*, were 'explained' in terms of secondary aspiration, with Tibetan invoked as a model: **mlata* > **mta* > **mtá*. The Gelao and Lachi deviant forms for 'die' were treated as a distinct intra-Kadai correspondence, with note made of the parallelism shown by Gelao *plă*, Lachi *pio* 'blood'. The only other *p-* form available at the time for either root was *rem pia* 'eye', cited for a Zhuang (Northern Tai) dialect (Liuzhou) by Ting (1929), and conveniently overlooked by me (all linguists have an intrapsychic protective device enabling them to scotch certain 'nonconforming' entries by not acknowledging their relationship). Certainly a prediction made at that time (1942) that both roots would ultimately be reconstructed with labial clusters would have been looked upon as excessively 'visionary', even for megalolinguistics.

As shown in Paiwanic (II), */C/ was introduced by Dyen as a cover symbol for the distinctive set of correspondences to Proto-Western Austronesian */t/ shown by these languages in a sizable number of roots, and retained by me as a symbol for 'cluster (undetermined)' (see Benedict 1979).

(III) Proto-Austro-Tai has **mapra* and **ma/pray* rather than **mapla* and **ma/play* in view of the fact that Saek has both clusters whereas Lakkia has only /pl/.

(IV) PKS **[]daa^A* 'eye': Sui *da^{11} ~ da^{13}*, Mak *daa^{13}*, T'en *ʔdaa^{13}* (reconstruction uncertain; all forms reflect an unvoiced initial, but not PKS **ʔdaa^A* since Sui and Mak regularly have *ʔd-* in other roots corresponding to Proto-Tai **ʔd-*); PKS **tay^A* 'die': Sui *tay^{11} ~ tay^{13}*, Mak *tai^{24}*, T'en *tai^{13}*, the short (single) vowel reflecting the absence of vocalic transfer, in contrast to Tai and Hlai. The remaining Kadai forms had been known from the beginning, of course, but had been downgraded in the 1942 line, which favored the parallel Pubiao forms (*te* and *tie*). As for the Proto-Austro-Tai reconstructions suggested by this, the appearance of medial *-l-* in Gelao points to the */pl/ cluster in the root for 'die', leaving */pr/ for 'eye'.

It can be seen from the discussion above that the Lakkia forms, while useful to confirm, are not essential for the above reconstruction. In a third basic root, however, a problem is posed by still another (incomplete) set of Kadai correspondences to Paiwanic */C/, and here Lakkia supplies the key form:

'weep': Proto-Western Austronesian **taŋits;* Paiwanic **Caŋits;* Lachi *cuŋ* < **caŋ[it]* (cf. Yabem (Papua: North Huon Gulf) *taŋ*), paralleling 'eye'; *mcu* < **mapra;* Proto-Tai **phray^B;* Southwest Tai/Central Tai **hay^B*, Northern Tai **tay^B* (secondary initial aspiration, with **phr-* contrasting with the disyllabic **ph-r-*). Li (1977) puts the forms in his Proto-Tai **thr-* table despite the nonconforming *h-* and *t-*, adding the note, "These words are put here merely as posing a problem to be solved" (p. 124) (cf. his Proto-Tai **tr-* for **pr-;* see fn. 7), from **pra[ŋ]i[t]* (see Benedict 1975:169 for loss of intervocalic **ŋ;* Proto-Tai lacks **-ait*). PKS **ʔŋe^B* < **ʔŋai^B:* Ong-Be *ŋai* ~ *ŋɔi* (high tonal series); Southern (Hlai) *ŋei,* White Sand (Hlai) *ŋai,* all reflecting glottalized replacement of the initial, with parallel loss of final **-t.* Lakkia *piẽ* 'weep' (*-iẽ* < **-yãi*) is unique in retaining the initial **p-* (**-y-* < **-r-* or **-l-*), with hallmark nasalization for an earlier nasal, while Laha reflects typical Kadai end-stress (canonical reduction on the left) rather than fore-stress associated with an initial cluster (Benedict 1975:151), with loss of the first syllable: *ɲit* ~ *ɲiet* < **ŋit* (palatalized before **i*), with *-t* for **-ts* (lacking in Kadai).

Now it is precisely this root for 'weep' that shows an unusual development in Atayalic (Formosa): Atayal *məŋilis* (Ci'uli *maŋilis*), Sedik *ləmiŋis,* analyzed in Benedict 1975 as re-infixed forms, although not without having carefully considered the alternative of regarding Atayal/Sedik *-l-* in this root as the reflex of a PAT */pl/* cluster, with infixed */m/* and showing metathesis in Atayal (Tsuchida 1976). Atayalic regularly has */s/* or */ts/* corresponding to PWA **/t/* and Pai **/C/;* cf. Atayal *ma/masa* 'eyeball', Paiwanic **maCa* 'eye'; Atayal *səlaq* (Ci'uli *tsalak*), Sedik *tsəlaq* 'field (wet)'; Proto-Western Austronesian **tanaʔ* ~ **tanəʔ* 'earth' (but note the Ngaja-Dayak doublet: *tana* 'field', *tanah* 'earth, land') (Paiwanic apparently lacks cognates for this root). The matter appears to have been settled by Tsuchida, who has uncovered an additional Proto-Austronesian root with reflexes as in 'weep':

PWA **tuhuy*

Itbayaten	*tohoy-ən*	'to thread a needle, skewer, string'
Tagalog	*tu:hog*	'to thread a needle, skewer, string'
Bikol and Samar-Leyte	*tohog*	'to thread a needle, skewer, string'
Cebuano	*túhog*	'to thread a needle, skewer, string'
Hiligaynon	*tóhog*	'to thread a needle, skewer, string'
(Oceanic) Tongan	*tu-i*	'to thread a needle'
(Formosa: Tsouic) Kanakanabu	*ts-um-a-tsu-úru*	'to thread a needle'
Paiwan	*ts-m-usu*	'to string beads'
Saisiyat	*söhö-ön*	'to thread a needle'
Atayal	*l-əm-oho*	'to thread a needle' (**/s/* > Ata. /h/ and **/γ/*, > ∅ Ata. are regular).

This root is represented in Kadai by a typical end-stress (canonical reduction on the left) form: SWT **son^A* 'to thread needle/plait/thrust through hole' (contra Benedict 1975, where it is erroneously placed under 'thrust through/into' along with the only true Proto-Tai cognate there: *zon^4 'push forward or into').

A distinct cluster must be reconstructed for Proto-Austronesian on the basis of this pair of roots, e.g., *C_2aɲi(t)s 'weep' and *C_2usuy 'to thread needle', as opposed to *maC_1a 'eye' and *ma/C_1ay 'die'. The fact that Atayalic has maintained the glide only in this one of the trio of (original) PAT */p/ + glide clusters provides a basis for reconstructing */pl/ for this cluster (in 'weep' and 'thread needle'), leaving */pl̥/ to be assigned to 'die' and */pr/ to 'eye', as above: *plaɲi(t)s 'weep'; *[plo]soy 'thread needle'; *ma/pl̥ay 'die' and *mapra 'eye'.

So much for the surprise; let us turn now to the confirmatory features of Saek. Saek *pr-* can also be of secondary origin, in contrast with the primary Proto-Austro-Tai clusters discussed above, as shown by the following root:

PWA *bul̥uq 'sp. of bamboo'

Formosa:	Tsouic/Paiwanic *bul̥uq 'a type of slender bamboo' (Paiwanic 'spear');
	SWT *took 'bamboo strip (withe)'
Central Tai:	Nung/Lungchow *phyook*, 'bamboo strip (withe)' (with *-h-* < *-r-*)
Northern Tai:	Wuming *ruk* 'bamboo strip (withe)'
	Saek *pruk⁴* 'bamboo strip (withe)'
Kam-Sui:	Mak *duk* (high tone series), 'bamboo strip (withe)' (the unvoicing of initial *b-* is a regular feature in Kadai, see Benedict 1975:154–55).

Note that only Nung/Lungchow (Central Tai group) show a distinction in initial reflex in this group and that for 'eye' (*th-* ~ *h-*; Thô has *th-* in both); the Proto-Tibeto-Karen reconstructions for these two roots appear to include a distinction between a *pr-* cluster and a *pVr-* sequence, neatly fitting with the etymologies of the two roots(!): *pra^4 'eye' < PAT *mapra; *p(o)rok 'bamboo strip' < PAT *bol̥oq (with vocalic transfer in Southwest/Central Tai). In a second root of the same shape Saek has initial *r-*, along with vocalic transfer, indicating that this is the Saek reflex for the sequence (rather than the cluster) initial:[7]

PWA		*buluŋ	'(large) leaf' (Ho. 'young (= large) leaves')
SW/CT		*tooŋ^A	'large leaf (especially of the banana)'
NT:	Wuming	röŋ	'large leaf (especially of the banana)'
	Saek	rɔɔŋ^2 < hrɔɔŋ^A < PT *p(o)roŋ^A from PAT *(m)boḷoŋ	'large leaf (especially of the banana)'

See Benedict 1975 for Miao-Yao cognates.

With PAT */ɣ/ rather than */ḷ/ (both generally > PT */r/) as medial, the following trio of roots present interesting contrasts in development, beginning with a re-prefixed root (first *b-, then the ubiquitous *qʔ > PT *ʔ-):

PWA		*b-iɣaŋ	'redden'
		(< *iɣaŋ	'red')
SW/CT		*ʔdeeŋ	'red'
		(/ee/ < */ia/)	
NT:	Wuming	ʔdiŋ	'dark brown, tan'
		(for $_1$*ʔriŋ, lacking in Wuming)	
	Saek	riiŋ^1 < *ʔriiŋ^A	'red' (vocalic assimilation)
KS:	Mak	laŋ^{13}	'red'
		(high tone series; apparently from *[p]yaŋ; cf. Saek 'rotten', below).	

Note that the Saek reflex (r-) is for the sequence (rather than the cluster), as might be anticipated in an originally prefixed (*b-) root, thus providing a bit of evidence for *b- as a productive prefix at the Proto-Kadai, or even later (Proto-Tai), level. The cluster prefix is indicated for the following root (see Benedict 1975 under 'spray'/ for the Miao-Yao cognates):

PWA *buya 'to spray' (Tg 'spit out'); Saek phrɔɔ^6 (*brɔɔ^B) 'to squirt (water from mouth)', from *brua^B (through vocalic transfer; cf. 'flesh/meat', below); the regular Kadai unvoicing of initial *b- (see roots above) does not

---

[7] Li (1977) reconstructs these roots rather differently, with initial *tl- for 'leaf' (a possibility at the Proto-Tai level, from a pre-Proto-Tai labial cluster), *pr- for 'bamboo strip' and *tr- for 'eye' and 'die'. He notes that Saek pr- for this last pair of roots indicates an original *pr- instead of *tr- but he does not comment on any possible distinction from the *pr- of 'bamboo strips' (and other roots with the same pattern of correspondences).

obtain here, indicating derivation from an originally reduplicated form (Benedict 1975:155–56): *buya/buya, reflected also in Oceanic: Ulawa (Sa'a dialect) hula/hula 'spring' (='the sprayer/squirter'). PT *ʔboo^C 'spring, well, mine' is possibly from this source (< *ʔbua^C < *q/bu[γ]a), but Benedict 1975 (under 'bubble') relates it rather to PWA *(m)bual 'spring, well' because of Kam-Sui forms which suggest an earlier final *-l.

PWA *buyuk 'spoiled', but note the Tagalog doublet: bugok 'spoiled', bulok 'rotten', the latter indicating a Proto-Western Austronesian doublet *buluk; Formosan: Pai/Ata *(ma/)buyuk 'rotten'; SW/CT *ʔdook, id.; NT *ʔduk, id.: Dioi duk, Po-ai nuk; KS: Mak ʔduk 'decayed, spoiled'. This root appears in Benedict 1975 with the reconstruction *(q/)boyok, an error for *(q/)bo[γ]ok since no mainland evidence for PAT */γ/ is cited. Saek has come to the rescue, however, with the unprefixed form plook 'rotten', with the cluster pl- rather than pr- for an original py- (cf. Mak 'red', above), suggesting that both */r/ and */γ/ will (prediction) have to figure in the final Proto-Kadai reconstruction schema. Now, thanks to Saek, we can retain the */γ/ in our Proto-Austro-Tai reconstruction for this root!

Saek does not maintain the primary PAT */ml/ cluster (nok⁶ 'bird') but it does preserve a secondary /ml/ (< */mb+V+glide/) in the following key Austro-Tai root:

Formosan: Paiwanic (Rukai) *bula/bula/i 'flesh, meat, animal'; SW/CT *nia^B 'flesh, meat, deer (meat)', but Thai (Siamese) has the doublet form bia < *ʔb[l]ia^B 'meat, deer' as well as phla < *bla^C 'seasoned raw meat' (from the reduplicated root, as in Rukai, with retention of voicing); Northern Tai: Po-ai noo (< *nua^C) 'flesh, meat' but the deviant Móng Cái region dialects described by Haudricourt (1960) have mo as well as no, pointing to an earlier *mlo (cf. KS mok ~ nok 'bird', Lakkia mlok, cited above, a primary Proto-Sino-Tibetan cluster), and Saek obliges with mlɔɔ⁵ < mlɔɔ^C 'flesh, meat', from *mlua^C < *mblua^C (with vocalic transfer; cf. 'spray/squirt', above); for the *B ~ *C tonal variation in this root, see Benedict 1975:196–97 (diagram on p. 197).

It can be seen from the foregoing that Saek has filled a lot of 'gaps' in the system! A labial cluster generally missing in Tai was actually reconstructed in the 1942 paper (Benedict 1975:457), on the basis of b- and d- variation in various Tai languages, in three basic roots (written there with lenis *b+l- initial and without tone marks): *ʔblian^A 'moon'; *ʔblii^A 'bile' and *ʔblook 'flower'. It was gratifying to see this cluster, despite its rejection by Shafer (1957),[8] finally 'come to life' in Saek: blian¹ 'moon', blii¹ 'gall bladder' (Haudricourt 1967 ʔbli 'bile') and blɔɔk⁶ 'flower' as well as in Lakkia: ʔblai 'bile' (but ʔbien 'moon'), especially since Austro-Tai etymologies are at hand for all three roots: PAT *(q/)(m)bul̥al 'moon';

---

[8]See footnote 3, p. 385.

*(q/)(m)pali 'bitter, bile' (note that Lakkia maintains the */a/ through vocalic transfer); *(/(q/)(m)b/l/u(w)aq 'fruit, flower' (the 1942 paper (fn. 50) compares with Bisaya *bolak*, Tagalog *bulaklak* 'flower').

Although Saek is outstanding in its retention of labial clusters, it also at times makes valuable contributions of other kinds; compare the following root:

Formosan: Paiwanic (generally) **kayaw* 'scratch (with fingernails)' but Thao reflects **k/m/uyaw;* the apparent cognate, SWT/NT (Dioi) **kaw^A* ~ CT **gaw^A* 'scratch (oneself)' has a short (single) vowel rather than the long (double) vowel anticipated from a PAT **(ŋ)kayaw* (PAT */ŋk/< PT */g/, paralleling */Nq/ > PT */ɣ/ via */G/ [Saek has /ɣ/], */nt/ > PT */d/ and */mp/ > PT */b/; regular loss of */ɣ/ in unstressed position: **(ŋ)ká(ɣ)aw).* To handle this problem, the Thao form was taken as primary and the general Paiwanic form as secondary (assimilated), with **(n)ku(ɣ)aw* yielding **(ŋ)kwaw* > **(n)kaw,* but the Benedict 1975 reconstruction was tentative: **(ŋ)k[u][ɣ]aw.* Saek has both *kaw^1* < **kaw^A* 'to scratch', an apparent loan from Tai, and *khwaaw^A* < **gwaaw^A* 'to scratch, claw', nicely confirming the first vowel of the reconstructed root, now **(ŋ)ku[ɣ]aw* (long /aa/ in Saek possibly through influence from a **ka[ɣ]aw* doublet, as in Formosan).

This paper concludes with an examination of that most celebrated of all Saek features: final *-l*. This hardly sounds exciting, to be sure, but it was so unexpected that Gedney (1976b) saw fit to devote an entire paper to the subject, with a provisional conclusion that "the evidence available to us points inescapably to inheritance of the *-n/-l* distinction from the protolanguage." Earlier in the same paper, however, the basic question of possible extra-Tai correspondences for Saek *-l* was disposed of in a rather offhand manner:

> Those who follow Dr. Paul Benedict in believing the Tai group to be genetically related to Austronesian have sometimes expressed an affection for this Saek final *-l*, because this makes at least one Tai language look more like Austronesian. But this idea does not get very far when one looks at specifics; for example, the common Tai classifier for things which is *ʔan^1* in Siamese has been alleged to resemble an Austronesian word having final *-n*, but this turns out to be one of the Saek words having final *-l*. (Gedney 1976b:4)

I must say, at the outset, that 'affection' hardly expresses the depth of my feelings for Saek final *-l*, and for Saek generally, I might add! I don't know just which 'specifics' Gedney has in mind, other than the example cited, but they could not have been from Benedict 1975:162, which points out that Saek *-l* serves as a reflex for five different Proto-Austro-Tai phonemes: */l ḷ r ɣ R/, also that final *-l* appears in White Sand (Hlai) Hlai and must be reconstructed for Proto-Kam-Sui in at least one root (see notes on 'stone', below). As shown above, Laha also has final -*l*, with at least one key Austro-Tai correspondence in the root for 'rain' (cognates apparently lacking in Tai and Kam-Sui). As pointed out in a note on Gedney's paper (Benedict 1976), there is fragmentary evidence (Pubiao reflexes) for a distinction of some sort with *-*l* versus *-*r* or *-*y* at the Proto-Kadai level. Note the following Laha dialects: Bản Bung, Noong Lay, Than-Uyên:

(2) Laha

	PWA	Paiwanic	BB	NL	TU	Pubiao	Pupeo	PKD
'rain'	*ʔu.ẓan	qudzal	zal	—	kzen	ðəu	—	*zal
'mouth/ estuary'	*muwa [r,γ]a	—	muol	mul	mɔn	mɔn	kəman	*mua[r]
'husked rice'	—	—	saal	saal	saan	—	—	*saa[r, l]

Notes: Laha/Pubiao/Pupeo 'mouth'; Proto-Western Austronesian 'estuary' (cf. German *Mündung*, French *embouchure*).

Saek *yaw⁶ saal²* (< **saal^A*) 'white (> husked) rice *(yaw⁶)*'; Dioi (NT) *hau san;* SW/CT **xaw^B saan^A* (source unknown, but early loan apparently ruled out by Laha forms; written *sar¹* in Siamese).⁹

The Saek forms became available only long after I had completed most of my PAT reconstruction, which in fact involved predictions as to which of these roots would have Saek cognates with final -*l* rather than -*n*. As Gedney points out, Saek has for some time been undergoing a process of replacement of the -*l* by -*n*, the corresponding final in the neighboring Tai languages, so that young Saek speakers now have only the final nasal. Saek at times has final -*n* where -*l* might be anticipated, as in 'moon' (above); in

---

⁹This root, of considerable cultural importance, appears to be related to Written Burmese *chan* 'husked rice', *ʔa-chan* 'kernel' (with PTB prefixed **a*-), from PBL **can¹* = **can^A* 'rice (paddy)' (cited by Bradley, (2)1:124). For the derived Written Burmese form meaning 'kernel' cf. Shan (under Burmese domination) *khaw-s'aan* (< SWT **xaw^B saan^A*) 'kernel of rice *(khaw)*. Proto-Burmese-Lolo final *-*n* is a regular reflex of PTB *-*l* as well as *-*r* (Benedict 1972b:fn. 54), hence the original (if this indeed a loanword) can be reconstructed with final *-[r,l] but the initials are divergent: possible **c*- versus **ts*- (Proto-Tai regularly has **s*- for PAT **ts*- but retains PAT **c*-). The tones agree and there is no discrepancy in vocalism since Proto-Burmese-Lolo (as generally reconstructed) lacks */aa/, which would simply be replaced with */a/. All in all, the evidence points to borrowing (perhaps at different times) from a third language which had */aa/ versus */a/ but with a marginal (at best) **c*- versus **ts*- distinction, as in Mon-Khmer (Benedict 1975:476–77).

one word ('fat/grease/oil', below) Thailand Saek (Gedney 1976b) has -*n* while Laos Saek (Haudricourt 1963) has -*l*. Note also the occasional doublet, as in the forms under 'lever/lift/net' (below) and *lil*⁶ ~ *lin*⁶ 'pangolin' < **hlil^C* or **lil^B* (tonal merging in Saek; SW/CT/NT [Dioi, Po-ai] **lin^C*, id.) In view of the replacement process that has been going on in Saek for some time it is evident that forms in -*l* are historically more significant than those in -*n*. A review of all such forms has yielded a significant result: without exception the likely Austronesian cognates involved (see Benedict 1975 for most of them) either have one of the five phonemes cited above (*/l ḷ r γ R/) corresponding to Saek -*l*, or in one case ('forest', below) have a reconstructible phoneme (*/l/) from this group in this position! The table below presents these roots in some detail.

(3)   Correspondences to Saek roots with -*l*.

	PAT	Paiwanic	PWA	SWT (CT)	Saek
'stone'	*(n)tril[ay]	*/Cilay (Paiwan)	—	*hrin^A (*thrin^A)	riil² < *hril^A
'string/num. classifier'	*[γa]sel	gasil (Atayal)	—	*sen^B	sɛl³ < *sɛl^B
'bee/sweet'	*(q/)wal[u]	*(q/)walu	—	*hwaan^A	vaal² > hwaal^A
'earth/field'	*(m)pralaq	səlaq (Atayal)	*tanə? *tanə?	*ʔdin^A	bal¹ < *ʔb[r]al^A
'(big) fly'	*ŋal[a] (/ŋala)	*ŋalaŋal (Saisiat)	—	nan (NT) (Yay)	nɛi² < hnɛi^A
'forest'	*[q]u(n)tal	—	*ʔutan	*thian^C	thual < *dual^C
'earthworm/eel'	*(n)tula	*tula	*[t]una	*ʔdian^A	tlual¹ < *tlual^A
'flea/louse'	*[ti]mula (/la)	*timula (Ilocano)	timel	*mlen^A	mlɛl⁴ < *mlɛl^A
'beat/hit/ hammer'	*pa(N)Gul	*puŋkul *puqu[l]	—	*yoon^{B/C}	khɔɔl⁶ < *yɔɔl^B
'lever, lift (net)'	*(n)tsu(w)aḷ	—	*sual	*soon^A	sɔɔl³ < *sɔɔl^B sɔɔn³
'stone'	*(n)tril[ay]	*/Cilay (Paiwan)	—	*hrin^A (*thrin^A)	riil² < *hril^A
'speak/teach'	*suaḷ	*sual	—	*soon^A	sɔɔl² < *sɔɔl^A
'worm/larva/ snail'	*[m]una[ḷ,γ]	*muna[ḷ,γ]	—	*hnoon^A	nɔɔl² > *hnɔɔl^A
'frog/toad/ tadpole'	*(ta)kar[a] (/qura) *(ta)Nqar[a]	takaru:ra (Kanakanabu) —	ka:l —	(WS Hlai) yal⁴- < *γal^A-
'dust'	*(qa/)mur	—	*ʔamur	*(h)mun^C	mul⁴ < *mul^A
'body hair/ feather'	*(N)qo(m)pur	*kupur (Thao)	—	*xon^A	pul¹ < *pul^A
'fat/grease/oil'	*(s)(i)may	*simay	—	*man^A	man⁴ < *mal^A (Haudricourt -maḷ)
'speak/sing/ crow'	*(N)qaγi	*kaγi	*kaγi	*xan^A	hal² < *xal^A
'sow (seed)/ scatter'	*tsa(m)ba[γ]	—	*səba[γ]	*hwaan^C	vaal⁶ < *hwaal^C

Linguistic Prediction: The Case of Saek

'hearth/firewood'	*(n)d[a]puy	—	*dapuy	*viin^A (*vun^A)	vil^1 < *fil^A
'to fly'	*(-)(m)pə[R] (/pR)	*/pə[R]/pə[R] (Paiwan)	—	*ʔbin^A (*ʔbon^A)	bil^1 < *ʔbil^A
'left (side)'	*(k-)weR[i]	*(ka/)wiRi	*k(a)/wiRi	—	veel^6 < *hweel^C
'lime'	*qapuR	—	ʔapuR	—	
	*NqapuR	—	*kapuR	*puun^A	
	*NqampuR	—	—	—	muul^6 < *hmuul^C

Notes on roots in (3):[10,11]

See Benedict 1975 for details, with addition of four new entries: 'string/number classifier (for string-like objects)'; 'fly' (Sai. 'big fly'); 'worm/larva/(Tai) snail (Sai.)'; and 'beat'.

'stone': final *-l apparently is to be reconstructed for Proto-Kam-Sui, with Sui, T'en and Kam all reflecting *d(y)in^A < *drin^A < *ntrin, but Mak reflecting *dwi^A < *dri^A *ntri[l].

'bee/sweet': Benedict 1975:230 erroneously cites Saek vaan (it was one of the Saek forms for which I thought the prediction [for Saek -l] had failed!).

'(big) fly': both the initial 'n- and the vocalism of Yay/Saek appear to be secondary; for the latter cf. 'flea/louse'.

---

[10]Cf. also Saek khal^4 < *gal^A 'classifier for spoons, pencils, saws' and SW/CT *gan^A 'handle' < PAT *[tsa] (ŋ)kal (PWA saŋkal 'handle of tool'). Saek also has kan^6 *ka[l]^C 'haft of knife', directly cognate with Dioi kan (< tone *C) 'button (of cap), peduncle (of fruit), handle (of pot cover)', and comparable also with a Lungchow form cited by Li: kan^2 < *kan^B 'handle, petiole'. These forms point to a PAT doublet *[tsa]kal, contrasting with PT *gan^A < *[tsa]ŋkal (PAT */ŋk/ > PT */g/). The forms with */aa/ vocalism cited in Benedict 1975 under 'handle' perhaps belong under 'branch', with possible contamination.

[11]See Benedict 1975:181 for PAT */γ/ versus */R/ (post-velar) and Benedict 1975:164 for PAT */l/ ('back' l) versus */L/ ('front' l), the latter pair corresponding to Dyen's */L/ and */N/ and to Dahl's */l/ and */ɬ/. The Benedict reconstruction is strongly supported by the wide range of Formosan data now available (cf. the remarks by Paul Li [7/30/79]):

> Your statement that [Dyen's] N is definitely *l is quite acceptable to me. Its reflexes in a number of Formosan languages are lateral fricative, either voiced or voiceless. What has been reconstructed as PA[N] *l by Dempwolff, Dyen, and Dahl should be the retroflexed *ḷ or flap *L as indicated by the phonetic reflexes in many Formosan languages.

PAT */l/ yields PWA */l/ while PAT */L/ yields PWA */L/ as an initial but PWA */n/ as medial or final in the scheme presented by Benedict 1975, but it now appears that Proto-Western Austronesian also maintained the distinction at the earliest level; cf. Dahl (1977:131), who shows that a distinctive /n/ reflex for PAN */L/ appears in initial position in several languages spread over Sulawesi (Celebes) from north to south and in Chamoro and the Philippines.

'earthworm/eel' and 'flea/louse': reduplication (complete or partial) is characteristic of Austro-Tai generally (see Benedict 1975:140–47).

'beat, hit, hammer': Paiwan *p-ən-aŋul* 'hit (with stick)', from **paNGul;* SWT **γoon^B* 'stick (for beating); mallet, hammer' but **γoon^C* 'beat, strike', from **γual* (typical vocal leveling) < **[p]aGul* (thru vocalic transfer); Central Tai has only **γoon^B* 'beat, strike, hammer (v.)' (with tone **B* of the noun) while Saek has only *khɔɔl^6* 'hammer, club', from **γool^B*.

'lever, lift (net)': Tagalog *sual* 'lever'; Fiji *tsua* < **nsua* 'stick for lifting net'; SWT **soon^A* 'to fish with (=lift) a landing net' (White Tai); Saek *sɔɔl^3* 'a kind of fish trap' ~ *sɔɔn^3* 'to scoop up (fish)' (doublet noted by Gedney).

'sow (seed)/scatter': final *-γ* indicated by the doublets in *-y* (see Benedict 1975 under 'spray').

'hearth/firewood': the Tai doublet **vun^A*, reflected both by Thô (Central Tai) and Ahom (Southwestern Tai), retains the back rounded vowel in this root.

'to fly': Paiwan: Makazayazaya dialect *mi/pərpər*, with final *-r* as reflex of PAN **-r* or **-R* but not **-γ* (< Paiwanic *-Ø;* see Benedict 1975:161); apparently from an original **sapər/pər* 'spread (wings)', an unusual doublet of PAN **sapəl* as represented by Sai. *s/om/apəl* 'lay mats'; see Benedict 1975 ('spread out') for another doublet: PAN **sa(m)pa[R]* (contra the Benedict 1975 reconstruction, as shown by Proto-Tsouic **-sapərə* 'lay mats'); Central Tai reveals a doublet in the Nung (Savina) forms: *ben *ʔbin^A* (Li cites *bin*) 'to fly' but *meŋ bön* < **ʔbon^A* 'winged (=flying) insect' (*meŋ*); Lakkia *pon* and Ong-Be *bɔ́n* < **pon^A* 'to fly' reflect the same Proto-Kadai vowel **/o/*, regularly from PAT **/ə/* as well as **/o/* (Benedict 1975:180–81), confirming the reconstruction **(-)pəR(/pəR)* for Proto-Austro-Tai, hence it appears that the /i/ ~ /ɨ/ ~ /e/ vocalism found generally in Tai (and Kam-Sui and Hlai) is secondary, apparently conditioned by the final **-R*. It is a curious fact that the three great language stocks of Southeast Asia all have similar roots for 'fly': PST **pur* (~ **pir* in Tibetan and Chinese); PMK **par*, PM **apir* (Benedict 1975:481–82).

'lime': a nasalized variant of the Austro-Tai root *(*NqampuR)* is reflected by what appears to be an old loan in Mon-Khmer, reconstructed by Shorto as PMK **kmpor* (Benedict 1975:483–84), yielding Saek *muul* through secondary nasalization (unusual but not unknown in Tai (cf. Benedict 1975 under 'belly' and 'vulva').

****

And so the game of prediction continues, and will continue on into the future so long as large chunks of Austro-Tai linguistic territory remain unexplored. The Miao-Yao languages, still poorly known, in many ways offer even greater challenges than Kadai. After all, Miao-Yao was really founded on only *one* root (PMY *day^C 'die' ~ *tay^C 'kill'), a doublet with 'pseudo-Sino-Tibetan' morphophonemics (!) (see Benedict 1972b:124–27 for the Proto-Tibeto-Burman alternation between intransitives or 'statives' with sonorant initial and transitives or 'causatives' with surd initial). Miao-Yao gives every appearance, in fact, of having been deliberately designed to obscure its core relationship with Austronesian and Kadai; for example, only dental stop reflexes were provided for the Proto-Austro-Tai labial stop + glide clusters, as far as can be determined (see above doublet), although for the */ml/ cluster in PAT *[ma]mlok 'bird' (above) a single (well-hidden) /m/ form was dangled before the comparativist (Yao all *nɔʔ < *nok; Miao generally *noŋ [assimilation of final], but the deviant Pa-hng has *hmu*). A master stroke of the diabolical design, however, was in having Kadai reduce to monosyllables mainly through end-stressing while having Miao-Yao carry out the same process through fore-stressing! This insures the development of 'split' cognates (Benedict 1975:137–38, 153), difficult enough to recognize even with Kadai or at times within Tai itself (cf. the forms for 'weep', above). For example, Proto-Tai *maw^A 'drunk' and Lachi *a/sŭ*, id., hardly impress as cognates unless one turns up the Proto-Austronesian root: *mabuçuk (see Benedict 1975:152 for the rule covering Tai forestress here). The game of predicting which forms might eventually be shown to belong together does not really come into its own, however, unless played on the grand scale afforded by Kadai and Miao-Yao, with their contrasting types of development, e.g., Proto-Tai *$ʔbia^{A~C}$ 'to poison fish' = 'fish with poison', (Southwest Tai 'poison/poisonous/to be poisoned'), from *[t]əba (SYL-I destressing followed by vocalic transfer), and PMY (Yao only) *dom^C < *tum(ba) 'fish with poison', with regular /o/ < *u and typical Miao-Yao initial voicing assimilation, both perfectly regular developments from PAT *(n)tu(m)ba, as reflected also in PAN *(n)tu(m)ba 'fish poison'. Perhaps somewhere in Southeast Asia there lies, still undiscovered, yet another language which will do for Miao-Yao what Saek and Lakkia have done for Kadai (a hope, rather than a prediction).

Appendix

1. The PAT *p + liquid clusters are now reconstructed as *pr in 'eye', *pl in 'die/kill', *pl̥ in 'weep', and others (see Benedict 1990).
2. The analysis of final -l can be greatly expanded as a result of the voluminous material now available on Hlai (Li) as well as on Laha. As is often the case in the field of comparative Kadai linguistics, however, the increase in material has complicated rather than simplified matters, with

Hlai itself serving as an excellent example. The early Hlai sources included one parallel to White Sand Hlai -a:l (Dogang Hlai fal 'nine') along with three instances of final -n replacement (Basadung Hlai, Lakkia, Laokwang fan). However the many recently recorded dialects/languages of this 'metalanguage' show exclusively vocalic reflexes, usually -aɨ or -eɨ, comparable with Savina's (1931) -əɨ (written o-u̇) for Southern/Central Dai. Baisha has -aɨ throughout while Xifang has -eɨ but the remaining dialects all exhibit some variation in reflexes, with the divergent Jiamao showing no fewer than four different reflexes. (4) presents the reflexes for eight dialects: Baoding/Zhongsha (reflexes merged), Heitu (close to Savina's Southern Dai, with preglottalized nasals > nasal rather than stop initials), Yuanmen, Tongshen, Qiandui, Baocheng, and Jiamao. Another aberrant dialect, Cunhua, not in the table, has $thɔ^3 < *tha^B$ 'low/short'.

(4)　Reflexes for eight dialects

	P-Hlai	WS Hlai	BD/ZS	HT	YM	TS	QD	BC	JM
'grandmother (F's M)'	*tsa:L^B	tɕa:l	aɨ	eɨ	eɨ	aɨ	aɨ	eɨ	ə
'grandfather (F's M sp.)'	*dza:L^B	ẓa:l		eɨ		aɨ			
'nine'	*fra:L^B	fa:l	aɨ	eɨ	aɨ	aɨ	aɨ	aɨ	ə
'child (gen.)'	+ *la:L^{A/B}	+ la:l	aɨ						
'return'	*ʔma:L^A	pa:l	eɨ	eɨ	aɨ	a:ɨ	eɨ	a:ɨ	ə
'know'	*ʔma:L^B	pa:l			aɨ		eɨ		
'near'	*pla:L^B	pla:l	aɨ	eɨ	aɨ	aɨ	aɨ	aɨ	a
'low/short'	*tha:L^B	tha:l	aɨ	eɨ	aɨ	aɨ	aɨ	aɨ	a
'rise'	*xwa:L^C	va:l	aɨ	eɨ	aɨ	a	aɨ	aɨ	a
'light, adj.'	*kha:L^C	kha:l	aɨ	aɨ	aɨ	aɨ	aɨ a+	aɨ	ɔ
'frog'	*ʔŋa:L^C	ka:l	aɨ	eɨ	aɨ	aɨ	aɨ	aɨ	ai

*-L is a cover symbol for the three liquids *-r, *-l, and *-ḷ and the velar (*-γ) and postvelar (*-R) fricatives, all possible (eventual) sources of the White Sand (Hlai) -l (see Benedict 1975:162–63), and all, except perhaps for *R, to be reconstructed for Proto-Hlai (*ḷ = Matisoff's *zh). Even the vowel length here, with support within Hlai only for 'return' (Tongshen -a:ɨ, Baocheng -a:i), is open to question despite the extra Hlai support furnished by 'child/grandchild' (below). Perhaps, although it seems unlikely, at least some of the reflex distinctions are based on proto-level vowel length, e.g.,

Proto-Hlai *-aL > JM -ə, with secondary lengthening in White Sand (Hlai) Hlai, versus *-aːL > JM -a. Conditioning by the initial appears to have played a role in some instances: -ei̯ rather than -ai̯ in Yunmen after initial dental (*ts- > t-) in 'grandmother' and in Baoding/Zhongsha after preglottalized *ʔm- in 'return' as well as the deviant Tongshen -a and Baocheng -ai̯ reflexes after medial -w- in 'rise'. Jiamao regularly has -ou for Proto-Hlai final *-a, hence it is clear that the Jiamao -a in 'near, low/short'; and 'rise' is a relatively late development. Jiamao -ɔ, on the other hand, is the regular reflex for Proto-Hlai *-aw after initial velars, hence for 'light' the development in Jiamao appears to have been *-aL > *-aw > -ɔ. Surely this suggests the reconstruction of final *-l̥ in this root at the Proto-Hlai level, yet the most likely Austronesian correspondences both have *-l rather than *-l̥: Paiwanic *saCaqal (cited in Benedict 1975:328–29) and Proto-Philippine (Zorc) *yăʔan < PAN-level *yaqa[n,l]. Even with the conditioning factors cited above, four different sets of *-L reflexes remain: *-L_1 for 'grandmother', 'nine', 'return' and 'know'; *-L_2 for 'near', 'low/short', and 'rise'; *-L_3 for 'light'; *-L_4 for 'frog'; also *L_{1-4} (indeterminate) for 'child'.

Laha is a far richer source for final -l, with -al as well as -aːl, along with -el (open vowel), -ol (open vowel), -l, -il, and -ul. A shift to final -n has taken place, it would seem, only in the dialect of Than-Uyên (see Benedict 1975:188–89), e.g., mul^4 'mouth', Bản Bung (Thuân-Châu) muol, but Than-Uyên mɔn. A sizable number of cognate sets show final -l forms in Saek and/or Laha and, less often, in White Sand Hlai but the correspondences are exceedingly complex, with frequent vocalic or final -n reflexes rather than -l, paralleling those found in other Kadai languages. The following table in (5) presents cognate sets involving the five Hlai final *-L's:

(5) Cognate sets with the five Hlai final *-L's

	'return/ come/go'	'near'	'low/below'	'light'	'[heavy]'	'frog'	'child/ grandchild'
P-Hlai	*ʔmaːL$^A_1$	*plaːL$^B_2$	*thaːL$^B_2$	*khaːL$^C_3$	*kʰin^A	*ʔŋaːL$^C_4$	*laːLa$^{A/B}_{1-4}$
Laha	ma^2		ta^6	kha^6	khal^6 khan^6	yal^{3}ʔ	laːl^3~ klaːl^3
Saek	ma^1		tɔ^3			yal^{2}ʔ	lam^1
PT	*(h)ma^A *mia^A		tai̯^{B}				*hlaːn^A
PKS	*ha^A	*phlai^C	*te^B	*khya^B	*khyan^A		*khlaːn^A
Lakkia	hã^5			kyie^3			khyaːn^1
O-Be (J)	mia			kho	khon		
(S)	nea$^{3/5}$			kho$^{3/5}$	khon^1		lan^1
(H)	nia^2(?)			khei$^{3/5}$	khien^1		lo^1~lan^1
Pubiao (Zhang)			te^{33}	khan^{13}	khän^{53}	-vän^{45}ʔ	läːn^{53}
(Chen)	hmie^{51}			khan^{13}	khan^{51}		

	'return/ come/go'	'near'	'low/below'	'light'	'[heavy]'	'frog'	'child/ grandchild'
Lachi				$kiā^{55}$		$-\eta ua^{53}$	
Gelao							
Gao	mu^1		xau^3	xen^1			klu^1
Aou			$xəu^{3/4}$	$xi^{3/4}$			
Hagei	$mo^{1/2}$						$tla^{1/2}$
Duoluo			$ko^{3/4}$	$qu\eta^{3/4}$			

Notes on (5):
Sources for O-Be data: (H) = Hashimoto; (J) = Jeremaissen; (S) = Savina. The Gelao dialects are: Gao (Wanzi), Aou (Pudi), Hagei (Qinglong), Duoluo (Liuzhi). Further comments on cognate sets in (5) follow.

'return/come/go': Hlai dialects show an apparent doublet root in -n: *$?min^A$ ~ (Jiamao) *$?mi\eta^A$ 'come', but it is not represented in available White Sand Hlai material, hence final *-L cannot be ruled out here. Proto-Tai also has a doublet: *$(h)ma^A$ 'come' ~ *mia^A 'return' (Lao ~ 'go'), the latter paralleling the Hlai doublet as a vocalic transfer form: Lakkia (< *hma^C) 'return' but Saek (and Northern Tai generally) and Kam-Sui 'come' ~ 'return' ('come back' ~ 'go back'); Ong-Be (vocalic transfer form, with mi- > ni-) and Gelao 'come' (< 'back') but Laha 'go' (< 'go back'); see Benedict 1991b for this complex root, a cognate of PAN (Blust) *$?(-um)a[\gamma,r]i$ (perhaps < *$?aRi$), which shows parallel incorporation in that family.

'heavy' (provides contrast with 'light'): final -l attested only in the Laha doublet, but some support here is furnished by a likely Austronesian cognate: cf. P-Rukai (Paiwanic) *$tikə[r,l]$ 'heavy', with $V_1 = *i$ supplying through vocalic transfer the palatalization indicated for this root.

'frog': Saek γal^2 '(comp.) toad', if cognate, points to a PKD-level *$?(N)GaL_4$ while the Pubiao and Lachi forms point rather to *$NGwal$, from an *$?u$- prefixed prototype *$?u$-$NGaL_4$.

'child/grandchild': Laha $la:l^3$ '[child of bow]' = 'arrow' (Tibeto-Burman has parallels), $kla:l^3$ 'grandchild', Be lo^1 'lad', lan^1 'grandchild'; Lakkia, Pubiao, Gelao 'grandchild'; Saek, Proto-Tai, Proto-Kam-Sui also 'nephew/niece'; apparently from a prototypical reduplicated *(qa-)la-la, with the ubiquitous Austro-Tai prefixed *qa-, PAT-level *?ulah: Saisiyat oläh 'grandson'; Proto-Atayalic *?ulaqi? 'child' (typical men's speech form, with -qi? for *-h), the *?u- in all likelihood an incorporated *?u- nominal marker, found also in PAN/PKD *(?u-)alak 'child' (see Benedict 1988:335).

With the possible exception of 'frog', none of the above cognate sets provides a final -l tie for the three languages most directly involved here: Hlai, Laha, and Saek, while only one ('child/grandchild') connects Hlai with either of the other two, again with a possible exception: Proto-Hlai *$xwa:L^C_2$

'rise' (cf. Laha əl^3 'raise [head]') . For Laha and Saek, however, six such sets are available in addition to 'husked rice' cited in the article.

'husked rice': Laha sa:l^3; Saek 'rice' + sa:l^1; Pubiao (Chen) qa-san^{51}; Gelao: Gao ('rice'+) su^1 (cf. klu^1 'grandchild'), all pointing to PKD *(qa-)sa:l^A (>/a:/ through vocalic transfer); cf. Puyuma ʔasal, from Proto-Paiwanic/PAN *qatsal or, perhaps better (cf. Kadai), *qa-tsal (ts- > s- is widespread shift in Kadai).

'forest': Laha məw^1 pal^1 'pig' (məw^1) 'of the wild/forest' (pal^1) = 'boar'; Saek thual^6 < NT *dial^C < PT *thial^C ~ *dial^C *thial^C ~ *dial^C < *ntial^C 'forest/jungle' ~ 'wilderness' ~ 'wild'; see article and Benedict 1975:296; also Benedict 1991a; Proto-Austronesian root now reconstructed all with aid of Paiwan qutsal *qu[C,C$_1$]al, (Blust), and the PAT-level etymon as *qu(m)plal.

'fat/grease/oil': Laha mal^1, id. ~ mnal^1 (< *mlal^1 < *m-1-al^1) 'fat/stout'; cf. also mal^2 'pleasant to the taste' (cf. higher fat content in top-grade steaks); Saek mal^2 (Haudricourt) ~ man^2 (Gedney) 'fat/grease/oil'; (see author's Proto-Kadai handout at the 1990 (Texas) 23rd ICSTLL for further details on this widespread -l-infixed etymon).

In the first pair of roots the correspondence is to PAN final *-l whereas in the third set it is to PAN final *-y (*simay) and in a fourth set it is probably to final *-R (Benedict 1975:393–94):

'to fly': Laha pəl^4; Saek bil^1; to the Benedict 1975 citations add the following: Buyang pi^{55}; Shidong pan^5; Lachi (comp.) phâ^{35}; Gelao: Gao phau^5 (< *pha^C).

Three other cognate sets appear to lack Austronesian cognates:

'twist': Laha pəl^1; Saek val^3; South/Central Tai *fan^B.

'yellow': Laha ŋil^3; Saek ŋiil^4 ['something yellow'] = 'tumeric' (cf. Germ. Gelbwurz; also PMP *küniŋ 'yellow' ~ *kunij 'tumeric' ~ [Chamic] 'yellow'); Pubiao nin (< *ŋin through assimilation); Lachi a-hni (written an hi); Proto-Gelao *ʔni$^{B/C}$; Gao nci^4, Duoluo ni$^{3/4}$ ~ ni$^{5/6}$. Contra the discussion in Proto-Hlai initial *ly (Benedict 1989), PKD *ʔŋiil$^{B/C}$ 'yellow' is probably to be interpreted as a metathesized derivative of PAT *kuli(n)jaŋ > via *kulin(jaŋ) > *kuliŋ > *ʔliŋ (regular CRL) > *ʔŋil. Without nasal increment, the same Proto-Austro-Tai root yielded quite different forms: Proto-Tai *hliaŋ^A; Proto-Hlai *(h)lyaŋ^A. Proto-Malayo-Polynesian also developed a doublet, far less striking in nature, based on the same factor: *kuniŋ < *kulin(jaŋ) 'yellow' versus *kunij < *kulij(aŋ) 'yellow' > 'tumeric'.

'shake': Laha sal^4 'shake (head)'; Saek sel^4 'shake (e.g., a bottle, fruit from tree)'; Dioi san^5, Southern Tai *san^C 'shake (intr.), tremble'.

Laha final -*l* appears in two other cognate sets that lack ties with Saek but do have Austronesian correspondences:

'deaf': Laha ŋal³, Than-Uyên ŋan, Bản Bung ka-ŋan (for the anticipated *-nal; cf. 'mouth', below); Gelao: Gao ŋan⁴, Liuzhi naŋ³/⁴; cf. PMP *bəŋəl, from PAT-level *bəŋəl.

'mouth': Laha mul¹, Then-Uyên mɔn, Bản Bung muol; Pubiao qa-mən⁴⁵ (Zhang Jungru) ~ men⁴⁵ (Chen Qiguang); Pubiao mon (Bonifacy) ~ ka-mu (Lajonquière); cf. PMP *mulmul 'put into the mouth and suck' (Blust 1969), from PAT-level *muḷmuḷ; probably from a prototype of SYL + muḷ shape, whence SYL + muḷmuḷ (denominalized through reduplication) > *muḷmuḷ (the well-known Austronesian 'drive towards disyllabism').

In two important etyma the Laha final -*l*, corresponding to vocalic or -*n* final in Saek, is of critical value in supporting posited Austro-Tai-level cognate sets:

'edible tuber': Laha mal¹; Saek man²; P-Hlai *m[wal]ᴬ 'sweet potato'; Pubiao (Chen) men³³ id.; cf. Proto-Polynesian *kumala id., famed in the anthropological literature of cross-Pacific speculation, analyzed in Benedict 1975:261–62 as 'cultivated crop'; the Proto-Hlai reconstruction remains uncertain even with the newer material now available but the final -*n* ~ -*ŋ* variation, found also in this material, points to a proto-level *-*l* while the *-*w*- (or *-*u*-) is readily interpreted as reflecting vocalic transfer in a root with $V_1 =$ *u.

'new': Laha maːl²; South/Central Tai *hmɨᶜ; NT (including Saek) *hnɔᶜ (< *hmrɔᶜ < *hmrauᶜ through typical leveling); Buyang maːn⁴⁴; PKS *hmaiᶜ; Lakkia wāi⁶ (cf. Sui hmai⁵ ~ hwai⁵); Ong-Be nau³/⁵; P-Hlai *ʔmaːnᴬ ~ *noᴮ (cf. the Tai doublet) ~ (Jiamao) ṭau⁴ (< *hrau⁴); cf. (Benedict 1975:344) PAN *(m)baɣu ~ *(m)baqaɣu, with *mb > /m/ a regular Kadai shift and with the medial *-q- apparently (contra the Benedict 1975 qa- analysis, not fitting for this verbal root) reflected in the initial *ʔ/h- of the Kadai forms.

A third set lacks Saek ties as well as Austronesian correspondences but does show final -*n* elsewhere in Tai:

'dust': Laha khoḷ⁵; PT *khu[n]ᶜ; Lao khun 'manure'; BT id. 'dust; manure'; WT, Tho id. 'dust'; Nung (Savina) khon ~ khun 'manure'.

In one further set, apparently without Saek cognate, Hlai significantly has final *-*n* ~ *-*ŋ* variation:

'shallow': Laha dəl³; cf. SWT *tɨɨnᴮ; Buyang tien⁵³; Be ʔdən³/⁵ < *tənᴮ/ᶜ; Proto-Hlai *thianᴮ ~ (Yuanmen) *thiaŋᴮ ~ (Jiamao) *daŋᴬ/ᴮ < *ntaŋᴬ/ᴮ; Pubiao dən¹³ (Chen); Gelao: Gao ten⁵, Aou (Pudi) len¹/² (contrast Gao xen¹, Pudi xi³/⁴ for 'heavy') in (5); note the curious resemblance to Proto-Waic dəl/r 'shallow' (above); Pubiao tian¹³ (Zhang).

Finally, special note must be made of Laha pul^4 'cook rice with steam', apparently reflecting an early Austro-Tai donor (D) source (DAC) of loans to Archaic Chinese; GSR-437j 饙 $p̯iwən/p̯iuən$ id. This is the anticipated Archaic Chinese form (see Benedict 1972b) and there is tonal agreement *(*A)* as well. Tai has an apparent cognate here: White Tai bun^1 'incomplete cooking of glutinous rice (by steam), making it into a pâté', from Proto-Tai-level *$ʔbun^A$. The Laha p- = PT *$ʔb$- correspondence, found also in 'to fly' (above), points to a proto-level *$ʔ(m)p$- (see Benedict 1975:393–94 for the latter root) but the likeliest Austronesian correspondence has *b-: Proto-Philippine (D. Zorc) *$buybuy$ 'cook wet rice'.

The above notes simply confirm the findings of the original article. The final -l of Saek, Laha, and Hlai (White Sand Hlai) can, in a given etymon, represent PAT-level *-l, *-$ḷ$, *-r, *-y, and apparently also *-R, but vocalic and -n finals are also found as reflexes even in these languages; rules governing the process here are hard to come by. Special conditions appear to play a role in some cases, e.g., *$laːl^A$ 'child' ~ *k-$laːl^A$ 'grandchild' is apparently of reduplicative origin (see above) while the medial *-$ḷ$- of PAT *$(m)buḷal$ 'moon' has perhaps led to uniform replacement of final *-l by -n in this root (see Benedict 1988:332). A much more serious problem, however, involves the determination of reflexes in the medial position, as in 'new' (above), with the formation of doublets through accentual variation (type undetermined). Note also 'village' (Benedict 1975:416), where a posited PAT-level *$(qa$-$)balu($-$a)$ (> PMP *$banua$) has yielded both PT/PKS *$ʔbaːn^B$, Lakkia $baːn^3$, Laha $baːn^1$ ~ $vaːn^1$, all from *qa-$bal(u)$ (through vocalic transfer), and Ong-Be $vo^{3/5}$, Proto-Hlai (Baoding, Zhongsha, Heitu) *baw^3 (< *$ʔbaw^B$) from *qa-$ba(l)u$, requiring the reconstruction of the disyllabic/prefixed *qa-$balu$ at the Proto-Kadai level.

References

Benedict, Paul K. 1942. Thai, Kadai and Indonesian: A new alignment in Southeastern Asia. American Anthropologist 44: 576–601.
———. 1972a. The Sino-Tibetan tonal system. In L. Burnet and J. M. C. Thomas (eds.), Langues et techniques, nature et société, 25–33. Paris: Klincksieck.
———. 1972b. Sino-Tibetan: A conspectus. Cambridge: Cambridge University Press.
———. 1973. Tibeto-Burman tones, with a note on teleo-reconstruction. Acta Orientalia 35:127–38.
———. 1975. Austro-Thai: Language and culture. New Haven: Human Relations Area Files Press.
———. 1976. A comparative note on Saek final *-l*. Paper circulated at the ninth Sino-Tibetan Conference, Copenhagen.
———. 1979. PAN consonant clusters. In P. B. Naylor (ed.), Papers from the Second Eastern Conference on Austronesian Languages, Ann Arbor, May 1976. Michigan Papers on South and Southeast Asia 15. The University of Michigan Center for South and Southeast Asian Studies.
———. 1988. Kadai linguistics: The rules of engagement. In Jerold A. Edmondson and David B. Solnit (eds.), Comparative Kadai: Linguistic studies beyond Tai, 323–40. Summer Institute of Linguistics and the University of Texas at Arlington Publications in Linguistics 86. Dallas.
———. 1989. Proto-Hlai initial **ly*. Kadai 1:1–4.
———. 1990. Japanese/Austro-Tai. Ann Arbor: Karoma.
———. 1991a. The wild in Kadai. Kadai 3:67–70.
———. 1991b. Kadai incorporated *-um- infix. Kadai 3:71–72.
———. Forthcoming a. A note on the loss of final stop in Karen. Linguistics of the Tibeto-Burman Area.
———. Forthcoming b. A note on reconstruction of Karen final *-s. Linguistics of the Tibeto-Burman Area.
———. Forthcoming c. A note on the reconstruction of Karen preglottalized surd stops. Linguistics of the Tibeto-Burman Area.
Blust, Robert A. 1969. Austronesian etymologies. Oceanic Linguistics 19(1–2):1–189.
———. 1970. Proto-Austronesian addenda. Oceanic Linguistics 9:104–62.
Bonifacy, Auguste. 1905. Étude sur les language parlées par les populations se la haute Rivière Claire. Bulletin de l'École française d'Extrême-Orient 5:306–23.
Dahl, Otto C. 1977–76. Proto-Austronesian. 2d ed. London: Curzon Press.
Dempwolff, Otto. 1934–1938. Vergleichende Lautlehre les austronesischen Wortschatzes. 3 Vols. Berlin: D. Reimer.

Dyen, Isadore. 1965. A lexico-statistical classification of the Austronesian languages. International Journal of American Linguistics 31(1):1–64.
Gedney, William. 1970. The Saek language of Nakhon Phanom Province. Journal of the Siam Society 58:67–87.
———. 1976a. On the Thai evidence for Austro-Thai, comparative analyses of Asian and African languages 6:65–81.
———. 1976b. Saek final *-l:* Archaism or innovation? Paper presented at the Ninth International Conference on Sino-Tibetan Languages and Linguistics, October 1976. Copenhagen.
Goodenough, Ward H. 1981. Culture, language, and society. Menlo Park: The Benjamin/Cummings Publishing Company, Inc.
Haudricourt, André-G. 1963. Remarques sur les initiales complexes de la langue sek. Bulletin de la Société de Linguistique de Paris 58:156–63.
———, ed. 1965. Le vocabulaire be de F. M. Savina. Paris: Bulletin de l'École Française d'Extrême-Orient 57.
———. 1967. La langue lakkia. Bulletin de l'École Française d'Extrême-Orient 62:165–82.
Li Fang-Kuei. 1940. The Tai dialect of Lungchow: Texts, translations and glossary. Institute of History and Philology, Monograph Series A 16. Taipei: Academia Sinica.
———. 1954. Consonant clusters in Tai. Language 30:368–79.
———. 1977. A handbook of comparative Tai. Honolulu: The University Press of Hawaii.
Liang Min. 1990. The Lachi language. Kadai 2:35–44.
Lunet de Lajonquière, Etienne. 1906. Ethnographie du Tonkin septentrional. Paris: E. Leroux.
Matisoff, James A. 1988. Proto-Hlai initials and tones: A first approximation. In Jerold A. Edmondson and David B. Solnit (eds.), Comparative Kadai: Linguistic studies beyond Tai, 289–321. Summer Institute of Linguistics and the Universtiy of Texas at Arlington Publications in Linguistics 86. Dallas.
Ostapirat, Weera. 1993. Proto-Hlai vowel system. M.A. thesis. Mahidol University (Bangkok, Thailand).
Ouyang Jueya and Zheng Yiqing. 1983. Liyu diaocha yanjiu [Research and survey of the Hlai language]. Beijing: China Social Sciences Press.
Savina, F. M. 1931. Lexique day-français accompagné d'un petit lexique français-day et d'un tableau des differences dialectales. Bulletin de l'École Française d'Extrême-Orient 31:103–99.
Shafer, Robert. 1957. Quelques equations phonetiques pour les langues li d'Hainan. Rocznik Orientalistyczny 21:385–407.

Shorto, Harry L. 1973. The vocalism of Proto-Mon-Khmer. Paper presented at the First International Conference on Austroasiatic Linguistics, Honolulu.
Simon, Walter. 1929. Tibetisch-chinesische Wortgleichungen, ein Versuch. Berlin Universität, Seminar für Orientalische Sprachen, Mitt., 32:157–228.
Solntseva, N. V. and Hoàng Văn Ma. 1986. Materalii sovetsko-vietnamskoe lingvisticheskoe ekspeditsii 1979 goda: Yazik Laxa. Moskva: Nauka.
Taylor, Doreen. 1970. Tamang segmental synopsis. In Austin Hale and Kenneth L. Pike (eds.), Tone systems of Tibeto-Burman languages of Nepal, 1:237–57. Urbana: University of Illinois.
Thurgood, Graham. 1991. Proto-Hlai (Li): A look at the initials, tones, and finals. Kadai 3:1–25.
Ting, V. K. 1929. Notes on the language of the Chuang in N. Kuangsi. Bulletin of the Museum of Far Eastern Antiquities. 1:61–64.
Tsuchida, Shigeru. 1976. Reconstruction of Proto-Tsouic phonology. Tokyo: Institute for the Study of Languages and Cultures of Asia and Africa.
Wang Li. 1952. Preliminary study of the language of the White Sand Hlai of Hainan (in Chinese). Lingnan Journal 2:253–300.
Zhang Junru. 1990. The Pubiao language. Kadai 2:23–34.

Abbreviations

Ata	Atayalic	PK	Proto-Karen
BB	Bản Bung	PKD	Proto-Kadai
BC	Baocheng	PKS	Proto-Kam-Sui
BD	Baoding	PM	Proto-Munda
BT	Black Tai	PMK	Proto-Mon-Khmer
C	cluster (undetermined)	PMP	Proto-Malayo-Polynesian
CLF	classifier	PMY	Proto-Miao-Yao
CRL	canonical reduction on the left	PST	Proto-Sino-Tibetan
CT	Central Tai	PT	Proto-Tai
HT	Heitu	PTB	Proto-Tibeto-Burman
JM	Jiamao	PWA	Proto-Western Austronesian
KS	Kam-Sui	O-Be	Ong-Be
Lh	Laha	QD	Qiandui
NL	Noong Lay	SWT	Southwest Tai
NT	Northern Tai	Tg	Tagalog
Pai	Paiwanic	TS	Tongshen
PAN	Proto-Austronesian	TU	Than-Uyên
PAT	Proto-Austro-Tai	WS	White Sand (Hlai)
Pb	Pubiao	WT	White Tai

PBL	Proto-Burmese-Lolo	YM	Yuanmen
P-Hlai	Proto-Hlai	ZS	Zhongsha

III. Central Tai

Implications of the Retention of Proto-Voiced Plosives and Fricatives in the Dai Tho Language of Yunnan Province for a Theory of Tonal Development and Tai Language Classification

Theraphan L-Thongkum
Chulalongkorn University
Bangkok, Thailand

1. Introduction. The southernmost Zhuang of Yunnan Province, China, comprises several related ethnic groups, including the Thu (Tho), Nong (Nung), Bu Sha (Northern Tai), Pu Yang, and Pu Piao. These ethnic groups are scattered in the southeastern part of Yunnan, near the Guangxi Zhuang Autonomous Region and North Vietnam. The Zhuang group which has been known locally as the Thu, Thu Liao, or Thu Lao speak a Central Tai

---

I would like to thank the Tai-Kadai Research Project of the Faculty of Arts, Chulalongkorn University for allowing me to use their language data; Pranee Kullavaanijaya, Gérard Diffloth, James R. Chamberlain, and Arthur S. Abramson for sparing their time for fruitful discussion; Jerold A. Edmondson for sending me a xeroxed copy of Zhang's article on the Wenma dialect of Zhuang (1987); and Korsak Thamcharonkij and Prapin Manomaivibool for translating Chinese documents.

language. They call themselves *Dai* /dai⁴¹/ or *Bu Dai* /bu⁴⁴ dai⁴¹/. There are also Northern Tai Zhuang speakers in Yunnan in Qiubei Prefecture who will not concern us here. The language data used for the analysis presented in this paper were collected in 1992 and 1993 by myself with the kind assistance of the Yunnan Institute of Nationalities. The research sites were Xinhuilong Village and Qixinguo Village in Wenshan County, and Luchaichong Village in Maguan County (see map 4). The Thu living in these three villages represent the three major subgroups of the Thu people of Yunnan. The Thu of Qixinguo Village call themselves *Mata*. Based on the survey of the Tai-Kadai Research Project of the Faculty of Arts, Chulalongkorn University, which I have been involved in since 1991, and the available published materials (e.g., Zhang 1987, Đặng Nghiêm Vạn, Chu Thái Sơn, and Lu'u Hùng 1984) the diagram illustrating the distribution of the Tho people, i.e., Dai Tho and Tai Tho, can be drawn as is shown in map 4. Those called Tai Tho represent the group whose language has lost the proto-voiced obstruents (plosives and fricatives): $*b > p$, $*d > t$, $*ɟ > c$, $*g > k$, $*v > f$, $*z > s$. The Dai Tho are the ones whose language still retains the proto-voiced obstruents (plosives and fricatives), but has lost consonant clusters, has been in the process of losing finals, and has developed nasalized vowels.[1]

Although Li (1960:958) says: "I avoid using such names as Chungchia, Chuang-chia, Thu (Tho), and the like, because they have been used too vaguely to be of scientific significance"; and some of my colleagues have warned me that the name *Tho* 土 should be avoided because it does not mean anything except 'local people', and *Tho Liao* 土僚 or *Tho Lao* 土佬 even have the bad connotation 'unrefined local people', I still think that the name *Tho* or *Thu* is very useful from a linguistic point of view, since it designates a group of people whose language possesses special tonal characteristics that make it different from other Central Tai languages.

There is no doubt that the Thu of Yunnan are closely related to the Tho of southwestern Guangxi and the Tày of North Vietnam (formerly called Thổ), especially the Cao Bằng Thổ (cf. Hoàng, this volume). Huffman (1986:619-20) gives an extensive bibliography of Tho language and linguistics. Haudricourt writes about Tho phonology in many articles (Haudricourt 1949, 1960, 1961, and 1972). He is the only linguist who pays serious attention to the data that can be extracted from "Les chants de mariage thổ recueillis dans la région de Cao Bằng" collected by

---

[1] Symbols for palatal consonants: [ɟ] = voiced palatal stop; [ʝ] = voiced palatal fricative; [ʄ] = voiced palatal implosive; [j] = voiced palatal approximant; [ʄ] = palatal affricate.

Nguyễn Văn Huyên (1946). The wedding songs contain some words that indicate the retention of the Proto-Tai voiced plosives and fricatives. It is regrettable that other specialists in comparative and historical Tai linguistics have not accorded due attention to Haudricourt's findings; for example, Chamberlain (1991:480-81) comments:

> Haudricourt does not cite the forms themselves; he merely refers to the glosses. Gedney, however, copied the original notebooks in Paris and I in turn copied all of the animal names from Gedney... The survey was not carried out by linguists, and much of the recording was impressionistic, done with the assistance of speakers of other Tai dialects and presumably some Vietnamese speakers. Also, in the points in question, there is considerable dialect mixing so it may not provide an entirely accurate picture. That the items for 'person' and 'owl' have voiced initials does seem to be consistent in this area, even though it is not apparent from the toponyms on the maps. Another point on the survey, 207IX.5, Thô of Moncay, has *cân* for 'person' and *gâu* for 'owl' and thus leaves open the question of accuracy of transcription.

In reconstructing Proto-Tai (PT) and Proto-Central-Tai (PCT), Li (1977) uses only the Tai Thô materials from Savina (1910) and Diguet (1910). He does not include any data from the Dai Tho dialect of Cao Bằng Province, Vietnam. The phonology and some patterns of sound changes in the Dai Tho dialect of Dazai village, Wenshan County, or the Wenma dialect of Zhuang has been studied by Zhang (1987).[2] She lists some of the words that still preserve the proto-voiced plosives and fricatives. For example:

(1)   *b: bi^{31} 'fat' $bəu^{31}$ 'evening meal' bi^{42} 'older sibling'
      *d: $duŋ^{31}$ 'copper' $duŋ^{33}$ 'stomach' $dəu^{42}$ 'ashes'
      *ɟ: $dzən^{31}$ 'fire tongs' $dzəy^{42}$ 'yes' $dzẽ^{42}$ 'artisan'
      *g: gun^{31} 'person' $gã^{33}$ 'lazy' gu^{33} 'pair'
      *v: $vɛi^{31}$ 'fire' ve^{31} 'incubate'
      *z: zi^{33} 'buy' ze^{31} 'wash (clothes)'
      *ɣ: $ɣo^{31}$ 'thatchgrass' $ɣən^{31}$ 'itchy'

---

[2] I had not known about Zhang's article on the Wenma dialect of Zhuang until May 1994 when I met Jerold A. Edmondson at the SEALS IV meeting in Bangkok. I would like to thank him for informing me and sending me a copy of this material.

Zhang says that the Wenma dialect of Zhuang is spoken by approximately 100,000 people who are scattered in six counties in the southeast corner of Yunnan Province: Wenshan, Malipo, Yanshan, Maguan, Kaiyuan, and Yuanyang. These people call themselves /dai²/. In Chinese history, they have been called *Thu Liao* 土僚 or *Thu Lao* 土佬. There are two major groups: *Hua Thu Liao* 花土僚 (Flowery Thu) and *Bai Thu Liao* 白土僚 (White Thu). Since 1949 the Thu have been regarded as a subgroup of the Zhuang nationality (Zhang 1987:10).

The content of this paper is divided into two main parts: (1) a reconstruction of initial consonants and tones in Pre-Tho with some examples of words having those initials and tones in Modern Tho drawn from three dialects of Dai Tho and a dialect of Tai Tho (Debao); and (2) comments on the theory of tonal development and Tai language classification.

2. Initials and tones in Pre-Tho and Modern Tho. From the data that I have collected in Wenshan and Maguan counties, Yunnan Province, and a portion of data found in Zhang (1987), the tones and most of the initial consonants in Pre-Tho can be reconstructed. To illustrate the types of sound changes that have occurred in Tho, especially in Dai Tho, Li's reconstruction of Proto-Tai and Proto-Central-Tai (Li 1977) has been used as the starting point. Based on the interaction between the phonation types or glottal states of the initial consonants and tones, Pre-Tho initials can be classified into four categories, just as has been done for Southwestern Tai. However, there are some differences, i.e., proto voiceless sonorants *(*m̥ *n̥ *ɲ̥ *ŋ̥ *w̥ *l̥ *r̥)* and fricatives *(*s *h)* are placed with other voiceless sounds in Row 2, not with aspirated plosives, which are in Row 1, as has been done for the Tai languages (Gedney 1972, 1979, 1985, and 1989).[3]

(2)   Row 1: Aspiration
        Voiceless aspirated plosives: *ph *th *ch *kh *khj

    Row 2: Voiceless
        Voiceless unaspirated plosives: *p *pj * t *c *k *kw *kj
        Voiceless nasals: *m̥ *n̥ *ɲ̥ *ŋ̥
        Voiceless fricatives: *s *h

---

[3]Regarding the phonetic terminology and concepts, I follow Ladefoged (1971:6–22); therefore, the term 'voiced implosive' will be used instead of 'preglottalized'. Such sounds are not alien to Tai-Kadai phonology; they can be found in Hlai or the Li language of Hainan as I determined when I worked on this language in May, 1992.

Row 3: Glottal (closure)
  Voiced implosives: *ɓ *ɗ *ʄ
  Glottal stop: *ʔ

Row 4: Voiced
  Voiced plosives: *b *d *ɟ *g *gj
  Voiced nasals: *m *n *ɲ *ŋ
  Voiced fricatives: *v *z *ɣ *ɣw
  Voiced approximants: *w *l *j
  Voiced trill/tap: *r

The following are the stages of initial consonant development from Proto-Tai (PT) > Proto-Central Tai (PCT) > Pre-Tho > Modern Dai-Tho (MDT) and Modern Tai-Tho (MTT) with some examples drawn from the three MDT dialects spoken in Luchaichong Village (LCH), Maguan County, Xinhuilong Village (XL), and Qixinguo Village (QG), Wenshan County, with an addition of data from the Dai Tho dialect of Dazai Village (DZ), Wenshan County (Zhang 1987). For Tai Tho, cognates from the dialect spoken in Debao County, Guangxi Province have been used. In some dialects of Dai Tho, e.g., the one spoken in Qixinguo Village, voiced plosives and affricates have been somewhat devoiced, i.e., fully voiced consonants have become partially voiced [b̥ d̥ d̥ʐ g̊].[4]

(3) ph (MDT, MTT) < *ph (Pre-Tho) < *ph phl/r (PCT) < *ph *phl/r *f *fr (PT)

	LCH	XL	QG	DB
'rain'	phən⁴¹	phən⁴¹	phɛn⁴¹	phon³¹ (DZ: phən³¹)
'dream'	phã⁴¹	phan⁴¹	phã⁴¹	phɔn³¹
'tie'	—	phək⁴⁴	—	phuk³³
'thin'	phũə⁴¹	phuəŋ⁴¹	phũə⁴¹	—
'burn'	phuə⁴¹	phəu⁴¹	phau⁴¹	—

---

[4] Tones are symbolized as follows 33' = glottalized tone (ended with glottal constriction); 33˜ = laryngealized or creaky tone; and 33¨ = breathy tone.

th (MDT, MTT) < **th* (Pre-Tho) < **th *thr* (PCT) < **th *thr *tr* (PT)

	LCH	XL	QG	DB	
'old (age)'	thəu³⁵	thəu³⁵	thau¹⁵	—	
'head'	thɯ⁴¹	thu⁴¹	thu⁴¹	thu³¹	
'tail'	thaŋ⁴¹	thaŋ⁴¹	theŋ⁴¹	thaŋ³¹	(DZ: thẽ⁵³)
'sweat'	thɯ⁴⁵⁴ˈ	thɯ⁴⁵³	thɯ⁴⁵⁴	thi³³	(DZ: thɯ⁵³)
'eye'	thɔ⁴¹	tho⁴¹	tho⁴¹	tha³¹	
'die'	tha⁴¹	thɔ⁴¹	thɔ⁴¹	thaai³¹	(DZ: thʋ³¹)

tɕh (MDT), *khj* (MTT) < **ch* (Pre-Tho) < **kh *x *xr* (PCT) < **kh *x* (PT)

	LCH	XL	QG	DB	
'needle'	tɕhən⁴¹	tɕhən⁴¹	tɕhen⁴¹	khjem³¹	(DZ: tshən³¹)
'feces'	tɕhə³⁵	tɕhə³⁵	tɕhi¹⁵	khjəi²⁴	

kh (MDT, MTT) < **kh* (Pre-Tho) < **kh *x *xr* (PCT) < **kh *x *xr* (PT)

	LCH	XL	QG	DB	
'leg, foot'	khɔ⁴¹	kho⁴¹	kho⁴¹	kha³¹	(DZ: kho³¹)
'body hair'	khən⁴¹	—	khun⁴¹	khɔn³¹	
'horn'	khəu⁴¹	khəu⁴¹	khau⁴¹	—	(DZ: khəu³¹)
'son-in-law'	khuəi⁴¹	khui⁴¹	khoi⁴¹	khi³¹	(DZ: khui³¹)
'kill'	khɔ³⁵	kho³⁵	kho¹⁵	khaa²⁴	
'sell'	kha⁴¹	khɔ⁴¹	khɔ⁴¹	khaai³¹	
'ride'	khi⁴⁵⁴ˈ	khi⁴⁵³	khi⁴⁵⁴	khwoi³³	
'knee'	khəu⁴⁵⁴ˈ	khəu⁴⁵³	khau⁴⁵⁴	khau³³	
'rice'	khau³⁵	khau³⁵	khau¹⁵	khau²⁴	(DZ: khau⁵⁵)
'joint'	khu³⁵	khəu³⁵	—	—	
'ascend'	khuən³⁵	—	khun¹⁵	khən²⁴	
'ear'	khɯ⁴¹	khu⁴¹	khu⁴¹	kheu³¹	
'stream'	khuəi³⁵	—	—	khui²⁴	
'laugh'	khɯ⁴¹	khu⁴¹	khu⁴¹	—	(DZ: khu³¹)

tɕh/kh (MDT) *khj* (MTT) < **khj* (Pre-Tho) < **khl *khr* (PCT) < **khl *khr* (PT)

	LCH	XL	QG	DB	
'ill, pain'	tɕhai³⁵	tɕhai³⁵	tɕhai¹⁵	—	
'six'	tɕhak³¹	tɕhak³¹	tɕhɔʔ³¹	khjok⁴⁴	(DZ: tsha³¹)
'egg'	khai⁴⁵⁴ˈ	khai⁴⁵³	kha⁴⁵³	khjai³³	

p (MDT, MTT) < **p* (Pre-Tho) < **p* (PCT) < **p* (PT)

	LCH	XL	QG	DB	
'mouth'	paʔ^{44}	paʔ^{44}	peʔ^{45}	paak^{44}	(DZ: pe^{53})
'wing'	piəʔ^{44}	piəʔ^{44}	piʔ^{45}	pik^{44}	
'duck'	pət^{33}	pet^{33}	peʔ^{22}	pat^{44}	(DZ: pe^{33})
'hundred'	paʔ^{44}	paʔ^{44}	paʔ^{45}	paak^{44}	
'eight'	piəʔ^{44}	piəʔ^{44}	piəʔ^{45}	pet^{44}	

p (MDT) *p/pj* (MTT) < **pj* (Pre-Tho) < **pl* (PCT) < **pl* (PT)

	LCH	XL	QG	DB	
'fish'	pɔ$^{21'}$	po$^{22'}$	po^{33}	pjaa^{52}	(DZ: po^{11})
'leech'	piəŋ$^{21'}$	piəŋ$^{22'}$	pin^{33}	pəŋ^{52}	(DZ: piŋ^{11})
'bark (n)'	puaʔ^{44}	puəʔ^{44}	—	pik^{44}	
'let go'	puəi$^{454'}$	puəi^{453}	puə^{454}	—	

t (MDT, MTT) < **t* (Pre-Tho) < **t* (PCT) < **t* (PT)

	LCH	XL	QG	DB	
'liver'	taʔ^{33}	taʔ^{33}	taʔ^{33}	tap^{44}	(DZ: ta^{33})
'fall'	tək^{33}	tək^{33}	tɔʔ^{22}	tɔk^{44}	
'weave (cloth)'	tã$^{454'}$	tã^{453}	tã^{454}	tam^{44}	

tɕ/ts (MDT) *ts* (MTT) < **c* (Pre-Tho) < **č* (PCT) < **č* (PT)

	LCH	XL	QG	DB
'heart'	tɕə$^{21'}$	tɕə$^{22'}$	tɕə^{33}	—
'seven'	tɕət^{33}	tɕet^{33}	tɕeʔ^{22}	tsat^{44}

k (MDT, MTT) < **k* (Pre-Tho) < **k *kl* (PCT) < **k *kl* (PT)

	LCH	XL	QG	DB	
'I'	kəu$^{21'}$	kəu$^{22'}$	kau^{33}	kəu^{52}	
'chicken'	kai$^{454'}$	kai^{453}	ka^{454}	kai^{44}	(DZ: kai^{55})
'nine'	kəu^{35}	kəu^{35}	kau^{15}	kau^{24}	
'branch'	kəŋ$^{454'}$	kə̃^{453}	kaŋ^{454}	ŋəŋ^{44}	
'crossbow'	kəŋ$^{21'}$	kəŋ$^{22'}$	—	kɔŋ^{52}	
'scratch'	kəu$^{21'}$	kəu$^{22'}$	kau^{33}	—	
'salt'	kɯ$^{21'}$	kɯ$^{22'}$	kɯ^{33}	kɿ^{52}	(DZ: ku^{11})
'far'	kuəi$^{21'}$	kuəi$^{22'}$	kuəi^{33}	kuəi^{52}	

k (MDT) kw (MTT) < *kw (Pre-Tho) < *kw (PCT) < *kw (PT)

	LCH	XL	QG	DB
'scrape'	$kuaʔ^{44}$	$kuaʔ^{44}$	—	$kwat^{44}$

$tɕ$ (MDT) < *kj (MTT) < *kj (Pre-Tho) < *k (PCT) < *k (PT)

	LCH	XL	QG	DB
'eat'	$tɕɯ̃^{21'}$	$tɕã^{22'}$	$tɕɯ̃^{33}$	$kjen^{52}$

m (MDT, MTT) < *$m̥$ (Pre-Tho) < *hm (PCT) < *hm (PT)

	LCH	XL	QG	DB	
'dog'	$mɔ^{21'}$	$mo^{22'}$	mo^{33}	maa^{52}	
'pig'	$mɯ^{21'}$	$mβu^{22'}$	$mɯ^{33}$	$məu^{52}$	(DZ: mu^{11})
'cloud'	$muək^{44}$	mok^{44}	$moʔ^{45}$	mok^{44}	
'fruit'	$maʔ^{44}$	$maʔ^{44}$	$meʔ^{45}$	$maak^{44}$	(DZ: me^{53})
'bear'	$mi^{21'}$	—	—	mui^{52}	
'smell'	$mən^{21'}$	$mən^{22'}$	—	—	
'new'	$mə^{454'}$	$mə^{453}$	$mə^{454}$	$mɔi^{44}$	

n (MDT, MTT) < *$n̥$ (Pre-Tho) < *hn (PCT) < *hn (PT)

	LCH	XL	QG	DB	
'skin'	$naŋ^{21'}$	$naŋ^{22'}$	$neŋ^{33}$	$naŋ^{52}$	(DZ: $nẽ^{11}$)
'insect'	$nũə^{21'}$	$nũə^{22'}$	$nũə^{33}$	non^{52}	
'rat'	$nɯ^{21'}$	$nu^{22'}$	nu^{33}	$nəu^{52}$	
'thorn'	$nã^{21'}$	$nã^{22'}$	$nã^{33}$	$naam^{52}$	
'one'	—	$nã^{453}$	$naŋ^{454}$	—	
'heavy'	$naʔ^{33}$	nak^{33}	$neʔ^{22}$	nak^{44}	(DZ: $nɛ^{33}$)
'thick'	$nɔ^{21'}$	$no^{22'}$	no^{33}	naa^{52}	

$ɲ$ (MDT, MTT) < *$ɲ̥$ (Pre-Tho) < *$hɲ$ (PCT) < *$hɲ$ (PT)

	LCH	XL	QG	DB
'grass'	$ɲɔ^{35}$	$ɲo^{35}$	$ɲo^{15}$	$ɲaa^{24}$

Proto-Voiced Plosives and Fricatives in Dai Tho

s/θ (MDT) ɬ (MTT) < *s (Pre-Tho) < *s (PCT) < *š (PT)

	LCH	XL	QG	DB	
'intestines'	θai³⁵	sai³⁵	θai¹⁵	ɬai²⁴	(DZ: sɛi⁵⁵)
'husked rice'	θã²¹'	saŋ²²'	θaŋ³³	—	
'two'	θəŋ²¹'	səŋ²²'	θoŋ³³	ɬoŋ⁵²	
'three'	θã²¹'	sã²²'	θã³³	ɬaam⁵²	(DZ: sã¹¹)
'four'	θi⁴⁵⁴'	si⁴⁵³	θi⁴⁵⁴	ɬi⁴⁴	(DZ: si⁵³)
'ten'	θəʔ³³	sət³³	θeʔ²²	ɬap⁴⁴	
'sour'	θən³⁵	sən³⁵	θen¹⁵	ɬam²⁴	
'tall, high'	θəŋ²¹'	səŋ²²'	θaŋ³³	ɬoŋ⁵²	
'ripe, cooked'	θəʔ³³	səʔ³³	θɔʔ²²	ɬok⁴⁴	(DZ: sa³³)
'wash (face)'	θui⁴⁵⁴'	səi⁴⁵³	θuəi⁴⁵⁴	—	
'weave (basket)'	θã²¹'	sã²²'	θã³³	ɬaan⁵²	

χ/h (MDT) h (MTT) < *h (Pre-Tho) < *h (PCT) < *h (PT)

	LCH	XL	QG	DB
'five'	χɔ³⁵	χo³⁵	ho¹⁵	haa²⁴
'weep'	χai³⁵	χai³⁵	ha¹⁵	haai²⁴

w (MDT, MTT) < *w̥ (Pre-Tho) < *hw (PCT) < *hw (PT)

	LCH	XL	QG	DB
'sweet, delicious'	wã²¹'	wã²²'	wã³³	waan⁵²

l (MDT, MTT) < *l̥ (Pre-Tho) < *hl (PCT) < *hl (PT)

	LCH	XL	QG	DB	
'back'	laŋ²¹'	laŋ²²'	leŋ³³	laŋ⁵²	
'grandchild'	lã²¹'	lã²²'	lã³³	laan⁵²	
'liquor'	ləu³⁵	ləu³⁵	lau¹⁵	lau²⁴	(DZ: ləu⁵³)
'iron'	lək³³	lək³³	lɔʔ²²	ljek⁴⁴	
'many'	la²¹'	lɔ²²'	lɔ³³	laai⁵²	(DZ: lɒ¹¹)
'close (eyes)'	laʔ³³	laʔ³³	laʔ²²	lap⁴⁴	

$s/ş/ɕ$ (MDT) < *$ɤ$ (Pre-Tho) < *hr (PCT) < *hr (PT)

	LCH	XL	QG	DB
'mushroom'	set^{33}	$şet^{33}$	$ɕeʔ^{22}$	—

b (MDT, MTT) < *$ɓ$ (Pre-Tho) < *$ʔb$ (PCT) < *$ʔb$ (PT)

	LCH	XL	QG	DB	
'leaf'	$bə^{21'}$	$bə^{22'}$	$bə^{33}$	$bɔi^{31}$	(DZ: $vəɣ^{11}$)
'bamboo tube'	$baŋ^{35}$	$baŋ^{35}$	—	—	
'village'	$bã^{35}$	—	$bã^{15}$	$baan^{24}$	
'to fly'	$bən^{21'}$	$bən^{22'}$	ban^{33}	ban^{31}	(DZ: $bən^{11}$)

d (MDT, MTT) < *$ɗ$ (Pre-Tho) < *$ʔd$ *$ʔbl/r$ (PCT) < *$ʔd$ *$ʔdl/r$ *$ʔbl/r$ (PT)

	LCH	XL	QG	DB	
'nose'	$daŋ^{21'}$	$daŋ^{22'}$	$deŋ^{33}$	$daŋ^{31}$	
'earth'	$dɛn^{21'}$	$dən^{22'}$	$dən^{33}$	—	
'asleep'	$daʔ^{33}$	$daʔ^{33}$	$deʔ^{22}$	dak^{44}	
'extinguish'	$daʔ^{33}$	—	—	dap^{44}	
'kick, jerk'	$dət^{44}$	$dət^{44}$	$dɛʔ^{45}$	—	
'bone'	$dək^{44}$	$dək^{44}$	$dɔʔ^{45}$	duk^{44}	(DZ: da^{53})
'mountain'	$duə^{21'}$	$duə^{22'}$	$duə^{33}$	doi^{31}	
'star'	$dau^{21'}$	$dau^{22'}$	dau^{33}	$daau^{31}$	
'red'	$diəŋ^{21'}$	$diəŋ^{22'}$	$diəŋ^{33}$	$deŋ^{31}$	
'black'	$dã^{21'}$	$dã^{22'}$	$dã^{33}$	dam^{31}	(DZ: $dã^{11}$)
'flower'	$dɔk^{44}$	dok^{44}	$dɔʔ^{45}$	dok^{33}	
'moon'	$duən^{21'}$	$duən^{22'}$	$duən^{33}$	—	

j (MDT) $ʝ$ (MTT) < *$ʝ$ (Pre-Tho) < *$ʔj$ (PCT) < *$ʔj$ (PT)

	LCH	XL	QG	DB	
'stand'	$jin^{21'}$	$jin^{22'}$	—	$jən^{31}$	
'cold, cool'	$jin^{21'}$	$jin^{22'}$	jin^{33}	—	
'medicine'	$jo^{21'}$	$jo^{22'}$	—	jaa^{31}	(DZ: jo^{11})

ʔ/γ (MDT) ʔ (MTT) < *ʔ (Pre-Tho) < *ʔ (PCT) < *ʔ (PT)

	LCH	XL	QG	DB	
'breast'	ʔəʔ³³	ʔəʔ³³	ʔɔʔ²²	ʔak⁴⁴	
'brain, marrow'	ʔuəʔ⁴⁴	ʔuəʔ⁴⁴	ʔoʔ⁴⁵	—	
'cough'	ʔai²¹'	ʔai²²'	ʔa³³	ʔai³¹	
'emerge'	ʔuəʔ⁴⁴	ʔuək⁴⁴	—	ʔok³³	(DZ: γuʋ⁵³)
'warm'	ʔuən⁴⁵⁴'	ʔuən⁴⁵³	γun⁴⁵⁴	—	
'soft'	ʔuən⁴⁵⁴'	ʔuən⁴⁵³	γun⁴⁵⁴	ʔon³³	(DZ: un⁵³)
'sugar cane'	—	—	—	ʔoi¹²˜	(DZ: γuai⁵⁵)

b (MDT) p (MTT) < *b (Pre-Tho) < *b (PCT) < *b (PT)

	LCH	XL	QG	DB	
'fat'	bi⁴¹	bβi⁴¹	b̥i⁴¹	pəi³¹	(DZ: bi³¹)
'older sibling'	bi⁴⁵⁴'	bi⁴⁴'	b̥i³¹	—	(DZ: bi⁴²)
'person, male'	—	bu⁴⁴'	—	po³³	

d (MDT) t (MTT) < *d (Pre-Tho) < *d *vl/r (PCT) < *d *vl/r (PT)

	LCH	XL	QG	DB	
'belly'	doŋ³³'	doŋ²⁴	d̥oŋ²²	toŋ¹²˜	(DZ: duŋ³³)
'river'	do⁴⁵⁴'	du⁴⁴'	—	taa³³	(DZ: do⁴²)
'stick'	dõu⁴⁵⁴'	dõu⁴⁴'	—	tau³³	
'copper'	doŋ⁴¹	doŋ⁴¹	d̥oŋ⁴¹	toŋ³¹	(DZ: duŋ³¹)
'Tai'	dai⁴¹	dai⁴¹	d̥ai⁴¹	—	
'ashes'	dəu⁴⁵⁴'	dəu⁴⁵³	d̥əu⁴⁵⁴	tau³³	(DZ: dəu⁴²)

ʥ (MDT) ts (MTT) < *ɟ (Pre-Tho) < *ɟ *g (PCT) < *ɟ *g (PT)

	LCH	XL	QG	DB
'name'	ʥɯ⁴⁵⁴'	ʥə⁴⁴'	ʥə³¹	—
'wipe'	ʥət³¹	ʥət³¹	ʥeʔ³¹	tsat³³
'squeeze'	ʥã³³	ʥã²⁴	ʥẽ²²	—

g (MDT) k (MTT) < *g (Pre-Tho) < *g (PCT) < *g (PT)

	LCH	XL	QG	DB	
'person'	guən⁴¹	guən⁴¹	g̥uən⁴¹	kɔn³¹	(DZ: gun³¹)

g (MDT) kj (MTT) < *gj (Pre-Tho) < *gr *gl (PCT) < *gr *gl (PT)

	LCH	XL	QG	DB	
'mortar'	$gək^{31}$	—	—	$kjɔk^{22}$	
'climb'	$gã^{41}$	$gã^{41}$	—	$kjaan^{31}$	

m (MDT, MTT) < *m (Pre-Tho) < *m (PCT) < *m (PT)

	LCH	XL	QG	DB	
'you'	$mɯ^{41}$	$mə^{41}$	$mə^{41}$	$mɔi^{31}$	
'horse'	$mɔ^{33'}$	mo^{24}	mo^{22}	$maa^{12˜}$	
'ant'	$mət^{31}$	$mət^{31}$	$mɛʔ^{31}$	$mɔt^{22}$	(DZ: $mɛ^{31}$)
'tree, wood'	$mai^{33'}$	mai^{24}	ma^{22}	$mai^{12˜}$	(DZ: mai^{33})
'round'	$mən^{41}$	$mən^{41}$	—	$mɔn^{31}$	
'tie'	$maʔ^{31}$	—	—	—	
'hand'	$mɯ^{41}$	$mβu^{41}$	$mɯ^{41}$	$moŋ^{31}$	(DZ: mu^{31})

n (MDT, MTT) < *n (Pre-Tho) < *n (PCT) < *nl/r (PT)

	LCH	XL	QG	DB	
'finger'	$niu^{33'}$	niu^{24}	niu^{22}	$niu^{12˜}$	
'otter'	$naʔ^{44}$	$naʔ^{33}$	—	—	(DZ: ne^{42})
'paddy field'	$nɔ^{41}$	no^{41}	no^{41}	naa^{31}	
'sleep'	$nũə^{41}$	$nũə^{41}$	$nũə^{41}$	non^{31}	
'sit'	$naŋ^{454'}$	$naŋ^{44'}$	$neŋ^{31}$	$naŋ^{33}$	(DZ: $nẽ^{42}$)
'bird'	$nək^{31}$	$nək^{31}$	$nɔʔ^{31}$	$nɔk^{22}$	(DZ: na^{31})
'water'	$nã^{33'}$	$nã^{24}$	$nã^{22}$	$nam^{12˜}$	

$ɲ/n$ (MDT, MTT) < *$ɲ$ (Pre-Tho) < *$ɲ$ (PCT) < *$ɲ$ (PT)

	LCH	XL	QG	DB	
'urine'	$ɲiu^{454'}$	—	$ɲeu^{31}$	$ɲeu^{33}$	
'two (twenty)'	$ni^{454'}$	$ni^{44'}$	ni^{31}	$ɲəi^{33}$	
'sew'	$niəʔ^{31}$	—	$niəʔ^{31}$	—	(DZ: $ɲa^{31}$)

ŋ (MDT, MTT) < *ŋ (Pre-Tho) < *ŋ (PCT) < *ŋ (PT)

	LCH	XL	QG	DB	
'snake'	ŋɯ⁴¹	ŋu⁴¹	ŋɯ⁴¹	ŋəu³¹	(DZ: ŋu³¹)
'silver'	ŋa⁴¹	ŋa⁴¹	ŋa⁴¹	ŋan³¹	

v (MDT) f (MTT) < *v (Pre-Tho) < *v (PCT) < *v (PT)

	LCH	XL	QG	DB	
'tooth'	va⁴¹	va⁴¹	va⁴¹	—	
'fire'	vai⁴¹	vai⁴¹	vai⁴¹	fai³¹	
'sky'	vɔ³³'	vo²⁴	vo²²	faa¹²˜	
'incubate'	—	—	—	fak²²	(DZ: ve³¹)

z/ʐ/ð (MDT) ɬ (MTT) < *z (Pre-Tho) < *z (PCT) < *z (PT)

	LCH	XL	QG	DB	
'left'	za³³'	ʐɔ²⁴	ðɔ²²	ɬɔi¹²˜	
'wash (clothes)'	zaʔ³¹	ʐaʔ³¹	ðeʔ³¹	ɬak²²	(DZ: ze³¹)
'wash'	—	—	ðau⁴¹	ɬaau³¹	
'buy'	zɯ²⁴	ʐɯ²⁴	—	ɬə¹²˜	(DZ: zɿ⁵⁵)

ɣ (MDT) j (MTT) < *ɣ (Pre-Tho) < *ŋw (PCT) < *ŋw (PT)

	LCH	XL	QG	DB	
'night'	ɣã⁴⁵⁴'	ɣã⁴⁴'	—	jam³³	(DZ: ɣã⁴²)
'itchy'	ɣə̃⁴¹	ɣən⁴¹	ɣən⁴¹	jen³¹	(DZ: ɣən³¹)
'thatchgrass'	—	—	—	jaa³¹	
'pull out of the mouth'	—	—	—	jaai³¹	

ɣw/ɣ (MDT) v (MTT) < *ɣw (Pre-Tho) < *ɣw (PCT) < *ɣw (PT)

	LCH	XL	QG	DB	
'neck'	ɣwo⁴¹	ɣwo⁴¹	ɣwo⁴¹	vo³¹	(DZ: ɣru³¹)
'word, language'	—	—	—	vaam³¹	
'buffalo'	—	—	—	vaai³¹	
'smoke'	—	—	—	van³¹	

w (MDT, MTT) < **w* (Pre-Tho) < **w* (PCT) < **w* (PT)

	LCH	XL	QG	DB
'day'	wã⁴¹	wã⁴¹	wã⁴¹	wan³¹

l (MDT, MTT) < **l* (Pre-Tho) < **l* (PCT) < **l *dl *dr* (PT)

	LCH	XL	QG	DB	
'blood'	luət⁴⁴	luət³³	luə³³	lut³³	(DZ: lue⁴²)
'tongue'	lɛn³³	lən⁴⁴	lɛn²²	lən¹²˜	(DZ: lən⁴²)
'child'	lək⁴⁴	lək⁴⁴	laʔ⁴⁵	luk³³	
'road'	lu⁴⁵⁴'	lu⁴⁴'	leu³¹	lo³³	
'forget'	lən⁴¹	lən⁴¹	lɛn⁴¹	—	
'nail'	lət³¹	lɛt³¹	leʔ³¹	lap²²	(DZ: lɛ³¹)
'wind'	lən⁴¹	lən⁴¹	lɛn⁴¹	lam³¹	(DZ: lən³¹)
'descend'	ləŋ⁴¹	—	—	lɔŋ³¹	(DZ: ləŋ³¹)
'steal'	laʔ³¹	laʔ³¹	leʔ³¹	lak²²	(DZ: lɛ³¹, le³¹)
'lick, smear'	la³³'	lɔ²⁴	lɔ²²	—	
'wash (dishes)'	laŋ³³'	laŋ²⁴	—	—	
'root'	laʔ⁴⁴	laʔ³³	leʔ³³	laak³³	(DZ: le⁴²)

l (MDT) *n* (MTT) < **ml* (Pre-Tho) < **ml/r* (PCT) < **ml/r* (PT)

	LCH	XL	QG	DB	
'saliva'	la⁴¹	lɔ⁴¹	lɔ⁴¹	naai³¹	(DZ: lɒ³¹)

ð/z̯/ɻ/z (MDT) *l* (MTT) < **r* (Pre-Tho) < **r* (PCT) < **r* (PT)

	LCH	XL	QG	DB	
'dry field'	ðai⁴⁵⁴'	z̯ai⁴⁴'	ɻai³¹	lai³³	(DZ: zei⁴²)
'house'	ðuən⁴¹	z̯uən⁴¹	ɻuən⁴¹	lun³¹	(DZ: zun³¹)
'long'	ði⁴¹	z̯i⁴¹	ɻi⁴¹	ləi³¹	(DZ: zi³¹)

The Tho language group seems to have more complex patterns of tone splits and mergers than the rest of Central Tai languages as can be seen in (5) and (6). The development of tones in Dai Tho and Tai Tho can be summarized as follows:

(4) Dai Tho   Tai Tho
     *A > A14   *A > A134
         > A23   > A2
     *B > B123 or B1234 (LCH)   *B > B134
         > B4   > B2
     *C > C123   *C > C123
         > C4   > C4
     *DL > DL123 or DL1234 (LCH)   *DL > DL134
         > DL4   > DL2
     *DS > DS14   *DS > DS123
         > DS23   > DS4

As a result, almost all of the MDT and MTT dialects have six tones, except the MDT dialect spoken at Luchaichong Village, which has five tones in nonchecked syllables, since there is only one tone in the B column. The fact that there is no split in the B tone column in the LCH dialect can be viewed in two ways: *B never splits, or, after it had split, the two resulting tones re-coalesced as a consequence of contact with the Han, who are the newcomers to the area. I am inclined to believe in the first explanation because of these reasons: Luchaichong Village is located in a remote area of Maguan County, Wenshan Prefecture; this big village is rather self-sufficient in terms of necessities, e.g., food and clothing, since the villagers grow their own crops, raise pigs and cattle, and weave cloth. Women and girls of all age groups still wear their native costume daily. Perhaps these indications are residues of a robust independence of spirit that allowed this Dai Tho group to manage to escape from the Great Tone Split, a linguistic epidemic that spread throughout Southeast Asia a thousand years ago! That is why the remnants of the Proto language, i.e., the *voiced series and the *B tone might still be preserved quite well.[5]

---

[5]Despite the data below, e.g., (5) and (6) it must be remembered that the Tho languages examined all show fairly unusual tone split patterns, such as the A1=A4 or A1=A34 mergers. But there are some other languages that have also been called Tho that do not have such tone split patterns. Most notably, perhaps, is the Tay of Cao Bằng described by Hoàng Vǎn Ma in his article in this volume. Ma's Tày seems to have a standard 123-4 split in all tones but B, which looks as if it is unsplit (or perhaps, first split then re-emerged).

There are also Diguet's Tho and Savina's Tay, at least as analyzed by F.-K. Li in his Handbook. Diguet's has a standard 123–4 split in all proto-tones, while Savina's has an A123=B4 merger. All this seems to mean that the unusual tone splits cannot be used on their own to define Tho as a linguistic group.

(5) Tone systems of the Tho language group

Central Tai: Tho Group

Dai Tho (LCH, Maguan)

*A	*B	*C	*DL	*DS
41		35		31
21'	454'		44	33
41		33'		31

(L-Thongkum, fieldnotes)

Dai Tho (XL, Wenshan)

*A	*B	*C	*DL	*DS
41				31
22'	453	35	44	33
41	44'	24	33	31

(L-Thongkum, fieldnotes)

Dai Tho (QG, Wenshan)

*A	*B	*C	*DL	*DS
41				31
	454	15	45	
33				22
41	31	22	33	31

(L-Thongkum, fieldnotes)

Dai Tho (DZ, Wenshan)

*A	*B	*C	*DL	*DS
31				31
	53	55	53	
11				33
31	42	33	42	31

(Zhang, 1987)

Tai Tho (Debao)

*A	*B	*C	*DL	*DS
31	33	24	33	44
52	44		44	
31	33	12˜	33	22

(L-Thongkum, fieldnotes)

Tai Tho (Tianbao, Funing)

*A	*B	*C	*DL	*DS
41	33	24	33	
34	44		44	44
41	33	13	33	31

(Kullavanijaya, fieldnotes)

(6) Tone systems of non-Tho language groups

Central Tai: Non-Tho Group

Nung (Lạng Sơn)

*A	*B	*C	*DL	*DS
33	15'	23˜	44	44
52	21¨	31'	22	22

(L-Thongkum, fieldnotes)

Nung (Maguan)

*A	*B	*C	*DL	*DS
15	22	21'	33	45
33	31	45	31	33

(L-Thongkum, fieldnotes)

Nung (Wenshan)				
*A	*B	*C	*DL	*DS
15	22	44	22	34
33	31	35	31	33

(L-Thongkum, fieldnotes)

S. Zhuang (Yuanjiang)				
*A	*B	*C	*DL	*DS
33	55	35	45	35
452	44	31	33	31

(L-Thongkum, fieldnotes)

S. Zhuang (Longzhou)				
*A	*B	*C	*DL	*DS
33	55	24	55	55
31	11	21	31	31

(Li, 1977)

S. Zhuang (Tiandong)				
*A	*B	*C	*DL	*DS
35	24	21	11	24
44	31	52	44	31

(Kullavanijaya and Chumnirokasant, 1986)

3. Comments on the theory of tonal development and Tai language classification. The retention of proto-voiced obstruents in Dai-Tho confirms that the cause of tone splits in Tai languages can be the voicing shifts of sonorants as well as that of obstruents, as has been pointed out by at least three linguists, Haudricourt (1961 and 1972), Matisoff (1973), and Chen (1992). Haudricourt (1972:65) says: "It seems that what is essential in order to obtain the two-way split of the tonal stem is the loss of aspiration in the sonorants: [hm hn hl . . .], for a Tho dialect exists (that of Cao Bằng) which has retained the voicing of the old voiced stops, now become voiced fricatives." Based on Haudricourt's hypothesis, Matisoff (1973:88) makes it more explicit by stating that "the voiced/voiceless opposition in syllable initial position must have swept through all the language families of SEA in the early centuries of the present millennium. Two tendencies were at work: the devoicing of previously voiced proto initials, and the voicing of previously voiceless nasals and other sonorants." He uses Standard Thai as a typical example of Southeast Asian languages in which the proto-voiced obstruents (stops and fricatives) have become voiceless aspirated stops and voiceless fricatives, and the proto-voiceless sonorants (nasals, semivowels, and liquids) have become voiced and merged with the proto-voiced sonorants. However, Matisoff does not say which of the two possibilities occurs first. Chen (1992) points out that in some Kam-Tai languages, e.g., Lakkja, the tone split must precede devoicing. According to Brown (1975) and Gedney (1991) the shift from the proto-voiced plosives *(*b* *d *ɟ *g) to voiceless aspirated plosives *(ph th ch kh)* in the Thai dialect of Sukhothai is quite recent; in other words, the alphabets or graphemes <พ ท ช ฅ> in Inscription One represent the sounds or phonemes /b d ɟ g/, not /ph th ch kh/ as in modern Thai dialects. This implies a case of tone split which occurs before the devoicing of proto-initial voiced plosives.

All of the scholars of Southeast Asian languages and linguistics, e.g., Haudricourt (1961, 1972), Matisoff (1973), Brown (1975), Mazaudon (1970), Li (1977), Henderson (1981–82), Gedney (1985), and Weidert (1987), seem to think along the same lines and agree on the hypothesis that the voiceless/voiced distinction in syllable-initial position can be a cause of tone splitting. However, it is interesting to see that whenever they want to illustrate this viewpoint, it is the plosive rather than the sonorant that is always selected as the example. As a result of this normal practice, experimental phoneticians, e.g., Lea (1973), Gandour (1974), Erickson (1975), Hombert (1978), and Hombert et al (1979), focus their experimental designs on the perturbations of voiceless/voiced initial stops on the raising/lowering of the fundamental frequency (F0) of the following vowels in many languages including Thai. This hypothesis has been well attested. There is a good physiological basis to support previous experimental findings. Abramson and Erickson (1992:4–5) give the following summary:

> We are convinced by the recent work of Anders Löfqvist and his colleagues (Löfqvist et al, 1989; Löfqvist and McGowan, in press) that responsibility lies with varying degrees of contraction of the cricothyroid muscle used for control of vocal-fold tension to maintain or suppress vibration. Greater amounts of tension to help suppress voicing upon opening the glottis, combined with aerodynamic consequences, will cause higher F0 values in the speech signal.

The audibility of the F0 differences caused by the perturbations of voiceless/voiced initial stop consonants has been questioned. However, Fujimura (1971), Hombert (1978), Abramson and Lisker (1985), Kohler (1985), Silverman (1986), and Whalen et al. (1990) have shown that F0 perturbations can influence judgments of voicing in stops in many languages. To examine the plausibility of historical arguments, Abramson and Erickson (1992) carried out experiments on the possible perceptual interaction between tones and initial stop consonants in Standard Thai. Based on their experimental findings, they conclude:

> By and large, then, our perceptual data seem to support the historical arguments concerning interactions between tone splits and voicing shifts. As pitch perturbations loomed larger in the consciousness of the community and gradually took on a distinctive function, one might suppose that the voicing states of initial consonants would have been reassessed perceptually and rearticulated to furnish new production norms. A combination of these factors would have brought about shifts in tonal and consonantal categories. (Abramson and Erickson, 1992:12)

It is obvious that the primary tone splits in the Tho language group resulted from the voicing of previously voiceless sonorants which in turn merged with the old voiced sonorants, or from the merging of previously voiced implosives with the old voiced plosives. Are such changes phonetically plausible? Of course, they are. In fact, it takes shorter steps for *m̥ and *ɓ to become /m/ and /b/, respectively, than *b to become /p/ or /ph/: *m̥ [m̥ᵐ] > /m/, *ɓ > /b/; *b (fully voiced) > *b̞ (partially voiced) > /p/; and *b > *b̞ (breathy voice) > *bɦ (voiced aspirated) > /ph/. It should work this way if the assumption is correct that sound changes occur gradually. Ladefoged (1971:11) says that "voiced and voiceless nasals and laterals occur in a number of languages. An acoustic analysis tells us that voicing began shortly before the closure was released. These sounds should be called partially voiced as opposed to fully voiced. Voiceless semivowels also have the voicing starting before the steady state of the vowel has begun." Since the so-called 'voiceless sonorants' are in fact partially voiced, it is rather easy for them to become fully voiced, especially when they precede vowels. Regarding the difference between voiced implosives (stops made with the glottalic ingressive airstream mechanism) and plosives Ladefoged says:

> The difference between implosives and plosives is one of degree rather than of kind. In the formation of voiced plosives in many languages, ... there is often a small downward movement of the vibrating vocal cords. This allows a greater amount of air to pass up through the glottis before the pressure of the air in the mouth has increased so much that there is insufficient difference in pressure from below to above the vocal cords to cause them to vibrate. An implosive is simply a sound in which this downward movement is comparatively large and rapid. (Ladefoged 1973:27)

When we investigate the tonal systems of many Southeast Asian tonal languages, it is not difficult to find the origin of the high tones or of the high tone series (odd-numbered tones). Obviously, the voicing of sonorants has an important role to play. In tonal Mon-Khmer languages that have two-tone systems, words having voiceless sonorants as initials always have high tone, whereas the ones with voiced sonorant initials have low tone. Examples can be drawn from Diffloth (1980).

(7) Kawa   Samtao

hmóŋ	m̥hóŋ	'hear'
hnám	n̥hám	'blood'
hɲáp	ɲ̥háp	'difficult'
hláʔ	l̥háʔ	'leaf'
hyáɔk	y̥hùk	'ear'
mèʔ	m̥àʔ	'mother'
ŋɔ̀k	ŋɔ̀k	'neck'
ɲɔ̀m	ɲùm	'sweet'
lɔ̀ŋ	lùŋ	'black'
yùm	yə̀m	'dead'

In general, Tai-Kadai languages have fully-developed tone systems: the six tones in Lakkja can be divided into tone categories: the high series tones (Tone 1 [453], Tone 3 [45], Tone 5 [33]) and the low series tones (Tone 2 [231], Tone 4 [214], Tone 6 [221]). Words with voiceless sonorant initials always have one of the three high series tones, or odd-numbered tones.

(8) Lakkja

High series tones				Low series tones		
n̥aŋ¹	453	'outside'		miə²	231	'hand'
l̥a³	45	'after'		niŋ⁴	214	'sit'
l̥oŋ¹	453	'to extinguish'		num⁶	221	'water'
w̥a:i⁵	33	'quick'		nɛn²	231	'silver'
ja:u³	45	'dry'		wan²	231	'day'
				liŋ²	231	'monkey'
				ja²	231	'ear'

(L-Thongkum 1991)

For Miao-Yao languages, the Mien dialects of the Yao branch have six tones. The dichotomy with high and low series tones is also applicable here: Tone 1 [33]; Tone 3 [354]; Tone 5 [13]; Tone 2 [31]; Tone 4 [231];

and Tone 6 [11]. In Mien-Yao, words having voiceless sonorants always carry the high tone series tones; for example:

(9)   Mien-Yao

High series tones			Low series tones		
l̥o^1	33	'big'	na:i^6	11	'ask'
n̥a^3	354	'bow'	ma:i^4	231	'buy'
m̥iən^1	33	'face'	n̪om^6	11	'dye'
l̥a:^{5}	13	'moon'	muŋ^4	231	'housefly'
m̥ei^3	354	'milled rice'	lwei^6	11	'lazy'
n̥a:ŋ^5	13	'cooked rice'	nɔm^2	31	'leaf'
			lau^2	31	'long time'
			lɔ^4	231	'look for'

(L-Thongkum 1993)

Burmese, a Tibeto-Burman language, has four contrastive tones (Thien Tun 1982). In the speech of my informant, Mr. Wen Go, the phonetic characteristics of these four tones are Tone 1 [32`], Tone 2 [453], Tone 3 [51˜], and Tone 4 [42']. Each of these four tones has two allotones, i.e., high [H] and low [L]. Syllables or words having voiceless sonorant initials always carry the high allotones, voiced sonorant initials carry the low allotones:

(10)   Burmese

n̥o^1	[1H]	'nose'	na^1	[1L]	'ill'
ŋ̥a^2	[2H]	'borrow'	ŋa^2	[2L]	'fish'
l̥a^3	[3H]	'pretty'	la^3	[3L]	'moon'
m̥eʔ^4	[4H]	'gadfly'	meʔ^4	[4L]	'dream'
l̥ai^4	[4H]	'seriously'	lai^4	[4L]	'flow'

Consonantal perturbation of F0 associated with obstruents (voiceless/voiced plosives) has been well attested in many languages. However, only a few phoneticians have paid attention to the effect of voiceless and voiced sonorants on the F0 or pitch of the following vowels. Maddieson (1983) and L-Thongkum (1990) did instrumental studies to demonstrate an interaction between the phonation types of the initial sonorants and the F0 of the following vowels in Burmese and Monic languages (Mon and Nyah Kur), respectively. Maddieson did some spectrographic measurements of the effect of voiceless and voiced sonorants (nasal and lateral) on

F0 of the following vowels in five pairs of Burmese words spoken by three speakers. He concludes that there was general difference in F0 at vowel onset between pairs of words which contrast in sonorant voicing, i.e., the voiced sonorants lower the pitch and the voiceless ones raise the pitch of the following vowel as expected. According to the findings of L-Thongkum syllables in Mon, a register language, have three different pitches: high, mid, and low. Voiceless nasals raise pitch of the following clear-voice vowels the most. The same phenomenon can also be found in Nyah Kur (Chao Bon), the only sister language of Mon. This helps us to predict the development of high tones in register languages like Mon and Nyah Kur when these languages become tone languages.

The evidence from many Southeast Asian languages belonging to different language families, Mon-Khmer, Tai-Kadai, Miao-Yao, and Tibeto-Burman, supports very well the plausibility that sonorants have an important role to play in pitch raising and lowering, in the same manner as obstruents. In some languages, e.g., the Tho group of Central Tai, voicing of proto-voiceless sonorants can cause tone split. To avoid homophones, two types of splitting are possible as illustrated in (11).

(11)   Two types of primary tone split in Tho

Rows	Type I			Rows	Type II	
1	*ph	ph	ph	1	ph	ph
2	*p *m̥ *l̥ →	p m l →	p m l	2	p m l →	p m l
3	*6	6	b	3	6	b
4	*b *m *l	b m l	b m l	4	b m l	p m l

It is likely that the splitting and merging of *A tone occurred first because this tone is unmarked, i.e., there are a large number of lexical items or words in the language which carried this tone before the voicing shift of initial consonants took place. The primary tone split in Central Tai languages can be Type I or Type II, depending upon the choice of each language. A mixed type is also possible, e.g., *A, *B > A12–34, B12–34; *C > C123–4, as in Tianbao and Debao.

4. Tai language classification. Because Maspero (1912) suggested that a careful study of the vocabulary of the different Tai languages might offer a better classification, Li (1960) selects a number of words from his comparative dictionary of twenty Tai dialects and classifies these dialects into three main groups: I. Southwestern, II. Central, and III. Northern. He uses three types of evidence: the distribution of vocabulary, the distribution of certain special phonological features in the vocabulary, and specific phonological developments characteristic of a certain group. He states clearly that Group II is not intermediate or transitional between I and III (Li 1960:956).

Chamberlain (1972) uses the *p/ph* criterion, i.e., **b > p* or **b > ph*, in classifying Southwestern Tai languages into two major branches, P and PH. Later on (Chamberlain 1975) he accepts Gedney's view, grouping Central and Southwestern Tai into one branch, namely, Southern Tai, and applies the same criterion to the classification of Proto-South-Central Tai (PSCT).[6] A series of rough chronological stages beginning with the earliest division of the Northern branch (NT) from the South-Central branch (SCT) is schematically represented as follows (here focusing only on the P group of the SCT branch):

---

[6]Gedney himself (1979 and 1989) seems to be especially cautious when he talks about the dichotomy in Northern/Southern Tai. He says: "We will for the sake of convenience use the term Southern Tai to refer to all the non-Northern Tai languages. This cover term Southern Tai for Central and Southwestern Tai may be regarded by some as awkward, ambiguous, or misleading; they are asked to keep in mind that it is intended only for temporary use in discussing the matters with which we are dealing" (Gedney 1979:3). Chamberlain (1972, 1973, and 1991) takes Gedney's idea in a serious way and uses it as a basis for his P/PH classification of Southwestern and South-Central Tai languages. Vickery (1991) uses Chamberlain's P/PH distinction as evidence to impugn the authenticity of Inscription One. As a result, not only Vickery but also Chamberlain are severely reproached by Gedney (1991).

(12)

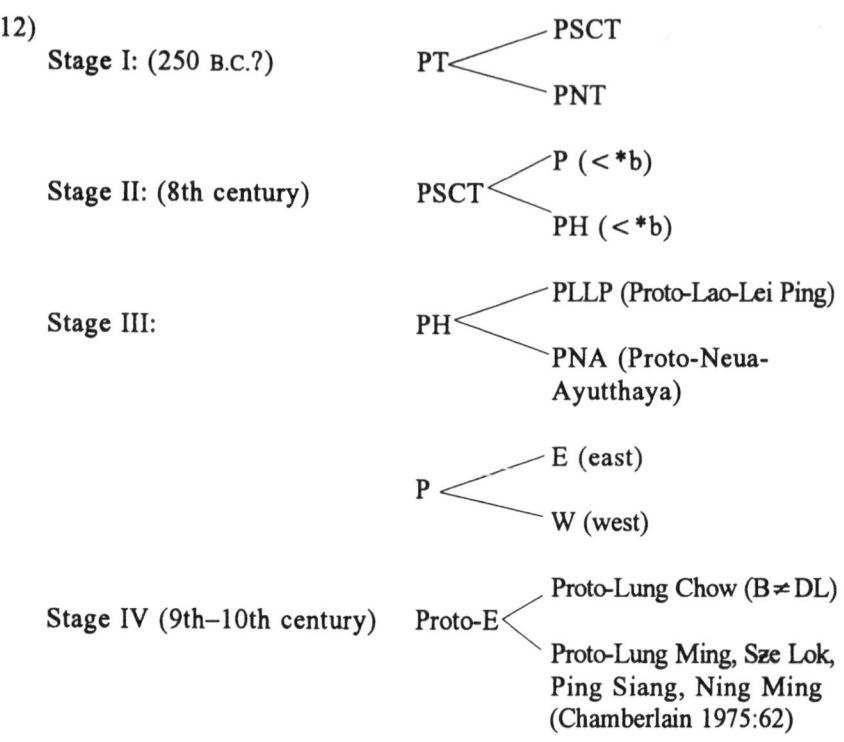

According to the above schema, we can see that *b becomes p around A.D. 700–800. How about the Dai Tho language group which still keeps the proto-voiced series: *b *d *ɟ *g *v *z *ɣ until today? Dai Tho is neither a P nor PH language, i.e., *b remains b, but a B language. Gedney (1991) gives a very negative comment on Chamberlain's classification, saying;

> The trouble with this classification is that it uses as its basic criterion something very late in the history of these languages, but Chamberlain wants to make it very early. It is as if a botanist were to propose abandoning the traditional classification of flowering plants into families and genera, and replacing it by two new big categories, those with yellow flowers and those with red flowers. (Gedney 1991:208)

Chamberlain (1991) defends his proposal for the P/PH classification and emphasizes its efficacy by stating confidently that "the P/PH distinction is enhanced even further as a meaningful linguistic isogloss and an historical boundary" (Chamberlain 1991:464). He also hypothesizes that the P group of the South-Central languages underwent the devoicing shift while still relatively unified in the east (homeland). This means that the devoicing shift occurs in the P group before the PH group. The evidence that can be drawn from Dai-Tho helps us prove that Chamberlain cannot be right.

5. Conclusion. Apparently, in Tho, the voicing of proto-voiceless sonorants *m̥ *n̥ *ɲ̥ *ŋ̥ *w̥ *l̥ *r̥ and the shifting of proto-voiced implosives *ɓ *ɗ *ʄ to voiced plosives b d j takes place before the devoicing of proto-voiced obstruents *b *d *ɟ *g *v *z *ɣ. This means that the merging of proto-voiceless sonorants with proto-voiced sonorants is the cause of primary tone split in Tho, not the devoicing of proto-voiced obstruents which is a rather late matter. Perhaps we can postulate the voicing shift of sonorants to account for the development of tones in all Central Tai languages.

Judging from the data in hand which I have collected myself, I think that Li's classification of Tai languages into three major branches, Northern, Central, and Southwestern, sounds more convincing and is more compatible with the reality of the tone splits. The Central branch has its own interesting history of phonological development; therefore it should be kept apart instead of being grouped together with the Southwestern branch. In spite of Gedney's negative comments on Chamberlain's classification of Tai languages in P/PH groups, I still think that it is a useful criterion, provided that the idea of B group is included and that some other criteria must also be applied, e.g., vowel shift, especially the diphthongs *ai *au *ia *ɯa and *ua, patterns of tone shift, and consonant shift. These typological features, to a certain extent, can reflect genetic relations among languages.

References

Abramson, A. S. and D. M. Erickson. 1992. Tone splits and voicing shifts in Thai: Phonetic plausibility. In Pan Asiatic Linguistics: Proceedings of the Third International Symposium on Language and Lingusitics, 1–15. Bangkok: Chulalongkorn University.
——— and L. Lisker. 1985. Relative power of cues: F0 shift versus voice timing. In V. Fromkin (ed.), Linguistic phonetics: Essays in honor of Peter Ladefoged, 25–33. New York: Academic Press.
Brown, J. Marvin. 1975. The great tone split: Did it work in two opposite ways? In J. G. Harris and J. R. Chamberlin (eds.), Studies in Tai linguistics in honor of William J. Gedney, 33–48. Bangkok: Central Institute of English Language.

———. 1980. The language of Sukhothai: Where did it come from? And where did it go? In Parittat (Social Science Review) Special Issue. Bangkok.

Chamberlain, James R. 1972. The origin of the Southwestern Tai. Bulletin des Amis du Royaume Laos. 7–8:233–44.

———. 1975. A new look at the history and classification of the Tai languages. In J. G. Harris and J. R. Chamberlain (eds.), Studies in Tai linguistics in honor of William J. Gedney, 49–66. Bangkok: Central Institute of English Language.

———. 1991. The efficacy of the P/PH distinction for Tai languages. In James R. Chamberlain (ed.), The Ram Khamhaeng controversy, 453–86. Bangkok: Siam Society.

Chen, M. Y. 1992. Competing sound changes: Evidence from Kam-Tai. In Pan Asiatic Linguistics: Proceedings of the Third International Symposium on Language and Linguistics, 16–27. Bangkok: Chulalongkorn University.

Đặng Nghiêm Vạn, Chu Thái Sơn, and Lư'u Hùng. 1984. Ethnic minorities in Vietnam. Hanoi: The Gioi Publishers.

Diffloth, G. 1980. The Wa languages. Linguistics of the Tibeto-Burman Area (5)2.

Diguet, Edouard 1910. Etude de la langue Thổ. Paris: A. Challemel.

Edmondson, Jerold A. 1994. Change and variation in Zhuang. In Karen Adams and Thomas Hudak (eds.), Papers from the Second Annual Meeting of the Southeast Asian Linguistics Society 1992, 147–85. Tempe: Program for Southeast Asian Studies, Arizona State University.

Erickson, D. M. 1975. Phonetic implications for an historical account of tonogenesis in Thai. In J. G. Harris and J. R. Chamberlain (eds.), Studies in Tai linguistics in honor of William J. Gedney, 100–111. Bangkok: Central Institute of English Language.

Fujimura, O. 1971. Remarks on stop consonants: Synthesis experiments and acoustic cues. In L. L. Hammerich, R. Jakobsen, and E. Zwirner (eds.), Form and substance: Phonetic and linguistic papers presented to Eli Fischer-Jørgensen, 221–32. Copenhagen: Akademisk Forlag.

Gandour, J. 1974. Consonant types and tone in Siamese. Journal of Phonetics 2:337–50.

Gedney, William J. 1972. A checklist for determining tones in Tai dialects. In M. Estelle Smith (ed.), Studies in linguistics in honor of George L. Trager, 423–37. The Hague: Mouton.

———. 1979. Evidence for another series of voiced initials in Proto-Tai. Paper presented at the Twelfth International Conference on Sino-Tibetan Languges and Linguistics, Paris. Also 1989 in R. J. Bickner, J. F.

Hartmann (eds.), Selected papers in Tai comparative studies. Ann Arbor: University of Michigan.

———. 1985. Confronting the unknown: Tonal splits and the genealogy of Tai-Kadai. In G. Thurgood, J. A. Matisoff, and D. Bradley (eds.), Linguistics of the Sino-Tibetan area: The state of the art. Pacific Linguistics Series C-87, 116–24. Canberra: The Australian National University.

———. 1991. Comments on linguistic arguments relating to Inscription One. In James R. Chamberlain (ed.), The Ram Khamhaeng controversy, 193–226. Bangkok: Siam Society.

Haudricourt, André-Georges. 1949. La conservation de la sonorité des sonores du Thai commun dans le parler Thô de Cao-bang. In Proceedings of the International Congress of Orientalists 21:251–52. Paris (Abstract).

———. 1960. Note sur dialectes de la région de Moncay (Vietnam du Nord). Bulletin de l'École Française d'Extrême-Orient 50(1):161–77.

———. 1961. Bipartition et tripartition des systèmes de tons dans quelques langues d'Extrême-Orient. Bulletin de la Société Géographique de Paris, 56(1):163–80. (English translation by Court, C. 1972. [Two-way and three-way splitting of tonal systems in some Far Eastern languages]. In J. G. Harris and R. B. Noss (eds.), Tai phonetics and phonology, 58–85. Bangkok: Central Institute of English Language.)

Henderson, Eugenie J. A. 1981–82. Tonogenesis: Recent speculations. Transactions of the Philological Society 1–24.

Hombert, J.-M. 1978. Consonant types, vowel quality, and tone. In V. A. Fromkin (ed.), Tone: A linguistic survey, 77–112. New York: Academic Press.

———, J. J. Ohala, and W. G. Ewan. 1979. Phonetic explanations for the development of tones. Language 55:37–59.

Huffman, Franklin E. 1986. Bibliography and index of Mainland Southeast Asian languages and linguistics. New Haven: Yale University Press.

Kohler, K. J. 1985. F∅ in the perception of lenis and fortis plosives. Journal of the Acoustical Society of America 78:199–218.

Kullavanijaya, P. and D. Chumnivohasant. 1986. The Chuang language of Du'an and Tiande (in Thai). In P. Kullavanijaya (ed.), Chuang: The Tai in the People's Republic of China. Part 1: Language, 26–55. Bangkok: Thai Language and Literature Center, Faculty of Arts, Chulalongkorn University.

L-Thongkum, Therapan. 1990. The interaction between pitch and phonation type in Mon: Phonetic implications for a theory of tonogenesis. Mon-Khmer Studies 16–17:11–24.

———. 1991. A preliminary reconstruction of Proto-Lakkja (Cha Shan Yao). Mon-Khmer Studies 20:57–89.

———. 1993. A view on Proto-Mjuenic (Yao). Mon-Khmer Studies 22:163–230.

——— and P. Kullavanijaya. 1981. The Chuang language of Debao (in Thai). In P. Kullavanijaya (ed.), Chuang: The Tai in the People's Republic of China. Part 1: Language, 9–25. Bangkok: Thai Language and Literature Center, Faculty of Arts, Chulalongkorn University.

Ladefoged, Peter. 1971. Preliminaries to linguistic phonetics. Chicago: The University of Chicago.

Lea, W. A. 1973. Segmental and suprasegmental influences on fundamental frequency contours. In Larry M. Hyman (ed.), Consonant types and tone. Southern California Occasional Papers in Linguistics, 1:15–70. Los Angeles: University of Southern California.

Li, Fang-Kuei. 1943. The hypothesis of a pre-glottalized series of consonants in Primitive Tai. Bulletin of the Institute of History and Philology 11:177–88.

———. 1960. A tentative classification of Tai dialects. In S. Diamond (ed.), Culture in history: Essays in honor of Paul Radin, 951–59. New York: Published for Brandeis University by Columbia University.

———. 1977. A handbook of comparative Tai. Honolulu: The University Press of Hawai.

Löfqvist, A., T. Baer, N. S. McGarr, and R. S. Story. 1989. The cricothyroid muscle in voicing control. Journal of the Acoustical Society of America 85:1314–21.

Maddieson, Ian. 1983. The effects of F0 of a voicing distinction in sonorants and other implications for a theory of tonogenesis. Journal of Phonetics 12:9–15.

Maspero, Henri. 1912. Études sur la phonetique historique de la langue annamite: Les initiales. Bulletin de l'École Française d'Extrême-Orient 12 (1):1–127.

Matisoff, James A. 1973. Tonogenesis in Southeast Asia. In Larry M. Hyman (ed.), Consonant types and tone. Southern California Occasional Papers in Linguistics, 1:71–95. Los Angeles: Linguistics Program, University of Southern California.

Mazaudon, M. 1974. Tibeto-Burman tonogenetics. Linguistics of the Tibeto-Burman Area 3(2):1–123.

Nguyễn Văn Huyên. 1941. Les chants de mariage thổ recueillis dans la région de Cao Bằng. Hanoi: EFEO.

Ohala, John J. 1973. The physiology of tone. In Larry M. Hyman (ed.), Consonant types and tone. Southern California Occasional Papers in Linguistics, 1:1–14. Los Angeles: University of Southern California.
———. 1978. Production of tone. In V. Fromkin (ed.), Tone: A linguistic survey, 5–39. New York: Academic Press.
Savina, F. M. 1910. Dictionnaire tay-annamite-français précéde d'un précis de grammaire tay et suivi d'un vocabulaire français-tay. Hanoi: Imprimerie d'Extrême-Orient.
Silverman, K. 1986. F0 segmental cues depend on intonation: The case of the rise after stops. Phonetica 43:76–91.
Thien Tun, U. 1982. Some acoustic properties of tones in Burmese. In D. Bradley (ed.), Papers in South-East Asian Linguistics, 8: Tonation. Pacific Linguistics Series A-26, 77–116. Canberra: The Australian National University.
Vickery, M. 1991. Pitdown skull: Installment 2. In James R. Chamberlain (ed.), The Ram Khamhaeng controversy, 333–418. Bangkok: Siam Society.
Weidert, Alfons. 1987. Tibeto-Burman tonology. Current Issues in Linguistic Theory, 54. Amsterdam: John Benjamins Publishing.
Whalen, D. H., A. S. Abramson, L. Lisker, and M. Mody. 1990. Gradient effects of fundamental frequency on stop consonant voicing judgments. Phonetica 47:36–49.
Zhang, Junru. 1987. Zhuangyu Wenma Tuyu de Yinlei Yanbian [Phonological changes in Wenma Patois of Zhuang]. Minzu Yuwen 5:10–18.

The Sound System of the Tày Language of Cao Bằng Province, Vietnam

Hoàng Văn Ma
Linguistics Institute, Vietnamese Institute of Social Sciences
Hanoi, Vietnam

The Tày nationality is concentrated in the central regions of northern Vietnam encompassing the provinces Cao Bằng, Lạng Sơn, Bắc Thái, Tuyên Quang, and Hà Giang (see map 4). Our investigations show that one can divide the Tày language into four vernacular areas.

Area 1: The central part of northern Vietnam including the sectors Thạch An, Ngân Sơn, and Chợ Rã in the southern part of Cao Bằng; Na Rì in the northern part of Bắc Thái; and Tràng Định in the northern part of Lạng Sơn. The language of this area is widespread making this variety the basis of Tày-Nùng.[1]

This contribution was translated and adapted by Jerold A. Edmondson and Anita Vũ. Many thanks also go to Mimi Barker for her help in the final version.

[1]It is common practice in Vietnam to use the term *Tày-Nùng* as if these languages were the same, whereas Nùng is another closely related Central Tai language of northern Vietnam. The speech of this area is apparently a kind of convergence formed from these two that has been the basis for speaking about Tày-Nùng.

Area 2: The eastern part of northern Vietnam including the remainder of the province of Cao Bằng except for Thạch An. The language of this area differs from Area 1 especially by virtue of the complex initials of the sound system.

Area 3: The southern part of northern Vietnam including the southern part of Lạng Sơn and the rest of Bắc Thái provinces.

Area 4: The northwest part of northern Vietnam most significantly including the provinces of Tuyên Quang and Hà Giang.

The description here is taken from that Tày of Area 2, specifically that variety of Tày found at Trùng Khánh in Cao Bằng. According to a number of researchers including some from outside Vietnam, the Tày language is best represented by the form found here, because in this place the language has retained the ancient sounds to greater degree than in other areas. For example, the number of initial segments in the Tày of Area 1 is twenty-four, but in Area 2 there are thirty-one. The people who have described this variety completely in synchronic terms have based that description on materials drawn from their own investigations carried out in the local areas and on the knowledge of the native speakers.

1. Structure of the syllable

In the Tày language, just as in other isolating languages of this area, the morphological boundaries correspond to the syllable boundary. The syllable is the smallest linguistic unit used to form meaning. The syllable can be analyzed into yet smaller linguistic units. Based on the functional components of the syllable, we can say that there are five elements to the Tày syllable: (1) the initial; (2) the nuclear vowel; (3) the medial; (4) the coda; and (5) the tone. One syllable, such as *thwaŋ¹* 'bamboo', includes all these components. Each segment can be manifested distinctively from others by means of place and manner of articulation. The main sonority of the syllable is carried by the vowel nucleus. Initials and codas also contribute to the development of the quality of syllables. The five parts above are also five parallel systems. Syllables are distinguished by features in each level of the system. The structure of the Tay syllable is as follows:

(1)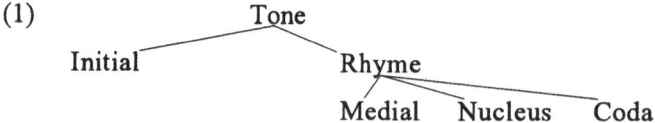

The two obligatory components are the tone and the syllable nucleus. The other elements are optional. Thus, the syllable in Tày has the following shapes:

(2) | Syllables | Saturated syllables | | Without medials | | Without initial | |
|---|---|---|---|---|---|---|
| with coda | thwaŋ¹ | 'bamboo' | nɐm⁶ | 'water' | ək² | 'chest' |
| without coda | twa¹ | 'right (side)' | sa¹ | 'to look for' | a¹ | 'aunt' |

The open syllable is a syllable without a coda; the nonopen syllable is a syllable with a coda. If the coda is formed by a voiceless stop, the syllable is 'closed'; if the coda is a sonorant or semivowel, the syllable is also defined as 'open'. These open syllables with codas include 'half-closed' (those that have nasal codas) and 'half-open' (those ending in semivowels) syllables.

2. System of sound contrasts

2.1. Initials. The system of consonant initials in the Tày of Cao Bằng includes thirty-one segments (the Tày at other locations has only twenty-four segments) that stand in mutual opposition and thus constitute a phonological contrast.[2]

(3)	stops								
	voiceless	plain	p	pj	t		c	k	
		aspirated	ph	phj	th			kh	
	voiced	plain	b	bj	d				
		preglottalized	ʔb	ʔbj	ʔd				
fricatives									
	voiceless		f		s			x	h
	voiced		v		z			ɣ	
nasals			m		n		ɲ	ŋ	
laterals									
	voiceless				ɬ				
	voiced				l				
Liquids					r				
Semivowels			w				j		

---

[2] Cao Bằng Tày is the only variety that has /j w r ɣ b d bj/.

The thirty-one initials usually function to begin the syllable; the following are examples of some initials:

(4)
p	pi^1	'year'	pa^2	'aunt'	paj^3	'crippled'			
ph	phi^1	'ghost'	pha^2	'blanket'					
b	bi^3	'older sibling'	ba^6	'to lean on'	baj^5	'to file'			
ʔb	$\mathit{ʔba}^3$	'to pour'	$\mathit{ʔbaj}^5$	'shovel, hoe'	$\mathit{ʔbe}^2$	'goat'			
pj	pja^1	'fish'	$pjaj^1$	'stem'	$pjɔj^3$	'to let go'	$pjɔk^3$	'belt'	
phj	$phja^1$	'mountain'	$phjɐk^2$	'vegetable'			$phjom^1$	'head hair'	
bj	bja^6	'knife'	$bjɔŋ^4$	'one half'	bje^4	'to reproduce'			
ʔbj	$\mathit{ʔbjaj}^5$	'to weed'	$\mathit{ʔbjɔk}^3$	'flower'	$\mathit{ʔbjɐt}^2$	'bend'			
f	fi^1	'lost sense of smell'	$ləw^2fi^1$	'wine without aroma'					
v	vaj^5	'handful'	$vɐn^6$	'to knead'	$vɛn^5$	'to shake, shiver'			
m	mja^4	'to smear'	$mjəw^5$	'betel'	$mjak^3$	'slick'			
w	wau^5	'buffalo'	$wɐn^5$	'day'	wi^2	'comb'	$wɛn^5$	'to chop around'	
t	ta^1	'to investigate'	ti^1	'to put down'	$taŋ^3$	'window'			
th	tha^1	'eye'	$thaŋ^3$	'to search'	thi^3	'shoe'			
d	da^3	'river'	$daŋ^5$	'road'	di^3	'location, place'			
ʔd	$\mathit{ʔda}^3$	'to scold'	$\mathit{ʔdaŋ}^3$	'white stripe'					
s	sa^3	'stove'	$saŋ^3$	'top, toy'	su^1	'ear'	$sɐk^2$	'to tend to'	
	sam^1	'to ask'							
z	za^1	'to hide'	$zien^3$	'lonesome'					
l	laj^1	'much'	lam^3	'to forget'					
ɫ	$ɫaj^1$	'to twirl on string'	$ɫam^1$	'three'	$ɫɔn^1$	'study'			
r	$ruan^5$	'house'	ru^6	'to buy'	raj^5	'to cut'	$ruŋ^3$	'bright, morning'	
j	ja^1	'medicine'	$jien^3$	'toilet'	$jɔn^5$	'rain-drenched'			
k	ka^1	'owl'	$kɛn^3$	'hard, not soft'	kin^1	'to eat'	$kɔ^1$	'kind of tree'	
kh	kha^1	'leg'	$khɛn^1$	'arm'	$khɔ^1$	'curved, bent'			
ɣ	$ɣən^5$	'people'	$ɣɔ^5$	'neck'	$ɣɯn^5$	'night'	$ɣaŋ^1$	'chin'	

2.2. Medials. In Cao Bằng Tày (and the remainder of Tày) there is a semivowel /u̯/ which serves as a medial in the syllable. This medial vowel can serve as the feature that distinguishes some words.

(5) $ŋwa^5$ 'yesterday' $ŋa^5$ 'sesame'
$kwaŋ^1$ 'deer' $kaŋ^1$ 'water barrel or vat'

The semivowel /u̯/ does not occur following labial consonants, but apical, laminal, and especially velar consonants do occur before it. Explaining these occurrences is a problem, but one can say that one of the sources is surely the requirement of reducing complications in phonetic structure.

(6) jwan¹   'to startle'   twak³   'briefly'   ŋwak³   'to go back'
     cwa²   'to touch'   khwa³   'trousers'   khwaŋ¹   'level, horizontal'
     kwa¹   'classifier for melon'   kwɛ¹   'calabash'   kwaŋ²   'wide, spacious'

2.3. Nucleus. In Cao Bằng the nucleus of the syllable is formed from a single vowel. If it occurs next to another vowel, it is no longer the peak on its own. The following segments can form the syllable nucleus:

(7) Nine long vowels: /i e ɛ u o ɔ ɯ ə: a/
     Two short vowels: /ə ɐ/
     Three diphthongs: /ie uo ɯə/

These fourteen sounds are contrastive based on vowel height, backness, rounding, and phonological changes.

(8) Nuclei

	front		back			
			unround		round	
high	i	ie	ɯ	ɯə	u	uo
mid	e		ə:	ə	o	
low	ɛ		a	ɐ	ɔ	

There is also length contrast: long vowels /a ə:/ contrast with short vowels /ɐ ə/:

(9) tan¹   'to harvest'   tən¹   'stupid'
     dan²   'dirty'   dɐn²   'to scratch'
     tə:n¹   'smooth, silky'   tən¹   'chair, light pole'

The major point about these two short vowels /ə ɐ/ is that they cannot stand alone to create the peak of the syllable, but always need a coda.

The vowels /ɔ o e i u ɛ/ can be combined to form long and short sequences, but length is not contrastive. When these vowels are put together with codas, they tend to be somewhat shorter than when they occur without codas. In other words, /o/ in po³ 'to compensate' is clearly longer than /o/ in pom¹ 'hot, warm'. The main point is that there are not two contrastive vowels /o/ and /ŏ/.

The vowel /ɔ/ generally does not distinguish long and short unlike other languages of the area such as Vietnamese; there is no justification to use different symbols to signify two /ɔ/'s in Tày and Nùng today, as are needed in Vietnamese. Aside from that, a length distinction for /ɛ/ exists in only one minimal pair: *khwĕt²* 'species of tree' and *khwet²* 'frog, toad'. Length distinctions may also be found in borrowings.

2.4. Codas. Coda segments end the syllable. These segments involve obstruance after the nuclear vowel in blocking the airstream. In Cao Bằng Tày there are nine segments that can function as the coda: /p t k m n ŋ u̯ i̯ ɯ̯/.

These nine codas form a sound subsystem with the contrastive features: obstruent~sonorant; nasal~non-nasal; labial~nonlabial; and alveolar~laminal.

(10) Coda segments

		Front		Back
Obstruents		p	t	k
Sonorants	nasal	m	n	ŋ
	non-nasal	u̯	i̯	ɯ̯

(11) Examples of coda segments

-p	*ap³*	'to bathe'	*cup²*	'hat, cap'	*nip³*	'to pick up with chopsticks'
-t	*ʔdit³*	'to jump'	*kat³*	'mustard greens'	*cut²*	'insipid'
-k	*nɐk²*	'heavy'	*ʔdek²*	'children'	*tuk²*	'ripe, cooked'
-m	*am³*	'peace'	*um²*	'to hold, pick'	*im³*	'full'
-n	*an³*	'to count'	*nen⁵*	'new year'	*tin¹*	'foot'
-ŋ	*ʔbaŋ¹*	'thin, not thick'	*liŋ⁵*	'monkey'	*nɔŋ⁶*	'y. sibling'
-i̯	*aj³*	'to want'	*thaj¹*	'to die'	*hɐj²*	'to cry'
-u̯	*ɐw¹*	'to take'	*khaw¹*	'white'	*tɐw¹*	'to link'
-ɯ̯	*ʔbəɯ¹*	'leaf'	*məɯ³*	'new'	*təɯ²*	'below'

In a number of items the nucleus and coda can combine in two ways to form long and short contrasts:

(12)   *pɐn¹*   'to separate'   *pan¹*   'to peel'

Three semivowels /u̯ i̯ ɯ̯/ correspond to the three vowels /u i ɯ/. In combinations with other vowels these segments form the syllable coda. When they combine in this way, they change phonological status from vowels to consonants. /u̯ i̯/ join in the rhyme with other vowels which have features of height, backness, and rounding unlike their own: /u̯/ follows front vowels /i e ɛ/ as well as central vowels /ə a ɐ/; i̭/ follows back vowels /u o ɔ/ as well as central vowels /ə a ɐ/.

The coda /ɯ̭/ behaves differently; it follows only /ə/. The restricted environment of /ɯ̭/ and the exceptional nature of its combination only with /ə/ causes us to suspect that, in the common ancestor language, there was only one form for /ɯ̭ ə/. However, the matter is uncertain and evidence is unpersuasive in regard to this theory of belonging and combining with other codas.

2.5. Tones. In Cao Bằng Tày there are six tones, distinguished according to height and contour.[3] According to custom, for description and study we have given each tone an arbitrary number. But others account for their significance in terms of working rules.

Tone 1. This tone is found at the highest level. From a high beginning it traverses a falling trajectory up to the syllable offset, i.e., 53. If the initial is a voiced sound there can be some rise before the fall.

(13) ma^1 'dog'
      mi^1 'bear'
      $pəi^1$ 'go, to'
      $ʔdɐŋ^1$ 'nose'
      waj^1 'cloud'

---

[3]Professor Ma's system of denoting tones corresponds to other systems as follows:

Ma	Li Fang-Kuei	Chinese System
1	A1	1
2	C1/DS1/DS2	3/7S/8S
3	B1/DL1	5/7L
4	B2	6
5	A2	2
6	C2/DL2	4/8L

Editors' note. We have made a few minor changes in interpreting Professor Ma's transcription. We have written /ə ɐ/ where he has /ɤ ǎ/. On the basis of comparative evidence we believe that the same phonetic value is intended. It is possible that he is using /ɤ ǎ/ as the phonetic value of ơ and â which would be used to render the Tày with these sounds if transcribed with Quốc Ngữ script. We have also reversed the respective transcription of /b d/ and /ʔb ʔd/ in light of evidence from other places. For example, $ʔbja^6$ 'knife' is cognate with Longzhou pja^4 = C4 < *bja and therefore should be bja^6, whereas $bjɔk^3$ 'flower' is cognate with Longzhou $ʔbjo:k^{7L}$ < *$ʔbj$.

Tone 2. This tone has a pitch that begins in the high-central range; from there its trajectory rises slightly upward, i.e., 34. All types of syllables can take this pitch shape, but it seems that no syllables that are long and closed are realized in this category.

(14) ma^2 'adult, grown up'
 mi^2 'abused, tired'
 $khɛw^2$ 'tooth'
 $pɐk^2$ 'to pierce'
 waj^2 'to swim'

Tone 3. This tone is also in the high set but lower than tone 1. From the mid-high range at the beginning of its trajectory it continues a slightly falling course, i.e., 43.

(15) ma^3 'pickle, to soak'
 mi^3 'to dip, vinegar'
 $mɐn^3$ 'stable, strong'
 naj^3 'to invite'
 waj^3 'to break down'

Tone 4. This tone is found in the tonal area lower than that of Tone 3. After starting, it continues on a trajectory that is nearly level across the syllable as it reaches the coda. The pitch is lower than mid, i.e., 33. It has some features of laryngealization.

(16) ma^4 'fading'
 mi^4 'taste, flavor, seasoning'
 $muoj^4$ 'grain, stone, seed'
 $mɐn^4$ 'to cast a spell'

Tone 5. This tone does not occur in closed syllables. Its pitch proceeds from a point lower than the level of Tone 4 and falls. It is a mid-low falling tone, i.e., 21.

(17) ma^5 'to go home'
 mi^5 'have, exist, there is'
 waj^5 'buffalo'
 $ŋu^5$ 'to sleep'

The Sound System of the Tày Language, Vietnam

Tone 6. This tone can be found in any syllable shape. It has a pitch starting at mid level. Over the course of the syllable it rises throughout its course. Its contour is 25.

(18) ma⁶   'horse'
      mi⁶   'jackfruit'
      luk⁶   'child'
      nɐm⁶   'water'
      maj⁶   'tree'
      lin⁶   'tongue'

We can compare and contrast the six tones with their height and contour as below:[4]

(19) Cao Bằng Tai Tones

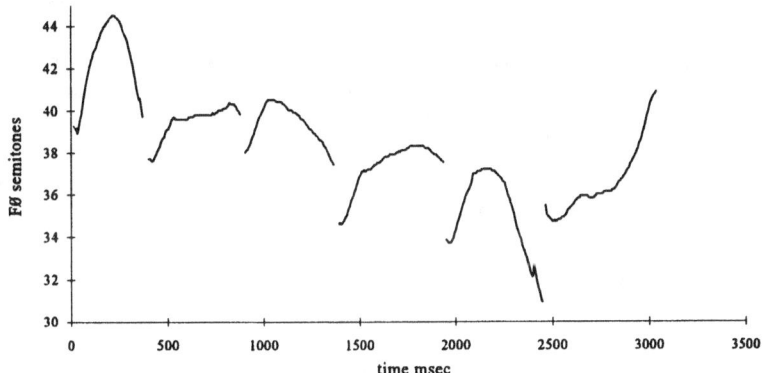

The occurrence of syllable types with tone category in Cao Bằng Tày can be portrayed as follows:

(20)
Syllable	Tone 1	2	3	4	5	6
open	+	+	+	+	+	+
half open	+	+	+	+	+	+
half closed	+	+	+	+	+	+
closed	−	+	+		−	+

---

[4]Editors' note: From the accompanying word list it can be seen that all obstruent consonant initials, including /p ʔb b s f/, are found in high tones in this language and all voiced obstruents are correspondingly found in low tones. This distribution confirms the claims in L-Thongkum (this volume) about the effect of voicing in Dai Tho languages.

3. Swadesh (200) word list in Tày of Cao Bằng Province, Vietnam

va^6	sky	ma^1	dog	$khop^2$	to bite, sting
pha^2va^6	cloud	pja^1	fish	kin^1	to eat
$tha^1wɐn^5$	sun	$ŋu^5$	snake	rak^3	to rain
haj^1	moon	$ʔduɯən^1$	earthworm	sup^3	to smell
$ʔdaw^1$	star	$thəw^1$	head louse	$nɐm^6$	to think
lom^5	wind	$mɛŋ^5vən^5$	a fly	ru^6	to know
$phən^1$	rain	$ʔdɐŋ^1$	nose	an^3	to count
$mɔk^3$	fog, mist	tha^1	eye	law^1	to fear
$yɐm^3/yɯɯn^5$	night	su^1	ear	$nɔn^5$	to sleep
$wɐn^5$	day	$thuo^1$	head	$jɐŋ^6$	to stand
pi^1	year	pak^3	mouth	$nɐŋ^3$	to sit down
$mak^3thɛp^3$	hail	$khɛw^2$	tooth	$pəj^1$	to go
$muɔj^1khaw^1$	snow	lin^6	tongue	$thəŋ^1$	to arrive, to come
$nɐm^6$	water	$phjom^1$	head hair	$dɛw^3$	tanned, shriveled
da^3	river	$yɔ^5$	neck	waj^2	to swim
$thom^1$	lake, pond	$ək^2$	chest	vu^5	to talk
haj^2	sea	$lɐŋ^1$	back	$lwəj^1$	to comb
tom^1/din^1	mud	$thuo^1cəɯ^1$	heart	$rɔ^6$	to push
$thin^1$	stone, rock	$mok^2, dɔŋ^6$	belly	lak^3	to pull
raj^5	sand	$łəj^1$	intestine	bom^3	to taste
$muɯn^3$	dust	$tɐp^2$	liver	tok^2	to drop, to fall
$phja^1$	mountain	$muɯ^5$	hand	$həɯ^2$	to give
$mɐj^6$	tree	kha^1	leg	$ɐw^1$	to take
$ʔdoŋ^1$	woods, forest	$thuo^1khɐw^3$	knee	raw^5	to wash
$ʔbəɯ^1$	leaf	$lɯət^3$	blood	pha^3	to chop
$pɯək^3$	tree bark	$ʔduk^3$	bone	$lam^3, phuk^3$	to tie
$ʔbjɔk^3$	flower	$nɐŋ^1$	skin	suk^2	to wipe
lak^3	root	nuk^6	meat, flesh	sat^3	to scrub
mak^3	fruit	bi^5	fat	$yɔn^6$	to hit, to beat
$muoj^4$	seed, grain	$ŋɐŋ^1$	spine	$tɐt^2$	to cut
$ɲa^2$	grass	$thaj^1$	to die	$tɐm^1$	to stab
$dəw^6$	stick	$daj^5cəɯ^1$	to breathe	yut^6	to dig
nok^6	bird	$diŋ^3$	to hear	$ʔdɐn^2$	to scratch
pik^3	wing	$ciem^3, ciew^3$	to look at	$tɐn^2$	to squeeze
$khon^1$	body hair	$phuoj^3$	to talk	phu^2zau^5	male, man
$sɐj^3$	egg	$khuo^1$	to smile, to laugh	$mɛ^3ɲiŋ^5$	female, woman
$thaŋ^1$	tail	kin^1nom^5	to suck	$miŋ^5$	people
lep^6	fingernail	$təw^3$	to spit out	$kəw^1$	father
$kɔk^3$	horn	$pəw^3$	to blow	$mɛ^3$	mother

The Sound System of the Tày Language, Vietnam

luk^6	child	kha^2	to kill	$lɯaŋ^1$	yellow
$phuo^1$	husband	$ʔdɔ^5 tuk^2$	to fight	haw^2	dry
mie^5	wife	$nɯŋ^3/dɛw^5$	one	$rɐm^5$	wet
$bi^3 zaj^5$	older brother	$tɔŋ^1$	two	men^1	smell bad
$bi^3 juŋ^5$	older sister	tam^1	three	$yəɯ^3$	swollen
$miŋ^5$	name	ti^3	four	tem^1	full
$kəw^1$	I, me	ha^2	five	$ɛ^5 tɔj^1$	dirty
$məɯ^5/məŋ^5$	you	cet^2	seven	yom^5	sharp
men^5/te^1	he, she, it	pet^3	eight	lu^4	dull
$rəw^5/bɔŋ^1 rəw^5$	all of us	tip^2	ten	$məɯ^4$	new
$ʔbɔŋ^1 men^5$	them	$ɲi^3 tip^2$	twenty	pom^1	hot
$kɯə^1$	salt	pak^3	hundred	$jen^5/daŋ^2$	cold
$huŋ^1$	to cook	$thuon^2$	all of it	$nɐk^2$	heavy
$vəj^5$	fire	laj^1	many, much, a lot	$jɐw^5$	straight
$məj^2$	to burn	ki^2	few	$mɛn^3/zə^3$	correct
$wɐn^5$	smoke	$nɔj^6$	a little bit	$ʔdəj^1$	good
$ʔdaw^3$	ashes	$luoŋ^1/kaj^2$	huge	raj^6	bad, ugly
$ʔdaŋ^5$	road	$i^2/eŋ^1$	small	$kɛ^3$	old
$zɯək^3$	rope	ri^5	long	twa^1	right
$ɲɐp^6$	to sew	$tɐm^3$	short	raj^6	left
$tɯa^2$	clothing	$mən^2$	round	$kwəj^1$	far
het^2	to work	$mjak^3/lɯən^2$	shiny	$səɯ^2$	near
$liew^3$	to play	na^1	thick	$taŋ^2$	different
ti^1	to sing	$ʔbaŋ^1$	thin	$nəj^2$	this
$ʔduŋ^3$	to dance	$kwaŋ^2$	broad	$men^2/zien^6$	that
$cɔŋ^1/tɔŋ^2$	to fight	$yɐp^6$	narrow	$ka^3 rəɯ^5$	who
ru^6	to buy	$ʔdɐm^1$	black	$tɐŋ^1$	what
dap^3	to teach	$ʔdeŋ^1$	red	$ʔbəw^3$	no
$bɐn^2$	to sell	$khaw^1$	white	$ʔdəɯ^1$	in(side)
$thəw^3$	to spread out	$khɛw^1$	green		

IV. Southwestern Tai Languages and General Tai

A Preliminary Examination of Tay Tac

Jean Donaldson and Jerold A. Edmondson

A description of Tay Tac allows for a preliminary comparison of Tay Tac with Gedney's (1964) comparative sketch of White, Black, and Red Tay. All four language varieties belong to the Southwestern Tai group in which Li (1960) places such languages as Siamese, Lao, Shan, and Ahom.[1]

The authors express their sincere appreciation to Dr. Hoàng Lương of the University of Hanoi, whose mother tongue is Tay Tac, for the word list upon which this paper is based. The list was elicited during Dr. Lương's visit to the U.S. for the 23rd International Conference on Sino-Tibetan Languages and Linguistics in October 1990. We are grateful to the University of Texas at Arlington for providing the travel funds that enabled Dr. Lương to participate in the conference.

[1]Tay Tac is spoken in Mường Tắc, a district of eastern Sơn La Province, Vietnam. Dr. Lương refers to his language as Tay Tac, following the Tai precedent of using the geographical location to identify a language variety. However, he calls it White Tay in English, apparently on the basis of nonlinguistic criteria, such as their dress. A photograph of Dr. Lương's wife depicts the Tay Tac white blouse, similar to that of the White Tay of Lai Châu except that the latter is adorned by silver buttons.

The spelling Tay [tɐj] follows the convention of Vietnamese and romanized alphabets based on Vietnamese in the use of -y and -i to distinguish *ay* [ɐj] from *ai* [aj]. Uniform usage in English publications has not yet been achieved for the spelling of Tay/Tai/Thay/Thai. The spelling Tay has been adopted for the varieties compared in this paper in deference not only to Dr. Lương, but also to Tay who object to the use of the romanization Tai for the name of their people, because without tone markings it is homophonous with the word for 'death'.

The general outline of this article is as follows:

Part 1. An examination of Tay Tac[2]—Donaldson
  1. Tay Tac phonology
    1.1 Consonants
    1.2 Vowels
    1.3 Tones
    1.4 Co-occurrence figures
  2. Tay Tac and White, Black, and Red Tay compared
    2.1 Consonants
    2.2 Vowels
    2.3 Tones
    2.4 Conclusion
Part 2. Instrumental analysis of Tay Tac—Edmondson
  1. Pitch contours of the tones
    1.1 The system of notation
    1.2 The 'voiced-low' situation
    1.3 Observations about the tone values of Tay Tac
  2. The rhymes of Tay Tac
    2.1 Syllables in Tay Tac
    2.2 Results of the F2-F1 versus F1 plot of rhymes in Tay Tac

Part 1: An examination of Tay Tac—Donaldson

1. Tay Tac phonology

Tay Tac is basically monosyllabic; an exceptional disyllabic word is sa^{B2}-$ləŋ^{A1}$ 'back'. The syllable pattern has an obligatory initial consonant, an obligatory nucleus consisting of vowel and tone, and an optional final consonant, CN(C).

There are no phonemic consonant clusters or vowel clusters. Aspirated and labialized consonants $th, kw, xw, ŋw$ occur only initially and are considered unit phonemes. Two types of diphthongs occur: the first type is considered a

---

[2]Language names are abbreviated as follows:
  T Tay Tac of the Tắc region of Sơn La Province, Vietnam
  W Tay Lay, also known as Tay Don or White Tay, of Lai Châu Province, Vietnam
  B Tay Dam or Black Tay of Sơn La, Vietnam
  R Tay Deng or Red Tay of Sam Neua Province, Laos (Gedney), and of Lang Chanh, Vietnam (Robert)

single vowel phoneme, and the second patterns as vowel plus consonant, since it is never followed by a consonant. To reflect the differing patterns or distributions, the final elements of the latter type, phonetically *i* and *u*, are analyzed as consonants and written as *y* and *w*. The first type of diphthong is restricted to the sequences *iə, ɨə, uə*, (cf. §1.2), which pattern like single vowel phonemes in that they may be followed by a consonant; e.g., *siəm^{A1}* 'spade', *siə^{A1}* 'tiger', *hɨək^{D1L}* 'gums', *nuət^{D1L}* 'beard, moustache'. The second type of diphthong consists of two phonemes, a vowel and semivowel. It is a sequence of any high, mid, or low vowel phoneme followed by a syllable-final semivowel, e.g., *y*[i] or *w*[u]; *nɨw^{C2}* 'finger', *saw^{A2}* 'twenty', *way^{A1}* 'rattan', *xɨəy^{A1}* 'son-in-law'. Li (1977:280) reports both types of diphthongs to be found in modern Tai dialects,

> One type consists of a high vowel *i, ɨ, u* as the first element and a lower vowel *a* or *ə*, as the second and occurs in open as well as closed syllables... The other type diphthong consists of a high vowel *i, ɨ, u*, as the second element, preceded by a lower vowel... This type occurs only in open syllables—not followed by any final consonant.

1.1. Consonants. There are twenty-two initial consonant phonemes, eight of which also occur syllable finally:

(1)   Consonants

    p   t   c   k   kw   ʔ
    f   th   s   x   xw   h
    b   d
    w   l   y
    m   n   ɲ   ŋ   ŋw

Initial consonants
  Voiceless stops: /p t c k kw ʔ/ *pa^{B1}* 'forest', *ta^{A1}* 'eye', *cay^{A2}* 'male (of humans)', *kəy^{B1}* 'chicken', *kwaŋ^{A1}* 'deer', *ʔəw^{A1}* 'to take'
  Spirants and aspirated stop: /f th s x xw h/ *fa^{A1}* 'wall', *tham^{A1}* 'to ask', *say^{A2}* 'sand', *xa^{A1}* 'leg', *xwa^{A1}* 'right (direction)', *ha^{A1}* 'to seek'
  Voiced stops: /b d/ *ba^{B1}* 'to spill', *dap^{D1L}* 'sword'
  Semivowels and lateral: /w [v] l y [z] ~ [j]/. Phonetically, the allophones of *w* are mutually exclusive: [v] occurs in syllable initial position and [w] in syllable final position. The allophones of *y* on the other hand, [z] and [j], fluctuate only in syllable initial position with only [j] occurring

syllable finally. wan^{A1} [van^{A1}] 'sweet', lak^{D1L} 'different', yan^{C1} [jan^{C1}] ~ [zan^{C1}] 'to fear'
Nasals: /m n ɲ ŋ ŋw/ ma^{A1} 'dog', na^{A1} 'thick', $ɲa^{C1}$ 'grass', $ŋa^{A2}$ 'tusk', $ŋwa^{B2}$ 'yesterday'

Final consonants
/p t k/ $ʔap^{D1L}$ 'to bathe', xat^{D1L} 'torn', sak^{D1L} 'pestle'
/w y/ in syllable final position have only the allophones [w] and [j], respectively; saw^{A1} 'young woman', fay^{C1} 'cloth'.
/m n ŋ/ sam^{A1} 'three', wan^{A1} 'sweet', $saŋ^{C1}$ 'side, edge'

1.2. Vowels. There are thirteen vowel phonemes in Tay Tac including three diphthongs *iə*, *ɨə*, and *uə*.

(2)
i	ɨ	u
iə	ɨə	uə
e	ə	o
	ɐ	
ɛ	a	ɔ

Front vowels and falling diphthong: /i iə e ɛ/ lin^{C2} 'tongue', $siəŋ^{A1}$ 'sound', wen^{A2} 'day', xen^{A1} 'arm', $xwen^{A1}$ 'to hang'
Central vowels and falling diphthong: /ɨ ɨə ə[ɜ]~[ə] ɐ a/ $fɨn^{A1}$ 'clothing (classifier)', $lɨəŋ^{A1}$ 'yellow', $siəŋ^{A1}$ 'to be pleased, happy', $kɐ^{B2}$ 'to swell', $ək^{D1S}$ 'chest', $dək^{D1S}$ 'late at night', $dɐk^{D1S}$ 'far', xan^{A1} 'to answer'
Back vowels and falling diphthong: /u uə o ɔ/ hu^{A1} 'ear', $huə^{A1}$ 'head', $muən^{B2}$ 'smile', hok^{D1S} 'six', $hɔk^{D1L}$ 'grey-haired'

Vowels are phonetically longer in an open syllable than in a closed syllable.

The two low central vowels differ in height, length, and distribution; ɐ never occurs in open syllables, but a does: ha^{A1} 'to seek'. Both a and ɐ occur in closed syllables, as the following contrasting pair demonstrates: $lɐk^{D2}$ 'to steal', lak^{D2} 'to pull'.

The allophones of ə similarly differ in height, length, and distribution, but they occur in mutually exclusive environments: close-mid [ɜ] in open syllables, open-mid [ə] in closed syllables. [ɜ] in T corresponds to the mid-central to high diphthong *əɯ* in W and B, e.g., T [$bɜ^{A1}$], W and B [bəɯ] 'leaf' (as will be exemplified in the comparisons in §2).

1.3. Tones. Tay Tac has a six-tone system on open syllables and syllables ending with a continuant, and a three-tone system on syllables ending with a final stop.

A Preliminary Examination of Tay Tac

Tone designations used herein follow that of the Proto-Tai system described by Li[3] (1977) in which A, B, C, and D refer to the four tones assumed to have been present in Proto-Tai: A, B, and C on syllables ending in a vowel, semivowel, or nasal, and tone D on syllables with a final stop, with the designation '1' in reference to proto-voiceless initial consonants and '2' to proto-voiced initial consonants. In Tay Tac, three tones occur with final stops, reflecting the assumed voiced/voiceless initial consonant and long/short proto-vowel divisions. On the D1 tones, S and L refer to proto-short and proto-long vowels, respectively, a distinction which is not made on the D2 tone. The Tay Tac tones are represented in (3), the (A, B, C) six tones on syllables ending in a continuant, and the (D) three tones ending with a final stop:

(3) Tay Tac tone representations

A1	B1	C1
A2	B2	C2

D1S	D1L
D2	

The table in (4) displays Tay Tac examples representing each of the twenty categories, or boxes, of Gedney's checklist for tones of Tay languages (1972). The vertical columns show the tones A, B, C, DS, and DL, while the horizontal rows from top to bottom are divided according to proto-initial consonants: voiceless friction, voiceless unaspirated, glottal, and voiced, respectively. As shown above, in Tay Tac the top three rows of each

---

[3]For the reader accustomed to another tone numbering system, we include for comparison with Li's tone designations the W romanizations of Minot (1940) and of Điêu and Donaldson (1970), the W and B romanizations by Hoàng and Tòng (1990) and by Martini (per Chabant 1951), the B romanization by Baccam et al. (1989), Gedney's transcription for Red Tay, and, according to Edmondson, the Chinese system. The vowel a is included to demonstrate placement of diacritics.

Li	W/Minot	W/D&D	W&B/H&T	W&B/Martini	B/B&F	R/Gedney	Chinese/je
A1	1. a	a	a	aa	a	1	1
B1	2. á	á	á	aax	á	2	5
C1	3. à	à	à	aaz	à	3	3
A2	4. ã	ã	ã	'aa	'á	4	2
B2	5. ā	ā	à	'aax	'a	3	6
C2	6. ạ	ạ	ạ	'aaz	'ạ	5	4
D1S	2. á	á	á	a	á	2	7
D1L	2. á	á	á	aa	á	2	9
D2S	4. ã	ạ	ạ	a	ạ	2(short)	8
D2L	4. ã	ạ	ạ	aa	'ạ	3(long)	8

(4) Tay Tac examples representing the twenty categories of Gedney's checklist for tones of Tay languages

	A		B		C		DS		DL	
voiceless friction	hu^{A1} xa^{A1} hua^{A1}	'ear' 'leg' 'head'	$sɯy^{B1}$ fa^{B1} $xɯw^{B1}$	'egg' 'split' 'knee'	$xɯw^{C1}$ sia^{C1} xa^{C1} $sɤy^{C1}$ ha^{C1}	'rice' 'shirt' 'to kill' 'fever' 'five'	$mɛt^{DIS}$ suk^{DIS} $fɤk^{DIS}$	'flea' 'cooked, ripe' 'green vegetables'	xa^{DIL} hap^{DIL} $hiək^{DIL}$	'torn, broken' 'carry on pole' 'gums'
voiceless unaspirated	pi^{A1} ta^{A1} kin^{A1}	'year' 'eye' 'eat'	pa^{B1} $kɤy^{B1}$ ke^{B1}	'forest' 'chicken' 'old'	pa^{C1} tom^{C1}	'aunt' 'to boil'	$tɤp^{DIS}$ kop^{DIS}	'liver' 'frog'	pik^{DIL} pot^{DIL}	'wing' 'lung'
glottal	bin^{A1} daw^{A1} $deŋ^{A1}$	'to fly' 'star' 'red'	ba^{B1} baw^{B1}	'shoulder' 'man, young'	ban^{C1} a^{C1}	'village, small' 'to open mouth'	ak^{DIS}	'chest'	ap^{DIL} bok^{DIL} dep^{DIL}	'to bathe' 'flower' 'sunshine'
voiced	$mɯ^{A2}$ $xway^{A2}$ na^{A2}	'hand' 'buffalo, water' 'rice field'	pi^{B2} po^{B2} $hɤy^{B2}$	'sibling, elder' 'male, father' 'field, dry'	$nɛm^{C2}$ $noŋ^{C2}$ mey^{C2} ma^{C2}	'water' 'sibling, younger' 'wood, tree' 'horse'	nok^{D2} $lɤk^{D2}$	'bird' 'to steal'	mit^{D2} luk^{D2} $liət^{D2}$ nok^{D2}	'knife' 'child' 'blood' 'outside'

column have fallen together, and words having proto-short and proto-long vowels have the same tone on words with proto-voiced initials.

An auditory description of Tay Tac tones as pronounced on a syllable in isolation follows in (5) with examples for both long /a/ and short /ɐ/, demonstrating the occurrence of both vowels with all tones except for the restriction on D1S and D1L. Examples are also given of Tay Tac vowels which occur before both D1S and D1L, in our data, /i u a/. An examination of the vowel /a/ on the six tones in open syllables indicated that glottalization affects the tone length: /a/ on tone C1 is a little shorter and on C2 significantly shorter than on the other four tones with open syllables.

(5) A1 Mid-low rising: ma^{A1} 'dog', $xɐn^{A1}$ 'to crow'

   B1 Low, slight fall, then rising: ma^{B1} 'to soak (rice)', $tɐm^{B1}$ 'short'

   C1 Mid to low falling with glottalization: ma^{C1} 'to rise (e.g, of a river)', $thɐm^{C1}$ 'cave'

   A2 High level: ma^{A2} 'to come', $xɐm^{A2}$ 'gold'

   B2 Mid level: ta^{B2} 'a place for washing', $hɐy^{B2}$ 'field'

   C2 High to mid falling with glottalization: ma^{C2} 'horse', $nɐm^{C2}$ 'water'

   D1S High with slight rise: $lɐk^{D1S}$ 'intelligent', sip^{D1S} 'ten', suk^{D1S} 'ripe, cooked'

   D1L Low level: lak^{D1L} 'different', pik^{D1L} 'wing', puk^{D1L} 'to plant'

   D2 Mid level: $lɐk^{D2}$ 'to steal', lak^{D2} 'to pull or drag'

Both the auditory (this section) and the instrumental (part 2, §1.3) analyses reflect the tone contrasts of Tay Tac. The instrumental analyses at times show more detail of the contour than what had been heard, on occasion detecting voicing which is too light to be heard. For example, on a word with B1 tone, rather than the customary rise, a low level variant was heard. When the difference was checked instrumentally, however, the low variant registered as low falling.

The analysis of tone sandhi is beyond the scope of this paper due to lack of opportunity to obtain enough data, but clear distinctions have been observed, similar to that described for B1 tone above. In addition, tone variation is frequently conditioned by an adjacent tone or juncture. For example, the C2 high to mid falling tone falls less before the A2 high tone than before a lower tone.

1.4. Co-occurrence figures. The following figures represent preliminary observations based on the word list obtained in October, 1990. X indicates co-occurrence and a blank space indicates a nonoccurrence. A dash marks a nonoccurrence which patterns in our preliminary data suggest may be expected to be found in additional data, e.g., when consonants occur with some '1' tones, their absence on other '1' tones may be due to insufficient data.

(6) Co-occurrences of tones with initial consonants

	A1	B1	C1	A2	B2	C2	D1S	D1L	D2
b-	X	X	X				X	X	
d-	X	X	X	X			X	X	
p-	X	X	X	X	X	X	X	X	X
t-	X	X	X	X	X	X	X	X	X
c-	X	X	–	X	X	X	X	–	X
k-	X	X	X	X	X	X	X	–	X
kw-	X	–	X	–	–	–	–	X	–
?-	X	X	X	X	–	X	X	X	–
f-	X	X	X	X	–	X	X	X	–
th-	X	X	X	X	–	X	X	X	X
s-	X	X	X	X	X	X	X	X	X
x-	X	X	X	X	X	–	X	X	–
xw-	X	X	X	X	X	–	–	X	–
h-	X	X	X	X	X	X	X	X	X
w-	X	X	X	X	–	X	–	X	X
l-	X	X	X	X	–	–	X	X	X
y-	X	X	X	X	–	–	–	X	–
m-	X	X	X	X	X	X	X	X	X
n-	X	X	X	X	X	X	X	X	X
ɲ-	–	X	X	X	X	X	X	–	–
ŋ-	X	X	–	X	–	–	–	–	X
ŋw-	–	–	–	–	–	–	–	–	–

/b/ and /d/ do not occur with the proto-voiced '2' series except in $dɛn^{A2}$ 'light' borrowed from Vietnamese.

A Preliminary Examination of Tay Tac

(7) Co-occurrence of tones with final consonants

	A1	B1	C1	A2	B2	C2	D1S	D1L	D2
-p							X	X	X
-t							X	X	X
-k							X	X	X
-w	X	X	X	X	X	X			
-y	X	X	X	X	X	X			
-m	X	X	X	X	–	X			
-n	X	X	X	X	X	X			
-ŋ	X	X	X	X	X	X			
-∅	X	X	X	X	X	X			

Occurrence of final stops is restricted to the D tone and final continuants to the A, B, and C tones.

(8) Co-occurrence of tones with vowels

	A1	B1	C1	A2	B2	C2	D1S	D1L	D2
i	X	X	X	X	X	X	X	X	X
iə	X	X	X	X	X	–	–	X	X
e	X	X	–	X	–	–	X		X
ɛ	X	X	X	X	X	X		X	X
ɨ	X	X	X	X	X	X	X	X	X
ɨə	X	X	X	X	X	X	X	X	X
ə[ɜ]	X	X	X	X	X	X			
ə[ə]	X	X	X	X	–	–	X		X
ɐ	X	X	X	X	X	X	X		X
a	X	X	X	X	X	X		X	X
u	X	X	X	X	X	X	X	X	X
ua	X	–	–	X	X	–	–	X	–
o	X	X	X	X	–	X	X		X
ɔ	X	X	X	X	X	X	X	X	X

/ə/ [ɜ] does not occur with a final consonant and thus does not occur with D tones. /e ə[ə] ɐ o/ do not occur with tone D1L; /a ɛ/ do not occur with tone D1S.

(9) Co-occurrence of initial consonants with vowels

	i	iə	e	ɛ	ɨ	ɨə	ə[ɜ]	ə[ə]	ɐ	a	u	uə	o	ɔ
b-	X	–	–	–	–	–	X	–	X	X	–	X	X	X
d-	X	–	–	X	–	X	X	X	X	X	X	–	–	–
p-	X	–	X	X	X	X	X	–	X	X	X	–	X	X
t-	X	–	X	X	–	–	X	–	X	X	–	–	X	X
c-	X	X	X	–	X	X	X	–	X	X	–	–	X	X
k-	X	X	–	X	–	X	X	X	X	X	X	X	X	X
kw-	–	–	–	–					–	X				
ʔ-	X	–	X	–	X	X	–	X	X	X	X	X	X	X
f-	X	–	–	–	X	–	X	X	X	X	X	X	X	–
th-	X	–	–	–	–	–	X	–	X	X	X	X	X	X
s-	X	X	–	X	X	X	X	X	X	X	X	X	X	X
x-	X	–	X	X	X	X	X	–	X	X	X	–	X	X
xw-	X	X	–	X					X	X				
h-	X	–	X	X	–	X	X	–	X	X	X	–	X	X
w-	–	X	X	X					X	X				
l-	–	–	X	X	X	X	X	X	X	X	X	X	X	X
y-	–	–	–	–	–	–	X	–	–	X	X	–	–	–
m-	X	X	X	X	X	X	X	–	X	X	X	X	X	X
n-	X	–	–	–	X	X	X	–	X	X	X	X	X	X
ɲ	X	–	–	–	–	X	X	–	–	X	X	–	–	–
ŋ-	X	–	–	–	–	X	–	X	X	X	X	X	–	–
ŋw-	–	–	–	–					–	X				

The labialized initial consonants and /w/ occur only with low central and front vowels.

(10) Co-occurrences of vowels and final consonants

	i	iə	e	ɛ	ɨ	ɨə	ə[ɜ]	ə[ə]	ɐ	a	u	uə	o	ɔ-
-∅	X	X	–	X	X	X	X			X	X	X	X	X
-p	X	–	X	X	–	–		–	X	X	X	X	X	X
-t	X	X	X	X	X	X		–	X	X	–	X	–	X
-k	X	X	X	X	–	X		X	X	X	X	–	X	X
-w	X	X	X	X					X	X				
-y					–	X			X	X	X	–	X	X
-m	X	X	X	X	X	–		–	X	X	X	–	X	X
-n	X	–	X	X	X	X		X	X	X	X	X	X	X
-ŋ	X	X	X	X	X	X		X	X	X	X	–	X	X

Front vowels do not occur with /y/, back vowels do not occur with /w/, low central vowels occur with both. [ə] and /ɐ/ do not occur in open syllables, [ɜ] only in open syllables.

2. Tay Tac and White, Black, and Red Tay compared

The dimension of Tay Tac is added to the correspondences from Gedney 1964, in which the three sound systems were compared with each other and with Siamese. Gedney's data for W (White Tay of Lai Châu Province, primarily Muong Te) and B (Black Tay) are basically consistent with ours[4] and are used herein unless another source is specified, e.g., (jd) for the author's field notes, (Dieu&jd) Điêu and Donaldson (1970), and (r) for Robert (1941).

W, B, and R, like T, are basically monosyllabic and have an obligatory initial consonant, an obligatory nucleus consisting of vowel and tone, and an optional final consonant, i.e., CN(C). In addition to the diphthongs of Tay Tac, W and B have a diphthong ending in the high central semivowel, əɰ, which corresponds to a mid central vowel in T and R.

The following correspondences are given in the same general order and, for ready comparison, similar sounds in W, B, and R are written in the same transcription as used for Tay Tac.[5] The tone column gives the tone for all four language varieties except when a tone designation is given in a specific column, at times merely indicating the coalescence of two tones (cf. 2.3).

---

[4]Field work in White Tay of Lai Châu province and Tay Dam or Black Tay was done by Donaldson under the auspices of the Summer Institute of Linguistics in Tùng Nghĩa, South Vietnam, 1960–1970, and with Tay who have resettled in the U.S., 1978–1988. Tay Tac data are limited to the author's transcription of the word list from Dr. Lương.

Special appreciation is extended to Joseph E. Grimes, Ph.D., for a number of comments which have benefited the first section of this paper. The author, however, bears responsibility for any errors.

[5]A single tone notation is used for all four varieties when they are in the same tone category. T, B, and R velar spirant is transcribed *x* (Gedney's *kh*), none of which have the *kh/x* contrast of W, and in agreement with Fippinger and Fippinger (1970) for B and with the R value assumed by *kh* in Robert's Vietnamese-based orthography, since Vietnamese *kh* is [x]. Initial w[v] is written w. Syllable initial w[v] and syllable final[w] are mutually exclusive in T, W, B, and R.

The ten vowels of T, W, B, and R are written *i, e, ɜ, ɨ, ə, ɐ, a, u, o, ɔ;* the three diphthongs in T, W, B, and R are *ia, ɨa,* and *ua* (Gedney's *ia, ɨa,* and *ua*); the W and B diphthong (Gedney's *ay*) is transcribed *əɰ*.

2.1. Consonants. T, W, B, and R share the same inventory of consonants, except that W has a series of initial voiceless aspirated consonants /ph ch kh khw/ not found in the other three varieties.

Correspondences for initial consonants. Correspondence groups for proto-voiceless initial consonants with tone category '1', i.e., A1, B1, C1 and D1, are normally listed first, then the proto-voiced '2' tones, A2, B2, C2, and D2. Voiceless stops /p t c k kw ʔ/ correspond in T, W, B, and R.

(11) | T | W | B | R | | |
|---|---|---|---|---|---|
| pa | pa | pa | pa | B1 | 'forest' |
| tɐp^{DIS} | tɐp | tɐp | tɐp$^{D1/D2S}$ | D1 | 'liver' |
| cep^{DIS} | cep | cep | cep$^{D1/D2S}$ | D1 | 'to hurt' |
| kop^{DIS} | kop | kop | kop$^{D1/D2S}$ | D1 | 'frog' |
| kuəy | koy | kuəy | kuəy$^{C1/B2}$ | C1 | 'banana' |
| kwaŋ | kwaŋ | kwaŋ | kwaŋ | A1 | 'deer' |
| ʔɔk^{DIS} | ʔɐʔ | ʔɔʔ | ʔɔɔk$^{D1/D2S}$ | D1 | 'to go out' |
| | | | | | |
| paw | paw | paw | paw | C2 | 'coconut' |
| pu | pu | pu | puu | A2 | 'betel' |
| taŋ | taŋ | taŋ | taŋ | A2 | 'road, way' |
| cay | cay | cay | cay | A2 | 'man, male' |
| cok | cok | cok | cok^{D2L} | D2 | 'mortar' |
| kən | kun | kon | kon | A2 | 'person' |

Scarcer and not included in Gedney's correspondences are /kw/ and /ʔ/ on the proto-voiced '2' tones, for which limited correspondences are added below. /kw/ does not occur in T; *kwa*^{B2} 'to visit' is possibly borrowed from Vietnamese *qua* 'to pass by'.

The two T demonstratives 'this' and 'that' have lost the initial /n/ retained in W and B. Possibly the frequent co-occurence of the final /n/ of the general classifier *ʔɐn*^{A1} before the initial /n/ of the demonstratives giving [ʔɐnːi] and [ʔɐnːɐn] influenced the loss of /n/, since there normally is no juncture or initial glottal stop in unstressed syllables phrase medially. In Lu and Lao the initial /n/ of 'that' has changed to *hɐn*^{C2}, which Li (1977:112) suggests may be due to dissimilation of nasals.

A Preliminary Examination of Tay Tac

(12)

T	W	B	R			
	kwa	kwa		B2	'to visit'	jd
ʔem		ʔem		A2	'mother'	jd
	(mɛ^{B2})ʔi^{B1}				'mother'	jd
ʔoŋ^{A2}/luəŋ	loŋ		luəŋ	A1	'big'	jd
ʔi	ni	ni	ni	C2	'this'	jd, r
ʔɐn	nɐn	nɐn	nɐn	C2	'that'	jd, r

Spirants /f th s x xw h/. W aspirated consonants /ph ch kh khw/ and fricatives /f s x xw/ have fallen together in T, B, and R. Lu shares the /ph/ /f/ and /kh/ /x/ contrasts (Li:1964).

T, W, B, R /f/ and W /ph/ T, B, R /f/. Words on '2' tones with aspirated initials are given, albeit without confirmed cognates:

(13)

T	W	B	R			
fa	fa	fa	fa	A1	'wall'	
fa	fa	fa	fa	B1	'palm, sole'	
fa	fa	fa	fa$^{C1/B2}$	C1	'cloud'	
fat	fat	fat	fat$^{D1/D2S}$	D1	'astringent taste'	
fɐk^{D1S}	fɐk	fɐk	fɐk$^{D1/D2S}$	D1	'sheath'	
fa	fa	fa	fa	C2	'sky'	
fa	pha	fa	fa	B1	'to split'	
fɐk^{D1S}	phɐk	fɐk	fɐk$^{D1/D2S}$	D1	'vegetable'	
fom	phum	fom	fom	A1	'hair (of head)'	
fuk	phuʔ	fuʔ	fuuk$^{D1/D2S}$	D1	'to tie'	
	phan			A2	'to hunt'	Dieu & jd
	phe			A2	'a shrew-mouse'[6]	Dieu & jd

T, W, B, R /s/ and W /ch/ T, B, R /s/:

(14)

T	W	B	R		
siw	siw	siw	siw	B1	'chisel'
sɔk^{D1L}	sɔʔ	sɔʔ	sɔk$^{D1/D2S}$	D1	'elbow'
suk^{D1S}	suk	suk	suk$^{D1/D2S}$	D1	'cooked, ripe'
sɐy	sɐy	sɐy	sɐy$^{C1/B2}$	C1	'intestines'
say	say	say	say	A2	'sand'

---

[6] Vietnamese *chuột chù*.

T	W	B	R		
sɐy	chɐy	sɐy	sɐy$^{C1/B2}$	C1	'fever'
sɐy	chɐy	sɐy	sɐy	B1	'egg'
sɔ	chɔ	sɔ	sɔ	A1	'to beg'
sɐŋ	chɐŋ	sɐŋ	sɐŋ	A1	'to imprison'
sɐw	chɐw	sɐw		A1	'dove'
saŋ	chaŋ	saŋ		B1	'top (to spin)'
sɔŋ	chɔŋ	sɔŋ		C1	'fish basket'
saŋ	chaŋ	saŋ	saŋ$^{C1/B2}$	C1	'side, ribs'
sɐp^{D1S}	chɐp	sɐp		D1	'to chase'
	chiŋ			A2	'to dispute over' Dieu & jd
	chɔn			C2	'to choose' Dieu & jd

T W B R /x/ and W /kh/ T B R /x/:

(15)

T	W	B	R		
xa	xa	xa	xa$^{C1/B2}$	C1	'to kill'
xat^{D1L}	xat	xat	xat$^{D1/D2S}$	D1	'torn'
xɐp^{D1S}	xɐp	xɐp		D1	'to sing'
xɐy	xɐy	xɐy	xɐy	A1	'tallow'
xɐw	xɐw	xɐw	xɐw	B1	'knee'
xɐw	xɐw	xɐw		C1	'to enter' jd
xɐw	khɐw	xɐw	xɐw$^{C1/B2}$	C1	'rice'
xɐy	khɐy	xɐy	xɐy	A1	'to open'
xop^{D1S}	khop	xop	xop$^{D1/D2S}$	D1	'to bite'
xun	khun	xun	xun	B1	'turbid, dust'

T W B R /xw/; T /xw/ W /khw/ B R /xw/; T, W, B, R /th/ and /h/:

(16)

T	W	B	R		
xwan	xwan[7]	xwan	xwan	A1	'axe'
xwa	xwa	xwa	xwa	A1	'right (hand)'
xwɐm	xwɐm/ xɐm	xwɐm	xwɐm$^{C1/B2}$	C1	'(to lie) face down' Dieu & jd

---

[7]For W 'axe', initial velar fricative /x/ (per Điêu and Donaldson) is used rather than initial velar aspirated stop /kh/ (Gedney 1964:16).

A Preliminary Examination of Tay Tac

T	W	B	R	
xwɐn	xwɐn[8]	xwɐn	xwɐn	A1 'spirit'
xwɛn	xwɛn	xwɛn	xɛn	A1 'to hang up'
xwiət[D1L]	khwet/khet	xiət	xiət[D1/D2S]	D1 'small frog'
thɐy	thɐy	thɐy	thɐy	A1 'plow'
ha	ha	ha	ha	B1 'heavy shower'
hay	hay	hay	hay	A1 '(to lie) face up'
hɔn	hɔn	hɔn	hɔn	C2 'hot'

The following /k x kw xw/ sets in the proto-voiced '2' tones in T, W, and R, have fallen together to Siamese /kh/ and B /k/, respectively (Gedney 1964:24).

(17)

T	W	B	R	
kən	kun	kon	kon	A2 'person'
xɐm	xɐm	kɐm	xɐm	A2 'gold'
xɔ	xɔ	kɔ	xɔ	A2 'neck'
xway	xway	kway	xway	A2 'water buffalo'
xwɐn	xwɐn/xɔn	kwɐn	xwɐn	A2 'smoke'
xwaŋ	xwaŋ	kwaŋ	xwaŋ	B2 'to throw fishnet'

Voiced stops /b d/ occur only on the proto-voiceless tones '1' in T, except for den[A2] 'light', a Vietnamese borrowing.[9]

(18)

T	W	B	R	
bin	bin	bin	bin	A1 'to fly'
biən	bən	biən	biən	A1 'moon, month'
bɔk[D1L] bɔʔ	bɔʔ	bɔk~wɔk[D1/D2S]		D1 'flower'
dək[D1S] dək	dək	dik	lik[D1/D2S]	D1 'late at night'

---

[8]Gedney has an alternate rendering for 'spirit', xɔn[A1], for which Điêu and Donaldson have the gloss 'a coffin containing a spirit'.

[9]The change of /d/ to Red Tay /l/ is mentioned by Gedney (1964:14) as is B and R /d/ /l/ and /b/ /v/ fluctuation; for the latter, see Fippinger and Fippinger 1970 as well. Fluctuation in T has not been confirmed.

Initial semivowels /w[v]/ and /y/:

(19)

	T	W	B	R		
	van	van	van~ban	van	A1	'sweet'
	vɐt^{D1S}	vɐt	vɐt	vɐt$^{D1/D2S}$	D1	'a cold'
	yu	yu	yu	yuu	B1	'to be (in a place)'
	yə	yəɯ	yəɯ		A2	'spider web'

Lateral /l/:

(20)

	T	W	B	R		
	lɐw	lɐw	lɐw	lɐw$^{C1/B2}$	C1	'alcoholic beverage'[10]
	lɐk	lɐk	lɐk	lɐk^{D2L}	D2	'to steal'

Nasals /m n ɲ ŋ ŋw/. The change from T, W, and B /ɲ/ to /y/ in R is broached by Gedney (1964:27) and Li (1977:173–80).

(21)

	T	W	B	R		
	ma	ma	ma	ma	A1	'dog'
	nam	nam	nam	nam	A1	'thorn'
	ɲə	ɲəɯ	ɲəɯ	yəə	B1	'big'
	ɲa	ɲa	ɲa	ya$^{C1/B2}$	C1	'grass'
	mɨ	mɨ	mɨ	mɨɨ	A2	'hand'
	na	na	na	na	A2	'rice field'
	ŋu	ŋu	ŋu	ŋuu	A2	'snake'
	nuŋ	nuŋ	nuŋ	yuŋ	A2	'mosquito'

---

[10] R tone in the word for 'alcoholic beverage' has been changed to C1 to conform with Gedney's tone chart (1964:8, 16).

Correspondences for finals. In W and B final /-k/ becomes glottal stop /-ʔ/ on words which had Proto-Tai long vowels, while T and R retain the /-k/.[11] As Haudricourt (1948 and 1956) noted, final /-k/ was lost when preceded by a long vowel in some Tay varieties, apparently before the vowel length contrast was lost.[12] Contrast of /ʔ/ with its absence is shown in the following pairs:

(22)

T	W	B	R		
ma	ma			B1 'to soak (rice)'	jd
mak	maʔ	maʔ		D1 'fruit'	jd
pu	pu	pu		B1 'grandfather, paternal'	
puk^{D1L}	puʔ	puʔ	puk$^{D1/D2S}$	D1 'to plant'	
	pi	pi		B1 'flute'	
pik^{D1L}	piʔ	piʔ	pik$^{D1/D2S}$	D1 'wing'	

Voiceless stops /-p -t -k/:

(23)

T	W	B	R	
sip^{D1S}	sip	sip	sip$^{D1/D2S}$	D1 'ten'
lek^{D1S}	lek	lek	lek$^{D1/D2S}$	D1 'iron'
cet^{D1S}	cet	cet	cet$^{D1/D2S}$	D1 'seven'
sək^{D1S}	sək	sək		D1 'war, enemy'
thək^{D1S}	thək	thək	thik$^{D1/D2S}$	D1 'young male animal'

---

[11] Gedney's three Red Tai glossaries (Hudak 1994) show that, with one exception, the Red Tai data that was originally compared with Tay Tac for this article reflects Gedney's Red Tai I glossary in the later work. Red Tai I has a final glottal stop apparently based on toʔ^2 'table'. Gedney had not posited a final glottal stop for Red Tai in his sketch of 1964, but commented, " 'Table' is another loanword, identified by Egerod as Swatow. Red Tai has borrowed many modern terms from Siamese and Lao, of which this is probably one." The Red Tai I glossary also has a final glottal stop in the reduced form of maak^2 'fruit' which is maʔ^2 = ma^2, maa^2; in bɔʔ^2 bɔn^2 'base of the throat'; and yaʔ^2 'yes', a probable borrowing from Vietnamese.

[12] Unlike B, in W due to the final glottal stop of tone A2 and the pitch similarity of tones A2 and D2, these two tones have coalesced on words having a final glottal stop, as indicated by the tone designation A2/D2. The glottal stop is not written since it is no longer phonemic. W words with tones B1 and D1, on the other hand, are clearly distinguished since only D1 has a glottal stop. (See also Donaldson 1963:40–45 for White Tay, Gedney 1964:36, Fippinger and Fippinger 1970, and Li 1977).

T	W	B	R		
dək^{D1S}	dək	dik	lik$^{D1/D2S}$	D1	'late at night'
hok^{D1S}	hok	hok	hok$^{D1/D2S}$	D1	'six'
viak	vɛ$^{A2/D2}$	via?	viak^{D2L}	D2	'work'
pik	pik	pik		D2	'to turn over'

Final semivowels /w ɯ y/. With the exception of the W and B diphthong /əɯ/, final semivowels, nasals, and open syllables are comparable in all four varieties of Tay under consideration.

The diphthong /əɯ/ in W and B is monophthongized to a mid central vowel in T and R (Robert, Gedney), which in T is the mid central allophone [ɜ], as in the word mə^{B1} [mɜ^{B1}] 'new'. (As Gedney notes, spoken Siamese has /ay/, not /əɯ/, but "the Siamese writing system has a different symbol for these words from the usual *ay* symbol, indicating that the distinction still existed at the time when the script was devised.") (1964:39)

T W B R /-w/:

(24)

T	W	B	R		
xɛw	xɛw	xɛw	xɛw	A1	'green'
daw	daw	daw	law	A1	'star'
xɐw	xɐw	xɐw	xɐw$^{C1/B2}$	C1	'to enter'
kɐw	kɐw	kɐw	kɐw$^{C1/B2}$	C1	'nine'

(25)

T /-ə/	W /-əɯ/	B /-əɯ/	R /-əə/		
bə	bəɯ	bəɯ	bəə	A1	'leaf'
cə	cəɯ	cəɯ	cəə	A1	'heart'
cə	cəɯ	cəɯ		C2	'to use, serve'
də	dəɯ	dəɯ	ləə	A1	'which, what, any'
fə	fəɯ	fəɯ		B1	'to daydream of'
hə	həɯ	həɯ	həə$^{C1/B2}$	C1	'to give'
mə	məɯ	məɯ	məə	B1	'new'
nə	nəɯ	nəɯ	nəə	A2	'yonder'
ɲə	ɲəɯ	ɲəɯ	ɲəə	B1	'big'
pə	pəɯ	pəɯ	pəə	C2	'female in-law'
sə	səɯ	səɯ	səə	A1	'clear, transparent'
sə	səɯ	səɯ	səə	B1	'to put'

A Preliminary Examination of Tay Tac

	T /-ə/	W /-əɯ/	B /-əɯ/	R /-əə/		
	tə	təɯ	təɯ	təə[C1/B2]	C1	'below, south'
	yə	yəɯ	yəɯ		A2	'spider web'
	xə	xəɯ	xəɯ	xəə[13]	B1	'dry'

Two exceptions are shown below in which [ɜ] corresponds to the W and B diphthong /ə/ rather than /əɯ/:

(26)   T   W   B   R

    kə [kɜ]   kə   B2   'amount'
    cə [cɜ]   cə   cə   A2   'time'

T W B R /-y/:

(27)   T   W   B   R

    kuəy   koy   kuəy   kuəy[C1/B2]   C1   'banana'
    nɨəy   nəy   nɨəy   nɨəy   B1   'tired'
    pɐy   pɐy   pɐy   pɐy   A1   'to go'
    nɔy   nɔy   nɔy   nɔy   C2   'small, few'

Nasals /-m -n -ŋ/:

(28)   T   W   B   R

    nɐm   nɐm   nɐm   nɐm   C2   'water'
    xɛn   xɛn   xɛn   xɛn   A1   'arm'
    muŋ   muŋ   muŋ   muŋ   A2   'to roof'

Open syllables:

(29)   T   W   B   R

    ha   ha   ha   ha   A1   'to seek'

2.2. Vowels. Except for /ɐ/, which is higher and shorter than /a/ and does not occur in open syllables, vowel length is written only in Red Tay as

---

[13]Noting Gedney's (1964:39) cover statement of the R correspondence to be without exception, we have changed R /əɯ/ in the word for 'dry' to /əə/.

transcribed by Gedney (1964:29–30) with reservations. (Robert 1941 did not indicate vowel length.)

Li (1977:280–84) notes that Proto-Tai diphthongs have monophthongized to mid vowels in, e.g., W, Lu, and Shan, a change not shared by T.

T, B, and R /iə ɨə uə/ and W /e ə o/:

(30)

T	W	B	R		
miə	*me*	*miə*	*miə*	A2	'wife'
siəŋ	*seŋ*	*siəŋ*	*siəŋ*	A1	'sound'
liəŋ	*ləŋ*	*liəŋ*	*liəŋ*	A1	'yellow'
huə	*ho*	*huə*	*huə*	A1	'head'
sɨə	*sə*	*sɨə*	*sɨə*$^{C1/B2}$	C1	'shirt'
suən	*son*	*suən*	*suən*	A1	'garden'
nuək^{D1S}	*noʔ*	*nuəʔ*	*nuək*$^{D1/D2S}$	D1	'deaf'

Li (1964) also refers to nasal umlaut, the raising of mid vowels to high in Lu, W, and some other Tay varieties before a nasal.

T, B, R mid vowels become W high vowels before a nasal:

(31)

T	W	B	R		
hen	*hin*	*hen*	*hen*	A1	'to see'
ŋən	*ŋin*	*ŋən*	*ŋən*	A2	'silver, money'
tom	*tum*	*tom*	*tom*$^{C1/B2}$	C1	'to boil'

T, W, B, and R mid vowels without final nasal:

(32)

T	W	B	R		
lek	*lek*	*lek*	*lek*$^{D1/D2S}$	D1	'iron'
bə	*bəɰ*	*bəɰ*		C1	'ignorant, stupid'
hok	*hok*	*hok*	*hok*$^{D1/D2S}$	D1	'six'

Exception: T, W /ə/ without final nasal became B, R /ɨ/:

| *dɨk* | *dək* | *dɨk* | *lɨk*$^{D1/D2S}$ | D1 | 'late at night' |

High and low front vowels /i ɛ/:

(33)

T	W	B	R		
pi	pi	pi	pii	A2	'fat'
tin	tin	tin	tin	A1	'foot'
sip^{DIS}	sip	sip	sip$^{D1/D2S}$	D1	'ten'
pik^{D1L}	piʔ	piʔ	piik$^{D1/D2S}$	D	'wing'
kɛ	kɛ	kɛ	kɛɛ	B1	'old (persons)'
mɛŋ	mɛŋ	mɛŋ	mɛŋ	A2	'insect'
pet^{D1L}	pet	pet	peet$^{D1/D2S}$	D1	'eight'

High and low central vowels /ɨ ɐ a/:

(34)

T	W	B	R		
mɨ	mɨ	mɨ	mɨɨ	C2	'day'
xɨn	xɨn	kɨn	xɨɨn	A2	'night'
mɨt	mɨt	mɨt	mɨɨt^{D2L}	D2	'dark'
tɐm	tɐm	tɐm	tɐm	B1	'short'
nɐm	nɐm	nɐm	nɐm	C2	'water'
ha	ha	ha	haa	A1	'to seek'
haŋ	haŋ	haŋ	haaŋ	A1	'tail'
ʔap^{D1L}	ʔap	ʔap	ʔap$^{D1/D2S}$	D1	'to bathe'

High and low back vowels /u ɔ/:

(35)

T	W	B	R		
pu	pu	pu	puu	A2	'mountain'
suk^{DIS}	suk	suk	suk$^{D1/D2S}$	D1	'cooked, ripe'
kɔ	kɔ	kɔ	kɔɔ	A1	'plant, tree'
hɔm	hɔm	hɔm	hɔɔm	A1	'fragrant'
cɔp^{DIS}	cɔp	cɔp	cɔɔp$^{D1/D2S}$	D1	'hoe'

2.3. Tones. Section 1.3 on Tay Tac tones introduces our adaptation of Li's system of tone designations which we use here for all four Tay varieties under discussion, where we are primarily concerned with comparing the tone systems of correspondences, rather than phonetic equivalents.

On tones A, B, and C, on open syllables and syllables ending in a continuant, White Tay, Tay Dam, and Tay Tac have a six-tone system with glottalization on tones C1 and C2. Red Tay (Gedney 1964) is reported to have a five-tone system with tones C1 and B2 falling together (herein designated C1/B2).[14] The two tone systems are depicted below:

(36)   W B T   R

A1	B1	C1
A2	B2	C2

A1	B1	C1/B2
A2	C1/B2	C2

On tone D, on syllables with a final stop, W, B, and R have a two-way split, W and B between D1 and D2. D2S and D2L are split in R, D1 combining with D2S in contrast with tone D2L. Thus, W, B, and R contrast with T's three-way split, as shown below, along with Siamese (Gedney 1964), which has a three-way split of D1, D2S, D2L, the reverse of Tay Tac's D1S, D1L, D2 split.

(37)   Siamese   W B   R   T

D1	
D2S	D2L

D1
D2

D1/D2S	
D1/D2S	D2L

D1S	D1L
D2	

W tones A2 and B2 are the same approximate level, but A2 has a final glottal stop. W words from tone category D2, in which final /-k/ is glottal stop, have therefore fallen together with A2 while the distinction between A2 and B2 with other final stops is neutralized.

The following list illustrates Tay Tac tone correspondences with W, B, and R. Red Tay C1/B2 and D2L refer to Gedney's R tone 3, and R D1/D2S to his R tone 2.

---

[14] Using Vietnamese diacritics, Robert distinguished four, rather than Gedney's five, R tones on open syllables and syllables ending with a continuant: $sɔng^{A1}$ 'two', hu^{C2} 'to know', and combining C1 and B2 as does Gedney, $ha^{C1/B2}$ 'five' and $pi^{C1/B2}$ 'older sibling'. Unlike Gedney, however, Robert's remaining tone combines B1 and A2 tones, both unmarked by a diacritic: $kɐy^{B1}$ 'chicken' and $fɐy^{A2}$ 'fire'. (Gedney describes the latter two tones as level and high, $kɐy^{B1}$, versus mid with slight and gradual fall, $fɐy^{A2}$.) Further data from a Red Tay speaker would be useful.

(38)

T	W	B	R	
sɔŋ^{A1}	sɔŋ^{A1}	sɔŋ^{A1}	sɔŋ^{A1}	'two'
pen^{A1}	pin^{A1}	pen^{A1}	pen^{A1}	'to be, become'
hɐw^{B1}	hɐw^{B1}	hɐw^{B1}	hɐw^{B1}	'to bark'
ha^{C1}	ha^{C1}	ha^{C1}	ha$^{C1/B2}$	'five'
hu^{A2}	hu^{A2}	hu^{A2}	huu^{A2}	'hole'
pi^{B2}	pi^{B2}	pi^{B2}	pi$^{C1/B2}$	'older sibling'
hu^{C2}	hu^{C2}	hu^{C2}	huu^{C2}	'to know'
cɔp^{D1S}	cɔp^{D1}	cɔp^{D1}	cɔp$^{D1/D2S}$	'hoe'
pik^{D1L}	pik^{D1}	pik^{D1}	pik$^{D1/D2S}$	'wing'
nok^{D2}	nok^{D2}	nok^{D2}	nok^{D2L}	'bird'
nɔk^{D2}	nɔʔ^{D2}	nɔʔ^{D2}	nɔk^{D2L}	'outside'

2.4. Conclusion. Tay Tac, although closely related, is distinct from White Tay, Tay Dam, and Red Tay, with a different tone system, to which Gedney, attaches the following significance,

> ... the most useful criterion for dialect boundaries within the Tai-speaking area is perhaps that of tonal systems; ... one may consider that he has crossed a dialect boundary if he finds an increase or decrease in the number of tones in the system, or if he finds that a list of morphemes in which the previously studied dialect agreed in tone is now distributed among two or more different tones. (1972:423)

The following is a list of tone and other phonological innovations which have been observed.[15]

---

[15]This list of comparisons does not include fluctuation of the [l] and [b] allophones of /d/ and /b/ in B (Fippinger and Fippinger) and similarly in R, only possibly in T, but not in W; fluctuation of the [z] and [j] allophones of initial /y-/ in W and, to a lesser degree in T and B, but not reported for R; fluctuation within W between /xw/ and /x/, or the isolated loss only in T of initial /n-/ on the demonstratives ni^{C2} 'this' and nɐn^{C2} 'that'. These occur within a particular variation and are in need of further study.

(39) T	W	B	R	Description of tone innovations
			R	1. On open syllables and syllables closed with a continuant, T, W, and B preserve the six-tone system which has changed in R to five tones.
T				2. On syllables with a final stop, W and B retain the simple two-way split between the D1 and D2. In T the D1 tone splits further between D1S and D1L, i.e., in words having Proto-Tai long versus short vowels.
			R	Conversely, in R D2 splits into D2S and D2L, with D1 and D2S then merging.
(40) T	W	B	R	Other innovations
			R	3. W preserves both the fricative and the aspirated consonant series /ph- ch- kh- khw-/ which has fallen together in T, B, and R with fricatives /f- s- x- xw-/.
		B		4. /k-/ and /x-/ and likewise /kw-/ and /xw-/ in the proto-voiced '2' tones in T, W, and R have fallen together in B /k-/ and /kw-/, respectively.
	W	B		5. On words which had Proto-Tai (and, per Gedney, both Siamese and R) long vowels, T and R preserve /-k/, which in W and B has become glottal stop /-ʔ/.
	W			6. Proto-Tai diphthongs preserved in T, B, and R as /iə ɨə uə/ have monophthongized to mid vowels in W.
	W			7. T, B, and R mid vowels have changed to high in W before a nasal.
			R	8. T, W, and B preserve /ɲ-/, which becomes /y-/ in R.
	W	B		9. W and B /əɰ/ is monophthongized in T and R.

In conclusion, we observe that the relationship of T to W, B, and R is comparable to that described by Gedney (1964:4) for W, B, and R.

> Whether White, Black, and Red Tai ought to be called three different languages or three dialects of one language is debatable. Each differs from the others in definite, identifiable ways.

This preliminary study indicates that Tay Tac is likewise closely related to White Tay of Lai Châu, Black Tay (Tay Dam), and Red Tay, while differing from each of them in 'definite, identifiable ways'. For linguistic purposes, it is appropriate to distinguish W and T, rather than use the term 'White Tay' for both.

Part 2: Instrumental analysis of Tay Tac—Edmondson

Several hours of recordings of Dr. Hoàng Lương's speech were made for instrumental study. The data for this sketch was elicted orally using White Tay prompts by Jean Donaldson. Dr. Lương was asked to respond by producing repetitions of the same lexical item. Both monosyllabic and disyllabic utterances were elicited.

A part of Dr. Hoàng Lương's utterances were recorded on audio tape of high quality and a part was digitized directly from the microphone. Audio recordings were made with a Sony TCM 5000 battery-operated professional quality cassette tape recorder. An Atus ATR20 low impedance unidirectional dynamic microphone was placed close to the mouth but sufficiently outside the airstream to avoid microphone blast. In order to discover the general prosodic patterns of Tay Tac, a number of diagnostic vocabulary items were studied first. These data were input from the microphone into the CECIL Hardware Unit (Computerised Extraction of Components of Intonation in Language, SIL, JAARS, Waxhaw, NC), which contains bandpass filters, an amplifier, and an 8-bit parallel interface to an AT-286 DOS computer. Once these data were captured in volatile computer memory and displayed on the screen, they were then saved on floppy disk medium for later editing and analysis. Since digitized files take up a considerable amount of disk space (20–30k/file), the use of audio and digital recording proved an effective method that combined the speed and economy of audio recordings with the precise, direct digital capture of some particularly distinctive examples. CECIL extracts pitch and plots this information on the computer monitor. Data files of this pitch track can be stored on the hard disk as well.

At a later time a compositing procedure was carried out on the data. In compositing, the common features of some syllables under study are extracted from a set of four or five repetitions. The procedure corrects for both *duration* (length of utterance) and *register* (mean pitch height) and removes any artifactual points before mean values are calculated. The resulting composited pitch trajectories are given in (41), (42), and (43). As a mnemonic of the historical and comparative situation, solid symbols on the curve represent syllables with proto-voiced initial consonants, whereas open symbols on the curve stand for syllables with original voiceless consonant initials. Fundamental frequency is given in semitones and time in milliseconds.

(41)   FØ plot of the Tay Tac A tones exemplified by 'dog' and 'to come'

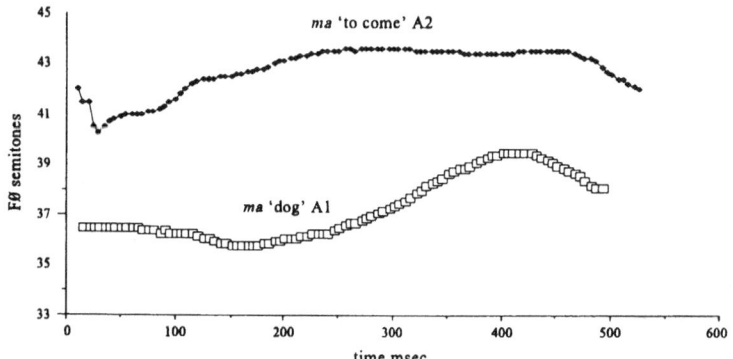

(42)   FØ plot of the Tay Tac B tones exemplified by 'to soak (rice)' and 'older sibling'

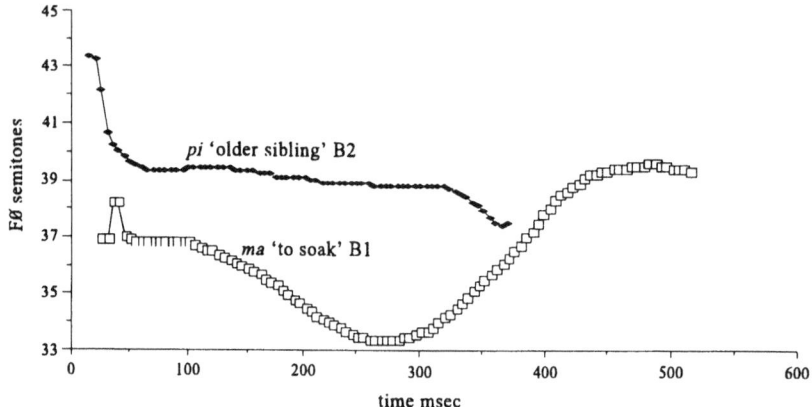

(43) FØ plot of the Tay Tac C tones exemplified by 'to rise' and 'horse'

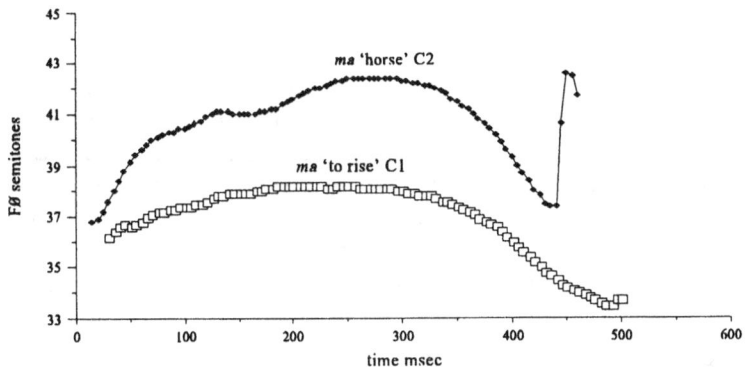

From Donaldson's experience with Tay varieties at other locations, it was anticipated that syllables in some tonal categories C1 and C2 would be accompanied by glottal constriction at the end of the syllable. Unfortunately, we were unable to undertake a direct study of this special voice quality by means of airflow or other techniques. Nevertheless, we believe there is evidence of it captured in the spike at the end of the word ma^{C2} 'horse' caused by the tightened glottal folds as the syllable approaches its end.

1. Pitch contours of the tones

1.1. The system of notation. In order to display the tone value or pitch contour of a representative set of lexical items, we selected a set with near minimal contrasts: ma^{A1} 'dog'; ma^{A2} 'to come'; ma^{B1} 'to soak (rice)'; pi^{B2} 'older sibling'; ma^{C1} 'to rise'; and ma^{C2} 'horse'. Originally, we planned to elicit a complete set with a *ma* syllable, including ma^{B2}. However, Tay Tac, unlike White Tay [Tay Don], does not have this lexical item. Therefore, pi^{B2} was substituted.

1.2. The 'voiced-low' situation. A glance at the plots in (41), (42), and (43) is instructive in showing that Tay Tac, like some others of the Tai stock, has the reflexes of original voiced initial consonants higher in pitch than the reflexes of original voiceless initial consonants; this situation has been called *voiceless low*. Members of the Tai Branch at many other locations in Thailand, Laos, Myanmar, Vietnam, and especially in Southern China show the opposite situation. Reflexes of the original voiced initial consonants have lower pitch today; in these varieties the *voiced-low principle* has prevailed (cf. Brown (1965, 1975) and Strecker (1979) for further discussion). To clarify the historical antecedent at a glance, blackened diamonds are used to plot syllables that once possessed voiced initial consonants and open squares are used to plot syllables whose roots possessed voiceless initials. As is immediately evident, Tay Tac has a voiceless-low heritage.

1.3. Observations about the tone values of Tay Tac. The pitch plots in (41), (42), and (43) leave the immediate impression of complexity of contour; with the exception of B2 none of them seem to be describable as simply level. The A1 tone has a smooth onset or a slight drop followed by a rise over about half the length of the syllable with a rather quick dropoff in fundamental frequency at the end. A2 is easily differentiated from A1. A2 rises to the highest level over the first third of its course and remains there. Tone B1 makes an overall impression of fall and rise. It begins just below the middle of tonal space and falls to the lowest level before rising to just above mid level. The two C tones feature glottalization throughout their course. The C2 is more strongly glottalized than C1, though both have it. In the pitch plot there are a few points at the end of each of the C2 syllables in which the glottal folds appear to be so tense that the fundamental frequency jumps up discontinuously to a higher level to form a horn at the end. The more weakly glottalized C1 has no such tense stoppage of voicing at the end of the syllable. The pitches of these two are very similar in contour, namely rise-fall except that C2 rises to a higher apex. The six pitches of these in terms of scale-of-five (Chao 1930) would be described as follows:

(44) A1 = 223   B1 = 213   C1 = 231
      A2 = 455   B2 = 33   C2 = 253

2. The rhymes of Tay Tac

2.1. Syllables in Tay Tac. Traditionally, studies of Kadai languages have been organized according to initial consonants and rhymes rather than vowels and consonants, which are the constituent members of the syllable. The rhyme is divided into an onset, nuclear vowel, and coda. A lexical item such as $tɐp^{D1}$ 'liver' would be divided into: t initial consonant and $ɐp$ rhyme. In Tay Tac there are, besides syllable final codas -p, -t, and -k, the nasals -m, -n, and -ŋ as well as -i (-y) and -u (-w). As has been indicated in part 1 §1.2 above, Tay Tac possesses nine contrastive simple vowel rhymes and many more nuclear vowel and coda combinations. Moreover, there are two onset glides that can occur before a nuclear vowel.

A set of examples illustrating each of the contrasts was selected from recordings. These were digitized with the CECIL Hardware Unit if they were not already in the computer files from the analysis of tone values. Each of these CECIL files was converted into a file format readable by the Mac-

Speech Lab II (GW Instruments, Inc.). With the MacSpeech Lab II software, spectrographic analysis using an LPC (Linear Predictive Coding) was conducted on the relevant syllables; five values of the first and second formant frequencies at evenly spaced intervals across the syllable were taken. These values were plotted using MS-Excel with F2-F1 plotted logarithmically on the horizontal axis and F1 on the vertical. Using the procedure described in Ladefoged (1964), these values were plotted in the third quadrant using a semilog projection. The examples used in these plots are:

(45) [i] pi^{A2} 'fat'
     [u] $pom^{A1}\ pu^{A2}$ 'mountain'
     [e] lek^{D1S} 'iron'
     [o] to^{A1} 'classifier for animals'
     [ɛ] $mɛ^{B2}$ 'mother, woman'
     [ɔ] $kɔ^{A1}$ 'classifier for trees'
     [a] pa^{B1} 'forest'

The data for the central vowels included the examples:

(46) [ɨ] $fɨn^{A1}$ 'classifier for clothing'
           $ʔɨn^{A1}$ 'wet'
     [ɜ] $kɜ^{B2}$ 'size'
           $tsɜ^{A1}$ 'heart'
     [ə] $fən^{A1}$ 'rain'
           $fəŋ^{A1}$ 'bee'
           $ŋən^{A2}$ 'silver'
     [ɐ] $fɐn^{A1}$ 'dream'
           $xɐm^{A2}$ 'gold'

2.2. Results of the F2-F1 versus F1 plot of vowels in Tay Tac.
Diagram (47) shows the plotting for the vowels of Tay Tac.

(47)

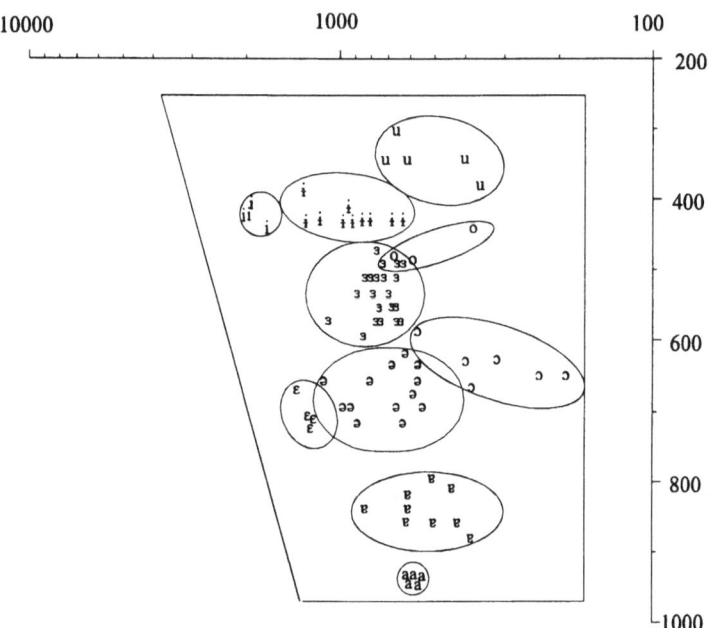

The most striking feature of the vowels of Tay Tac is the complete set of central vowels. In phonetic terms there are four /ɨ ɜ ə ɐ/. The high central vowel /ɨ/ has sometimes been described as high back unrounded, i.e., /ɯ/, but Dr. Lương displayed a more centralized form of unrounded vowel. The vowel /ɜ/ is also surprising. The word tsɜ 'heart' in Tay Tac corresponds to Siamese /tsai/ (whose rhyme is written with ใ in the Thai script) and Shan /tsaɯ/, cf. also Sanfang Zhuang, where it is realized as /ɤ/ in Wei/Edmondson, this volume. Li (1977:289) gives as the root for this word PT *tsau. The Tay Tac realization of the diphthong /auɯ/ is the monophthong /ɜ/. The tendency to monophthongization in Tay Tac is quite evident in a number of rhymes, whereby the resulting value falls in height between the two elements in the diphthong of the proto language. For example, Tay Tac has pi^{42} 'fat' for *bu̯i and to^{41} 'classifier for animals' for *tua.

References

Baccam, Don, Faluang Baccam, Hung Baccam, and Dorothy Fippinger. 1989. 'Păp Pe Khót 'Quám Táy-Ăng-kít [Tai Dam-English, English-Tai Dam Vocabulary Book]. Eastlake, Colo.: Summer Institute of Linguistics.

Benedict, Paul K. 1975. Austro-Thai: Language and culture. New Haven: Human Relations Area Files Press.

Brown, J. Marvin. 1965. From ancient Thai to modern dialects. Bangkok: Social Science Association Press of Thailand. Reprinted 1985 in Brown, From Ancient Thai to modern dialects and other writings on historical Thai linguistics. Bangkok: White Lotus Co., Ltd.

———. 1975. The great tone split: Did it work in two opposite ways? In J. G. Harris and J. R. Chamberlain (eds.), Studies in Tai linguistics in honor of William J. Gedney, 33–48. Bangkok: Central Institute of English Language.

Catford, J. C. 1977. Fundamental problems in phonetics. Bloomington: Indiana University Press.

Chabant, Edmond and Diew-Cingx Gnimz (Điêu, Chính Nhìm). 1951. Cours de langue 'Tai.

Điêu, Chính Nhìm and Jean Donaldson. 1970. Păp san khăm pák Tãy-Keo-Eng: [Ngữ-vựng Thái-Việt-Anh] [Tai-Vietnamese-English vocabulary]. Saigon: Department of Education.

Donaldson, Jean. 1963. White Tai phonology. M.A. thesis, Hartford Seminary Foundation, Hartford, Conn.

Edmondson, Jerold A. and Li Shaoni. 1991. Voice quality and inverse filtering in the Bai language of Yunnan Province. In Dai Qingxia (ed.), Proceedings of the International Conference on Yi-Burmese Languages, Xichang, Sichuan, August 1991.

Fant, Gunnar. 1959. The acoustics of speech. Proceedings of the Third International Congress on Acoustics, Stuttgart.

———. 1970. Acoustic theory of speech production. The Hague: Mouton.

———. 1983. The voice source—acoustic modeling. Speech Transmission Laboratory Quarterly Progress and Status Report (STL-QPSR) No. 4/1982:1–27.

Fippinger, Jay and Dorothy Fippinger. 1970. Black Tai phonemes with reference to White Tai. Anthropological Linguistics 12(3):83–97.

Gedney, William J. 1964. A comparative sketch of White, Black, and Red Tai. The Social Science Review (Bangkok). Special Number 1:1–47. Reprinted 1989 in R. Bickner et al. (eds.), Selected papers on comparative Tai studies. Michigan Paper on South and Southeast Asia. Center for South and Southeast Asian Studies 29. Ann Arbor: The University of Michigan.

———. 1972. A checklist for determining tones in Tai languages. In M. Estelle Smith (ed.), Studies in linguistics in honor of George L. Trager, 423–37. The Hague: Mouton.

Haudricourt, André-Georges. 1948. Les phonèmes et le vocabulaire du thai commun. Journal Asiatique 236:197–238.

———. 1956. De la restitution des initiales dans les langues monosyllabiques: Le problème du thai commun. Bulletin de la Société de Linguistique de Paris 52:307–22.

Hoàng, Trân-Nghịch and Tòng Kim Ân. 1990. Từ Diển Thái-Việt. Hà Nội: Nhà Xuất Bản Khoa Học Xã Hội.

Hudak, Thomas John, ed. 1994. William J. Gedney's Southwestern Tai dialects: Glossaries, texts, and translations. Michigan Paper on South and Southeast Asia. Center for South and Southeast Asian Studies 42. Ann Arbor: University of Michigan.

Ladefoged, Peter. 1964. A course in phonetics. New York: Harcourt Brace Jovanovich

Laver, John. 1980. The phonetic quality of voice. Cambridge: Cambridge University Press.

Li, Fang-Kuei. 1960. A tentative classification of Tai dialects. In S. Diamond (ed.), Culture in history: Essays in honor of Paul Radin, 951–59. New York: Published for Brandeis University by Columbia University Press.

———. 1964. The phonemic system of the Tai Lu language. Bulletin of the Institute of History and Philology 35:7–14.

———. 1977. A handbook of comparative Tai. Honolulu: The University Press of Hawaii.

Li Shaoni and Ai Jierui (Jerold A. Edmondson). 1989. Yunnan Jianchuan Baiyu yinzhi he yindiao anliang [Voice-quality settings and pitch in the Bai language of Yunnan Province]. Zhongyang Minzu Xueyuan Xuebao 70–74.

Minot, Georges. 1940. Dictionnaire tay blanc-français avec transcription latine. Bulletin de l'École Française d'Extrême-Orient 40 (1)1:–237.

———. 1949. Vocabulaire français-thay blanc et éléments de grammaire, 2 vols. Publication de l'École Française d'Extrême-Orient.

Robert, R. 1941. Notes sur les tay deng de Lang Chanh (Thanh-hoa-Annam). Institut Indochinois pour l'étude de l'homme. Mémoire 1. Hanoi: Imprimerie d'Extrême-Orient.

Sarawit, Mary. 1973. The Proto-Tai vowel system. Ph.D. dissertation. University of Michigan.

Strecker, David. 1979. Higher falls more: A tonal sound change in Tai. Computational Analyses of Asian and African Languages 11:30–84.

'Near' and 'Far' in Tai

William J. Gedney

Editors' preface

The following article was originally prepared for the Seventh International Conference on Sino-Tibetan Languages and Linguistics, held at Georgia State University in October of 1974. It was never published.

We have attempted to reduce the space it occupies on the printed page without sacrificing the wealth of data cited, mostly by relegating to footnotes cognate forms that are transcribed identically to forms cited in the body of the paper. We have omitted a part of the introduction explaining the proto-Tai tonal system and the notation used. The reader is directed to the introduction of this volume for these matters; note that we here retain Professor Gedney's tonal notation, except that where he writes A1a, A1b, B1a, B1b, etc. we write A1, A1m, B1, B1m. We have converted names of large or well-known Chinese places to Hanyu Pinyin transcription (e.g., Guangxi Province), but have retained Gedney's spelling of some place-name designations he cites (e.g., Sz Lok). Names of ethnic groups and languages are also as in Gedney's original paper, but the reader can consult the introduction of this volume for information about the current conventions regarding spelling.

For Siamese *klay^1* (mid level tone) 'far' and *klay^3* (falling glottalized tone) 'near', differing only in tone, forms which appear to be cognate are found in almost all languages and dialects of the Tai family, with only occasionally a sporadic instance here or there of replacement of one or the other of these two words by some completely different word.

In the case of 'far' it would be satisfactory for many of the daughter languages to regard Siamese *klay¹* as a direct reflex of something like proto-Tai **klay⁴;* that is, in much of the Tai-speaking area the forms for 'far' are perfectly compatible with a reconstructed proto-form **klay⁴*. But in the northeastern part of Vietnam and adjacent parts of Guangxi Province in China a form *kwaɯ* occurs. This has been noted by scholars in comparative Tai studies, and suggestions, as we shall see later, have been made for a reconstructed proto-form that would accommodate both the *kl-* and the *kw-* forms of this word.

In the case of 'near' the situation is more troublesome. Throughout a large part of the Tai-speaking domain, including much of Tai-speaking Guangxi, the forms of the word for 'near' show various initials which cannot be reconciled with the *kl-* of Siamese *klay³*. Rather, in this area the forms seem to resemble in their initials other words for which initial clusters have been reconstructed consisting of a fricative or aspirated stop followed by a liquid, perhaps something like **khr-, *khl-, *xr-,* or **xl-*. Although a few of these forms have been noted in the literature as variants, the extent of the problem appears not to have been recognized.

If, for this large area, we find it necessary to reconstruct a form with initial **khr-* or the like in the word for 'near', then which is older—this form or the form with initial **kl-* suggested by Siamese *klay³*? Can the *kl-* forms be the result of contamination from the word for 'far'? But what then of the *kl-* ~ *kw-* alternation in words for 'far'?

For a good many years, in the course of fieldwork and in studying older published materials, I have been troubled by the forms encountered for 'near' and 'far', and have felt that this was something that had to be looked into. The purpose of this paper is to assemble and examine available data on these two words from field notes and published sources. At the very least we may hope that such a study will afford us a clearer picture of the facts, and we may be able to formulate theories as to the prehistory of one or both words.

In the listing of forms, geographical locations or language names are given at the left and sources at the right. WG in the sources refers to my own fieldnotes.

When the transcription in a printed source does not permit certain interpretation, the original spelling is cited in quotation marks. Otherwise transcription has been normalized; that is, forms from various sources have been retranscribed according to my usual system. Symbols used are, it is hoped, self-explanatory, but note that *y* here is the high front unrounded semivowel, corresponding to the high front vowel *i*, while *ɯ* is the high back unrounded semivowel corresponding to the high back unrounded vowel, here transcribed *ɨ*.

'Near' and 'Far' in Tai   269

Tones are not marked or mentioned if in the particular language or dialect the form has the historically normal tone. The indication NT means that the source does not mark tones at all.

To give some preliminary organization to the data, we follow the three-fold classification of Tai languages of Li (1959, 1960), although we find that for neither of our two words do the main geographical divisions correspond exactly to his grouping.

'Far' in the Southwestern languages. For purposes of comparison with cognates of Siamese *klay* 'far', the forms of two other words with initial *kl-* in Siamese apparently reflecting original **kl-* are cited: *klaaŋ* 'middle' (tone A1m) and *klaa* 'rice seedling' (tone C1m). Forms of the word 'nine' (Siamese *kaaw*, tone C1m) are cited as an example where no one has ever found reason to suspect any other original initial than plain **k-*. And since we know that when we get to the Central languages we will find forms for 'far' with initial *kw-*, the word 'wide' (Siamese *kwaaŋ*, tone C1b) is cited as an example of a word which universally has initial *kw-* except in dialects that altered all *kw-* initials to *k-*.

(1)

Language or location	'far'	'middle'	'rice seedling'	'nine'	'wide'	source
Ahom	'klai'	'klang'		'kau'	'kwāng'	Barua 1920[1]
Tairong	'kai'			'kau'		Grierson 1904[2]
Khamti	'kai'	'kâng'		'kau'	'kâng'	Needham 1894[3]
Shan						
Hsi Paw	kaɯ	kaaŋ	kaa	kaw	kwaaŋ	WG[4]
Keng Tung	kaɯ	kaaŋ	kaa	kaw	kaaŋ	WG

---

[1] All NT identical forms for 'far' in Brown 1837; for 'far, middle, nine' in Grierson 1902, 1904. For Ahom 'far' Grierson 1904 has *klai*, written *kai*. The Ahom dictionary (Barua 1920) cites this word in the introductory matter but surprisingly not in the body, nor does the more recent Ahom lexicon (Barua and Phukan 1964) have it. Ahom sources cite a number of other words for 'far'. For 'wide' Barua 1920 has *kwāng*, pronounced *kāng*.

[2] The same source includes identical forms for these two words in Nora and Aitonia, also in Assam.

[3] All NT identical forms for all except 'wide' (substituting *ā* for *â*) in Brown 1837 ('far' only), Hodgson 1850 has *kaü* for 'nine', Grierson 1902, 1904. Cushing 1914 gives Khamti *kaaŋ* 'wide'.

[4] Identical forms in Cushing 1914 (unspecified location); for Moeng Nai (minus 'rice seedling' and 'nine') in Bandhumedha 1964.

Language or location	'far'	'middle'	'rice seedling'	'nine'	'wide'	source
Chinese Shan						
Chefang	kaɯ	kaaŋ	kaa	kaw	kaaŋ	WG[5]
Khün	kaɯ	kaaŋ	kaa	kaw	kwaaŋ	WG[6]
Lue	kaɯ	kaaŋ	kaa	kaw	kwaaŋ	WG[7]
Tai Nuea						
Moeng Vo	kaɯ	kaaŋ	kaa	kaw	kaaŋ	WG
Thailand						
Bangkok	klay	klaaŋ	klaa	kaaw	kwaaŋ	WG[8]
Chiengmai	kay	kaaŋ	kaa	kaw	kwaaŋ	WG[9]
Tak	kay	kaaŋ	kaa	kaaw	kwaaŋ	Sautter 1970
Nong Khai	kay	kaaŋ	kaa	kaw	kuaŋ	WG[10]
Phu Thai of Sakon Nakhon	kay	kaaŋ	kaa	kaw	kwaaŋ	WG
Lao						
Sam Nuea	kay	kaaŋ	kaa	kaw	kwaaŋ	WG[11]
White Tai	kay	kaaŋ	kaa	kaw	kwaaŋ	Điêu & Donaldson 1970[12]
Black Tai	kay	kaaŋ	kaa	kaw	kwaaŋ	Diguet 1895[13]
Red Tai	kay	kaaŋ	kaa	kaw	kwaaŋ	WG

It seems clear that no matter how thoroughly we search in the Southwestern area, we find nothing among cognates of our word for 'far' but initial *kl-* where such clusters have been preserved, as in Ahom, the Standard Thai or

---

[5] Identical forms for Moeng Khon (minus 'wide') in WG.

[6] Identical forms (minus 'middle' and 'nine') in Egerod 1959.

[7] WG's forms are identical in both Chieng Rung and Moeng Yong; identical forms for Chieng Kham in Weroha 1974.

[8] Bangkok = Siamese or Standard Thai; identical forms for Surat in WG; for Songkhla (minus 'rice seedling' and 'nine') in Chantavibulya 1956, 1959).

[9] Identical forms for Chiengmai minus 'middle', 'wide') in Suntharakun 1962; for Chiengrai in Purnell 1963.

[10] Identical forms for Udorn and Ubon in WG; for Sakon Nakhon and Nyo of Tha Uthen ('far' and 'nine' only) in WG.

[11] Identical forms for Lao (unspecified location) in Guignard 1912; for Luang Prabang in Roffe 1958; for Sam Nuea and Pak Seng in Chamberlain 1973; for Xieng Khouang (except 'wide' written *kwaŋ*) in WG.

[12] Identical forms in WG (minus 'far', see next footnote) and in Minot 1940 (minus 'far' and 'rice seedling').

[13] Identical forms in WG (minus 'far'). My White Tai informants use another word for 'far': *dak* (tone D1m). My Black Tai informants also use this other word, and Fippinger and Fippinger 1970 cites it, but Diguet cites our word, as indicated.

Siamese of Bangkok, and the Southern peninsular dialects; and initial *k-* at places where the liquid has regularly been lost in such clusters. There is not the slightest hint anywhere of positive evidence of the *kw-* initial that we find when we go on to examine forms for 'far' in languages of the Central area.

'Far' in the Central languages. Tai languages are spoken all across the extreme north of Vietnam. White Tai, Black Tai, and Red Tai at the western end of this strip have been dealt with above in the Southwestern group. Dialects midway along this strip, for example around Lào Cai and Hà Giang, belong to the Central group, as do Thổ and Nùng in the extreme East, and also Tai dialects across the border in Guangxi Province in China.

Throughout the dialects of this Central group forms for 'far' with initial *kw-* are prevalent, though not universal:

(2)
Language or location	'far'	'middle'	'rice seedling'	'nine'	'wide'	'source'
Lào Cai area						
Pa Kha	kway	caaŋ	caa	kaw	—	WG
Western Nùng	kay	caaŋ	caa	kaw	kaaŋ	WG[14]
Hà Giang area						
Claire River	kway	caaŋ	caa	kaw	kwaaŋ	Savina 1910[15]
Thổ						
That Khe, Lạng-sơn	kway	caa	caa	kaw	kwaa	WG
Po Muc, Lạng-sơn	cay	caa	—	kaw	—	WG
Lạng-sơn	kway	ca (sic)	—	kaw	—	Gordaliza 1908[16]
Cao Bằng	kway	caaŋ	caa	kaw	kwaaŋ	Diguet 1910
Nùng	kway	kyaaŋ	caa	kaw	kwaaŋ	Savina 1924
Bắc Giang, near That Khe	cay	caaŋ	caa	kaw	—	WG

---

[14]Identical forms in Western Nùng of Mường Khương and of Bản Lao.

[15]WG has identical forms in Hà Giang (minus 'wide') and Yên Bình (minus 'middle' and 'wide').

[16]Gordaliza's Thổ word for 'far' has the wrong tone, assumed to be a recording error or a misprint. Maspero (1911:167) cites the Black Tai and Thổ forms for 'far' from these same sources, but has accidentally transposed the two words.

Language or location	'far'	'middle'	'rice seedling'	'nine'	'wide'	'source'
Guangxi						
Longzhou	kway	kyaaŋ	kyaa	kaw	kwaaŋ	Li 1940[17]
Ningming	kyay	kyaaŋ	kyaa	kow	kwaaŋ	WG
Sz Lok	kyay	cf. kyɔɔŋ 'drum' (A1m)		kaw	cf. kwaa 'to pass' (B1m)	WG

Reviewing our forms for 'far' in the Central area, in both Vietnam and Guangxi, the extent of forms with initial kw- corresponds so closely to Li's tentative definition of this Central group as to provide corroborative evidence for the correctness of his classification.

Forms for 'far' with initial k- in Western Nùng, a displaced variety of Nùng far to the west of other varieties of this language, appear to present no problem, as the forms for the word 'wide' show that *kw- has been changed to k-. Older initial *kl- has become c-, as in 'middle' and 'rice seedling'. So Western Nùng kay 'far' may be assumed to agree with the other Central kway forms.

But my Thổ notes from Po Muc and my Nùng notes from Bắc Giang show an initial c-, which apparently goes back to *kl- rather than *kw-. Ningming and Sz Lok in Guangxi treat the word 'far' in the same way. Ningming and Sz Lok have a number of odd forms that agree with Northern Tai rather than with Central, and this may be another, but we know of no reason why a Thổ dialect and a Nùng dialect in northeastern Vietnam should behave in this way.

'Far' in the Northern languages. Tai languages of the Northern group are found in the provinces of Guangxi, Guizhou, and Yunnan in southern China. Bouyei material is from forty points in southern Guizhou cited in a valuable Chinese work. My Yay data come from an extension of the Northern Tai area into Vietnam in the vicinity of Lào Cai. Saek, spoken in some villages far to the south in Nakhon Phanom Province in Thailand and across the river near Thakhek in Laos, is a displaced language of this Northern Tai group.

It seems apparent that Tai languages of the Northern group agree with those of the Southwestern group in having initial kl-, or a reflex of an earlier *kl-, in the forms for 'far'. A few points in the Bouyei material (29 and 31 in particular) are troublesome, and these, together with points 34–36 and

---

[17] WG has identical forms for Piang Siang and Longming; also for Leiping except that 'rice seedling' is caa.

'Near' and 'Far' in Tai 273

perhaps others, invite a special study of all words having initials reflecting an earlier *k-, *kl-, or *kw-; however, this is beyond the scope of our present investigation.

(3)

Language or location	'far'	'middle'	'rice seedling'	'nine'	'wide'	source
Wuming	klay	klaaŋ	klaa	kaw	kwaaŋ	Li 1954, 1956
Zhuang	kyay	kyaaŋ	kyaa	kow	kwaaŋ	Guangxi 1960[18]
Yay	cay	caaŋ	caa	kuu	kwaaŋ	WG[19]
Saek	tlay	tlaaŋ	tlaa	kuu	—	WG
Bouyei						Chin. Acad. 1959a
Points 11, 38	cay	caaŋ	caa	cuu	kwaaŋ[20]	
Points 21, 25–26, 28	kay	kaaŋ	kaa	kuu	kaaŋ	
Point 31	kay	kaaŋ	khaa	kaw	kwaaŋ[21]	
Other points[22]	cay	caaŋ	caa	kuu	kwaaŋ	

Reconstruction of 'far'. Two possible theories suggest themselves to account for the occurrence of kw- forms in the Central languages but kl- forms in the Southwestern and Northern languages, with a few kl- forms occurring also in some Central dialects. One theory is that the parent language had a special initial cluster in this word of which kw- is the regular development in one area and kl- in the rest. The other theory is that the parent language itself had variation, with both *kway and *klay to be reconstructed. But this second explanation seems merely to push the problem farther back: how then did proto-Tai come to have the two forms?

The earliest attempt in the literature to deal with the problem is apparently Haudricourt (1948:217). (Wulff (1934:205) refers to the Siamese word and Maspero (1911:167) deals with forms for 'far', but neither tackles the kl- ~ kw- problem). Haudricourt reconstructs proto-Tai *kwl- for this word. Li

---

[18]Identical forms in Dioi (Esquirol and Williatte 1908), except that 'nine' is kuu. Note that the Northern words for 'wide' have tone B1m rather than C1m as in Southwestern and Central languages. The Dioi dictionary, whose transcription, though complicated, is otherwise consistent and reliable, infuriatingly fails to distinguish short â and long ââ.

[19]Identical forms in Po-ai (Li 1954, 1965), minus 'wide'.

[20]Identical forms at Points 12, 17, 18, 19, except for 'nine' (12 cew, 17 kew, 18 and 19 kuu) and 'middle' (18 kaaŋ).

[21]Identical forms at 27, 32, 33, 34, 35, except that 27 and 32 have kew 'nine', 33 has kaa 'rice seedling', 34 has khew 'nine', and 33 and 35 lack forms for 'nine'.

[22]Includes 1–10, 13–16, 20, 22–24, 39–40. We have omitted points 29, 30, 36, 37.

(1954:376) suggests that the Longzhou form goes back to *klw-. Haudricourt (1965) disregards the kw- problem and reconstructs *klay.

The reconstructions *kwl- and *klw- would seem to be identical. Since in modern Tai languages what we commonly transcribe kw- is actually a velar with simultaneous lip-rounding, either of these reconstructions would have to mean an initial k- with lip-rounding, followed by -l-.

But some object to a special reconstruction with only a single example. Happily in the course of the present investigation I have turned up another word that shows the same kl- ~ kw- alternation, but with a much more restricted geographical area for the kw- form. This is the Tai word for 'ringworm', of which the following forms have been noted, all with tone D1m.

(4) 'ringworm'
     Southwestern languages

   khaak   Khün (WG), Lue of Chieng Rung and of Moeng Yong (WG), Lue of
            Chieng Kham (Weroha 1974), Chieng Rai (Purnell 1963)
   khaa?   Chiengmai (WG)
   klaak   Bangkok,[23] Ko Samuy, Surat (all WG)
   kaak   Tak (Sautter 1970), Ubon (WG), Nong Khai (WG), Lao (Guignard
            1912), Luang Prabang (WG), Vientiane (WG), Xieng Khouang (WG),
            Sam Nuea (WG and Chamberlain 1973), Pak Seng (Chamberlain 1973),
            Red Tai (WG)
   kaa?   White Tai (Minot 1940, also Điêu and Donaldson 1970), Black Tai
            (WG, also Diguet 1895)
   'kak'   (NT) Cheminaud 1906

   Central languages

   caak   Western Nùng (WG), Claire River (Savina 1910), Nùng (Savina 1924)

   kwaak   Thô of Cao Bằng (Diguet 1910)
   kyaak   Longming (WG)

   Northern languages

   kyaak   Zhuang (Guangxi Study Committee of Zhuang 1960)
   caak   Yay (WG)
   laak   Saek (WG)

There are two anomalies in these forms for 'ringworm' which seem to be irrelevant to our kl- ~ kw- problem. One is the kh- initial in Khün, Lue, and

---

[23]Parenthetically, Wulff (1934:100) cites 'ringworm' in another connection, and gives a false Siamese form g'lāk`, which would have to be modern *khlaak.

Northern Thailand. (Shan forms for 'ringworm' have not been found either in published sources or in my own fieldnotes). This *kh-* may be due to assimilation, because in this area (and indeed in a much wider area, including Bangkok) the word commonly occurs attached to the word for 'excrement', as in Siamese *khii³ klaak²*. The other anomaly is Saek *laak*. That this is genuine is shown by the fact that I find it in my fieldnotes recorded on a number of different occasions, with different informants. No possible explanation of this Saek form has occurred to me.

The rest of the forms show *kl-*, or initials reflecting an earlier *kl-*, everywhere except in the Thổ of Cao Bằng recorded by Diguet, where the initial is *kw-*. This tempts us to reconstruct proto-Tai **kwl-* for 'ringworm', as for 'far'. But why the greatly restricted geographical area of *kw-* in 'ringworm' as compared with 'far'?

We are here reminded that other sporadic instances of initials with *-w-* are known to occur in this Cao Bằng and Hà Giang area of Vietnam, in the cognates of Siamese *-day¹* 'ladder', *saay⁵* 'late in the morning', and *lay⁵* 'to flow'. A glance at these forms shows that they do not help us much, except to show that in these languages 'far' and 'rice seedling' often agree in initial.

One modern Tai language, Wuming (Li 1956), has an initial cluster *klw-*, but as noted above, 'far' has initial *kl-* in Wuming. Most of the Wuming *klw-* words are not readily recognizable as native Tai words. One that is recognizable, *klwaaw* 'spider' (lost in Siamese), has tone A1, not A1m, in dialects that make a tonal distinction here, and has the varied initials (cf. Ping Siang *-khyaaw*, Hà Giang *saaw*, Longming *-laaw*) that characterize initial reflexes of original clusters of fricative or aspirated stop plus liquid in row 1 of the tone chart rather than the 1m or middle row where 'far' belongs.

There has not yet been a thorough investigation of proto-Tai initials involving *-w-* or lip-rounding. When such a study is undertaken, it will have to tackle the problem presented by these instances of *kw-*, *sw-*, *dw-*, *lw-*, etc., in the modern Central area. It will not be easy to account for the varied geographical distribution of the *-w-* forms.

Our study of Tai forms for 'far' not only has failed to give us firm answers to the questions we knew of when we started, but has opened up new problems. Before leaving 'far' to examine forms for 'near', we list the forms for the words we have been examining in other languages believed to be somehow more remotely related to the Tai family. Tones are disregarded because tonal correspondences have not been completely worked out, though progress has been made by Li (1965) and Oshika (1973). Retranscription has been ventured only where the facts are clear.

(5)

Language or location	'far'	'middle'	'rice seedling'	'nine'	'wide'	source
Sui of Li-Ngam	—	taa	kaa	chuu	—	Li 1965[24]
Mak	cɔy	taa	cii	cəw	—	Li 1948
Kam	kaay, lyaay	taaŋ-taa	kaa	cuu	khwaa	Chinese Academy 1959b
T'en	kee	taa	kyaa	kuu	—	Li 1968
Be	loi	—	la	ko	—	Haudricourt 1965
Hlai (Li)	lay	chang	—	pauɰ, phauɰ	beng	Savina 1931

Tai words for 'near'. The main problem with Tai words for 'near', as mentioned in the beginning, is that while in much of the Tai-speaking area forms occur which seem, like Siamese *klay³*, to reflect an original initial **kl-* cluster, on the other hand in some dialects of Lao, in White, Black, and Red Tai, and throughout the Central group of Tai languages forms are found which seem to reflect a different type of initial, perhaps something like **kh* or **x* followed by a liquid.

In the forms for 'near', in both the two large divisions just referred to, the first problem, which is really no problem at all, involves the diphthong. In Siamese the word ends in the diphthong *ay*, but in many Tai dialects outside Thailand the word has a diphthong ending with a high back unrounded semivowel, here written *ɰ*. There seems to be no reason to doubt that 'near' had a diphthong *aɰ* in the parent language (the Siamese writing system, dating from the 13th century C.E., retains a special symbol ใ in 'near' and other words that formerly in Siamese, and presently in other dialects, have the diphthong *aɰ*).

There is an area in eastern Laos extending into the Red Tai area of Vietnam where *aɰ* has changed to a monophthong, a back unrounded mid vowel here written *əə*[25]. This *əə* monophthong also replaces *ay* in the intrusive Phu Thai dialects in Northeastern Thailand and in Saek.

To show that 'near' does indeed belong to the set of *aɰ* words, we note in our lists of forms another very common *aɰ* word, 'leaf' (Siamese *bay¹*). 'Near', as stated earlier, normally has tone C1m.

---

[24] Identical forms in Sui of Rongjiang and of Pyo, except that 'rice seedling' is *dyaa* in the former, *ʔdi* in the latter.

[25] Guignard's much-cited Lao dictionary (Guignard 1912) cites 'near' and other *aɰ* words with this monophthong. Our fieldnotes confirm that Xieng Khouang, the chief source of Guignard's data, is in this *əə* area. However, Guignard states that the monophthong is found in other areas where we know for certain that the pronunciation is *ay*, indicating that he heard both *əə* and *aɰ* as *əə*.

'Near' and 'Far' in Tai   277

Since for some areas we suspect that the forms for 'near' reflect not an original initial *kl- but *kh or *x followed by a liquid, we need to compare other words believed to reflect original initial clusters of these types. Li (1954) affords us guidance here. For his proto-Tai *khl- we cite the forms for 'to imprison' (tone A1). For his proto-Tai *khr- we cite the forms for 'egg' (tone B1). For his proto-Tai *xr- we cite the forms for 'ear'. His proto-Tai *xl- is not relevant here, as its reflexes are everywhere plain initial l-.

'Near' in the Southwestern Tai languages.

(6)

Language or location	'near'	'leaf'	'to imprison'	'egg'	'ear'	source
Assam (all NT)						
Ahom	'klai'	'baü'	—	'khrai'	—	Grierson 1902[26]
	'tai'	'baü'	—	'khai', pronounced 'khrai'		Barua 1920
Tairong, Nora	'kaü'	—	—	—	'hu'	Grierson 1904
Aitonia	'kaü', 'tai'	—	—	—	'hu'	Grierson 1904
Khamti	'kaü'	'kaü'	—	'khai'	'hú'	Grierson 1904[27]
Shan	kaɯ	maɯ, waɯ	khaŋ	khay	huu	Cushing 1914
Chinese Shan						
Chefang	kaɯ	maɯ	khaŋ	khay	huu	WG[28]
Khün	kay	—	—	khay	—	Egerod 1959[29]
	—	bay	khaŋ	khay	huu	WG

---

[26]Identical forms in Hodgson 1850 (except báu 'leaf'), Grierson 1904 (cites both klai and tai for 'near').

[27]Forms identical except for the diacritic on 'ear' in Needham 1894 (hù); Grierson 1902 (hū) and Grierson 1904 (hú), the latter citing 'near' as tai. The latter form in Khamti and Ahom (above) is here assumed to be unrelated to our word. Some Ahom sources give another word for 'near' cognate with the forms cam and sam found in many other Tai languages. Cushing 1914 gives Khamti khaŋ 'to imprison'.

[28] Identical forms in Moeng Khon (WG). In Shan the usual word for 'near' is sam (tone A1m). In many dialects our word occurs either not at all or only in combination with sam.

[29]Egerod's Khün word kay 'near' has the same tone mark as the word for 'egg'; we assume a typographical error in the diacritic.

278   William J. Gedney

Language or location	'near'	'leaf'	'to imprison'	'egg'	'ear'	source
Lue						
Chieng Rung	kay	bay	khaŋ	khay	huu	WG[30]
Tai Nuea	kaɯ (cf. caɯ 'heart')	—	khaŋ	khay	huu	WG
Thailand						
Bangkok	klay	bay	khaŋ	khay	huu	WG
Surat[31]	klaay	bay	khaŋ	khay	huu	WG
Chiengmai	kay	bay	khaŋ	khay	huu	Suntharakun 1962[32]
Nong Khai	kay	bay	khaŋ	khay	huu	WG[33]
Phu Thai of Sakon Nakhon	khəə	bəə	khaŋ	khay	huu	WG
Nyo of Tha Uthen	kəə	bəə	—	—	huu	WG[34]
Lao	khəə, kay	bəə, bay	khaŋ, saŋ	khay	huu	Guignard 1912
Luang Prabng	kay	bay	—	khay	huu	Roffe 1958
Vientiane	kay	bay	khaŋ	khay	huu	WG
Sam Nuea	khəə	bəə	khaŋ	khay	huu	WG
Sam Nuea	kəə	bəə	khaŋ	khay	huu	Chamberlain 1973[35]

---

[30]Identical forms in Moeng Yong (WG) and Chieng Kham (Weroha 1974).

[31]Surat regularly lengthens *ay* to *aay* and *aw* to *aaw* in reflexes of tone *C: *khaaw* 'rice'; *thaaw* 'old'; *haay* 'weep, give'; *daay* 'to obtain'; but not in tone *A: *ay* 'to cough'; *cay* 'hear'; or tone *B: *khay* 'egg'. Lengthening changes like this are usual in Peninsular dialects, which differ, however, as to which parts of the system are affected. Such lengthened forms in the Southern Peninsula, where they are the result of regular changes, are apparently the source of irregular, sporadic lengthened forms in a few common words in modern Bangkok Thai.

[32]Identical forms for Chiengmai (minus 'imprison') in WG; for Chiengrai in Purnell 1963; for Tak in Sautter 1970; for Phras ('near' and 'leaf' only) in Simmonds 1965.

[33]Identical forms (minus 'imprison') in Ubon (WG).

[34]Identical forms (minus 'ear') for Nyo (no location given) in Simmonds 1965.

[35]Identical forms for Pak Seng (Chamberlain 1973), and (minus 'imprison') for Xieng Khouang (WG).

'Near' and 'Far' in Tai

Language or location	'near'	'leaf'	'to imprison'	'egg'	'ear'	source
White Tai	cay	bay	chaŋ	chay	huu	WG[36]
Black Tai	say	bay	saŋ	say	huu	WG[37]
Red Tai	khəə	bəə	saŋ	say	huu	WG[38]

The Lao and Red Tai form *khəə* 'near', and White Tai *cauɟ*, Black Tai *sauɟ*, bring us to one of the main topics of this investigation. Li (1954:376) cites Lao *khəə*, 'apparently a dialect form', and suggests that this came probably not from proto-Tai *kl- but from *khl-. Apparently in Lao the form *khəə*, as opposed to *kauɟ* or *kay*, is restricted to a particular area that includes Sam Nuea, i.e., that dialect of Lao closest geographically and linguistically to Red Tai. (Indeed, some Sam Nuea informants call their speech Red Tai). Guignard seems to have gotten the form *khəə* from Xieng Khoang cf. Xieng Khouang nearby. Guignard's inclusion of *saŋ* (typically a Black or Red Tai form) in addition to *khaŋ* 'to imprison', raises questions as to how typically Lao his material really is.

Lao and Red Tai *khəə*, White Tai *chauɟ*, and Black Tai *sauɟ* cannot reflect the original initial *kl- that must be assumed for all the other Southwestern languages. Rather, these forms must be examined in connection with the Central forms. Here is an instance where Li's division between Southwestern and Central breaks down.

'Near' in the Central languages. In the Central area we see another word for 'near', with initials that can have nothing to do with the *kl-* of Siamese *klay³*, in all its varied glory.

(7)

Language or location	'near'	'leaf'	'to imprison'	'egg'	'ear'	source
Lào Cai area						
Pa Kha	say	bauɟ	saŋ	khay	suu	WG
Western Nùng	chauɟ	bauɟ	chaŋ	chay	chuu	WG[39]

---

[36] Identical forms cited in Minot 1940 and Điêu and Donaldson 1970.

[37] Identical forms (minus 'near' and 'imprison') in Diguet 1895. White and Black Tai also use *cam* (tone A1m) for 'near', cognate with Shan forms referred to earlier. Diguet gives only this word for 'near', but my informants give both *cam* and *say*.

[38] Identical forms for 'near' and 'leaf' in Degeorge 1927–28.

[39] WG records identical forms in Western Nùng of both Mường Khương and of Bản Lao.

Hà-Giang area						
Hà-Giang	chaɯ, saɯ	baɯ	saŋ	khay	suu	WG[40]
Claire River	ʃaɯ	bay	ʃaŋ	khay	suu	Savina 1910
Thô						
That Khe, Lạng-sơn	saɯ	baɯ	haŋ, saŋ	khyay, say	huu, suu	WG
Po Muc	saɯ	baɯ	—	say	suu	WG[41]
Nùng	saɯ	baɯ	haaŋ, saaŋ	khyay	khyuu, suu	Savina 1924[42]
Bắc Giang	caɯ	baɯ	haŋ	hay	huu	WG
Guangxi						
Piang Siang	khyaɯ	baɯ	haŋ	khyay	huu	WG[43]
Leiping	caɯ	baɯ	haŋ	khyay	vuu	WG
Sz Lok	khaɯ	baɯ	—	lay	khɔw	WG
Longming	kyaɯ	maɯ	laŋ	lay	low	WG

Are we to put these forms for 'near' with 'to imprison', for which Li (1954) reconstructed proto-Tai *khl-? Or with 'egg', for which he reconstructed proto-Tai *khr-? Or with 'ear', for which he reconstructed proto-Tai *xr-? Study of the array of forms seems to show closer agreement with 'to imprison' than with the other two items, but there are disturbing exceptions.

A number of possible explanations suggest themselves for the failure of these data to show clear conclusions. One would be that dialect mixture has been so active as to render impossible any clear conclusions. Surely this inference should not be allowed unless all other lines of attack fail.

Another possibility is that we did not here, and Li did not in his 1954 article, include enough other words to permit firm conclusions. Indeed, Li (1954:379) tells us that he omitted scores of forms for lack of data from key dialects, presumably of the Central group in particular. Our 'near' data suggest that a special study of all these groups of words which are suspected of reflecting an original *kh or *x initial plus liquid is badly needed, drawing upon all available material and perhaps even necessitating further fieldwork to provide a finer geographical grid for the isoglosses.

There is another even more alarming possibility, that we do not yet have a firm enough picture of the entire system of proto-Tai velars (and perhaps

---

[40] Yên Bình (WG) also has *say* 'near' and *suu* 'ear'.
[41] Identical forms in Cao Bằng (Diguet 1910).
[42] Savina's Nùng dictionary has *saaŋ, haaŋ* 'enfermer' with a long vowel. Li 1954 silently corrects to *haŋ*.
[43] Identical forms (minus 'imprison') in Longzhou (Li 1940), and in Ningming (WG) with the exception of *khyow* 'ear' (cf. Sz Lok, below).

'Near' and 'Far' in Tai   281

also post-velars?), with or without -w- or liprounding, to provide a basis for studying the clustering of these velars with liquids.

It is tempting to postulate, on the basis of the material presented above, a tentative reconstruction of the proto-Tai form for 'near' of the shape *khlaɯ, on the basis of the fairly close agreement of 'near' with 'to imprison'. But Li's evidence for proto-Tai *khl is not without its weaknesses. He cites three examples: 'to imprison', 'hard' (Siamese $khɛŋ^5$), and 'kind of basket' (Siamese $khɔŋ^3$). My data for 'hard' (which I will spare the reader here) do not usually show agreement with 'to imprison'. And words for 'basket' are so numerous in all dialects of this area that they are risky to use as evidence; one often feels that he can find some sort of basket name of something like whatever phonological shape he needs at the moment. This Siamese word refers to a narrow-necked fish creel. Printed dictionaries and glossaries are usually not precise enough to insure that we are getting the term for exactly this kind of basket.

But in spite of these problems, there can be no question that in the area which includes all of the Central languages plus White, Black, and Red Tai, and including parts of Laos, the word for 'near' reflects some sort of aspirated or fricative initial in cluster with a liquid, and certainly not the *kl- required by the other Southwestern languages.

'Near' in the Northern languages.

(8)
Language or location	'near'	'leaf'	'to imprison'	'egg' (tone A2)	'ear'	source
Wuming	klaɯ	ʔbaɯ	klaŋ	ray	rɨɨ	Li 1956
Zhuang	kyaɯ	baɯ	kyaŋ, haŋ	kyay	rɨɨ	Guangxi 1960
Dioi	kyaɯ	baɯ	kyaŋ	kyay	ɬɨa	Esquirol 1908
Po-ai	caɯ	maɯ	—	cay	ɬɨɨ	Li 1954, 1965
Yay	caɯ	baɯ	caŋ	cay	rɨa	WG
Saek	tləə	bəə	thraŋ	—	rua	WG
Bouyei						Chinese Academy 1959
1–2, 4, 19	caɯ	baɯ	caŋ	cay	rɨa	
3, 14	cay	bay	caŋ	cay	rɨɨ[44]	
31, 34	khaa	baa	kaŋ	kay	yii	
36	khɨɨ	bɨɨ	caŋ	kii	—	

---

[44]Editor's note: Here we omit that large portion of the Bouyei data cited which reconfirms the agreement in initial among 'near', 'imprison', and 'egg', usually as *c* but occasionally as *k* (points 21, 26–28). The varieties also vary in their reflexes of the rhymes; *aɯ* and *ay* in 'near' and 'leaf', and mostly *ɨa* and *ɨɨ* in 'ear'.

Study of these Northern forms suggests a startling conclusion. They can be reconciled with the initial *kl- required by the majority of Southwestern languages, except for Bouyei points 30–36, where both initials and vowels are aberrant. Li 1954 did indeed list Northern forms for 'near' under proto-Tai *kl-.

But a comparison with 'to imprison' and 'egg' (not 'ear', where our material confirms Li's decision to put 'ear' in another list) shows that 'near' agrees also very closely with forms for these two words. Only the Saek form 'to imprison' and the Wuming form 'egg' are really troublesome.

Coalescence of such proto-Tai pairs as *khl- and *kl- in the Northern languages would not be surprising, since the contrast between plain *kh- and *k- is lost in this branch of Tai. Tonal criteria do not help us because no Northern language is known which distinguishes 1 tones from 1m tones.

I suspect that further study of other words that behave like Saek *thraŋ* 'to imprison' will force us to reconstruct an aspirated initial cluster for this group, but an unaspirated *kl- for 'near' in the Northern group of languages; but it must be admitted that the data presented in the present study are inconclusive.

As in the case of 'far', we should not leave 'near' without glancing at forms in languages believed to be more remotely related:

(9)

Language or location	'near'	'leaf'	'to imprison'	'egg'	'ear'	source
Sui of Li-Ngam	phyay	waa	—	kay	qhaa	Li 1965[45]
Mak	phyay	vaa	caŋ	cay	chaa	Li 1948
Kam	—	paa	—	kəy	khaa	Chinese Academy 1959b
T'en	taaw	waa	—	kay	khaa	Li 1968
Be	lê	—	—		sa	Haudricourt 1965
Hlai (Li)	lauɯ, plauɯ	bəuɯ	—	—	thai, yai	Savina 1931

These non-Tai forms do not help much, especially in view of the paucity of data for 'to imprison'. But the forms for 'near' at least suggest that it is more likely that at some pre-Tai period the initial of 'near' was more probably a complex cluster like *khl- than the simpler *kl-.

---

[45]Identical forms in Sui of Rongjiang and of Pyo, except that 'leaf' is *vaa* in the latter.

'Near' and 'Far' in Tai   283

Conclusions. We have seen that investigation of these two words by the methods used here raises many questions requiring further research. But some inferences seem clear.

'Far' must go back to *klay in the Southwestern branch and the Northern branch, but to *kway in virtually all the languages of the Central branch; if we are to reconstruct a proto-form to accommodate both, it has to be something like *kwlay.

'Near' in most of the Southwestern area reflects an earlier *klauɟ, but in eastern parts of this area and all the Central area the forms reflect something like *khlauɟ. Northern forms could go back to either original.

In any case, Siamese[46] $klay^{33}$ 'far' and $klay^{41}$ 'near' show an identity of all phonological features except tone which surely cannot be original. One is tempted to infer that contamination has taken place, that an earlier different form for 'near' was altered at some time as a result of frequent use in the phrase with 'far', just as Indo-Europeanists tell us that some of the low number words in Germanic and Italic have contaminated each other.

Other such instances of initial contamination are not unknown in Tai languages. Li (1971) has shown that Siamese $yaay^{33}$ 'maternal grandmother' probably owes its modern initial to frequent use with yaa^{41} 'paternal grandmother'.

'Right (hand)' (Siamese $khwaa^{24}$) and 'left (hand)' (Siamese $saay^{55}$) have the same initial in some Central dialects in Guangxi, including Li's Longzhou material, and also some Central dialects in northern Vietnam. Contamination appears to have brought this about, as if the frequent Siamese phrase $saay^{55}$ $khwaa^{24}$ 'left and right' were to come to be pronounced $saay^{55}$ saa^{24}.

Some of the problems with individual forms of our two words in other parts of the Tai area may also be explained by contamination, but too many unknowns still beset the total picture of the history of 'near' and 'far' in Tai to allow us to do much guessing as to which form contaminated the other at what points and when.

If the other form for 'near', the one reflected in White Tai *chay* and elsewhere, once existed in Siamese, and if it had been preserved, it would have the form in modern Siamese $*khay^{42}$ (not $*khray^{42}$ as erroneously in Gedney 1964:42), homonymous with $khay^{42}$ 'fever'. There is another common Tai word meaning 'swollen' that Siamese has lost which would also have the form $*khay^{42}$ (tone B2) in Siamese. It seems likely that this word for 'swollen' went out of use because of the homonymy with the word for 'fever'; one can imagine constant problems of ambiguity in speaking of invalids that would have led to replacement of the inherited word for

---

[46]Editor's note: In this final section we use the Chao 5-step pitch scale to write the Siamese tones to help clarify the points being made about modern tone categories.

'swollen' to avoid confusion with the word for 'fever'. But it is difficult to see how these factors would have affected the word for 'near'. In any case no such homonymy would have come about in other languages such as Shan where the *auɰ* diphthong has not changed to *ay;* yet Shan has *kauɰ* 'near' from earlier **klay*, rather than the form with aspirated initial.

Editors' afterword

Since the present paper was written, several works have appeared which touch on the problems that Professor Gedney discusses here. Although these subsequent publications do not deal directly or primarily with the problems of 'near' and 'far', we feel it worthwhile to call readers' attention to them.

First and most important is Li's *Handbook of Comparative Tai* (1977). Previously, in the article cited by Gedney (Li 1954), Li listed both 'far' and 'near' under proto-Tai **kl-*, but with notes suggesting that Longzhou *kwai* 'far' 'comes probably from proto-Tai *klw-'*, and that Longzhou *khjai*[47] and Lao *khəə* 'near' are from proto-Tai **khl-*. The same article also proposes a separate proto-Tai **kr* and **khl*, but cites only three examples of each.

In (Li 1977), **kr* and **khl* have grown to include six and ten examples respectively. Li has also modified his analysis of both 'far' and 'near'. 'Far' remains under **kl-*, but the reconstruction with -w- medial is now rejected:

> the CT dialects show rounding after the velar, not apparent in other dialects. This rounding occurs with other initials also so that the reconstruction of a labiovelar in this type of correspondence cannot be systematically carried out. (Li 1977:222)

Li does not give examples of "this rounding ... with other initials," but we can infer that he had in mind examples like those cited by Gedney in the present paper as occurring in the Cao Bằng/Hà Giang area. We here cite some of Li 1977's examples, followed by the Siamese cognate to illustrate the more widespread nonrounded form:

---

[47]We convert this and the following Lao form into the transcription Li (1977) uses. The 1954 article has Longzhou 'near' as *khjâə* in the chart (376); the subsequent note mentions 'Longzhou ... *khja'* which must be a misprint.

(10) Language or
location   'ladder'   'late morning'   'flow'

Tày   duei   thoai, xoai   lôêi
Thổ   duei   swaai   luei
Tianbao   —   tooi   lai
Po-ai   —   —   lwai
Siamese   daai   saai   lai

Note that the presence of rounding extends into Northern Tai for 'flow', as shown by the Po-ai cognate. When Li rules out reconstructing a labiovelar for sets like these, he is contrasting them with other sets (including 'wide'), which have more extensive evidence of lip rounding in all three branches, and for which he does reconstruct a full range of labiovelars (Li 1977:236–42).

'Near' in Li 1977 has been taken out of *kl and listed under *kr, which has also acquired two other etyma ('sieve' and 'to snore'), giving it a total of six examples. Now Li states that the Southwestern dialects, except for Lao and White Tai, and the Northern Tai forms "all indicat[e] *kl-." Lao, White Tai, and all the Central forms "indicat[e] *khr- < *kr-," with the aspiration attributed to the influence of *-r-, a development well attested for proto-Tai *r in other environments, both medial and initial. The 1954 paper's suggestion of *khl for the Lao, White Tai, and Central Tai forms has been changed, probably because the ten examples of *khl cited in Li 1977 are consistent in showing aspiration throughout the Southwestern languages, not just in Lao and White Tai.

Li states (1977:225) that *kr examples are 'rare', that there is "some confusion between kl- and kr-" (for example, Siamese has kl- in three etyma and kr- in three), and that this *kr section includes "some doubtful examples" that "are listed ... for future investigation." It may not be too wide of the mark to see the difference between 1954 and 1977 as reflecting a decision on Li's part to retain the irregularity of his *kr and to use it as a parking place for a few other irregular velar-liquid sets.

Note that in both cases Li has not so much solved the problems as taken note of them and indicated to what portions of his reconstructed proto-Tai system they are relevant. The differences between Li's and Gedney's handling of these two problems are no doubt in part differences in style, but they surely also reflect the different purposes of Li's compendium covering the entire reconstructed system, contrasted with Gedney's detailed exploration of one pair of etyma together with that portion of the proto-phonological system occupied by velar-liquid clusters.

As for the non-Tai Kadai languages, considerable progress has been made in both available data and in reconstruction. For Kam-Sui, we can add the following forms from Mulam (Wang and Zheng 1980), Maonan (Liang 1980), and Sui (Zhang 1980): Mulam ce^1, Maonan ci^1, Sui $?di^1$ 'far'; and Mulam $phyəi^5$, Maonan $phjai^5$ 'near'. Thurgood (1988) reconstructs proto-Kam-Sui 'far' *$kla:i^4$ (irregular vowel), agreeing with 'rice seedling', and 'near' as *$phlai^5$, agreeing with 'blood' and 'ashes'.

For Hlai we add the following sampling of forms, all from Ouyang and Zheng 1983:

(11)   Baoding   Heitu   Tongshi   Qiandui

'far' lai^1 lai^1 lai^1 lai^4
'near' $plau^3$ leu^3 $plau^3$ pau^3

For these Matisoff (1988) reconstructs initials and tones: 'far' *l with tone 1; and 'near' *pl with tone 3. In connection with the latter it may be relevant to point out that proto-Hlai lacks both *p and *phl, and has no velar-liquid clusters.

References

Bandhumedha, Banchob. 1964. Characteristics of the Shan language compared with the Thai language of Bangkok. Social Science Review, special number (14 December 1964):146–84. (in Thai)

Barua, B. and N. N. Deodhai Phukan. 1964. Ahom lexicons (based on original Tai manuscripts). Gauhati: Dept. of Historical and Antiquarian Studies in Assam.

Barua, Golap Chandra. 1920. Ahom-Assamese-English dictionary. Calcutta: Printed at the Baptist Mission Press.

Brown, N. 1837. Alphabets of the Tai language. Journal of the Asiatic Society of Bengal 6:17–21.

Chamberlain, James R. 1973. A comparative wordlist of the Sam Nuea and Pal Seng dialects of Northern Laos. ms.

Chantavibulya, Vichin. 1956. The differences between the language of Bangkok and the language of Songkhla. (in Thai) M.A. thesis. Chulalongkorn University.

———. 1959. The phonology of the syllable in Songkhla, a Southern Thai dialect. M.A. thesis. University of London.

Cheminaud, Guy. 1906. Nouveau dictionnaire français-laotien. Tulle: Crauffon.

Chinese Academy of Sciences. 1959a. Report on the investigation of the Bouyei language. Beijing: Kexue Chubanshe.

———. 1959b. Concise Kam-Chinese dictionary (preliminary draft). Guiyang: Guizhou Minzu Chubanshe.
Cushing, Josiah Nelson 1914. A Shan and English dictionary. 2nd ed. Rangoon: American Baptist Mission Press.
DeGeorge, J.-B. 1927-28. Proverbes, maximes et sentences tays. Anthropos 22:911-32 and 23:596-616.
Điêu Chính Nhìm and Jean Donaldson. 1970. Păp san khăm pák Tãy-Keo-Eng: [Ngữ-vựng Thái-Việt-Anh] [Tai-Vietnamese-English vocabulary]. Saigon: Dept. of Education.
Diguet, Édouard. 1895. Étude de la langue taï; Précédée d'une notice sur les races des hautes régions du Tonkin. Hanoi: F. H. Schneider.
———. 1910. Étude de la langue thô. Paris: Augustin Challamel.
Edmondson, Jerold A., and David B. Solnit, eds. 1988. Comparative Kadai: Linguistic studies beyond Tai. Summer Institute of Linguistics and the University of Texas at Arlington Publications in Linguistics 86. Dallas.
Egerod, Søren. 1959. Essentials of Khün phonology and script. Acta Orientalia 24:123-46.
Esquirol, Joseph and Gustave Williate. 1908. Essai de dictionnaire dioi-français reproduisant la langue parlée par les tribus Thai de la haute Rivière de l'Ouest suivi d'un vocabulaire français-dioi. Hong Kong: Imprimerie de la Société des Missions Etrangères.
Fippinger, Jay and Dorothy Fippinger. 1970. Black Tai phonemes, with reference to White Tai. Anthropological Linguistics 12(3):83-97.
Gedney, William J. 1964. A comparative sketch of White, Black and Red Tai. The Social Science Review 1:1-47.
Gordaliza, T. 1908. Estudio sobre el dialecto Thô de la región de Lang-Sön. Anthropos 3:512-32.
Grierson, G. A. 1902. Notes on Ahom. Zeitschrift der Deutschen Morgenländischen Gesellschaft 56:1-59.
———. 1904. Linguistic survey of India II. Mon-Khmer and Siamese-Chinese families (including Khassi and Tai). Calcutta: Office of the Superintendent of Government Printing.
Guangxi Study Committee of Zhuang. 1960. Zhuang-Chinese lexicon. rev. ed. (in Chinese). Nanning: Guangxi Minzu Chubanshe.
Guangxi. 1960. See Guangxi Study Committee of Zhuang.
Guignard, Théodore. 1912. Dictionnaire laotien-français. Hong Kong: Imprimerie de Nazareth.
Haudricourt, André-Georges. 1948. Les phonèmes et le vocabulaire du thai commun. Journal Asiatique 236:197-238.
———, ed. 1965. Le vocabulaire bê de F. M. Savina. Paris: Bulletin de l'École Française d'Extrême-Orient 57.

Hodgson, B. E. 1850. Aborigines of the north and east frontier. Journal of the Asiatic Society of Bengal 19:309–16.

Li Fang-Kuei. 1940. The Tai dialect of Lungchow: Texts, translation, and glossary. Institute of History and Philology Monograph Series A 16. Taipei: Academia Sinica

———. 1948. Notes on the Mak language. (in Chinese) Bulletin of the Institute of History and Philology 19:1–80.

———. 1954. Consonant clusters in Tai. Language 30:368–79.

———. 1956. The Tai dialect of Wuming (Texts, translations, and glossary). Bulletin of the Institute of History and Philology Monograph Series A 19. Shanghai: Academia Sinica.

———. 1959. Classification by vocabulary: Tai dialects. Anthropological Linguistics 1–2:15–21.

———. 1960. A tentative classification of Tai dialects. In S. Diamond (ed.), Culture in history: Essays in honor of Paul Radin, 951–59. New York: Published for Brandeis University by Columbia University.

———. 1965. The Tai and the Kam-Sui languages. Lingua 14. Reprinted in G. B. Milner and Eugénie J. A. Henderson (eds.), Indo-Pacific linguistic studies. Part I Historical linguistics, 148–79. Amsterdam: North Holland Publishing Co.

———. 1968. Notes on the T'en (Yanghwang) language. Part 3: Glossary. Bulletin of the Institute of History and Philology 40:397–504.

———. 1971. On Siamese *jaai*. Bulletin of the Institute of History and Philology 42:337–39. Taipei: Academia Sinica.

———. 1977. A handbook of comparative Tai. Oceanic Linguistics Special Publication 15. Honolulu: University Press of Hawaii.

Liang Min. 1980. Outline of Maonan. (in Chinese) Beijing: Minzu Chubanshe.

Maspero, Henri. 1911. Contribution à l'étude du système phonétique des langues thai. Bulletin de l'École Français d'Extrême-Orient 11:153–69.

Matisoff, James A. 1988. Proto-Hlai initials and tones: A first approximation. In Edmondson and Solnit, eds. 289–321.

Minot, Georges. 1940. Dictionnaire tày blanc-français avec transcription latine. Bulletin de l'École Français d'Extrême-Orient 40:1–237.

Needham, Jack F. 1894. Outline grammar of the Tai (Khâmtî) language as spoken by the Khâmtîs residing in the neighbourhood of Sodiya. Rangoon: Superintendent Government Printing.

Oshika, Beatrice Reyes Teodoro. 1973. The relationship of Kam-Sui-Mak to Tai. Ph.D. dissertation. University of Michigan.

Ouyang Jueya and Zheng Yiqing. 1983. Liuy diaocha yanjiu [Research and survey of the Hlai language]. Beijing: Zhongguo Shehui Kexue Chubanshe.

Purnell, Herbert C. 1963. A short Northern Thai-English dictionary (Tai Yuan). Chiengmai: Overseas Missionary Fellowship.
Roffe, G. Edward, and Thelma W. Roffe. 1958. Spoken Lao, book two. Washington: American Council of Learned Societies.
Sautter, Mary. 1970. A Tai dialect: Tak. ms.
Savina, F. M. 1910. Dictionnaire tày-annamite-français précede d'un precis de grammaire tay et suivi d'un vocabulaire français-tay. Hanoi: Imprimerie d'Extrême-Orient.
———. 1924. Dictionnaire étymologique français-nùng-chinois. Hong Kong: Imprimèrie de la Société des Missions Etrangères.
———. 1931. Lexique ɗay-français accompagné d'un petit lexique français-ɗay et d'un tableau des différences dialectales. Bulletin de l'École Français d'Extrême-Orient 31:103–99.
Simmonds, Edward H. S. 1965. Essays in honor of E. H. S. Simmonds.
Suntharakun, Benchawan. 1962. The phonemes of the Chiengmai language. (in Thai) M.A. thesis. Chulalongkorn University.
Thurgood, Graham. 1988. Notes on the reconstruction of proto-Kam-Sui. In Edmondson and Solnit (eds.). 1988:179–218.
Wang Jun and Zheng Guoqiao. 1980. Mulaoyu jianzhi [Sketch of the Mulam language]. Beijing: Minorities Publishing House.
Weroha, Seree. 1974. Tai Lue-English dictionary. ms.
Wulff, Kurt. 1934. Chinesisch und Tai: Sprachvergleichende Untersuchungen. (Danske Videnskabernes Selskab. Historisk-Filiologiske meddelelser 20:3). Copenhagen: Levin and Munksgaard.
Zhang Junru. 1980. Outline of Sui. (in Chinese) Beijing: Minzu Chubanshe.

Tai-Kadai Arthropods:
A Preliminary Biolinguistic Investigation

James R. Chamberlain
Chulalongkorn University

> The wanderer hears the tiny sound
> And weeps. The wife left desolate
> Feels more than string or stirring flute
> The cricket chirping of her mate.
> Tu Fu

Introduction. The purpose of this study is to provide a foundation for additional research into the relationship between Tai-Kadai speakers and that phylum of organisms known as Arthropoda. It is an inquiry the scope of which is not limited exclusively to comparative and historical linguistics (although it does aim at reconstruction, not only of linguistic forms but also of biogeographical prehistory of the families involved) and which seeks to include and explicate the higher order structures suggested by so-called cognitive anthropology as they relate to the zoological and vegetal environment in both synchronic and diachronic dimensions. In addition, to some

---

Editors' note: A few definitions of terms may be useful. (1) *taxon* (plural *taxa*): morpheme designating a living thing or a class thereof. (2) *paronyms:* words descended from a common root. (3) PHT (proto-Hlai-Tai): the parent language of Tai-Saek-Be, Kam-Sui-Lakkia, and Hlai. See appendix 2 for a list of abbreviations.

extent this approach is premised on a perceived need for the inclusion of language in providing explicit definitions of the relationship between humans and environment which have so far eluded anthropologists and biologists alike. By comparison with other faunistic groups, we seem to know least about arthropods in Tai languages, in spite of their ubiquity, their obvious biologic importance, and the existence of large lexical inventories in the various languages. It is hoped that this paper will at least serve as an introduction and perhaps even as a stimulus to further investigation and analysis.

Biogeographically speaking, the modern Tai-Kadai languages are found within the Oriental (Zoogeographic) Region which was originally delineated by nineteenth century naturalist Alfred Russel Wallace.[1] It extends to India and Pakistan in the west, and is bounded to the southeast by the Wallace Line (so named by T. H. Huxley who modified the line to exclude most of the Philippines except Palawan); that is, it includes Java, Bali, and Borneo, but not the Celebes, the Lesser Sundas, and Timor. These latter, together with the Philippines, comprise the domain of 'Wallacea', those islands which fall between the Sunda and Sahul continental shelves and whose fauna derives from both the Oriental and Australasian regions (Udvardy 1969). The northern boundary of the Oriental Region with the Palearctic is not quite so easily defined. MacKinnon (1974) suggests that it runs from the Hindu Kush mountains, and includes Yunnan and Sichuan, to Formosa. For the area which concerns most of the Tai-Kadai languages the Yangtze river may suffice as the northern frontier.

The floral regions, at least those mapped by Good (1964), do not completely match the zoogeographic ones, and thus the Sino-Japanese region dips south of the Tropic of Cancer into northern Laos and Vietnam before cutting northeast to Japan. The Ryukyus, Formosa, and Hainan, however, all belong to the region of continental Southeast Asia. To the south, the Malaysian region encompasses the Philippines, New Guinea, and most of Indonesia and Malaysia.

Oriental faunistic mapping further distinguishes three sub-regions: the Indian, with links to the Ethiopian region of Africa; the Indochinese, with links to the Palearctic; and the Indo-Malayan (also Malayo-Indonesian) which has evolved its indigenous fauna in a rain forest habitat that has remained relatively stable since the Pliocene (MacKinnon 1974; Gressitt 1970; Udvardy 1969). The Indochinese sub-region includes Assam, Burma, Southern

---

[1]The term Tai-Kadai is used here to include the four ethnolinguistic families of Be-Tai, Kam-Sui-Lakkia, Hlai, and Kadai. While the relationship of the first three families to each other is fairly obvious, if problematical, the interrelationships of languages in the fourth grouping such as Lachi, Laqua, and Gelao, remains unclear.

China, Laos, Northern Thailand, Vietnam, the Ryukyu Islands, Taiwan, and Hainan (Gressitt 1970); that is, virtually all of the extant Tai-Kadai languages fall into this sub-region with the exception of those dialects found in southern Thailand, which is included with the Indo-Malayan area.

From previous studies carried out by the author on mammals, reptiles, and amphibians it was found that within the Indochinese sub-region at least two major criteria further constrain faunal composition, coastal versus interior distribution, and north or south distribution relative to the Tropic of Cancer. For example, there are a paucity of squirrel species and genera found along the coast, compared to a great diversity further inland, whereas the highly conspicuous saltwater crocodile and the large sea turtles are [were] confined to the coastal areas. The Varanidae (monitor lizards) and many mammalian forms are found only to the south of the Tropic. In cases such as these, the linguistic forms used by the various ethnolinguistic groups to refer to these organisms, when viewed in a comparative frame, become good indicators of historical movements and length of habitation.

The Arthropoda have been divided into ten classes, but only five of these are relevant to the present study: Crustacea, Chilopoda (centipedes), Diplopoda (millipedes), Arachnida (spiders, scorpions), and Insecta. The majority of lexical items in Tai-Kadai languages which refer to arthropods predictably relate to the class of insects, and this class represents a considerable number of forms in the vocabulary of most speakers. In spite of the fact that the insect fauna of the Oriental and Palearctic regions vary considerably—the ties between Palearctic and Nearctic or Nearctic and Neotropical being much stronger—insects are older and radiated much earlier than vertebrates (Udvardy 1969:272). All twenty-nine orders of insects are represented in the major zoogeographical regions of the world, and thus recognition of morphological characters that differentiate the various types is often restricted to the higher taxonomic categories of order and family. That is, generic and specific differences may be known to biologists working with a microscope, but are otherwise invisible to a nonscientist. This situation contrasts sharply with that of the vertebrates where significant differences at lower taxonomic levels are more easily discernible.

Arthropod biolinguistics. The type of study undertaken here has been referred to elsewhere (Chamberlain 1992) as biolinguistic. Equal weight is accorded to semantic reconstruction (in addition to phonological reconstruction) and that evidence may be used in reconstructing both the earlier common biolinguistic system and the biogeographical prehistory of Tai-Kadai groups as it relates to the history and prehistory of Southeast Asia (here taken to include that portion of China south of the Yangtze). The present paper is confined to the Arthropoda. It attempts to delineate the broad patterns suggested by the data available to the author at the time of writing, while at the same time highlighting gaps in the linguistic record for this lexical domain. The data are presented in appendix 1 in the form of 99 cognate sets, or potential cognate sets, at various levels of time-depth, for example Proto-Tai-Kadai, Proto-Hlai-Tai, Proto-Hlai, Proto-Kam-Sui, Proto-Kam-Tai, Proto-Bê-Tai, and Proto-Southwestern Tai.

Given the relatively similar habitats of the Tai-Kadai languages within a single zoogeographical subregion, from the perspective of comparative and historical linguistics, we should expect a correspondingly large number of faunal lexicon with cognates among the various languages. In support of this supposition, in 1977, working only with photographs, the author recorded over 800 animal names from a Black Tai informant who considered himself to be a town dweller, and almost comparable large corpora were gathered from Tai Vat, Western Nùng, and Yay informants as well. It is perhaps a comment on the state of the art in Tai-Kadai field studies that such disproportionately low numbers of zoological terms appear in the sources on these languages available to date. Example (1) below shows numbers of animal names occurring in comparative reconstructions, and therefore reflects only forms for which cognates are known, but even these are indicative of an overall imbalance when compared to the Black Tai.

(1) Numbers and percentages of animal names in comparative reconstructions

Source and Corpus	#/% Zool.	#/% Arthrop.	Arthrop. = %Zool.
Li (1977) [TAI] 1,320	66/5.0%	21/1.59%	31.82%
Thurgood (1988) [KS] 361	34/9.42%	10/2.77%	29.41%
Thurgood (1991) [HL] 740	53/7.16%	21/2.84%	39.62%

Part of this discrepancy is due no doubt to the Nearctic (North American) and Palearctic (European and Chinese) biases of linguists who have worked on Tai-Kadai languages. This would likewise account for the proportionately higher numbers of arthropods whose representatives in all zones share common morphological characteristics. Distinctions between such categories as spider, scorpion, centipede, millipede, beetle, bug, grub, butterfly, caterpillar, grasshopper, cricket, cicada, flea, louse, tick, fly, mosquito, ant, bee, wasp, and hornet are generally recognized by both linguist and informant. But identifying features of the hog badger, tree shrew, bamboo rat, gibbon, macaque, langur, slow loris, palm civet, binturong, serow, goral, gaur, kating, barking deer, monitor, agamid, hornbill, hoopoe, trogon, and coucal are less well known; lexemes for these organisms appear with less frequency in recorded material even though they may occur regularly in the daily life of the native speaker. Furthermore, one suspects that if a similar chart were prepared for the botanical side of the biota as reflected in extant Tai-Kadai lexicons, the ratios would be even worse.

It must be remembered, however, that the biological organism as represented in human language has little to do with the organism itself. The role played by the representation of the organism in human thought determines its classificatory status which may or may not agree with scientific biological classification. This does not mean that scientifically naive speakers are not capable of recognizing morphological similarities and differences in animals and plants, but it means that in natural language other factors take precedence. In some Tai languages soft shell turtles are classified as fish, apparently to render them edible; pythons are usually not classed as snakes; and domestic chickens and ducks are not called birds as are their wild counterparts. As Charles Pyle (1991) has pointed out, a dove may be a symbol of peace only to a human, not to the dove.

Folk biological taxonomists have developed a nomenclature which is convenient in spite of an underlying overreliance on physical features and the ignoring of much linguistic evidence (cf. Berlin et al 1973, Brown 1984, Chamberlain 1992). At the highest end of the taxonomic hierarchy the term UNIQUE BEGINNER (UB) is used for taxa equivalent to a biological kingdom. Following this, terms which are used to refer to larger taxonomic classes (such as bird, fish, snake) are designated as LIFE FORM (LF). Languages may lack some or all of these levels. However, it is a universal that all languages possess GENERIC (G) level taxa, primary lexemes such as *stork, robin,* or *magpie* in English. Such taxa as these may be broken down further by adding SPECIFIC (S) and even VARIETAL (V) taxa, secondary lexemes roughly equivalent to species and subspecies in biological parlance, for example, *adjutant stork,* and *greater adjutant stork* or *lesser adjutant stork.*

In the Tai system, Unique Beginnner is represented by paronyms of PT *$tua \sim dua^4$*. Organisms for which Life Forms exist, that is, bird, fish, snake, arthropod, mollusk, are referred to by expressions of the type: (UB) + LF + G + (S); for example in Lao, /(too^{A2}) nok^{DS4} pet^{DS2}/ 'wild duck, grebe.' For organisms without LF markers, for example, domestic animals, auspicistic birds, mammals, some other arthropods, amphibians, and turtles, UB + G + (S) is the preferred structure, as in Black Tai /too^{A2} paat^{DL2} sa-laŋ^{A1} khew^{A1}/ 'green-backed Rhacophorus frog'.

With reference to Arthropods, we shall see that there is a distinction between those organisms whose designation contains the LF marker, PT *$mleŋ^4$*, and those without. The extent to which this same type of system may operate in Kam-Sui, Hlai, and Kadai is impossible to determine from the available published sources because the complete expressions are usually not provided. Judging from Li's T'en material, the term /nuei/ 'insect' is used in this way, and in Savina's Day (Hlai) /mêi/ or /vàng/ might function in a similar manner, as in the minimal pair, /cử lống mêi d[r]ờp/ 'spider,' and /cử lống dờp/ 'centipede'. But /mêi/ 'mother' is used with other animals as well, for example 'bat'. The use of 'mother' in animal names is also common in Western Nùng. In both T'en and Hlai, the LF markers for bird, fish, and snake are used as in the Tai system described above, leading one to the conclusion that the Arthropod Life-Form would behave in the same way as well. When more data on usage becomes available, it will be interesting to compare the major families to see if LFs occur with the same organisms in each family.

Tai-Kadai Arthropods As rich in arthropod life as the Oriental Region may be, these creatures appear to have had relatively insignificant effects on the ritual life of Tai-Kadai inhabitants. Eberhard (1968:187) makes mention of *Ch'iung-ch'an,* the cicada god, and associates this animal with the south of China, but neither details nor contexts are provided. More attention is devoted by this author to *ku* magic, a southern practice, wherein the 'five poisonous animals', the frog, the snake, the centipede (enemy of the snake), the scorpion, and the gecko (enemy of the scorpion) are placed in a pot to fight each other, the victorious animal becoming the most powerful for *ku* magic during the coming year. In some texts, according to Eberhard (p. 159), the spider may replace the scorpion. I have speculated elsewhere (1977) that Eberhard's 'frog' is really a toad, and that the snake in question is a krait (*Bungarus*). All of these five animals tend to have disyllabic taxa in Tai languages.

Ku was originally a form of love magic prepared by southern women, and was fatal to men who did not return to the woman at the 'specified time'. The centipede, as well as being used in the preparation, also served as protection from the poison. The souls of persons killed by *ku* would serve its owner as slaves; they partially resembled humans in form and were referred to as 'gold silkworms'. These souls could not function as ancestral spirits unless the owner was killed, which might involve burying her (usually a woman) up to the neck, covering the head with wax, and burning it. By some definitions, the meaning of *ku* was in fact 'the soul of a dead person whose head had been spitted on a pole'. In other areas it simply meant 'snake'. The primary geographical distribution of *ku* was south of the Yangtze in Guizhou, Guangxi, Guangdong, Yunnan, and Hunan. Eberhard writes:

> The first well-described *ku* magic of political importance took place in the year 134 B.C., and here magicians from Yüeh played the principal role. Intimations of sexual irregularities are made in the texts. The *ku* magic itself seems to have consisted, at least in part, of

magic human figures buried under the road which the emperor, the intended victim, was supposed to take. At that time Yüeh most probably meant people from Kuangtung. In *Randvölker* it was shown that the *ku* magic occurred rarely among the Yao and Miao in the strict sense of these terms, but frequently among the Chuang and Li, and not infrequently among the Liao. It was decided to consider the *ku* magic as typical for the Chuang. (1969:152)

The magic preparation was carried out on the fifth day of the fifth month, a time also associated with that other denizen of darkness, the owl, whose name [(K403) MC *$g'i̯au$- (qu tone = Tai B tone)] means 'the spitted one' (Eberhard 1969:160). This is certainly close to the PT reconstructed form /*gaw^C/ (Southwest, Central) or /*taw^A/ (Northern) (cf. Li 1977) (note that the tone category is already irregular in Tai). Unfortunately, I do not know the etymology of *ku*, but a variant may be preserved in the Southwest forms for 'millipede' (Diplopoda, 13), or in 'spider' (6, 7). A Chinese form for 'centipede', which in folklore is the well-known enemy of the snake and antidote for *ku*, (K1284) MC *$nguo$ (A) < *ngu, is a good contact form for PT *$ɲïa/ɲu^A$ 'snake', a semantic displacement that may explain why this word is not found in Kam-Sui, Hlai, and Kadai.

This sort of semantic confusion may also underlie Eberhard's statement (p. 365) that drum skins may be made from the skin of large 'centipedes', and that the flesh is edible. (His sources here are a seventeenth century citing of a Tang work, and one from the tenth century. Eberhard himself was somewhat predisposed to a lack of precision when referring to animals, as are Chinese sources generally when discussing the south.) I have never heard of centipedes being eaten per se, but among the various Tai groups they are frequently preserved in local alcohol and taken to increase one's vitality and sexual prowess.

Schafer (1967:210) cites a Tang source of A.D. 745 which speaks of an enormous "centipede" that "washed ashore" in Canton and provided 120 catties (180 lbs) of meat, leading us to believe that some other organism was originally the referent of the Chinese taxon. (Indeed, both mentionings, by Eberhard and Schafer, of gigantic 'centipedes' would be more suitable to pythons, the skins of which are used for drumheads and the flesh of which is edible.)

Schafer (pp. 111, 210) likewise finds the Tang sources generally deficient in arthropod lore, remarking only on the eating of live shrimps as a southern trait, and a small creature known by many Chinese names, such as 'short fox, sand mouther, shooter'. This latter is described by one Tang source as being the size of a chicken egg, shaped like a dung beetle, with a horn one inch long, and having four wings with which to fly, all of which perfectly fits the rhinoceros beetle (*Coleoptera, Dynastinae,* 20), a possibility overlooked by Schafer. These beetles are used for fighting in Thailand and Laos, much like crickets in China.

Yin-Ch'i Hsu (1928-29) provides extensive information on cricket rearing in China, especially along the coast. He even provides a glossary of some 67 varieties of fighting cricket, most of which refer to a single species, *Gryllodes berthellus* Sauss. The fighting species in the Palearctic, North and East China are the aforementioned and sometimes *Gryllus mitratus,* Burm., while in the Oriental *Gryllus chinensis* Weber and *Liogryllus bimaculatus* De G. are used. In China crickets were also raised for their voices, but only in the North and East. In the South katydids are kept for this purpose instead. This interest in crickets is shared to some extent by Tai speakers, a fact that may explain the large numbers of *Gryllidae* taxa in the data. Yin-Ch'i Hsu lists 39 species of crickets occurring along the Chinese coast from Suzhou and Peking to Hainan. These are grouped into 17 genera and 7 subfamilies.

Arthropod edibility varies from location to location, between languages, between organisms, even between villages. It may be fair to say that, in general, arthropophagy increases among Tai speakers as one moves south. Thus, in addition to such roles as forest nutrient recycling for the *Cerambycidae* or pollination for the *Hymenoptera,* arthropods serve as a major source of protein for Tai-speaking populations, particularly those of the Southwest and Central branches of the family.

The data. The linguistic data on Tai-Kadai arthropods is presented in appendix 1 in the form of cognate sets. Taxa of the Specific level, that is, taxa composed of a Generic plus a secondary lexeme have not usually been included. Likewise, arthropod taxa which occur only in a single recorded form in one language have not been included. In fact, there are a very large number of such taxa, which is undoubtedly an indication of the very preliminary stage in which we are currently working, waiting as it were for some comparative and historical linguist cum ethno-entomological systematist fieldworker to come to our rescue and get things sorted out. Based on this evidence, however, impoverished as it is, we may still venture a few prefatory observations, albeit tentative ones.

To begin with, regarding the existence of an arthropod LF, it would appear as if derivatives of PT *mleŋ have come to serve this function in varying degrees dependent upon a somewhat amorphous set of criteria, a condition which may arise from its relatively recent emergence as a higher order taxon. As may be seen from the data of set (15), several Central dialects spoken in the Bắc Giang and Cao Bằng area of Vietnam, as well as across the border in Longming, have glosses of 'housefly' for this form. This implies a semantic transition from 'fly' to 'insect', a metonymical transition of a type well-recorded by the folk biological taxonomists, whereby the specific comes to represent the general (as, for example, when 'oak' becomes the word for 'tree' as it apparently has in some Native American acorn cultures). The only problem with this supposition is that there is already an extensive set of cognates in Tai languages for 'housefly' (set 32), though they are irregular in initial and tone. It is therefore conceivable that the original PHT (Hlai-Tai) taxon for 'housefly' was a disyllabic expression of which the first syllable became the LF marker for certain categories of arthropods generally, and the second was preserved only in Tai with resultant contamination from the first syllable. The first syllable is still present in all dialects where the second occurs. Whatever explanation is ultimately accepted, the arthropod LF differs from bird, fish, and snake in that the usage is not so readily explainable.

(2) Life-Form usage by Arthropod classes and orders

UB + G	(UB) + LF + G
CRUSTACEA	
ARACHNIDA	Scorpiones
CHILOPODA (centipedes)	
DIPLOPODA (millipedes)	
Isoptera (termites)	Isoptera (adult fly)
Hymenoptera (ants, bees)	[LF + honey = bee (45)]
Lepidoptera	
butterfly-1 (C, N)	butterfly-1 (SW)
Odonata	(dragonfly-1)
Coleoptera (C, N)	
(beetles)	Coleoptera (SW)
Dictyoptera (C, N)	Dictyoptera (SW)
(cockroaches, mantids)	
Diptera (flies)	Muscidae (housefly)
Culicidae (Mosquito)	(some C)
Homoptera (cicadas)	
Orthoptera	grasshopper-2
	cricket-2
Hemiptera (bedbugs)	Hemiptera (waterbugs, stinkbugs)
Siphonaptera (fleas)	
	Megoloptera (Dobson's flies)
	Neuroptera (antlions, lacewings)

In Chamberlain (1992) it was shown that zoological taxonomies operate according to a principle of ANTHROPROXIMITY, but in that paper only the horizontal axis was discussed whereby LF marks distinguish those organisms least similar to humans in physical form and familiarity. It was suggested there that the marking of Bird, Fish, and Snake in fact parallels other universal marking trends such as plural and gender. The third member of such categories occuring in language (actually second in numerical ordering) such as dual or neuter, and which become the most highly marked, are logically analogous to the occurrence of MAMMAL and WUG (worm + bug) in biological taxonomies. As may be seen in (3) below, in the case of invertebrates we are confronted with the vertical dimension of the anthroproxemic principle since arthropods, annelids, and mollusks (Wugs) are very unlike humans in physical form and yet remain in opposition to Bird, Fish, and Snake as regards marking.[2] Arthropods are at least possessed of the character of bilateral symmetry and, phylogenetically, a more highly evolved segmentation which has given rise to a recognizable head and abdomen. This seems to have influenced their taxonomic position to the extent that when the LF marker does occur with invertebrate taxa it is with arthropods as opposed to annelids. (Mollusks have a separate LF which may be much older.)[3]

We notice in (2) above that the overwhelming tendency is towards the UB + G configuration with notable exceptions as indicated.[4] This may in fact be somewhat deceptive in terms of actual numerical occurrence of the various categories, given especially the considerable volume of arthropods in the Oriental Region, and the occurrence of the LF taxon in speech. This may also reflect the emergent character of the LF as well, especially when in several cases, as in the Coleoptera, Dictyoptera, and butterfly-1 of (2), LF usage differs between branches, especially Central and Northern versus Southwest.

There is yet another integral pragmatic element relating to this particular LF which may derive from its historical semantic associations with the

---

[2]This separation of LFs on the basis of marking is evident from the work of Brown (1984) although he has not drawn the same conclusions. Brown has demonstrated that Mammal and Wug should be treated separately from Bird, Fish, and Snake. For further discussion see Chamberlain (1992).

[3]Note: PH *$tshei^1$* 'clam, snail'; and PKS *$khruui^1$* 'cowry [money], shellfish'. The PT form is problematical. Li (1977) claimed the cognate does not occur in the Northern branch, yet it is clearly glossed in his own Wuming materials. Thus we are faced with SW *$hɔy$, C *hoy, and N *$θay$, for which I can find no other good analogous correspondence sets; perhaps PT *$hruay^A$.

[4]In the case of Araneae (spiders) several taxa are found with the LF markers not noted on the chart. These include the well-known /$mɛɛŋ^{A4}$ mum^{A4}/ (lit. 'LF + corner') in Lao and Thai, as well as the Mène form found in set 8. The Yay cognate is dubious. A few other such exceptions may exist in the data, but they do not obscure the general pattern.

housefly. In some Tai languages, for example Lao, the LF may be used pejoratively to refer to people, or it may be used to signify a strange or unfamiliar small creature whose true appellation is not known. This may account for its being used throughout the Tai dialects with such groups as scorpions and Hemipterids, the larger and more conspicuous representatives of which are probably confined to a range south of the Tropic.[5]

In the following schema, revised only slightly from Chamberlain (1977, 1992), the arthropods are thus illustrated in relation to other categories of faunal taxa.

(3) Proto-Tai zootaxonomic scheme

Human → ↓ Vertebrates	Γ = UB + G	Γ = (UB) + LF + G
	Anthroproxemic Generic taxa	Bird *nrok (A) Fish *plaa (A) Snake *nguu/ngïa (A)
Invertebrates	Arthropods Annelids	Mollusk *hruay (A) Arthropods *mleng (A)

In this diagram, the category of LF is defined both grammatically (Γ = grammar) and by its marked position as more remote from human. On the horizontal axis the more highly marked Arthropod LF is opposed syntactically to other arthropods represented only by Generics, while on the vertical axis it stands opposite Bird, Fish, and Snake. Its ambiguity vis-à-vis the more clearly anthroproxemic generic taxa is perhaps justified, at least at this stage of our research, because of an apparent recent emergence into the LF dominion. It should be noted that among the vertebrates in the upper left box of the chart are found the mammals, many birds with perceived special auspicistic characteristics such as eagles and crows, turtles, lizards, pythons, amphibians, and domestic animals. Thus, scientific categories such as bird or snake, like arthropods, have representatives on both sides of the chart.

---

[5]It might be mentioned, however, that of the three best-known families of Hemipterids, the *Belostomatidae* (giant waterbug) (35) and the *Pentatomidae* (stink bugs) (37) are large and highly edible, whereas the *Cicimidae* (bedbugs) (36) are tiny but in close proximity to humans. In the case of the first two the LF marker is used in all Tai dialects, whereas it is never used for bedbugs. In other words, this order of insects conforms well to the anthroproxemic principle as described in Chamberlain 1977 and 1992.

Some of the material included in the data illustrates a common use of secondary lexemes or semantic content. The form for mantis (25), which takes the lexeme 'horse', is found in all Tai branches and is assumed to have had this form at the level of proto-Tai.[6] The sole *Phasmida* (walking stick, 95) entry shows that these organisms were perceived in two very separate languages as carrying dead bodies or spirits, though the phonological forms are not cognate. Finally, in set (10), the scorpion has been classified as a crab.

Conclusion. As stated from the outset, this paper should be viewed as the starting point for future study of Tai-Kadai Arthropoda, a gathering together and organizing of available data, and noting of a few structural patterns. This will hopefully be of some value to field researchers as a guide to where attention might be most usefully focused, in providing more meaningful glosses, and for comparative and historical studies generally. There is much more to be done.

In comparison with other zoological fields, particularly the mammals, reptiles, and amphibians which I have already sought to examine (1977, 1980, 1981a, 1981b), the arthropods do not leave such a neat geographical trail, at least not so far. This is mostly due to the dearth of definitive technical materials available on the distribution of arthropods which are necessary to such generalizations and to the ubiquitous nature of the arthropod classes and orders. Whereas vertebrate species and ranges are fairly well recorded, the insects themselves in many cases have yet to be discovered. As an example, entomologist J. Rondon (in Gressitt et al 1970), remarks that so far 1,144 species of longicorn beetles are recorded for only part of the country of Laos and estimates that the total will be over 2,000. In the single family of Cerambycidae, 454 are described and of these, 195 are new to science. Many of the longicorns are large and conspicuous, yet in our data

---

[6]The use of other animal taxa in naming is not random. The Tai data clearly show that the naming of biological organisms, particularly at the Specific and Varietal levels, is not arbitrary but falls into patterns which appear to be universal in nature and are also based upon the principle of anthropocentric distance. Essentially there are three categories of biological taxa expanding outward in succession away from human, as may be seen in the scheme below, where G1 = animals without LF taxa, G2 = animals dominated by LFs, and P = plants.
    HUMAN > G1 > G2 > P
The naming constraint simply works in reverse; in terms of physical form, P may be named after G (1 or 2), G2 may be named after G1 but not after P, G1 may be named after neither G2 nor P. This sort of larger systemic pattern can only be discovered by looking at whole systems and by expanding the universe of discourse to include linguistic context (Chamberlain 1977, 1993).

they are represented by a paltry four taxa in sets (18) and (19) and even these are problematical. Such is the state of the art at this time.

Perhaps of greater immediate value is the biolinguistic contribution (or foundation) that may be offered to the study of the culture and environment relationship in the structure of biological taxonomies. The position of the arthropod LF marker and its opposition to Bird, Fish, and Snake on the one hand, and to anthroproxemic generics on the other, helps to round out the general picture that is emerging of classification and naming and the semantic position of Generics and Life-forms as structurally homologous with more familiar categories such as plural, tense, pronouns, and gender. Ideally, it is the structure of this system, this biology or grammar (in the epistemological sense), which might be targeted by those seeking to sustain biological diversity; for interaction between man and the environment is composed of a linguistic fabric[ation] including its potential for creative innovation, as opposed to the actual organisms themselves, whose scientific nature remains strategically secondary. To this way of thinking ecology is redefined to include human language, *si diis placet*.

Appendix 1

The data are presented here according to the biological taxonomy of Class, Order, and Family. These have been placed in alphabetical order with the non-Insecta classes preceded by 'Arthropoda.' (Crustacea are found at the end.) The English common name follows each entry.

Not all of the sets are phonological cognate sets. Some (e.g., 25, 26, 95) are grouped together because they share a common semantic structure. Forms in parentheses are classifiers. Bracketed forms are alternates.

The tones have mostly not been regularized owing to the problem of differing qualities of data. In some cases, however, where variation is especially prolix, the forms have been regularized and set off by braces {xxx} to show where this has been done.

The sources for the data and the abbreviations utilized are to be found in appendix 2. See map 5 for a key indicating the locations of the EFEO survey of 55 dialects done in 1938. This data is available by courtesy of Prof. Georges Condominas who loaned them to William J. Gedney (sometime before the availability of xerox machines) who in turn copied every word, 600 forms from 55 dialects, by hand.

Generally speaking, this data is much more developed for Tai than for the other families of Tai-Kadai. It is hoped that with the increased amount of fieldwork being carried out in that portion of Southeast Asia known as southern China, the many gaps in our data will begin to be filled.

1. Anoplura [body louse]
   Southwest: BT: *men⁴ (too¹)*; TV: *men³ (?) (too¹)*; Lao: *men⁴⁴ (too^A2)*; Siamese: *len¹*
   Central: WN: *man⁴ (tii¹)*; LM: *min⁴ (tuu¹)*; NùngS: *mền (tu)*; TayS: *màn tong (tu)*
   Northern: Yay: *nan⁴ (tua⁴)*; Dioi: *nan⁴⁴ (toueu⁴⁴)*; also *men^A1* 'petite poux ou de puce'; *men^A1 leuk^D1 gue^A1* 'mioche [mite ?]'; SaekG: *mlɛl⁴*; Mène: *men⁴ (too¹)*; WM *nan²*
   Be: BeS: *diên*
   Kam-Sui: PKS **nan¹*; T'en: *nan¹³ (ne)*
   Hlai: PH **than¹*

2. Anoplura [chicken louse (1)]
   Southwest: BT: *hay⁴ (too¹)*; Lao: *hay⁴⁴ (too^A2)*; Siamese: *ray¹*
   Central: WN: *day⁴*; LM: *lay⁴ (tuu¹)*; TayS: *lầy (tu)* 'maringouin'
   Northern: Yay: *ri⁴*; Dioi: *thoui⁴⁴ (toueu⁴⁴)*; SaekG: *rii⁴*; Mène: *hay⁴*; WM: *roi²*
   Kam-Sui: PKS **mprai¹*; T'en: *ʔbai³⁵ (ne)*
   Hlai: PH **zau/zo³* (Mat.)
   Other: Chinese: AmoyD: *koe-tâi* 'sort of insect smaller than flea, bred on fowls'

3. Anoplura [chicken louse (2)]
   Southwest: BT: *min¹ (too¹)* 'a kind of chicken louse also found on horses, larger than /hay⁴/.'
   Central: TayS: *mửn (tu)* 'maringouin'

4. Anoplura [head louse]
   Southwest: BT: *haw¹ (too¹)*; TV: *haw¹ (too¹)*; Lao: *haw^A1 (too¹)*; Siamese: *haw⁵*
   Central: WN: *thaw¹ (tii¹)*; LM: *thau¹*; LP *hau¹*; TayS: *thâu/hâu (tu)*
   Northern: Yay: *đaw¹ (tua⁴)*; Dioi: *thaou^A1, men^A1 thaou^A1*; SaekG: *rau²*; Mène: *haw⁴ (too⁴)*; WM *rau¹*
   Be: BeS: *(kot)*
   Kam-Sui: AC: *təu¹*
   Hlai: PH **srou¹*

5. Arthropoda, Arachnida, Acarina [tick]
   Southwest: BT: *hep⁷ (too¹)*; Lao: *hep^DS1*; Siamese: *hep²*; Ahom: *rip-rup; [phiw]*

Central: WN: *thep⁶*; LM: *ʔip³*; NùngS: *[tu méng pe]*; TayS: *hấp (tu)*
Northern: Dioi: *sip^D1 (toueu^A4)*; SaekG: *rip⁴*; Mène: *hep⁶ (too¹)*
Other: Viet: *rệp* 'bedbug'

6. Arthropoda, Arachnida, Araneae [spider, gen.]
   Southwest: BT: *siŋ⁴ saaw¹ (too¹)*; TV: *siŋ⁴ saaw⁴ (too¹)*; LMY: *koŋ³ kwaaw¹*; WT: *chiŋ² chaaw¹*
   Central: WN: *chuŋ¹ chaaw¹ (mee⁵)*; LM: *cii² laaw¹, laaŋ³ laaw¹ (tuu¹)*; LP: *caak⁵ haaw¹*; LC: - *khjaaw¹*; NùngS: *sing sao (tu)*; TayS: *sinh sao (tu), sâm sao*
   Northern: Yay: *cuŋ¹ caaw² (tua⁴)*; Dioi: *kouao⁴ diang⁴ (toueu²)*; SaekC: *thung thao*; SaekG: *thruŋ⁶ thraaw²*; Mène: *kiŋ⁴ kaaw⁴*; WM: *tu klwaaw¹*
   Kam-Sui: Mak: *tə tçwaau*
   Kadai: PB: *ku⁵³ zaau²¹³*; Lachi: *mia³³ çuŋ¹¹ çiau³⁵*
   Other: Chinese: AmoyD: *ti-tu*

7. Arthropoda, Arachnida, Araneae [spider, large jungle]
   Southwest: BT: *kuu² (too¹)*; TV: *kuu⁴ [?] (too¹)*

8. Arthropoda, Arachnida, Araneae [spider, sp.]
   Northern: Yay: *yiaŋ² (tua⁴)* 'animal similar to squirrel but larger'; Mène: *yeŋ² (mɛŋ⁴)* 'kind of spider'

9. Arthropoda, Arachnida, Scorpiones [scorpion (1)]
   Southwest: BT: *ŋɔt⁵ (too¹)*; Lao: *ŋɔɔt^DS4 (mɛɛŋ^A4)*
   Northern: SaekC: *ngòt*; Mène: *ŋɔɔt² (mɛŋ⁴)*

10. Arthropoda, Arachnida, Scorpiones [scorpion (2)]
    Southwest: TV: *puu⁴ liŋ⁴ (too¹)*
    Central: WN: *puu⁴ leŋ⁴ (tii¹)*
    Northern: Dioi: *paou^A1 po^A1 (toueu)*, also *toueu² ak¹ o⁴*

11. Arthropoda, Arachnida, Scorpiones [scorpion (3)]
    Southwest: BT: *ŋaw⁴ (mɛŋ⁴)* 'centipede'; Lao: *ŋaw^A4 (mɛŋ^A2)* 'large scorpion'; MM: *vaw^A4 (mɛɛŋ^A2)*
    Northern: SaekC: *ngạo (meng)*

12. Arthropoda, Chilopoda [centipede]
    Southwest: BT: *cak-kheep* (Li); TV: *khaaŋ¹ khep⁷*; Lao: *khii^B1 khep^DS2*; *cii khep^DS2*; Siamese: *ca-khep²/ta-khaap²*

Central: WN: *chii¹ cep⁷ (mee⁵)*; LM: cii³ *lyap³ (tuu¹); tuu¹ kip³; cuu³ kip³;* LC: *cii-khip;* NùngS: *khi khếp (tu);* TayS: *khinh khếp (tu);* Thổ: *kai-theep* (DL1)
Northern: Yay: *θip⁷ (tua⁴);* Dioi: *sip^{D1} (toueu^{44});* SaekC: *kĩ thib;* Mène: *khep/hep⁶;* Po-Ai: *ɬip;* Ling-yün: *ɬit* (Li says N dialects indicate PNT **s-*)
Be: BeS: *zop*
Kam-Sui: PKS **khryap⁷, *khyap⁷*
Hlai: PH **rʔiip⁷;* DayS: *díp/dríp (cứ lống-)*

13. Arthropoda, Diplopoda [millipede (1)]
    Southwest: BT: *kɨɨ¹ (boŋ³);* Siamese: *kiŋ³ kɨɨ¹;* Ahom: *ku* 'a worm'
    Central: TayS: *khư (tu bống)* 'larvae of terrestrial insects'
    Other: GSR (95h) **g'i̯o/g'i̯wo / k'ü* 'millipede'

14. Arthropoda, Diplopoda [millipede (2)]
    Southwest: MM: *tɨk taw* [?]
    Central: WN: *caw³ (mee⁵ phaa² ʔi-);* TayS: *cháo (tu xu); tu tám tâu*
    Northern: Yay: *saaw² (tua⁴ vəy² -)*
    Other: GSR (46m) **tsi̯o/tsi̯wo* 'millipede'

15. Arthropoda, Insecta [insect, arthropod LF]
    Southwest: BT: *meŋ⁴;* TV: *mɛŋ⁴;* Lao: *mɛɛŋ⁴⁴;* Siamese: *ma-lɛɛŋ¹;* Ahom: *miŋ/mleŋ* 'a glow worm'
    Central: WN: *mɛŋ⁴;* LM: *meeŋ⁴ (tuu¹)* 'housefly'; LP: *mɛɛŋ⁴;* NùngS: *mèng;* TayS: *mèng;* ThổBG (4): *mèng* 'housefly'; ThổCB (10): *mèng* 'housefly'; NùngCB (15): *nêng (tu)* 'housefly'
    Nùng-an: (13): *néng* 'housefly'
    Northern: Yay: *neŋ⁴* 'insect; mosquito'; Dioi: *neng²;* SaekG: *mɛɛŋ⁴;* Mène: *mɛŋ⁴*
    Be: BeS: *ming, ning, mêng* 'insect'
    Hlai: PH **wiiŋ³* 'a fly' (DayS: *méi vàng;* BD: *-hweeŋ³;* HT: *-vaaŋ³*) 'a fly'
    Other: GSR (742s-t) **mâng / mang / meng* 'gadfly, horsefly';[7] GSR (1181e) **mung / mung: / meng* 'midge, mosquito'

---

[7]Not being a Chinese specialist I include Karlgren's GSR and MC forms here only with extreme caution, but also with no small degree of fascination since regular patterns of correspondance do occur. For example, the GSR final velar stop corresponding to PT C-tone, as in GSR (1041t) **gi̯og / ji̯äu* 'owl' (PT **γ ~ gaw^C*); (1069r) **glôg / lâu* 'spirits with sediment' (PT **hlaw^C*); (1063a-c) **môg / mau* 'male' (PT **b ~ phuu^C*).

16. Arthropoda, Insecta [worm, larvae, wug][8]
    Northern: Dioi: *douai¹/dai¹* 'larve de gros charançon des bamboo'
    Kam-Sui: PKS **dzuui²* 'snake'; AC: *nui²* 'worm, bug'; Mak: *nui* [mid-fall] *(tə)* 'worms'; T'en: *nuei³⁵ ʔzaap³¹ jaa¹³* 'kind of worm'

17. Coleoptera [grub, beetle larvae, gen.]
    Southwest: BT: *duaŋ³ (too¹)*; Lao: *duaŋ^C3 (too^A2)*; Siamese: *duaŋ³*
    Central: WN: *duŋ³ (tii¹)*; LM: *nuuŋ³ (tuu¹ noon¹)*; TayS: *duúng (tu)* [used also for bee larvae]
    Northern: Yay: *duŋ⁶ (tua⁴)*; SaekG: *duaŋ³*; Mène: *duaŋ³ (too⁴)*

18. Coleoptera, Cerambicidae [Cerambycid (1)]
    Southwest: BT: *ʔaa¹ ʔit⁷ (mɛŋ⁴)*
    Northern: Mène: *ʔiit² faay³ (mɛŋ⁴)*

19. Coleoptera, Cerambycidae [Cerambycid (2)]
    Southwest: TV: *ŋɔɔt² (too⁴)*
    Northern: Mène: *ta-ŋeet² (mɛŋ⁴)*

20. Coleoptera, Dynastinae [rhinoceros beetle]
    Southwest: BT: *ŋuaŋ⁴ (mɛŋ⁴)*; MM: *kwaaŋ^B* 'fighting beetle'; Lao: LBNG: *kwaaŋ^B2 (mɛŋ^A2)*
    Central: WN: *ŋaaŋ⁵ [?] (tii¹)*; TayS: *nguang (tu)* 'Coléoptère terreste'
    Northern: Yay: *ŋaaŋ² ʔaa¹ (tua⁴)*
    Other: Viet: *con ca cuông*

21. Coleoptera, Hydrophillidae [water scavenger beetle]
    Southwest: BT: *niaŋ² (too¹)*; TV: *niaŋ² (too⁴)*; Siamese: *niaŋ² (mɛɛŋ¹)* 'whirligig or gyrinid water beetle'; WT: *neŋ^B1 (mɛŋ^A4)*
    Central: WN: *ñiŋ³ [?] (tii¹)*; NùngS: *niếng (tu - nạm)*
    Northern: Yay: *ciaŋ⁵ (tua⁴)*

---

[8]Semantic coalescence of snake and worm is said by Brown to be common throughout the world's taxonomies, as in fact it seems to have been in Germanic, e.g., Anglo-Saxon <wyrm> 'serpent, dragon, worm,' although IE {netr-}, AS <nædre> 'adder' seems to refer unambiguously to 'snake'. This should, then, be assumed with caution; more precise glosses from Kam-Sui would be helpful.

22. Coleoptera, Lampyridae [firefly (1)]
    Southwest: BT: *hiŋ⁴ hɔy³ (too¹)*; TV: *hiŋ⁴ hɔy³ (too⁴)*; Lao: *hiŋᴮ¹ hɔɔyᶜ¹ (tooᴬ²)*; Siamese: *hiŋ⁵/² hɔɔy³*
    Central: TayS: *hiếng hoi* [tone?] *(tu)*; LC: *hiŋ* [mid] *hooi* [rise]

23. Coleoptera, Lampyridae [firefly (2)]
    Central: WN: *dɔŋ² dit⁷ (mee⁵)*; TayS: *lung líp (tu)*
    Northern: Yay: *rɔŋ⁵ rip¹ (tua⁴)*; Dioi: *thong¹ (toueu²)*
    Kam-Sui: AC: *nap⁷ niŋ³* 'lightning bug'

24. Dictyoptera, Blattaria [cockroach]
    Southwest: BT: *saap² (mɛŋ)*; WT: *sát (tú mĕng)*; TV: *saap² (mɛŋ)*; Lao: *saapᴰᴸ¹ (mɛɛŋ)*; Siamese: *saap² (malɛɛŋ)*; Ahom: *caap (miñ)*
    Central: WN: *'aap² (tii¹)*; LM: *caap² / saap² (tuu¹)* [differentiates two kinds of cockroach, /saap²/ is small and grey and causes musty smell in clothes]; LC: *ɬaap*; NùngS: *xláp (tu)*; TayS: *sáp / tháp*
    Northern: Yay: *'θaap² (tua⁴)*; Dioi: *souap¹*; Mène: *ka-saap² / caap² (mɛŋ⁴)*; Po-Ai: *ɬaap*
    Be: BeS: *k'a-lap*
    Kam-Sui: AC: *swap⁷*

25. Dictyoptera, Mantidae [praying mantis (1)]
    Southwest: BT: *mɛŋ⁴ maa⁶*; TV: *mɛŋ⁴ maa⁶*; Lao: *mɛŋᴬ⁴ maaᶜ⁴*
    Central: WN: *tak⁷ maa⁶*; NùngS: *tu ma mí*; TayS: *tu càn ma; tu míng ma*
    Northern: Yay: *tua⁴ tak⁷ ma-liɨ⁴*; Dioi: *tak¹ maa³*; Mène: *mɛŋ⁴ maa⁵*

26. Dictyoptera, Mantidae [praying mantis (2)]
    Kam-Sui: Kam-CZ: *pui¹ (te⁵)*; Kam-ZG: *cai³ (ma⁴)*

27. Diptera [maggot, worm, gen.]
    Southwest: BT: *nɔn¹ (too⁴)*; Lao: *nɔɔnᴬ¹ (tooᴬ²)*; Siamese: *nɔɔn⁵*
    Central: WN: *non¹* 'caterpillar'; LM: *noon¹ (tuu¹)* 'worm'; NùngS: *non (tu)*; TayS: *non (tu)*
    Northern: Yay: *nɔn¹ (tua⁴)*; Dioi: *gnien¹ (toueu²)*; SaekC: SaekG: *nɔɔl²*; Mène: *nɔn⁴* 'worm, maggot'; WM: *nên¹*
    Kam-Sui: PKS *ʔnuun¹*; T'en: *nuen³⁵ (ne)*
    Hlai: PH *hñʔan²*; DayS: *hên (cứ lống)*

Tai-Kadai Arthropods

28. Diptera [fly, very small, hovers around eyes]
    Southwest: BT: *mii⁴* (tone?) *(mɛŋ⁴)*; TV: *mii²* *(mɛŋ⁴)*; Lao: *mii^B1* *(mɛŋ)*;
    Siamese: *vii⁵* *(malɛɛŋ¹)*

29. Diptera, Chironomedae, Orseolia oryzae [gall midge]
    Southwest: Lao: *bua^B3* *(mɛɛŋ^A4)*
    Northern: Mène: *bua²* *(mɛŋ⁴ -)* 'the red bug'

30. Diptera, Culicidae [mosquito (1)]
    Southwest: BT: *ñuŋ⁴* *(too¹)*; TV: *ñuŋ⁴* *(too⁴)*; Lao: *ñuŋ^A4* *(too^A2)*;
    Siamese: *yuŋ¹*; Ahom: *ñuŋ*
    Central: WN: *ñuŋ⁴* *(mɛŋ⁴)*; LM: *yoŋ (tuu¹)*; NùngS: *nhùng (tu)*; TayS:
    nhùng (tu mèng)
    Northern: SaekC: *nhung*; SaekG: *ñuŋ⁴*; Mène: *ñuŋ⁴*
    Be: BeS: *núng*
    Kam-Sui: Mak: *ñuŋ* [hi-fall] *(tə)*
    Hlai: PH **ñuuŋ¹* 'fly; mosquito'; DayS: *nhuóng (mề i vàng)*

31. Diptera, Culicidae [mosquito (2)]
    Northern: Yay: *hap⁸ (tua⁴ neŋ⁴)*; Dioi: *gniap¹ (toueu² neng²)*
    Kam-Sui: T'en: *[tsjaam⁴⁴]?*

32. Diptera, Muscidae [housefly]
    Southwest: BT: *ŋuan⁴/ŋwan⁴* *(mɛŋ⁴)*; WT: *mun⁴* *(mɛŋ⁴)*; TV: *van (mɛŋ⁴)*;
    Lao: *van^A4* *(mɛɛŋ^A4)*; Siamese: *wan¹* *(mlɛɛŋ¹)*
    Central: WN: *fan⁴* *(mɛŋ⁴)*; LP: *fən⁴* *(mɛɛŋ⁴)*; NùngS: *phần (tu míng)*;
    TayS: *phùn (tu mèng)*
    Northern: Yay: *ñan¹* *(neŋ⁴)*; SaekC: *me nhell*; SaekG: *ñel²*; Mène: *hon³*
    (cf. 15 'insect')

33. Diptera, Phlebotomus [sandfly]
    Southwest: BT: *hin³* (?) *(too¹)*; TV: *hin⁶* *(too⁴)*; Lao: *hin^C4*; Siamese:
    rin⁴; Ahom: *rin* 'flea'
    Central: LM: *lin³ (tuu¹)*; LP: *łin⁵ (mɛɛŋ⁴)*; NùngS: *lền*; TayS: *lin (tu
    míng)*
    Northern: SaekC: *hin*
    Other: Viet: *rĩn (con)*

34. Diptera, Tabanidae [gadfly, horsefly]
   Southwest: BT: *liaʔ²*; TV: *liat² (too⁴)*; Lao: *liak^DL1 (mɛɛŋ⁴⁴)*; Siamese: *liap²*
   Central: WN: *lət² (tii¹)*; LM: *niik² (tuu¹)*; NùngS: *cước (tu)* 'taon'; TayS: *lước (tu)*
   Northern: Yay: *liak² (tua⁴)*; Dioi: *neue.¹*; SaekG: *liap⁶*; Mène: *liat²*
   Kam-Sui: AC: *ŋək⁸*; T'en: *pjaak²² (ne)*
   Hlai: PH **lyʔaak⁷*
   Kadai: Pubiao *qa⁰ taak⁴⁵*

35. Hemiptera, Belostomatidae [giant waterbug, Belostome]
   Southwest: BT: *daa¹ (mɛŋ⁴)*; TV: *daa⁴ (mɛŋ⁴)*; Lao: *daa⁴³ (mɛŋ⁴⁴)*; Siamese: *daa¹ (mlɛɛŋ¹)*
   Central: WN: *daa¹ (tii¹)*; NùngS: *da (tu)* 'lucane'; TayS: *da (tu míng)* 'hydrophile'
   Northern: Yay: *daa¹ (nɛŋ⁴)*; Dioi: *taa¹ (souap¹* 'cockroach') 'insect resemblant à la blatte'; Mène: *daa⁴ (mɛŋ⁴)*
   Other: Chinese: MC: *da* 'Alligator sinensis'; Viet: *kì dà* 'Varanus salvator (water monitor)'

36. Hemiptera, Cimicidae, Cimex lectularius [bedbug]
   Southwest: BT: *hiat⁵ (too¹)*; TV: *hiat⁵ (too⁴)*; Lao: *hiat^DL4 (too^A2)*; Siamese: *riat³*
   Central: WN: *lət⁵ (tii¹)*; LM: *liit⁵ (tuu¹)*; TayS: *lượt (tu)*
   Northern: Yay: *diat⁵ (tua⁴)*; Dioi: *theuet¹ (tueue²)* 'punaise'; SaekG: *ruat⁶*; Mène: *hiat²*
   Be: BeS: *zêat*
   Kam-Sui: [PKS **hñiŋ¹*]
   Hlai: PH **kip⁷* (Mat.)
   Other: Lakkia: *jiet⁷*

37. Hemiptera, Pentatomidae [stink bug]
   Southwest: BT: *kɛŋ⁴ (mɛŋ⁴)*; TV: *khɛŋ⁴ (mɛŋ⁴)*; Lao: *khɛɛŋ⁴⁴ (mɛɛŋ⁴⁴)*; Lao Roi-et: *sɛɛŋ (mɛɛŋ)*; Siamese: *khrɛɛŋ¹*; Ahom: *cɛŋ* 'a kind of insect'
   Central: WN: *cɛŋ⁴ (tii¹ mɛŋ⁴)*; LM: ; NùngS: *kêng (mèng)*
   Northern: Yay: *kɛŋ⁴ (tua⁴ nɛŋ⁴)*; Dioi: *keng¹ neng²* 'punaise des bois'; Mène: *kɛŋ⁴ (mɛŋ⁴)*; Po-Ai: *keeŋ*; Hsi-lin: *nɛŋ⁴⁴ keeŋ⁴⁴*
   Kam-Sui: AC: *dziŋ¹* 'stinkbug' (also: *kwaŋ⁵* 'kind of flying stink bug')
   Other: GSR (713a-b) **g'i̯ang / g'i̯ang / k'iang* 'kind of insect'

38. Homoptera, Cicadidae [cicada (1)]
    Southwest: BT: cak^7 can^2 (too^1); TV: cak^7 can^2 (too^4); Lao: cak^{DS2} can^{B2}; Siamese: cak^4 (ka) can^2; Ahom: *chak-chan* 'an ant [?]'
    Other: GSR (147z) *$d\underset{\sim}{j}an$ / $\acute{z}\underset{\sim}{j}än$ / *ch'an* 'cicada'; GSR (866o) *$d'ieg$ / $d'iei$ / $t'i$ 'cicada'

39. Homoptera, Cicadidae [cicada (2)]
    Southwest: BT: $ŋwaaŋ^6$ $(mɛŋ^4)$; Lao: $ŋuaŋ^{C4}$ $(mɛɛŋ^{A4})$
    Central: WN: $ŋaaŋ^5$ [?] $ʔaa^2$; LM: $vaaŋ^4$ (tuu^1) [?]

40. Hompotera, Cicadidae [cicada (3)]
    Central: LM: pit^5 (tuu^1)
    Northern: Yay: pit^8 (tua^4); Dioi: pit^1
    Kam-Sui: AC: mat^{7b} 'grasshopper'[?]

41. Homoptera, Cicadidae [cicada (4)]
    Southwest: TV: $ka\text{-}len^4$ (too^4); Lao: $ka\text{-}len^{A4}$ (too^{A2})
    Central: TayS: *lìn (tu míng)* 'cigale'

42. Hymenoptera [bee (1)]
    Southwest: BT: $fəŋ^3$ (too^1); TV: $phəŋ^3$ (too^4) ; Lao: $phəŋ^{C1}$ (too^{A2}); Siamese: $phɨŋ^3$; Ahom: *phrɛŋ* 'honey'
    Central: LM: $phyəŋ^3$ (tuu^1); TayS: *pêâng*
    Northern: Mène: $phəŋ^3$ 'beeswax, bee'; GiayHG (20): *phîêng*
    Kam-Sui: AC: fe^3 'beehive'[?]
    Other: Chinese: AmoyD: *phang* 'bee, wasp'; Karlgren MC: *p'i[w]ong* (A) 'bee, wasp'

43. Hymenoptera [bee (2)]
    Southwest: WT (27): *mɨm*; TV: mim^6 (too^4); Lao: mim^{C4} (too^{A2})

44. Hymenoptera [bee (3)]
    Central: NùngCB: (15) *rui (tu)*
    Nùng-an: (13) *rùi*
    Northern: Yay: $rɨay^1$ $(tua^4)/dɨay^1$ [JRC]; SaekC: *me rái*; SaekG: $rooy^2$; NhắngLK (35): *rươi (táa)*
    Hlai: Pai-sha: *kuai*; DayS: *cói*
    Kadai: PB: qa^0 $zəi^{33}$; GL: *zei* [mid-high level]

45. Hymenoptera [bee, honey (1)]
    Central: LC: *t'əəŋ* 'sugar'; NùngS: *thương (tu míng)*; TayS: *thương* 'miel' {LF + *thiaŋ*} 'bee': ThôBG (1, 3, 5); TayBK (6); ThôBK (8); Cao Binh (12); ThôCB (16); NùngLS (29, 30); ThôLS (31–33); ThôMC (43) {*thiaŋ* + LF} 'honey': TayBK (6); ThôBK (7–9); ThôCB (10, 11, 14, 16–18); Cao Binh (12); NùngLS (29, 30); ThôLS (31, 33); ThôMC (42–3); ThôQY (46)
    Northern: Yay: *tiaŋ⁴* 'sugar'/ *tiaŋ⁶* [JRC]; Dioi: *teuang²* (*toueu²*) 'wild bee' Cao Lan: (44, 45) *tàng (-pháng)*; (50) tong *(-long tên)* Nùng-an: (13) *tin*
    Kam-Sui: PKS **daaŋ²*
    Hlai: DayS: *thŏng*
    Other: Chinese: MC: *d'âng* 'sugar'

46. Hymenoptera [honey (2)]
    Southwest: ThaiLK (40): *biit*; ThaiYB (51): *mịt*
    Central: ThôTQ (49): *mịt*

47. Hymenoptera [honey (3)]
    Southwest: ThaiLK (41): *ngọt*; [Thai?]YB (55): *ngọt*

48. Hymenoptera [hornet]
    Southwest: BT: *tɔɔ² (too¹)*; TV: *tɔɔ² (too¹)*; Lao: *tɔɔ^{B2} (too^{A2})*; Siamese: *tɔɔ²*; Ahom: *to* 'a hornet'
    Central: WN: *too² (tii¹)*; LM: *too² (tuu¹)*; NùngS: *tó (tu)*; TayS: *tó* (tu)
    Northern: Yay: *tɔɔ² (tua⁴)*; Dioi: *to¹ (toueu²)*; SaekC: SaekG: *tɔɔ⁶* 'wasp'; Mène: *tɔɔ² (too⁴)*; Po-Ai: *too^{B1}*
    Kam-Sui: AC: *lau¹* 'big wasp'; PKS (Thurgood) **ʔdlu¹* (A)
    Hlai: **plou¹*; DayS: *lắu (cứ lống mềi -)*
    Other: Mon: *tho [thow]* 'kind of hornet'; Chinese: AmoyD: *thɔ̂-kàng-phang* 'sort of bee with nest in ground'; Viet: *tŏ vŏ* 'wasp; mason-bee'

49. Hymenoptera [wasp (1)]
    Southwest: BT: *tɛn² (too¹)*; TV: ; Lao: *tɛɛn^{A2} (too^{A2})*; Siamese: *tɛɛn¹*
    Central: WN: *thɛn¹/theŋ¹*; LM: *pheeŋ¹ (tuu¹)* [?]; NùngS: *then (tu)*; TayS: *then (tu)*; LC: *pheen¹*; ThôBG (4): *phen*; ThôYB (54): *teng (tú)*
    Northern: Yay: *tin⁴ (tua⁴)*; Dioi: *tin² (toueu²)*; SaekG: *thiil⁴*; Mène: *tɛn⁴ (too⁴)*; WM: *tin²*
    Kam-Sui: AC: *din¹*; T'en: *tin¹³ (ne)*
    Hlai: PH **thiñ*

50. Hymenoptera [wasp (2)]
    Southwest: Lao: *yay^A3*; WT: *yay^A3*
    Central: TayS: *dây/giày (tu míng)* 'espèce de guêpe à corps étranglé'
    Northern: Yay: *ñay¹ (tua⁴ neŋ⁴)* 'a wasp that makes mud nests on walls';
    Dioi: *diaɨ⁴ (neng²)*; Mène: *yay⁴ (mɛŋ⁴)* 'wasp, hornet, yellow with red waist'

51. Hymenoptera, Formicidae [ant, gen.]
    Southwest: BT: *mot⁴ (too¹)*; TV: *mot⁸ (too⁴)*; Lao: *mot^DL4 (too^A2)*;
    Siamese: *mot⁴*; Ahom: *mat*
    Central: WN: *mat⁸ (tii¹)*; LM: *mət⁴ (tuu¹)*; NùngS: *mọt (tu)*; TayS: *một (tu)*
    Northern: Yay: *mat⁸ (tua⁴)*; Dioi: *mot¹*; SaekC: ; SaekG: *mɛk⁶*; Mène: *mot⁷ (too⁴)*
    Be: BeS: *mo*
    Kam-Sui: PKS **mwit*; T'en: *met³¹ (ne)*
    Hlai: PH **mʔu*; DayS:
    Kadai: KelaoB: *mi gờ* [comp. Mulam: *myət⁸*]
    Other: Lakkia *mot⁸*

52. Isoptera [termite (1) adult]
    Southwest: BT: *maw⁵ (mɛŋ⁴)*; TV: *maw² (mɛŋ⁴)*; Lao: *maw^B4 (mɛɛŋ^A4)*
    Central: WN: *maw⁵ (mɛŋ⁴)*

53. Isoptera [termite (2), white ant]
    Southwest: BT: *puaʔ² (too¹)*; TV: *puak² (too⁴)*; Lao: *puak^DL2 (too^A2)*;
    Siamese: *pluak²*
    Central: WN: *cuk² (tii¹)*; LM: *pjuuk² (tuu¹ mət⁴)*; LP: *cuuk⁵*;
    NùngS: *cuốc (tu)* 'fourmis blanches'; TayS: *puốc (tu)*
    Northern: Yay: *suk³* [G]; *sup⁷ (tua⁴ mat⁸)* [JRC]; Dioi: *chouk¹ (mot¹)*;
    SaekC: *puek (thua)*; SaekG: *ca-pluk⁴*; Mène: *puak²*
    Hlai: PH **pluak⁷*; DayS: *lụ (cứ lổng)*

54. Isoptera [termite (3)]
    Southwest: BT: *mɔt⁵ (too¹)*; TV: *mɔɔt⁵ (too⁴)*; Lao: *mɔɔt^DL4 (too^A2)*;
    Siamese: *mɔɔt³*
    Central: WN: *mot⁵*; LM: *moot⁵ (tuu¹)*; NùngS: *mọt (tu)* 'charançon'
    Northern: Yay: *mot⁵*; SaekG: *mɔɔt⁵*; Mène: *mɔɔt²*
    Kam-Sui: AC: *mot⁸* 'insect that eats books'

55. Lepidoptera [butterfly (1)]
Southwest: *{(kaap^{DL}) bɨa ~ bəə^C}* BT, WT(D), Lao {LF + *bɨa ~ bəə^C*} TV, WT (27, 28), ThôBG (2)
Southwest ~ Central: {UB + *bɨa ~ bəə*} YB (51, 53–55)
Central: {UB + *bɨa^C*} TayS, NùngS, ThôBG (1, 3), ThôBK (8, 9), ThốCB (11), ThốLS (31), ThốTQ (49) {UB + *bəə^C*} ThốMC (42, 43), ThốLK (41) {UB + *bɨi^C*} NùngBG (5), NùngLS (29), ThốLS (32) *(báng) bưa* ThốHG (22); *(binh) bả* ThốBG (4) *(bụm) ba* NùngCB (15)
Central ~ Northern: *(bung) bá* Nùng-an (13)
Northern: *{(buŋ^{B/C}) baa^C}* Saek, Dioi, Yay, Nhắng (34, 35) *{(boŋ) baaŋ}* GiayHG (20) *{(bum^B) baa^C}* WM
Kam-Sui: (*ʔbum* [rise]) baa [high] Mak *(ʔbəm^5) baa^3* AC: *paa^{35}* (*pin^{44}*) T'en
Hlai: BD: *hwou^1;* YM: *mvou^4;* TS: *gwou^1* 'moth'
Kadai: GL: *p'au* [mid-fall] *p'au* [mid-rise]
Other: BY: *(bət^{55}) ba^{42};* Ch. Amoy: *boé(-iah), bé(-iah)*

56. Lepidoptera [butterfly (2)]
Southwest: {(LF + *ka[ap]*) + *bii^C*} Lao {UB + *bii^C*} ThaiHB (23), ThaiLK (40) {UB + *vii^C* (?)} ThaiHB (24, 25)
Central: {UB + *bii^C* (?)} TayBK (6), ThôBK (7, 8), NùngHG (19), ThốHG (21), ThốLS (33), NùngLK (36–39), ThốQY (5) *(bung) bii* ThốTQ (49) {UB + *vii^C* (?)} ThốCB (10, 12, 14, 17, 18) {UB + *pii^C* (?)} ThốMC (43) {UB + *phii^C* (?)} ThốCB/LS (16) *{(kap^D) fi}* NùngLS (30), SZ(Ed) {*(b-/p-/ph- + -t^D)* + *fii^C* (?)} Cao Lan (44, 45, 50)
Northern: (UB + *bii^C*) NhắngLK (34) [borrowed from WN?]

57. Lepidoptera [butterfly (3)]
Southwest: *{kaap^D (bɨa ~ bəə^C)}* BT, WT, Lao
Central: *{kap^D (fi^C)}* NùngLS (30), SZ(Ed)

58. Lepidoptera [butterfly (4)]
Central: *báng (bưa)* ThốHG (22); *báng (bi)* ThốTQ (49); *binh (bả)* ThốBG (4)
Central ~ Northern: *bung bá* Nùng-an (13)
Northern: *{buŋ^{B/C} (baa^C)}* Yay, Saek, Dioi, NhắngLK (34, 35), NZ(Ed) *bồng (bạng)* GiayHG (20)
Hlai: DayS: {LF + *mướng*}

59. Lepidoptera [butterfly (5)]
    Central: NùngCB (15): *bụm (ba)*
    Northern: WM: *ʔbum* [rise] (*ba* [rise])
    Kam-Sui: Mak: *ʔbum* [rise] *ba* [high]; AC: *ʔbəm⁵ (ba³)*
    Other: Viet: *bươm bướm*

60. Lepidoptera [butterfly (6)]
    Southwest ~ Central: Cao Lan (44, 45): *pệt (phử)*; Cao Lan (50): *phệt (phử)*
    Kadai [?]: BY: *bət⁵⁵ (ba⁴²)*

61. Lepidoptera [butterfly (7)]
    Central: LM: *huu⁴ tee⁴ (tuu¹)*
    Hlai: Pai-Sha: *taam* [mid] *teʔ* [mid]

62. Lepidoptera [caterpillar, gen.]
    Southwest: BT: *boŋ³ (too¹)*; TV: *boŋ³ (too⁴)*; Lao: *boŋ^{C3} (too^{A4})*;
    Siamese: *buŋ³*; Ahom: *buŋ* 'silkworm'
    Central: LM: *moŋ³ (tuu¹)*; TayS: *bůng (tu non)*; *bống (tu)*
    Northern: SaekC: *vŏng*; SaekG: *vɔŋ⁶*; Mène: *boŋ³*
    Other: Chinese: Amoy: *búng* 'sort of insect'; also *bán, tɔ-bun* 'a worm'

63. Lepidoptera [caterpillar, sp.]
    Southwest: BT: *haan¹ (too¹)*
    Central: TayS: *han (tu), (tu non)*

64. Lepidoptera [caterpillar, stinging]
    Central: WN: *pheŋ³ (tii¹)*
    Northern: Yay: *piaŋ³ (tua⁴)*; Dioi: *piang³ (toueu²)*

65. Lepidoptera [silkworm (1)]
    Southwest: BT: *mɔn⁶ (too¹)*; TV: *mɔn⁶ (too⁴)*; Lao: *mɔɔn^{C4} (too⁴)*;
    Siamese: ; Ahom:
    Central: WN: ; LM: *muun⁵ (tuu¹ caam⁵)*; NùngS: *mọn (tu)*; TayS: *mọn (tu)*

66. Lepidoptera [silkworm (2)]
    Central: WN: *θaw¹ (meŋ⁴)*
    Northern: Yay: *θaaw¹ (tua⁴ neŋ⁴)*
    Other: Viet: *dâu* (A) 'mulberry'; *đào* (A) 'young girl'

67. Megaloptera [hellgramite, Dobson's fly]
   Southwest: BT: *ʔyaa¹ təə² (mɛŋ⁴)*; TV: *ñaa⁵ təə³* (?) *(too⁴)*

68. Neuroptera, Myrmeleontidae [antlion]
   Southwest: BT: *kay² kɔm³ (mɛŋ⁴)*; TV: *kay² kɔm³ (mɛŋ⁴)*

69. Odonata [damsel-fly]
   Southwest: BT: *pɔɔ¹* [?] *(mɛŋ⁴)* 'adult white ant termite'; WT: *pɔɔ⁴⁴ (nɔn⁴¹)* 'insect at edible stage where wings have just formed' [nymph]
   Northern: Mène: *pɔɔ⁴ (mɛŋ⁴)*

70. Odonata [dragon-fly (1)]
   Southwest: {LF + *bii^C*} WT, TV, Lao, Ahom {UB + *bii^C*} BT, ThaiYB (52), ThaiLK (40) {*bii* + (?/*bo*)} ThaiHB (23, 24, 25)
   Central: {LF + *bii^C*} ThôBG (2) {UB + *bii^C*} ThôMC (42), ThôYB (54) {LF + *pii^C*} ThôBG (4), ThôBK (9) {UB + *pii^C*} MuongBG [sic] (1), ThôBG (3), ThôLS (32), ThôMC (43) {LF + *ph/fii^C* NùngBG (5) {UB + *ph/fii^C* NùngLS (29, 30), ThôLS (31, 33), NùngS, LP, SZ (Ed) *(pung⁴) pey⁶* LM *(póng) pí* ThôHG (22), ThôCB (11) *[poong pì]* *(pung) pi* TayS *(pàng) pừi* Cao Lan (44, 45) *(bang) bừi* Caolan (50) *(pŏm) pi* ThôTQ (49) *(lam* [low]) *vaai* [low fall] LC
   Central ~ Northern: Nùng-an (13): *(bung) bí*
   Northern: {UB + *pii^C*} Dioi, GiayHG (20) *(piiŋ²) pei⁶* NZ(Ed) {*bii^C* + *(bum^B)*} Saek, Mène
   Hlai: Pai-sha: *(saam* [high]) *tʃ'i* [high] (belongs here?)
   Other: Amoy: *bé(-iah), boé(-iah)*

71. Odonata [dragon-fly (2)]
   Central: ThôTQ (49): *pŏm (pi)*; LC: *lam* [low] (*vaai* [low fall])
   Northern: SaekG: *(bii³) bum²*; Mène: *(bii³) bum²*
   Hlai: Pai-sha: *saam* [high] (*tʃ'i* [high]) [?]

72. Odonata [dragon-fly (3)]
   Central: LM: *puŋ⁴ (pey⁶)*; ThôHG (22) *póng (pí)*; ThôCB (11) *[poong pì]* TayS *pung (pi)*; Cao Lan (44, 45) *pàng (pừi)*; Cao Lan (50) *bang (bừi)* Nùng-an (13): *bung (bi)*

73. Odonata [dragon-fly (4)]
   Central: {UB + piŋ^B (/C?)} WN, NùngHG (19), ThổHG (21), NùngLK (36–39) {piiŋ^B + (pei^C)} SZ(Ed)
   Northern: {UB + piŋ^B} Yay, NhắngLK (34, 35)

74. Odonata [dragon-fly (5)]
   Central: {LF + kwaaŋ^A} Thổ/TayBK (6, 7, 8) {UB + kwaaŋ^A} ThổMC (43) {(kwiŋ^B)/(kiŋ^B) kwaaŋ^A} Cao Binh (12), ThổCB (14, 16, 17, 18), ThổMC (42)

75. Odonata [dragon-fly (6)]
   Southwest: ThaiHB (23): *(tú) bí-bò*; ThaiHB (24, 25): *(tú) bí-ò*

76. Odonata [dragon-fly (7)]
   Southwest/Central [?]: ThaiYB (51): *(tua) chỉ chuồn;* Yên Bay [unidentified] (55): *(tua) chuồn-chuồn*

77. Odonata [dragon-fly (8), larvae]
   Southwest: BT: *niaw^3 (too^1);* TV: *niaw^3 (too^1);* Lao: *niaw^{C3} (too^{A2})*

78. Orthoptera, Acrididae [grasshopper (1)]
   Southwest: {tak^{DS} (ten^4)} all SW languages except Ahom: *teñ*
   Central: {UB + tak^{DS}} NùngLK (36–39) {UB + thak^{DS}} ThổBK (9), ThổCB (11, 14, 17), Cao Binh (12), Nùng-an (13), ThổHG (22), ThổMC (42), ThổTQ (49) {tak^{DS} (ten^4)} ThổBG (2), ThổLK (41), ThổTQ (49) {thak^{DS} (then^4)} ThổCB (10, 16) {thak^{DS} (than^4)} ThổBK (7, 8, 9), ThổTQ (49) *thác (giáng)* ThổCB (16)
   Nùng-an: (13): *(tu) thạc*
   Northern: {UB + tak^{DS}} Yay, Dioi, GiayHG (20), NhắngLK (34, 35) WM: *(rak^5)*
   Kam-Sui: PKS **thrak^7;* AC: *djaak^{7b} ka-^{3} waai^2* 'kind of grasshopper' (also: *djaak^{7b} hwaai^5* 'cricket' [glosses not dependable]); Ten: *zjak^{35} (ne)*
   Kadai: BY: *tak^{44} (li^{53})*

79. Orthoptera, Acrididae [grasshopper (2)]
   Central: NùngLS (29): *then (tu);* ThổBG (3): *meng ten (tu);* ThổBK (6, 8): *meng ten (tua);* ThổLS (30): *manh then (tua);* ThổLS (33): *meng then;* ThổHG (21): *then (ti)*

80. Orthoptera, Acrididae [grasshopper (3)]
    Central: WN: lum^3 $(tii^1$ tak^7-); NùngS: luồm (tu); TayS: luúm (tu);
    ThồBG (1): luồm (tu); ThồBG (4): lồm (tu); NùngCB (15): lum (tu);
    ThồLS (32): lum
    Caolan: (44, 45): lùm làu; (50): lám (tá)
    Northern: Yay: $luam^5$ [?] $(tua^4$ tak^7-)

81. Orthoptera, Acrididae [grasshopper (4)]
    Southwest: WT(27): tấp khoang
    Central: ThồYB: (tú méng) cáp quang; ThồLS (31): (tua) cáp cooang;
    ThồLS (33): (tua) cháp cháo; ThồMC (43): (tu) cạp sản

82. Orthoptera, Grillidae [cricket (1)]
    Southwest: BT: cii^4 hit^5; TV: cii^2 $hiit^5$ (small); Siamese: $ciŋ^3$ $riit^2$
    Central: NùngS: cá lít (tu); TayS: chi rit/lịt (tu); ThồBG (2): chí hit;
    ThồCB (17, 18): (tuo) khí-lít; ThồHG: (tu) chí-rít
    Northern: Mène: cii^2 $hiit^2$ (probably SW borrowing)
    Be: BeS: hit 'sauterelle'

83. Orthoptera, Gryllidae [cricket (2), large]
    Southwest: BT: $kuŋ^2$ (cii^4); TV: $kuŋ^2$ (cii^2); MM: $kuŋ^{B2}$ $(ci?-)$; ThaiYB
    (51, 52): (tua) chi cháng; ThaiLK (40): (tú) chí cháng
    Central: ThồBG (2): (tú) chí còng; ThồLK (41): chí cháng; ThồYB (54):
    (tô méng) chí cáng
    Other: Chinese: GSR (1172e') *g'i̯ung/g'i̯wong/k'iung 'cricket'; MC:
    g'i̯[w]ong 'cricket, locust' [K470]; Viet: con cùng

84. Orthoptera, Gryllidae [cricket (3)]
    Central: {(cak) cay} ThồCB (11, 14, 16, 18), Cao Binh (12) {(tak) tay}
    NhắngLK (34), NùngLK (37, 38), YayG 'small cricket that does not
    fight' ThồQY (46) míng giày; ThaiYB (53) [SW] (tú) sáy

85. Orthoptera, Gryllidae [cricket (4)]
    Southwest: {tak (tian)} ThaiHB (23, 24, 25)
    Central: {cak (cay)} ThồCB (11, 14, 18), Cao Binh (12) {tak (tay)}
    NhắngLK (34), NùngLK (37, 38) thác (cháy) ThồCB (16) {tak (ngaw)}
    NùngLK (39), ThồLK (41)
    Northern: {tak (ngaw)} NhắngLK (35) {tak (nan)} YayHG (20) {thak
    (tan)} Nùng-an (13)

86. Orthoptera, Gryllidae [cricket (5)]
 {(tak) ngaw} NhắngLK (35) NùngLK (39), ThổLK (41), YayG 'cricket used for fighting'

87. Orthoptera, Gryllidae [cricket (6)]
 Southwest: *{(tak) tian}* ThaiHB (23, 24, 25)
 Central: {UB + *dan*} NùngLK (36)
 Northern: *{(tak) nan}* YayHG (20) *{(thak) tan}* Nùng-an (13)

88. Orthoptera, Gryllidae [cricket (7)]
 Central: *{kay (taw)}* ThổMC (42), ThổLS (31, 32) *{khay (taw)}* NùngBG (5) *{kay (naa)}* ThổBK (8), ThổLS (33) *{kay (k'm)}* ThổBG (4) Cao Lan (13): *{ka[a] (taw)}*
 Other: GSR (533a–d) **g'iwəd / yiwei-* 'kind of cricket'

89. Orthoptera, Gryllidae [cricket (8)]
 Central: *{(kay) taw}* ThổMC (42), ThổLS (31, 32) *{(khay) taw}* NùngBG (5) Cao Lan (44, 45, 50): *{(ka[a]) taw}*

90. Orthoptera, Gryllidae [cricket (9)]
 Central: *{ʔɔn mɔn}* ThổMC (43), NùngLS (30), ThổBK (8), ThổCB (10, 18) *{ʔon mɔn)* ThổBK (7, 9) *{ʔuan mɔn}* ThổBG (1, 3)

91. Orthoptera, Gryllidae [cricket (10)]
 Central: ThổTQ (49): *(tu) chí-lé;* NùngLS (29): *chảm ri;* ThổLS (31): *chảm ri;* ThổBG (8): *(tua) tùm ri*

92. Orthoptera, Gryllotalpidae [mole cricket (1)]
 Southwest: BT: *sɔn⁴ (cii²);* Lao: *sɔɔn^A4 (ka-)/(cii^B2)/(mɛɛŋ^A4);* MM: *cɔɔn^A4 (mɛɛŋ^A4)*
 Northern: Mène: *cɔn⁴ (mɛŋ⁴)*

93. Orthoptera, Gryllotalpidae [mole cricket (2)]
 Northern: Mène: *dəə⁴ (too⁴ ka-)*
 Other: GSR (123.1) **glu/ləu* 'mole cricket' [??]

94. Orthoptera, Tettigoniidae [katydid]
 Southwest: BT: *man⁴ (mɛŋ⁴);* TV: *man⁴ (mɛŋ⁴):* ThaiHB (23): *(tú) mành tặc ten*
 Central: NùngHG (19): *tác khẩu mận*

Northern: Mène: *man⁴ (mɛŋ⁴)*
Kam-Sui: T'en: *zjak³⁵ man³⁵* 'kind of grasshopper'

95. Phasmida, Phasmatidae [walking stick]
    Central: TayS: *tu hám khoan*
    Northern: Mène: *mɛŋ⁴ haap² phii⁴*

96. Siphonaptera [flea]
    Southwest: BT: *mat⁷ (too¹)*; TV: *mat⁷ (tua⁴)*; Lao: *mat^DS1 (too^A2)*; Siamese: *mat²*
    Central: WN: *mat⁷ (tii¹)*; LM: *mat³ (tuu¹)*; NùngS: *mát (tu)*
    Northern: Yay: *mat⁷ (tua⁴)*; Dioi: *mat¹ (toueu²)*; SaekG: *mat⁴*; Mène: *mat² (too⁴)*
    Be: BeS: *mot*
    Kam-Sui: PKS **k-hmat⁷*; T'en: *mat³⁵ (ne)*
    Hlai: PH **mʔoot⁷*; DayS: *mát (cử lống)*
    Kadai: Lachi: *[maam¹¹]*

97. Arthropoda, Crustacea [crab]
    Southwest: {UB + *puu^A*}
    Central: {UB + *puu ~ pow^A*}
    Northern: {UB + *paw^A*} Yay, Dioi, Saek

98. Arthropoda, Crustacea [shrimp (1)]
    Southwest: {UB + *kuŋ^C*}
    Central: {UB + *kuŋ ~ koŋ^C*}
    Northern: {UB + *kuŋ^B*} Yay, Saek, WM {LF + *koŋ^B*} Dioi [LF = *neng²*]
    Bê: *zoang*

99. Arthropoda, Crustacea [shrimp (2), small]
    Southwest: Shan: *ŋew⁴*
    Central: WN: *yiiw⁴ (tuu¹)*; LP: *yiiw⁴*; LM: *yiiw⁴*; LC: *yiiw²*; TayS: *(tu) cúng nghiều, (tu) nghiều*
    Kam-Sui: T'en: *ŋjuu³⁵ (ne)*

Tai-Kadai Arthropods

Appendix 2: Sources

The first list below contains language names and sources abbreviated with letters only. Language abbreviations including a numeral in parentheses, such as GiayHG (20), are contained in the second list below. For abbreviations followed by EFEO, see the third list.

1. Language names and sources

AC	[Ai-Cham] (Shi Lin and Cui Jianxin 1989)
AmoyD	[Amoy of Douglas] (Douglas 1899)
BeS	[Bê, Savina] (Savina 1965)
BK	(Bernhard Karlgren)
BT	[Black Tai] (author's fieldnotes)
BY	[Buyang] (Liang Min 1990)
DayS	[Day of Savina] (Savina 1931)
Dioi	(Esquirol and Williate 1908)
GL	[Gelao] (Hé 1982)
GSR	[Grammata Serica Recensa] (Karlgren 1957)
Hsi-Lin	(Li 1977)
Kam-CZ	[Chezhai Kam] (Zheng and Yang 1988)
Kam-ZG	[Zhanglu Kam] (Zheng and Yang 1988)
Lachi	(Liang Min 1990)
Lao	(Laos, Ministry of Education 1962)
LBNG	[Luang Prabang Lao] (author's fieldnotes)
LC	[Lungchou] (Li 1940)
LM	[Lung Ming] (Gedney fieldnotes)
LMY	[Lue of Meuang Yong] (Gedney's fieldnotes)
LP	[Lei Ping] (Gedney fieldnotes)
Mak	(Li 1943)
Mat.	(Matisoff 1988)
MC	[Middle Chinese, Karlgren] (Karlgren 1923)
Mène	(author's fieldnotes)
MM	Kam Meuang from Meth 1965 1 14 20 83 92
NùngS	[Nùng, Savina] (Savina 1924)
Pai-sha	? (Wang Li and Qian Sun 1951)
PB	[Pubiao] (Zhang Junru 1990)
PH	[Mat.] [Proto Hlai of Matisoff] (Matisoff 1988)
PH	[Proto-Hlai] (Thurgood 1991)
Po-ai	(Li 1977)?
PKS	[Proto Kam-Sui] (Thurgood 1988)

SaekC   [Saek, Cuaz] (Cuaz 1904)
SaekG   [Saek, Gedney] (Gedney fieldnotes)
Siamese   (author fieldnotes, Gedney fieldnotes)
SZ (Ed)   [Sz Lok] (Gedney's fieldnotes)
T'en   [Yanghwang] (Li 1968)
TayS   [Tay, Savina] (Savina 1910)
Thổ BG   (Gedney)
Thổ CB   (C. Brown)
TV   [Tai Vat] (author's fieldnotes)
WM   [Wuming] (Li 1956)
WN   [Western Nùng] (author's fieldnotes)
WT   [White Tai] (Donaldson 1970)
Yay   (author's fieldnotes Gedney 1991)

2. Index to the 1938 EFEO Questionnaire

1. Mường of Bắc Giang (I.1)
2. Thổ of Bắc Giang (I.2)
3. Thổ of Bắc Giang (I.3)
4. Thổ of Bắc Giang (I.4)
5. Nùng of Bắc Giang (I.5)
6. Tày of Bach Thông, Bắc Cạn (II.3)
7. Thổ of Bắc Cạn (II.4)
8. Thổ of Bắc Cạn (II.5)
9. Thổ of Bắc Cạn (II.6)
10. Thổ of Lóc Giang Cao Bằng (III.1)
11. Thổ of Bảo Lạc, Cao Bằng (III.2)
12. Cao Bình (III.2)
13. Nùng-an of Cao Bằng (III.3)
14. Thổ of Cao Bằng (III.5)
15. Nùng of Cao Bằng (III.5)
16. Thổ of Cao Bằng and Lạng Sơn (III.7)
17. Thổ of Cao Bằng (III.8)
18. Thổ of Cao Bằng (Cao Bình, Nước Hai, Nguyễn (III.9)
19. Nùng of Hà Giang (IV.1)
20. Giay of Hà Giang (IV.4)
21. Thổ of Hà Giang (IV.6)
22. Thổ of Hà Giang (IV.7)
23. Thái or Thổ Mai Đa Hòa Bình (V.5)
24. Thái or Thổ Mai Đa Hòa Bình Mai Thương (V.6)
25. Thái or Thổ Mai Đa Hòa Bình Quy Dức (V.6)

26. Thái Noir, Lai Châu (VI.2)
27. Thái Blanc, Lai Châu (VI.3)
28. Thái Blanc, Lai Châu (VI.4)
29. Nùng of Lạng Sơn (VII.1)
30. Nùng of Lạng Sơn (VII.2)
31. Thổ of Lạng Sơn (VII.6)
32. Thổ of Lạng Sơn (VII.7)
33. Thổ of Lạng Sơn (VII.8)
34. Nhắng of Mường Khương Lào Cai (VIII.4)
35. Nhắng of Chapa Lào Cai (VIII.5)
36. Nùng of Mường Khương Lào Cai (VIII.6)
37. Nùng of Mường Khương Lào Cai (VIII.7)
38. Nùng of Mường Khương Lào Cai (VIII.8)
39. Nùng of Bảo Tháng Lào Cai (VIII.9)
40. Thái of Lào Cai (VIII.13)
41. Thổ of Bảo Tháng Lào Cai (VIII.14)
42. Thổ of Bình Liêu Móng Cái (IX.5)
43. Thổ of Móng Cái (IX.6)
44. Màn Cao Lan, Phu Thọ (XI.7)
45. Màn Cao Lan, Tiên Ả (XI.8)
46. Thổ of Hoành-Bồ, Quảng Yên (XIII.5)
47. Thái Noir of Phù Yên, Sơn La (XIV.1)
48. Thái Noir of Sơn La (XIV.2)
49. Thổ of Chiêm Hoá Tuyên Quang (XVI.1)
50. Màn Cao Lan of Yên Sơn Tuyên Quang (XVI.2)
51. Thái of Trại Hút, Yên Bái (XIX.5)
52. Thái of Yên Bái (XIX.2)
53. Thái Noir of Than Uyên Yên Bái (XIX.5)
54. Thổ of Yên Bái (XIX.6)
55. unidentified Yên Bái (XIX.7)

3. EFEO language abbreviations

Hà Giang	(HG)
Hòa Bình	(HB)
Lai Châu	(LCh)
Lạng Sơn	(LS)
Mường Khương	(MK)
Lào Cai	(LC)
Bắc Giang	(BG)
Bắc Cạn	(BC)

Cao Bằng   (CB)
Cao Bình   (BH)
Móng Cái   (MC)
Tiên Á   (TA)
Quảng Yên   (QY)
Sơn La   (SL)
Tuyên Quang   (TQ)
Yên Bái   (YB)

References

Berlin, Brent, Dennis Breedlove, and Peter Raven. 1973. General principles of classification and nomenclature in folk biology. American Anthropologist 75:214–42.

Brown, Cecil H. 1984. Language and living things: Uniformities in folk classification and naming. New Brunswick N.J.: Rutgers University Press.

Chamberlain, James R. 1977. Proto-Tai zoology. Ph.D. dissertation. University of Michigan.

———. 1980. Proto-Tai zoology: Amphibians. Paper presented at the Thirteenth International Conference on Sino-Tibetan Languages and Linguistics, University of Virginia, 1980.

———. 1981a. Proto-Tai zoology: Chelonians. Péninsule 2:245–82. Paper presented at the Twelfth International Conference on Sino-Tibetan Languages and Linguistics, Paris, 1979.

———. 1981b. Proto-Tai zoology: Serpentes. Paper presented at the Fourteenth International Conference on Sino-Tibetan Languages and Linguistics, University of Florida, Gainesville, 1981.

———. 1992. Biolinguistic systematics and marking. In Pan-Asiatic Linguistics: Proceedings of the Third International Symposium on Language and Linguistics. 3:1279–93. Bangkok: Chulalongkorn University.

Cordominas, Georges. 1980. L'espace social a propos de l'Asie du Sud-Est. Paris: Flammarion.

Cuaz, M. J. 1904. Etude sur la langue laocienne. Hong Kong: Imprimerie de la Société des Missions Etrangères.

Điêu, Chính Nhǜm and Jean Donaldson. 1970. Pǎp san khǎm pòk Tǎy-Keo-Eng: [Ngữ-vựng Thời-Việt-Anh] [Tai-Vietnamese-English vocabulary]. Saigon: Department of Education.

Douglas, Carstairs. 1899. Chinese-English dictionary of the vernacular or spoken language of Amoy with the principle variations of the Changchow and Chin-chow dialects. London: Presbyterian Church of England.

Eberhard, Wolfram. 1969. The local cultures of South and East China. Leiden: E. J. Brill.
Edmondson, Jerold A. and David B. Solnit. Comparative Kadai: Linguistic Studies beyond Tai. Summer Institute of Linguistics and the University of Texas at Arlingtion Publications in Linguistics 86. Dallas.
Esquirol, Joseph, and Gustave Williatte. 1908. Essai de dictionnaire dioi-français. Hong Kong: Imprimerie de la Société des Missions Etrangères.
Good, Ronald D. 1964. The geography of flowering plants. London: Longmans.
Gressitt, J. Linsley. 1970. Biogeography of Laos. Pacific Insects Monograph 24. 573–626.
———, J. A. Rondon, and Stephan von Breuning. 1970. Cerambycid-beetles of Laos [Longicornes du Laos]. Pacific Insects Monograph 24. Honolulu: Bishop Museum.
Hè Jiashan, ed. 1982. Gelao language. Beijing: Ethnographic Institute Publications.
Hudak, Thomas J., ed. 1991. William J. Gedney's The Yay language: Glossary, texts, and translations. In Thomas J. Hudak (ed.), Michigan Papers on South and Southeast Asia 38. Ann Arbor: University of Michigan Center for South and Southeast Asian Studies.
Karlgren, Bernhard. 1923. Analytic dictionary of Chinese and Sino-Japanese. Paris: P. Geuthner. (Dover Edition, 1974, New York).
———. 1957. Grammata Serica Recensa. Stockholm: Museum of Far Eastern Antiquities, Bulletin 29:1–332. (Reprinted 1964, Göteborg: Elanders Boktryckeri Aktiebolag).
Laos, Ministry of Education. 1962. Wachananukom Phasa Lao. Vientiane: Ministry of Education Press.
Li Fang-Kuei. 1940. The Tai dialect of Lungchow: Texts, translations and glossary. Institute of History and Philology Monograph Series A 16. Taipei: Academia Sinica.
———. 1943. Notes on the Mak language. Institute of History and Philology Monograph Series A 20. Taipei: Academia Sinica.
———. 1956. The Tai dialect of Wu-Ming: Texts, translation, and glossary. Bulletin of the Institute of History and Philology Monograph Series A 19. Shanghai: Academia Sinica.
———. 1968. Notes on the T'en or Yanghwang language: Glossary. Bulletin of the Institute of History and Philology 40:397–504.
———. 1977. A handbook of comparative Tai. Honolulu: The University Press of Hawaii.
Liang Min. 1990a. The Buyang language. Kadai 2:13–22.
———. 1990b. The Lachi language. Kadai 2:35–44.

MacKinnon, John R. and Kathy MacKinnon. 1974. Animals of Asia: The ecology of the Oriental region. New York: Holt, Rinehart and Winston.

Matisoff, James A. 1988. Proto-Hlai initials and tones: A first approximation. In J. Edmondson and D. Solnit, eds. 289–321.

Pyle, Charles. 1991. Natural logic. ms.

Savina, F. M. 1910. Dictionnaire tày-annamite-français précede d'un precis de grammaire tay et suivi d'un vocabulaire français-tay. Hanoi: Imprimerie d'Extrême-Orient.

———. 1924. Dictionnaire étymologique français-nùng-chinois. Hong Kong: Imprimerie de la Société des Missions Etrangères.

———. 1931. Lexique day-français accompagne d'un petit lexique français-day et d'u tableau des differences dialectales. Bulletin de l'École français d'Extrême-Orient 31:103–99.

———. 1965. Le vocabulaire bê. A.-G. Haudricourt, ed. Paris: l'École français d'Extrême-Orient.

Schafer, Edward. 1967. The vermillion bird. Berkeley: University of California Press.

Shi Lin and Cui Jianxin. 1989. Ai-Cham-English glossary. Kadai 1:25–62.

Thurgood, Graham. 1988. Notes on the reconstruction of Proto-Kam-Sui. In J. Edmondson and D. Solnit, eds., 179–218.

———. 1991. Proto-Hlai (Lí): A look at initials, tones, and finals. Kadai 3:1–49.

Udvardy, Miklos D. F. 1969. Dynamic zoogeography: With special reference to land animals. New York: Van Nostrand Reinhold Co.

Wang Li and Qian Sun. 1951. Hainandao Baisha Liyu chutan. Lingnan Science Journal 2(11):254–300.

Yin-Ch'i Hsu. 1928–1929. Crickets in China. Peking Society of Natural History Bulletin 3:5–43.

Zhang Junru. 1990. The Pubiao language. Kadai 2:23–34.

Zheng Guoqiao and Yang Quan. 1988. The sounds of Rongjiang Kam. In J. Edmondson and D. Solnit, eds. 45–58.

The Emergence of the Length Distinction in the Mid-front Vowels *e-ee* in Thai

Puttachart Dhananjayananda
Department of Linguistics, Chulalongkorn University
Bangkok, Thailand

Introduction

The Proto-Southwestern Tai vowel system, reconstructed by Li (1977:259–61) and Sarawit (1973:97) shows the length distinction for all high vowels and mid-low vowels as follows:

(1)   *i   *ii   *ɨ   *ɨɨ   *u   *uu
              *e   *o
              *εε   *a   *aa   *ɔɔ

When compared with the vowel systems of the daughter languages in the Southwestern Tai group, it is found that in all the daughter languages except Thai only the mid-low vowels *a-aa* possess the length distinction.[1] The vowel system of Thai[2] is different from those of other Tai languages in that it consists of nine pure vowels, all of which contrast in length. The Thai vowel system can be represented as follows:

---

[1]This paper is a revised version of a paper with the same name originally published in 1992 *Pan-Asiatic linguistics*. Vol. III. Bangkok: Chulalongkorn University Printing House.

[2]'Thai' in this paper refers to Standard Thai.

(2)
```
       i    ii   ɨ    ɨɨ   u    uu
       e    ee   ə    əə   o    oo
       ɛ    ɛɛ   a    aa   ɔ    ɔɔ
```

Li (1977:260–61) claims that the vowels *ee ɛ oo ɔ* might have been introduced into the Thai vowel system through borrowing or secondary developments.

In order to test Li's claim, the documents of the Sukhothai period (Inscription I) and of the present period (Royal Institute Dictionary B.E. 2525 [A.D. 1982]) are investigated. I found that in the Sukhothai period only two written forms are used to represent the vowel *e* or *ee*: <เ->³ ทเล /thalee/ 'sea'; <เ-C> เตม /tem/ 'full'. Four written forms are used, however, in the present period: <เ-> เจดีย์ /ceedii/ 'pagoda'; <เ-C> เหตุ /hèet/ 'cause'; <เ-ˇC> เด็ก /dèt/ 'to pluck (flowers)'; <เ-ะ> เตะ /tè?/ 'to kick'. It is hypothesized, therefore, that the length distinction of the vowel *e-ee* may have emerged at some time between the Sukhothai and the present period. A study to locate the more specific time of the emergence of the length distinction of mid and low vowels in Thai should thus be very interesting.

This study investigates when the length distinction of the mid-front vowels (*e-ee*) emerged, and whether borrowing is a significant factor in such emergence.

Research Methodology

In this study, the orthographic forms used to represent the vowel *e-ee* (<เ->; <เ-C>; <เ-ˇC>; <เ-ะ>), which may be accompanied by each of the following markers: ˊ ˇ ˜ ˙)[4] are drawn from ten selected documents during five periods (Sukhothai, Ayudhaya, Early Bangkok, Middle Bangkok, and present).[5] After that the data are compared with lexical items in other Tai dialects and also in other languages so that the types of words can be specified. A hypothesis on the emergence of the length distinction for the mid-front vowels *e-ee* is given at the end.

---

[3] The hyphen <-> represents the initial consonant. Thai words are given both in Thai orthography and in a transcription of modern pronunciation, using the Haas system modified by substituting final stops /p t k/ for Haas' /b d g/.

[4] Words which are written <เ-> co-occur with all tone marks. Although all combinations are collected in the present study, words in proto-tones B and C cannot be considered. I have removed from consideration items from these two groups because Thai orthographic conventions do not allow length to be shown when vowels *e-ee* (เ-) co-occur with the tone marks corresponding to proto-tones B and C. So all the example words used in developing conclusions drawn here are in proto-tones A or D.

[5] I assume that the documents of the Sukhothai, Ayudhaya, and Bangkok periods reflect successive stages in the development of a single variety of the language.

The Occurrence of Written Forms Used for *e-ee*

The data are grouped according to two factors: forms and types of words.

First the data are put into five groups according to different orthographic forms of the vowel *e-ee*. This is to study the development of these written forms, which are as follows:

(3) 1. <เ->   เฉ /chěe/   to incline
     2. <เ-C>   เลศ /lêet/   trick
     3. <เ-C> ~ <เ็-C> เปน ~ เป็น /pen/ to be
     4. <เ็-C>   เข็ด /khèt/   ball of cotton
     5. <เ-ะ>   เกะ /kè?/   short

The third type above shows the variation of written forms <เ-C> and <เ็-C>.

The following table displays the count of different written forms of the vowel *e-ee* in five periods (the numbers for each form in the table refer to numbers of different words. E.g. the number 2 for Inscription I forms <เ-> refer to two different words ทเล /thalee/ and เจดิย์ /ceedii/).

(4) Occurrence of written forms used for *e-ee*

Period	A.D.	Documents	Written forms					Total
			<เ->	<เ-C>	<เ-C> ~ <เ็-C>	<เ็-C>	<เ-ะ>	
Sukhothai	1292	Inscrip.I	2	9	—	—	—	11
	1341–67	Srichum	4	27	—	—	—	31
Ayudhaya	1686	Kosa Paan	12	27	3	3	—	45
	1728	Pamok	1	11	—	—	—	12
Early Bk.	1804	3 Sealed Laws	33	101	14	2	—	150
	1825–27	Rama III	23	77	11	2	1	114
Middle Bk.	1854	Dict.Ling.	200	263	5	97	12	577
	1891	Dict. 2434	191	336	6	75	4	612
Present	1927	Dict. 2470	233	350	—	130	17	730
	1982	Dict. 2525	222	409	2	137	20	790

As one can see, only two forms <เ-> and <เ-C> occurred in the Sukhothai period. During the Ayudhaya and Middle Bangkok periods, there was variation between forms <เ-C> ~ <เ็-C>. And at the same time, there is occurrence of the non-varying representation <เ็-C>. The form <เ-ะ> appears last, in the Early Bangkok period.

Second, in order to discover if different written forms are dictated by different types of words, the data are assigned to three groups according to whether they are cognates, new formations, or borrowings:

(5) a. Cognates: Words with Tai cognates specified by Sarawit (1973) and Li (1977), for example:

เจ็ด /cèt/ 'seven'
เปลว /pleew/ 'flame'

b. New formations: Words that are neither cognates nor loanwords, for example:

สะเก็ด /sakèt/ 'fragment'
เลก /lêek/ 'man'

c. Loanwords: Words borrowed from other languages, for example:

เซ็น /sen/ 'to sign' (English)
เทวา /theewaa/ 'angel' (Pali)

The data in (6) show the counts of word types for different forms of the vowel *e-ee* over the course of the five periods.

(6) Occurrence of written forms used for *e-ee* in cognates (C), new formations (N), and loanwords (L) in the five periods

Documents	<เ->			<เ-C>			<เ-C>~ <เ̆-C>			<เ̆-C>			<แ>		
	C	N	L	C	N	L	C	N	L	C	N	L	C	N	L
Inscription I	—	—	2	6	—	3	—	—	—	—	—	—	—	—	—
Srichum	—	1	3	10	2	15	—	—	—	—	—	—	—	—	—
Kosa Paan	—	1	11	14	4	9	1	—	2	1	1	1	—	—	—
Pamok	—	—	1	1	3	7	—	—	—	—	—	—	—	—	—
3 Sealed Laws	—	9	24	16	31	54	7	1	6	1	—	1	—	—	—
Rama III	—	2	21	10	20	47	6	—	5	1	—	1	—	1	—
Dictionary Ling	—	99	101	8	107	148	—	2	3	28	50	19	—	10	2
Dictionary 2434	—	43	148	8	69	259	1	4	1	26	32	17	—	4	—
Dictionary 2470	—	80	153	11	128	211	—	—	—	37	60	33	—	14	3
Dictionary 2525	—	92	130	8	182	219	—	2	—	34	72	31	—	15	5

The data demonstrate that the form <เ-> was first used for Pali and Sanskrit loanwords and later for new Thai words. The form <เ-C> is used for cognates, new formations, and loanwords. But during the Ayudhaya and Early Bangkok periods some cognates, new formations, and loanwords experienced gradual change in the written forms of their vowels from <เ-C> to <เ̊-C>. Although there was a time when <เ̊-C> existed in free variation with <เ-C>, the form <เ̊-C> increases in occurrence as we approach the present period. Beyond that, it seems that the form <เ-ะ> arose abruptly in the Middle Bangkok period. However, there are only a few examples of this form.

The Occurrence of Distinct Forms

In considering whether different sounds are different phonemes, the principle of phonemic analysis is used; that is, minimal pairs such as เพ็ญ /phen/ 'full' and เพล /pheen/ 'noon' must be found. Since the present research is based on orthographic forms, the minimal pairs used in this article are pairs of orthographic forms with identical initial consonant symbols, final consonant symbols, and tone markers, but with different vowel symbols. For example:

(7) เล็น /len/ 'white louse' : เลน /leen/ 'mud'
     เช็ก /chét/ 'to wipe'   : เชษฐ /chêet/ 'pre-eminent'[6]

In (8) below all pairs of distinct written forms are grouped according to types of words in each pair. The abbreviations used for any group consist of two letters identifying the word types; for example C-C = both forms are cognates; C-N = one is cognate, the other is a new formation; and C-L = one is cognate, the other is a loanword.

(8) Occurrence of distinct written forms grouped by types of words

Types and Paired Forms	Documents			
	Dict. Ling.	Dict. 2434	Dict. 2470	Dict. 2525
1. C-C				
เห็น /hěn/ 'see' : เหน /hěen/ 'weasel'	+	—	—	—
2. C-N				
เหล็น /lěn/ 'great grandchild' : เหลน /lěen/ 'lizard sp'	+	—	—	—

---

[6]Editors' note: As the author states, these are orthographic minimal pairs. The reader will notice, here and in (8) below, that the modern spoken forms also make minimal pairs when the final consonant is nasal, as in /len : leen/, but that the many syllables with final stops, as /chét : chêet/, are not minimal pairs since they differ in tone as well as vowel length. It can plausibly be argued that the high tone of /chét/ and the falling tone of /chêet/ are, in syllables ending in stops, variants conditioned by vowel length (there is no */chêt/). Hence /chét : chêet/ is underlyingly also a minimal pair.

เล็ก /lék/ 'small' : เลก /lêek/ 'able-bodied man'	+	+	+	+
เอ็น /ʔen/ 'tendon, sinew' : เอน /ʔeen/ 'lean, slant'	+	+	−	+
เด็ก /dèk/ 'child' : เดก /dèek/ 'shake, tumble'	−	−	−	+

3. C-L

เผ็ด /phét/ 'spicy' : เผท /phêet/ 'misfortune'	+	−	−	−
เม็ด /mét/ 'seed' : เมศ /mêet/ 'sheep, Aries'	+	−	−	−
เม็ด /mét/ 'seed' : เมท /mêet/ 'butter'	−	+	−	+
เล็น /len/ 'lice' : เลน /leen/ 'mud, loam'	+	+	+	+
เห็ด /hèt/ 'mushroom' : เหตุ /hèet/ 'reason, cause'	+	+	+	+
เล็ด /lét/ 'ooze, seep' : เลส /lêet/ 'trick, fraud'	−	+	−	−
เจ็ด /cèt/ 'seven' : เจด /cèet/ 'intellect'	−	+	−	+
เช็ด /chét/ 'wipe' : เชษฐ /chêet/ 'pre-eminent'	−	+	+	+
เด็ด /dèt/ 'pluck' : เดช /dèet/ 'flame, heat'	−	+	+	+
เล็บ /lép/ 'fingernail' : เลป /lêep/ 'stroke gently'	−	+	+	+
เข็ม /khěm/ 'needle' : เขม /khěem/ 'cheerful'	−	−	+	−
เจ็ด /cèt/ 'seven' : เจฏ /cèet/ 'servant'	−	−	+	−
เกล็ด /klèt/ 'scale' : เกลศ /klèet/ 'lust'	−	−	+	+
เม็ด /mét/ 'seed' : เมตร /méet~mét/ 'meter' (unit measure)	−	−	+	+
เล็ด /lét/ 'seed' : เลท /lêet/ 'stroke, smear'	−	−	+	+
เบ็ด /bèt/ 'barbed hook' : เบส /bèet/ 'base'	−	−	−	+
เป็ด /pèt/ 'duck' : เปต /pèet/ 'ghost'	−	−	−	+

4. N-L

เล็ง /leŋ/ 'aim, gaze' : เลง /leeŋ/ 'gambler'	+	−	−	−
เข็ด /khèt/ 'afraid to re-offend' : เขต /khèet/ 'area'	+	−	+	+
เก็จ /kèt/ 'colored glass' : เกศ /kèet/ 'hair, mane'	−	+	+	+
กะเล็ด /kasèt/ 'a kind of fish' : เกษตร /kasèet/ 'cultivated land'	−	−	+	+
ละเบ็ง /labeŋ/ 'noisy' : ละเบง /labeeŋ/ 'to compose'	−	−	+	+
เพ็จ /phét/ 'dwarfed' : เพศ /phêet/ 'gender, form'	−	−	+	+
เกร็ง /kreŋ/ 'tense' : เกรง /kreeŋ/ 'fear, revere'	−	−	+	−
เก็จ /kèt/ 'colored glass' : เกตุ /kèet/ 'flag'	−	−	−	+
เม็ก /mék/ 'Eugenia grata' (a plant): เมฆ /mêek/ 'cloud'	−	−	−	+

5. N-N

เคล็น /khlen/ 'caress' : เคลน /khleen/ 'mud'	+	−	−	−
เข็น /khěn/ 'push' : เขน /khěen/ 'raised'	+	+	+	+
ระเบ็ง /rabeŋ/ 'a form of dance' : ระเบง /rabeeŋ/ 'pound'	−	+	+	+
เร็ง /reŋ/ 'rapid' : เรง /reeŋ/ 'reckless'	−	−	+	−

6. L-L

เพ็ชร /phét/ 'diamond' : เพท /phêet/ 'divine knowledge'	+	+	−	−
เข็ญ /khěn/ 'trouble' : เขน /khěen/ 'forearm shield'	+	−	+	+

เว็จ /wét/ 'feces' : เวจร์ /wêet/ 'reed'	+	—	+	+
เสร็จ /sèt/ 'finished' : เสษ /sèet/ 'remainder'	+	+	+	+
เท็จ /thét/ 'false': เทศ /thêet/ 'region'	+	+	+	
เว็จ /wét/ 'feces' : เวธ /wêet/ 'perforation'	—	+	—	—
เซ็น /sen/ 'to sign' : เซน /seen/ 'Zen'	—	—	—	+

7. L-N

เจ็น /cen/ 'go out' : เจน /ceen/ 'skillful'	—	+	—	—
เพ็ญ /phen/ 'full' : เพล /pheen/ 'monks' midday mealtime'	+	—	+	+
เอ็ง /ʔeŋ/ 'oneself' : เอง /ʔeeŋ/ 'without cause'	—	+	+	+

From (8), it can be seen that 80% of 46 pairs of distinct written forms are loanwords. This reveals that borrowing is probably the most important factor in the emergence of the length distinction of the mid-front vowels in Thai.

Conclusion

The development of the length distinction in the mid-front vowels *e-ee* may be summed up as follows:
(1) The presence of form <เ-C> and absence of form <เ็-C> in the Sukhothai period indicates that proto-Southwestern Tai *e may have been pronounced either long or short. The variation of *e might have been free variation (*e freely pronounced long or short) or conditioned variation (*e pronounced long or short depending on syllable structure). Such variation may have persisted until the Early Bangkok period.
(2) During the Ayudhaya period and the beginning of the Middle Bangkok period, the fluctuation of written forms <เ-C> and <เ็-C> shows that the language had changed, and scribes were hesitating between traditional spellings and more accurate spellings. However, the form <เ็-C> finally prevailed for the short vowel /e/, while <เ-C> came to be used for the long vowel /ee/.
(3) In the Middle Bangkok period there is an increase of new formations with the written forms <เ-> <เ-C> <เ็-C> and <เ-ะ>. This means that there are two distinct phonemes /e/ and / ee/.

Data Sources

Sukhothai:
1. caarýk phɔ́ɔ khǔn raamkhamhɛ̌ɛŋ (Inscription I)
2. caarýk wát sǐichum (Wat Srichum Inscription)

Ayudhaya:
3. prawàt koosǎapaan lɛʔ còtmǎaj hèet kaan dəən thaaŋ paj faràŋsèet (Autobiography and Letter of Kosa Paan)
4. caarýk wát paamôok (Wat Pamok Inscription)

Early Bangkok:
5. kòtmǎaj traa sǎam duaŋ (Three Seals Law)

	6.	còtmăaj hèet rátchakaan thîi săam (King Rama III Records)
Middle Bangkok:	7.	Dictionarium linguae thai sive siamensis; interpretatione latina, gallica et anglica illustratum. Pallegoix, Jean Baptiste, 1854.
	8.	Dictionary B.E.– 2434, Ministry of Education [A.D. 1891]
Present:	9.	Dictionary B.E. 2470, Ministry of Education [A.D. 1927]
	10.	The Royal Institute Dictionary B.E. 2525 [A.D. 1982]

References

(in Thai)

Boonphan, C. et al. 1981. Bangkok-Chiangmai dictionary. Bangkok: Department of Linguistics, Chulalongkorn University.

Chandhaburinarunat, Phrachaoboromawongthoe Kromphra. 1977. Pali-Thai-English-Sanskrit dictionary. Bangkok: Mahamakot-Rachawithayalai.

Institute of Southern Thai Studies. 1982. Southern Thai dialect dictionary. Songkhla: Srinakarinwirote University.

Kullavanijaya, Pranee 1989. Thai-Chuang dictionary. Bangkok: Language and Literature Center, Chulalongkorn University.

———, Witthaya Chirotkun, and Kalaya Tingsabadh, M. R. 1984. Vocabulary of six Tai languages. Bangkok: Language and Literature Center, Chulalongkorn University.

Leerawat, M. 1982. Comparative Thai dictionary: Bangkok-Chiangmai-Lü-Black Tai. Chiangmai: Faculty of Humanities, Chiangmai University.

Naksakun, K. 1983. Thai-Khmer dictionary. Bangkok: Faculty of Arts, Chulalongkorn University.

Phra Maha Veeravongsa. 1972. Northeastern Thai-Bangkok dictionary. Bangkok: Thai Watana Panich.

Ratanakul, Suriya and L. Daoratanahong. 1987. Thai-Lawa dictionary. Nakhon Pathom: Institute of Language and Culture for Rural Development, Mahidol University.

Sriwiset, P. 1978. Kui-Suai-Thai-English dictionary. Bangkok: English Language Center, Chulalongkorn University.

(in English)

Bandhumedha, Banchob. 1987. Tai Phake-Thai-English dictionary.

Echols, J. M. and S. Hassan. 1975. An Indonesian-English dictionary. Ithaca and London: Cornell University Press.

Gedney, William J. n.d. Comparative Tai word list. ms.

Halliday, M. A. R. S. 1922. A Mon-English dictionary. Bangkok: Siam

Society.
Headley, R. K. 1977. Cambodian-English dictionary. Washington, D.C.: Catholic University of America Press.
Hornby, A. S. 1974. Oxford advanced learner's dictionary of current English. London: Oxford University Press.
Kerr, A. D. 1972. Lao-English dictionary. Washington, D.C.: Catholic University of America Press.
Li, Fang-Kuei. 1977. A handbook of comparative Tai. Honolulu: The University Press of Hawaii.
McFarland, G. B. 1944. Thai-English dictionary. Stanford: Stanford University Press.
Sarawit, Mary E. S. 1973. The Proto-Tai vowel system. Ph.D. dissertation. University of Michigan.
Shorto, H. L. 1962. A dictionary of spoken Mon. London: Oxford University Press.
Thongkum, Theraphan L. 1984. Nyah-Kur (Chao-Bon)-Thai-English dictionary. Bangkok: Chulalongkorn University Printing House.
Wilkinson, R. J. 1959. A Malay-English dictionary. London: Macmillan.

Comparative Shan

Jerold A. Edmondson and David B. Solnit
University of Texas at Arlington and University of Michigan

> Remnants of the non-absorbed and non-Sinicised parts of larger stocks of several races, gradually driven southwestward, these tribes [the Shan] are now scattered, on a large area, into an undefined number of fragments, intermingled to a great extent, and often difficult to trace individually up to their original stems.
>
> The Cradle of the Shan Race
> Terrien De Lacouperie

Background and history

Shan has usually been taken to refer to those Tai languages spoken in Shan State of Myanmar (Burma), Dehong Prefecture of Yunnan Province, China, as well as the adjoining areas of Ruili, Gengma, Menglian, and Mengding Counties, Yunnan, and parts of Mae Hong Son and Chiangrai Provinces of northern Thailand. In the past, the Tai groups of India, upper Myanmar, and even those in distant Guangdong Province, China, were sometimes spoken of as SHAN. Dr. Josiah Cushing (1888b:5–7) uses Shan in a more restrictive

---

We would like to express our thanks to Professors Somsonge Burusphat and Suujaritlak Deepadung of Mahidol University, Bangkok Thailand, and to Ed Robinson of Chulalongkorn University for their help in obtaining some of this data and comments on a draft of this paper.

sense distinguishing among the Khamti, Chinese Shan, and the Burman Shan, which he says belong to a northern group, in opposition to the Siamese and the Lao of the southern group. In this paper we will focus on those languages of Burma and China that have been called Shan, exclusive of Khamti (see map 6). We had hoped to include Khamti data, but our efforts to find a mother-tongue speaker have as yet been frustrated.

Older sources such as Cushing (1888b), Grierson (1928), Carthew (1952), Seidenfaden (1958), and Min Naing (1960) concentrate largely on Assam and northern Burma, and portray a mixed picture. Cushing regards the variation in Shan to be of no importance. He does remark on Burmese influence on the language in the west at Samkah, and names as 'noticeable dialects' Khɯn at Kengtung and Lɯ at Kenghong [Chianghong, Jinghong], the latter is mostly he says the result of admixtures from Lao. But authors subsequent to Cushing generally agree in seeing Khɯn and Lɯ as distinct from Shan, a view that we follow also.

Grierson divides the Shan by geography, not by ethnicity, into (1) the northwestern extending from the Tropic of Cancer to just 25 miles south of the city of Myitkyina and all the way to the Manipuri border; (2) the northern, located somewhat farther east dwelling on the east side of the Irawaddy River and reaching south to a place called Mong Tung,[1] and (3) the southern also east of the Irawaddy. In the northeast, on the protuberance projecting from China along the Shweli toward the Salween, live the Tai Mao or Chinese Shan. Seidenfaden (1958) calls the Chinese Shan the Tai Tayok[2] or Tai Khe, or Tai Nɯa (Nüa/Nə) and distinguishes them from their western cousins, the Tai Moi, Tai Khamti, and various Tai Yai (Cis-Salween and Trans-Salween in Myanmar.[3]

---

[1]Cushing (1888b:511) lists $məŋ^{44}$ $thuŋ^{41}$ 'Möngtung, a small Shan principality south of Hsipaw'. Since we will be discussing Southwest Tai languages in this paper, we will use the Gedney system to notate tones, e.g., A1234, B1234, etc. Splits are indicated as in A1-23-4, which claims that A1 ≠ A2 = A3 ≠ A4.

[2]Burmese /təyou?/ (spoken) <tərup> (written) 'Chinese'. Seidenfaden gives what may be a folk etymology, saying that Tayok is a contraction of Tai Hok Chao 'Tai of the Six Chao or Kingdoms', referring to the six Tai groups which made up the confederation of the Nanzhao (Nanchao; the seventh group was the Tibeto-Burman Mosu or Naxi). there is today considerable doubt as to whether the Nanzhao was a Tai Kingdom (cf. Chamberlain 1975 and Luce 1985). Chinese opinion today is that the Nanzhao was ruled by a Tibeto-Burman group, though there is also no doubt that there were many Tai speakers in this area too.

[3]We have changed Thai to Tai in some of these citations for the sake of consistency of reference. The two names are separated by a sound change, in which *d → th some places and t elsewhere. In speaking of the Tai groups in China, we have exceptionally used the name *Tai*, even though the Hanyu Pinyin transcription requires *Dai* for the same reason. Both *Tai* and *Dai* are pronounced with an unaspirated voiceless stop.

According to Brown (1965), the Shan language can be divided into three major varieties: (a) northern, centered on the city of Lashio in Myanmar; (b) southern, centered on Taunggyi; and (c) eastern, centered on Chiangtung (Kengtung) in the Golden Triangle (Brown 1965:88), If we assume that the latter is Khun, then that leaves a northern-southern distinction in Brown's Shan.[4]

Min Naing (1960) in a Burmese publication continues the three-term system of affiliation found in Cushing, distinguishing the Shan, Khamti, and Shan-Chinese (Shan-Tayok). This same view is found in Lowis (1919), Enriques (1933), and a recently published volume entitled *National Races of the Union of Myanmar* (Tint Hswei 1992). Chinese scholars generally use the term *Dai* for all the Southwest Tai groups without mentioning *Shan* or dwelling on affiliations outside Chinese borders.

The consensus of these older sources is that what we call Shan in the narrow sense is to be distinguished from Khamti to its west, from Khun and Lu to its east, and, we may add, from Tai Yuan (Northern Thai, Kammuang) to its south. To the north are groups formerly called 'Chinese Shan', later Nüa [nɯə, nɤ/ə] 'upper', which are somehow distinct from Shan pure and simple. Within Shan in the narrow sense a north-south division is made by Grierson and Brown; however, as we have noted Grierson's scheme is geographic, not linguistic, while Brown simply asserts his division without giving linguistic or any other kind of evidence.

The Shan are often regarded as the first of several groups to leave China for Southeast Asia. As a consequence, they are often referred to as the Tai Long 'the great Tai'; other groups to the south, including the Siamese, are called the Tai Noy 'lesser Tai'. One Shan native speaker scholar as well as Prof. F. K. Lehman (p.c.) have told us that within Burma they further distinguish between the Tai Long east of the Irrawaddy and the Tai Leng west of the Irrawaddy near Katha. In Irving Glick and Sao Tern Moeng (1991:656) there is a glossary entry for the $taj^{A4}n\partial^{A1}$ 'Chinese Shan' (Shan who are near the border between the Shan State and China), $taj^{A4}nɔj^{C4}$ 'the Thai', and the taj^{A4} jau^{B3} 'the name the Thai use to designate the Shan'.

---

[4]Brown cautions that his "information is limited", and his "eastern" is especially difficult to interpret. The language "centered at Chiantung" ought to be Khun rather than Shan, but Brown states that the one dialect he does cite as "Chiang Rai," which seems to be fairly typical Shan in the narrow sense, is spoken in a village "which migrated from Chiangtung [in the 1930s]." But he does not say whether he regards this Chiang Rai as representing his "eastern Shan."

According to Cushing, the sixth century Shan descended from Southern Yunnan into the Nam Mau or Shweli Valley,[5] establishing a kingdom called Müng Mau Long with the capital at Si Lan (30 miles from Namhkam on the Shweli River). This capital was moved in A.D. 1204 to Müng Mau, which is often written as *Maingmaw*, following Burmese spelling. From there they spread south and east. The northwest Shan are the group from which several westward migrations have emanated. The most famous of these groups are the Ahom invaders of Assam, now effectively extinct as a speech community, who ruled there before being absorbed by the Indo-Aryan majority. *Ahom* may be a later version, via a not-unusual shift of *s* to *h*, of the name *Assam*, which in turn probably is simply another incarnation of Syam (see Introduction to this volume). Later there were other immigrants, the Tai-Phakes, Tai-Aiton, Turung, Khamyang, and Nora (cf. Diller 1992). Northward migration took the Shan into territory of the Kachin, a Tibeto-Burman group of Upper Myanmar. These Shan became the Tai Khamti.

More recent work on the Shan and some Southwest Tai relatives

The areas focused on by the older sources, the Tai territories of Myanmar, northern Laos, and Assam, have not been freely open to linguistic investigation for several decades. More recent work has come largely from the Chinese side. Thus, the study of this ethnolinguistic region has proceeded from opposite sides at separate periods, adding to the difficulty of telling where the various subgroups among the Shan dwell, what they are called (by themselves and outsiders), and how they relate developmentally to one another and to other Tai groups of the area. Recently Diller (1993) has contributed important new information on the situation of the Tai groups of India.

Probably the most extensive and accurate studies of these groups in recent years, beginning in the 1950s, has taken place in China concerning the rather large number of linguistic groups all calling themselves *Tai*, although there has been no attempt until recently to analyze how these groups fit together linguistically. Elsewhere (Solnit and Edmondson 1994) we have surveyed the past decade of this work; we will here summarize some points most relevant

---

[5]Shweli is the Burmese name of this river, which finds reasonable echo in the Yunnanese pronunciation of the Chinese characters 瑞麗 still used as the name of a very small county to the southwest of Dehong prefecture. Since /shwei/ in Burmese is 'gold', there may also be a connection to the name of the town of Namhkam, perhaps 'gold water' in Shan. Lehman notes, however, that in Shan the river is always *nam ma(a)w*, while *nam kham* is only used for the name of the town (p.c.)

to the question of Shan and its delimitation and subgrouping. However, we would emphasize that much concerning these matters remains unclear.

The official Chinese designation Daizu essentially includes all Southwestern Tai speakers of China, all located in Yunnan with a few small exceptions. Of these, the groups located along the southwestern border with Burma are of interest to us here. In the present Chinese classification they are known as the Dehong 'dialect' *(fangyan)* of the Dai language. There is undoubtedly a close correspondence between this Dehong Dai and the groups known outside of China as Nüa/Chinese Shan, although we do not assume that the denotations of the two terms overlap exactly. For a recent description of Dehong Dai and its lexicon see also Luo Yongxian (to appear).

The scholar and Tai Prince, Zhou Yaowen, (1983:10) brings in data concerning the types of scripts in traditional use (pre-1948) among Tai speakers in China. Among others, he notes (1) the *Tai Nuua* [Nə], Upper, or Dry [dry field] Tai of Dehong Prefecture use the $to^{A2}lik^{D2S}$ [lik^{D2S} 'Shan script'], (TL) script; (2) the *Tai Tau*, Lower, or Water [wet field] Tai of Ruili (Shweli) and Mengding Counties use the $to^{A2}pɔŋ^{B4}$ (TP) script. The $to^{A2}pɔŋ^{B4}$ script is exactly the same as the Southern Shan script of the Burman Shan and of Cushing's dictionary. The TL script represents nineteen initial consonants, whereas the TP script has only seventeen. These are in their traditional order: < k x ŋ ts s n̯ t th n p ph m j l v (s) h (h) ʔ >. Two graphs for < s h > in TL were found in the original seventeenth century Shan script, although the two graphs had phonetic values that are homophonous (Wang 1984:310). These two were used for conventional spelling differences and do not reflect a difference of initial consonant or high versus low tone, as is found in the Sipsong Panna script of the Tai Lɯ and, of course, in the better known Tai scripts of Southeast Asia. Indeed, neither the TL or the TP script originally marked tones in any way, and the vowel signs failed to show several distinctive features, such as vowel height (Cushing 1888b:9–10; cf. also Egerod 1957, and Wang 1984:310–17). The TP script has been reformed starting in 1955 to distinguish all vowels and tones unambiguously. This required adding several new vowel signs, as well as tone marks written at the end of the syllable: < no mark, colon, comma, semicolon, period >. Thus: ဝၣ *ma^{A1}* 'dog'; ဝၣ: *ma^{A4}* 'to come'; ဝၣ, *ma^{B1}* 'to soak rice'; ဝၣ; *ma^{C3}* 'to be crazy'; ဝၣ. *ma^{C4}* 'pony, horse'. (For more details see Egerod 1957.) For varieties of the language that have six tones, the sixth tone—category 6—is signified by the symbol ៖, as in ဝၣ៖ *ma^{B4}* 'an exclamation' (cf. Glick and Moeng 1991).[6]

---

[6]This symbol, ultimately a descendent of the Indic *visarga*, is akin—in form, not necessarily in value—to similar elements in other Indic scripts of Southeast Asia, including Mon, Burmese, Siamese (Standard Thai), and Khmer.

Most recently, a comprehensive classification of Dai is proposed by Luo Meizhen (1993). She divides the Dai language *(Daiyu)* into four 'dialects' *(fangyan)*:

(a) Xishuangbanna: the Tai Lɯ of Sipsong Panna
(b) Dehong
(c) Jinping, an extension of the Black and White Tai into China from Vietnam
(d) Hongjin, a new group including communities scattered across central and eastern Yunnan, as well as a few in Sichuan just north of the Yangzi.

Some of these are further divided into local vernaculars *(tuyu)*. Dehong has two, Mengshi (Mangshi) to the north (and west), and Meng-Geng (named for the two centers Gengma and Menglian) to the south and east.

Based on the older sources as well as the recent work of Zhou Yaowen and Luo Meizhen, it may be reasonable to state that Shan in the narrow sense, or Shan Proper, is largely confined to Burma. What remains unclear are the internal divisions of this Shan Proper, and the relation of Shan Proper to Nüa/Chinese Shan. We now turn to recently recorded data from several locations, after which we will see what these data do towards clarifying the two points just mentioned.

Shan tones and initials in panlectal perspective

In 1991, 1992, and 1993 we were able to obtain data from seven informants who represent at least four Tai languages spoken in three countries. We list them and analyze them in rough south-to-north order.

Data on Panglong Shan were obtained from a 34 year-old Buddhist monk in the monastery on the northern outskirts of Mae Sariang, Mae Hong Son Province, Thailand. Panglong is located about 40 kilometers east of Taunggyi in southern Shan State of Myanmar. A second informant, a 39 year-old woman from a neighboring village, provided a similar but distinctive location. Both of these informants had arrived in Thailand less than two years before the data were gathered.

We also interviewed briefly two apprentice monks from the Marble Temple in Bangkok Thailand, who had recently come from Mae Hong Son Province in northern Thailand. The sixteen year-old apprentice was from a village called Naisoi and the twelve year-old apprentice was from Tophae.

The next two locations are in Upper Burma on the Shweli River just across the border from China. Ms. Kham Jai of Longkong near Namhkam was interviewed on a ferry traveling up the Irrawaddy River as she was returning from visiting relatives in Katha, Myanmar. She was 39 years old at the time of the interview and referred to her ethnicity as Tai Mao. Her speech showed similar features to Mau Haung, a 45 year-old male resident in Bangkok, who originally came from Mu-se, upstream 25 kilometers on the Shweli from Namhkam and just across the river from Ruili in Yunnan Province, China.

The speech of the two locations just described has been referred to as Tai Mao or Mau (Harris 1975, Young 1985), Mao being the local name of that stretch of the Shweli river. Harris writes *tay maw⁴*, where 4 = tone A4, while Cushing (1888b) has *nam^{C4} maaw^{44}* 'the Shweli River' (p. 354) and *məŋ^{44} maaw^{44}* 'Möngmow, Shan principality in southwestern China' (p. 512). Young also cites /máau/ 'the Shan state called Mau' (p. 236), where the acute accent marks tone A4 (cf. *táa* 'smear', *náa* 'ricefield'). F. K. Lehman (p.c.) suggests a connection with the word /waaw^{B1}/ 'valley, interspace between two mountains' (Cushing).

Northernmost is the speech of Ms. Guo Yuping of Mangshi (Luxi). Ms. Guo was about 30 years old at the time of the interview in July 1991. Mangshi is located in Dehong Dai Autonomous Prefecture, Yunnan Province, China about 175 kilometers to the northeast of Lashio.

For the purposes of rapid comparison in the pitch plots shown in the charts below, original voiced initials are given with filled boxes and voiceless with empty boxes. In the dead tone categories, diamonds signify syllables with original short vowels, and boxes, original long vowels. In referring to tone categories we use the numerals 1234 to designate the four initial consonant types delineated by Gedney (voiceless friction, voiceless unaspirate, glottalized, voiced). Thus A23 designates a tone that is the reflex of proto-tone A as conditioned by voiceless unaspirated and glottalized initials.

Southern types

In Pinlon (Panglong) Burmese Shan the A tone is split into two reflexes. The A123 category, exemplified in vocabulary items such as *phon^{41}* 'rain', *lin^{41}* 'soil', begins at about mid level, falls to a position just below the mid and then rises to the highest level, i.e., 325, using Chao's five-step tone scale. The A4 tone category as is found in the words *na^{44}* 'wet field' and *saːi^{44}* 'sand', and has a value that begins at about the mid level and rises very slightly toward the end, i.e., in Chao's system, 44. The B4 and the C123 tones have pitch trajectories that seem to merge; the distinctive feature may be a rapid glottal constriction in C123 that can at times even be released to form a quasi-syllable. The pitch shapes begin slightly higher than mid, are level across most of the syllable, and then drop at the end. They could be portrayed as 332 in Chao's system.

The C4 in a word such as nam^{C4} 'water' starts above mid level and drops to the lowest level, i.e., 41. There is some weak glottal constriction at the end of these syllables. The B123 tone value as in $thəu^{B123}$ 'bean' is mid to low falling, not starting as high as the C123 tone, perhaps 221.

Of the dead tone pairs, DL and DS, the DS pair is higher in pitch than the DL pair, and within each pair, syllables with an original voiced initial consonant are higher in pitch than syllables with original voiceless initial consonants. In the DS set, the item mot^{D4S} 'ant' $[<*m-]$ would be assigned a value 53 and the item mat^{D1S} 'flea' $[<*hm-]$ would receive a tone value 35. In the DL set, muk^{D4L} $[<*m-]$ 'mucus' is perhaps a 33 tone, with mok^{D1L} 'cloud' $[<*hm-]$ a 31 tone.

(1) Pinlon (Panglong) A tone pairs

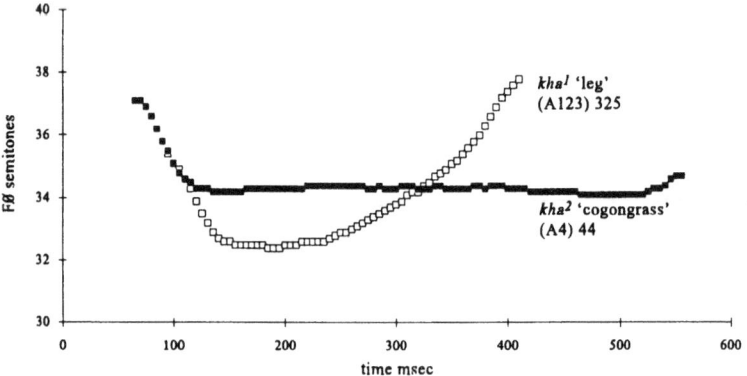

(2) Pinlon (Panglong) B tone pairs

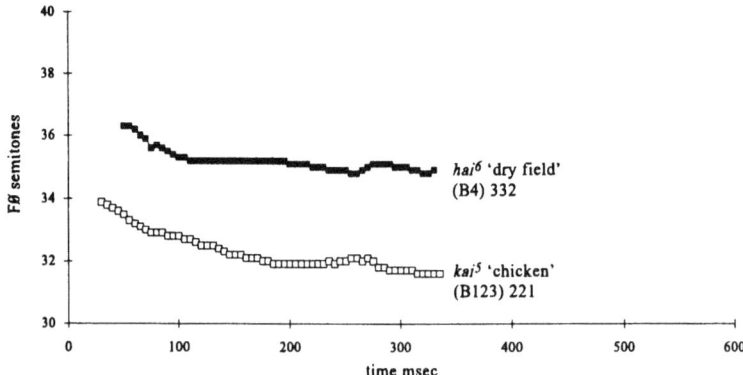

(3) Pinlon (Panglong) C tone pairs

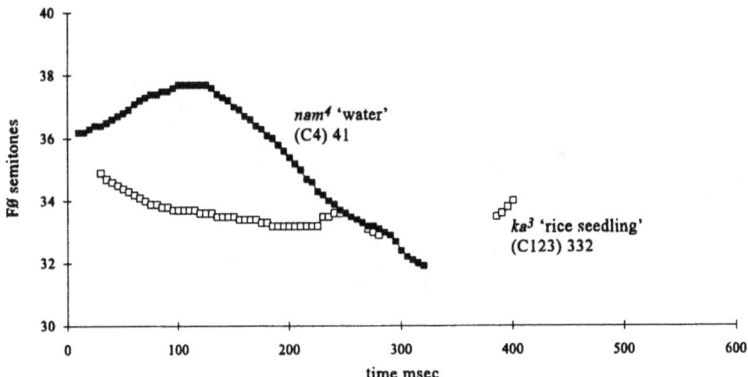

(4) Pinlon (Panglong) DS and DL tone pairs

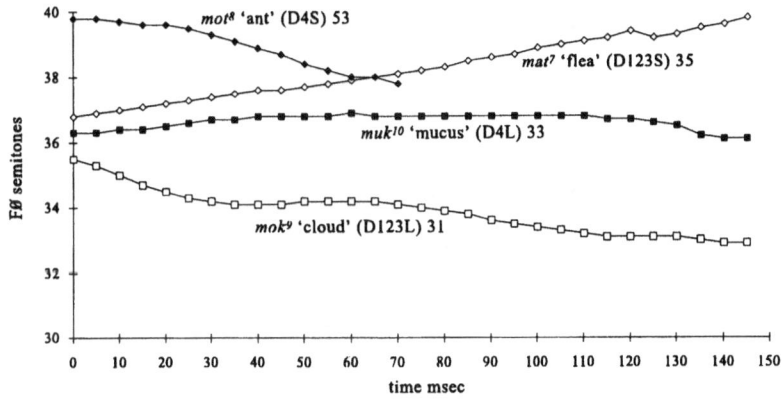

The data on Mae Hong Son Shan showed a very similar system of tonal organization to that found in Pinlon (Panglong): A123 = 325; A2 = 44; B123 = 221; B4 = C123 = 332; C4 = 41; D123S = 33; D4S = 53; D123L = 21; and D4L = 55.

(5) Mae Hong Son A tone pairs

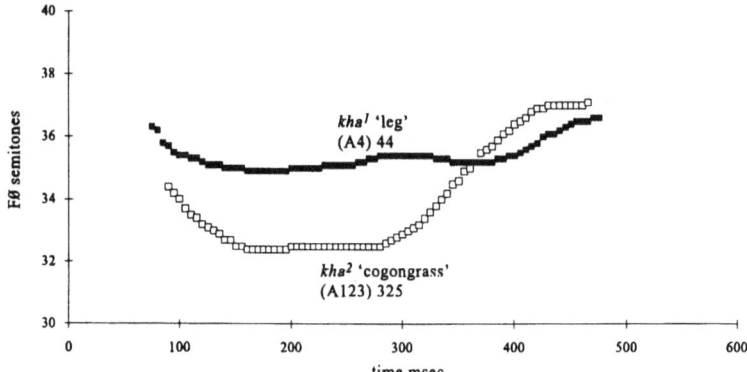

(6) Mae Hong Son B tone pairs

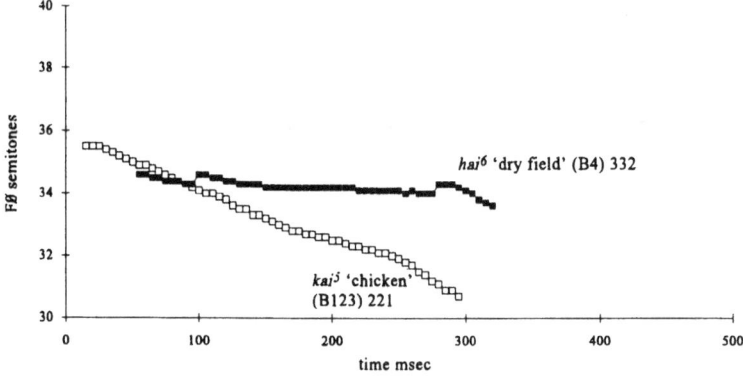

(7) Mae Hong Son C tone pairs

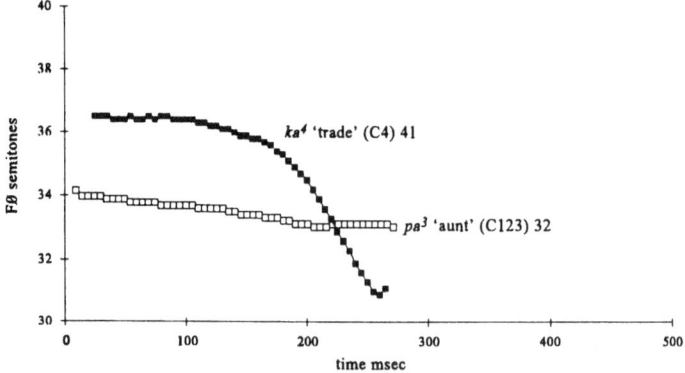

(8) Mae Hong Son DL and DS tone pairs

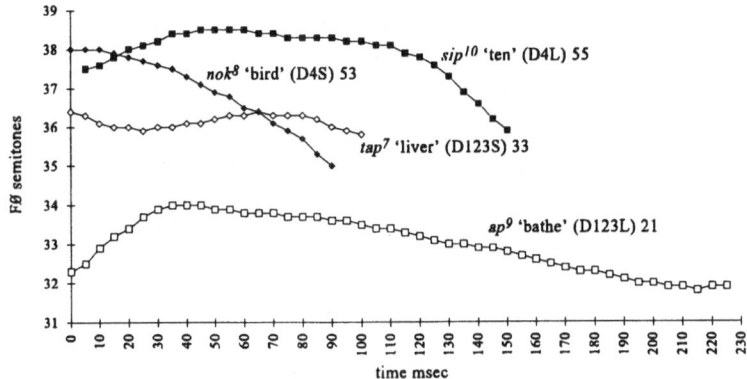

The Mae Hong Son Shan tone categories illustrated by pa^{C2} 'aunt' and hai^{B4} 'dry field' have similar values, but may be distinguished by glottal constriction in the C tone category, although this feature is not especially prominent. Four dead tones seem to be differentiated.

Cushing's dictionary (1888b) is based on the speech of Laihka and Mongnai. Li (1977) gives the following interpretation of the tone values:

(9) A123   35
     A4   55   D123S
     B123   11 or 21   D123L
     B4 = C123 33   D4L
     C4   53   D4S

We have interpreted the tonal descriptions in Glick and Moeng (1991) and assigned them these values:

(10) A123   13
     A4   55   D123S
     B123   11 or 21   D123L
     B4 = C123 33   D4L
     C4   43   D4S

Egerod's (1957) characterization, based on work with Shan speakers from various locations (Hsipaw, Mong Tung, Ke-hsi Mansam, Nam Hu), agrees quite well, although it is less detailed in that the A123 and C4 tones are called simply 'rising' and 'falling' respectively. Egerod also states that B4 = C123 may be slightly falling, and that A4 may be slightly rising.

Northern varieties

Mangshi (Dehong Dai) is very clearly quite different from the first two discussed. It shares some common features of phonology and lexicon, but there are also obvious differences.

(11) Mangshi tone A trajectories

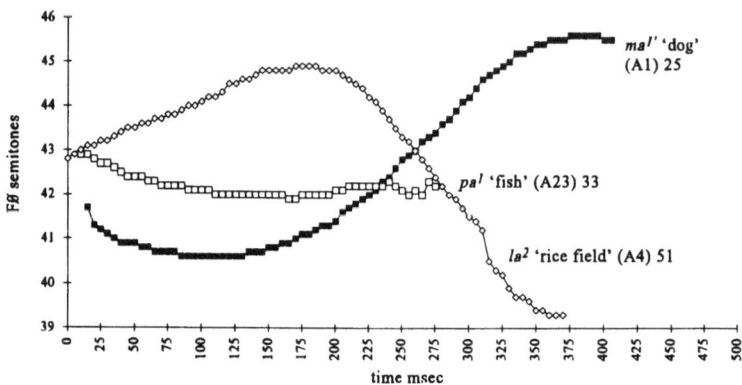

(12) Mangshi B tone pairs

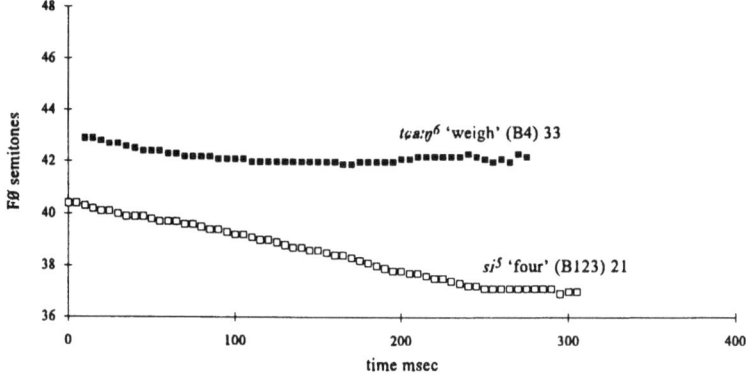

(13) Mangshi C tone pairs

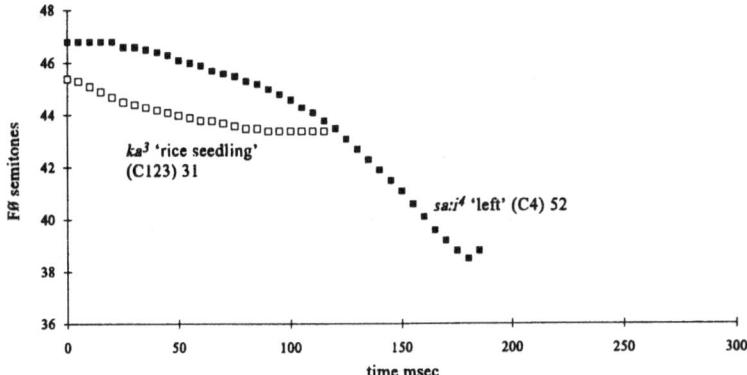

(14) Mangshi DL and DS trajectories

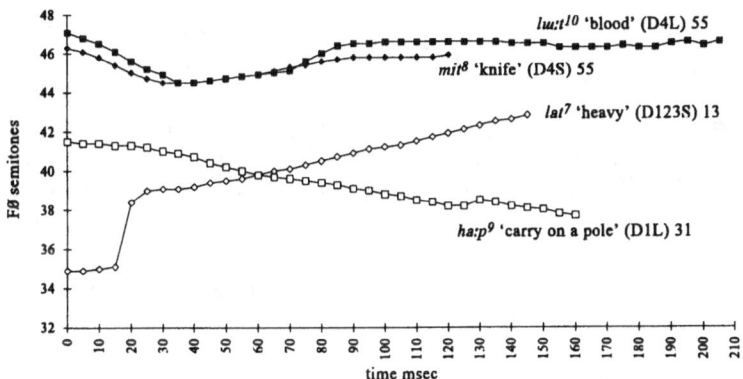

Mangshi possesses different splitting of the original tones than is found in the two southern varieties. Lexical items in the original category Gedney calls 'voiceless friction' (i.e., proto A1) receive a tone value of 25, as in fa^{35} 'mud', ma^{35} 'dog', xa^{35} 'right (not left)'. The original voiced category A4 has the shape of the mirror image of A1 or 51. The two categories A2 and A3 have a pitch trajectory differing from both A1 and A4, which is, however, identical to that of the B4 category with a value of 33, so that pa^{33} 'fish' and ta^{33} 'eye' have the same tone value as $tcan^{33}$ 'weigh'.

In the B category, B123 have a value 21 and are relatively long in duration. As just mentioned, the B4 category has the same value today as the A2 and A3, namely 33.

In the C category both reflexes in Mangshi are of shorter duration than A and B and finish with obvious glottal constriction. The historical C123 tone as in ha^{C1} 'five', lau^{C1} 'wine' is very short with a value of 31?. The C4 category in the word $sa:i^{C4}$ 'left' is slightly higher in pitch, namely 52?.[7]

The dead tones D4S and D4L have merged with a value of 55, though there may be a nearly imperceptible vowel length distinction. D123S has a value of 13 and D123L a value of 31.

Mangshi consonants. Mangshi show several remarkable features not found in the Southern varieties. The voiced continuants /m l/ are not simple nasals and liquids but rather have the phonetic forms [m^b] and [l^d], respectively, of post-stopped consonants. This sound change would presumably be a secondary development, as it seems to have transpired equally in vocabulary items that originally possessed nasal and liquid initials and also in items that came from row 3, the 'preglottalized' initials, so that today /m/ and /ʔb/ merge to [m^b] and /n l ʔd/ merge to [l^d]. The effect of these 'post-stopped nasal' initials can be seen clearly in (14) above in the Mangshi Dai dead tone categories. The items m^bit^{D4S} 'knife' and l^dut^{D4L} 'blood' show a pronounced pitch depression transition right after release. This change is reminiscent of a development in Chinese noted by Karlgren (1929) in which n → n^d and m → m^b in North China, a stop intruding between a nasal and following vowel. More examples are: l^di^{43} 'good, gallbladder', m^ba^{B3} 'shoulder', l^da^{B1} 'scold, abuse'. At the same time n → l^d as in l^da^{44} 'rice field', $l^doŋ^{C4}$ 'younger sibling', $l^dɐk^{D1S}$ 'heavy', as well as in cases of original laterals and nasals; cf. l^dom^{44} 'wind' and m^bu^{A1} 'pig'. Thus the Mangshi initial /l^d/ can be a reflex of *ʔd, *hn, *n, *hl, or *l. Parallel shifts for labials have produced examples such as m^bu^{A1} 'pig', from *hm. The two southern Shan types at Mae Hong Son and Pinlon (Panglong) do not have this post-stopped nasal feature. Moreover, Mangshi Shan distinguished between /ph f/ clearly. Guo Yuping produced the following data pairs: pha^{41} 'eye excrement' versus fa^{41} 'mud'.

The tones in the Namhkam and Mu-se varieties resemble Mangshi in terms of their patterns of tone splitting. The A tone has tripartition—A1–23–4—all yielding distinctive pitch trajectories. Like at Mangshi, at Namhkam and Mu-se A23 merges with B4. There were surprising differences in tone values and details of the consonants in these places that are only about 25 kilometers apart on the Shweli River.

Namhkam and Mu-se consonants. In regard to consonants Namhkam and Mu-se also merge original /m/ and /ʔb/ to /m/, as in Mangshi. The parallelism between the places is not complete, however; in Namhkam /hn n l ʔd/ merge,

---

[7]We write a glottal stop after the tone letter transcription to emphasize that this tone value has constriction as a contrastive feature.

to be sure, but they merge to /n/ and not to /l/; whereas in Mu-se the product of the merger is usually /l/. The post-stopped nasals that are such a prominent feature of the speech of Guo Yuping from Mangshi are found in the Mu-se speaker in only a small number of words. Were it not that one was expecting to find them, they would be easy to overlook. In Mu-se the word for 'bone' luk^{D3S} < *?d had the post-stopped feature, i.e., was pronounced [l^{d}uk^{D3S}]. In Namhkam it is quite evident in /n/ but not in /m/. Thus, in Namhkam we heard $n^da\text{:}t^{D4L}$ 'blood'; $n^du\text{:}k^{D4L}$ 'bone', and n^dom^{A4} 'wind'. Sometimes we also heard simple /l/ initials.

Our consultants produced both /f ph/ for items elsewhere having /f/; in these cases /ph/ predominated, e.g., $phai^{A4}$ 'fire'. The Namhkam speaker also demonstrated a rule that labializes the initial before the rhyme -oŋ; e.g., $\eta o\eta^{C4} \rightarrow \eta wa\eta^{C4}$ 'younger sibling'; and /-ia/ in Namhkam was /-e/.

Harris (1975) describes a Tai Mao of Namhkam that differs slightly from that described here. It agrees on the variation between /ph/ and /f/, and the tone system having the A23 = B4 merger found in Mangshi. By contrast it has a single reflex for the C tone, not showing any split. In addition, it keeps n and l distinct, e.g., laŋ 'back', naŋ 'skin' (both tone A1), and the reflex of *?d is l rather than n (e.g., $laaw^{A3}$ 'star', lay^C 'get, obtain', luk^{D3S} 'bone').

Namhkam and Mu-se tones. The dead tones in both Namhkam and Mu-se seem to have divided completely to give a total of four reflexes, unlike in Mangshi, which has only three.

(15) Namhkam tone A trajectories

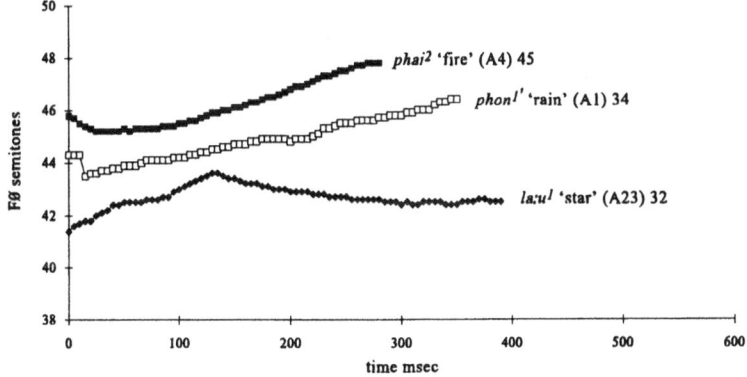

(16) Namhkam tone B pairs

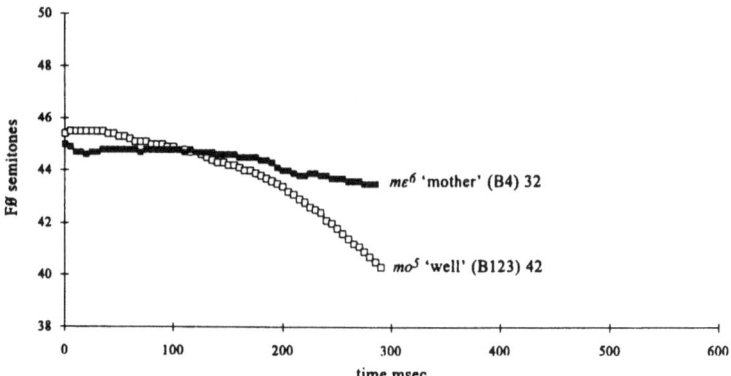

(17) Namhkam tone C tone pairs

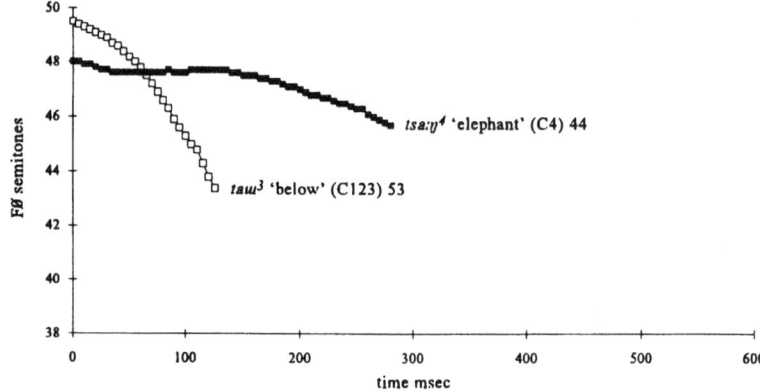

(18) Namhkam tones DL and DS pairs

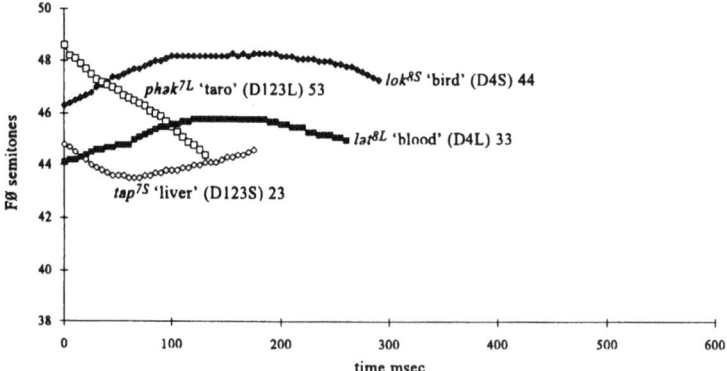

Mu-se has three tone reflexes in the A tone with a splitting pattern A1-23-4. In (19) the A23 tone with tone value 44 lies between the trajectories of A1 with tone value 55, e.g., *la*^{A1} 'thick' and A4 with tone value 334 *kha*^{A4} 'cogongrass', which is high and level.

For tone *B we found values B123 equal to 31 and the B4 tone had a value identical to A23 of 44, as shown in (20) below.

The tones C123 and C4, *la*^{C1} 'face' and *lam*^{C4} 'water' are 41 and 54, respectively, as shown in (21). Both are very short and end in glottal catch.

The dead tones in Mu-se are densely packed in the tone space with values that are not very different. The values we ascertained are: *lok* 'bird' (D4S) 55; *la:t* 'blood' (D4L) 44; *pet* 'duck'(D2S) 34; and *lu:k* 'bone' (D3L) 23, as shown in (22) below.

(19) Mu-se tone A pairs

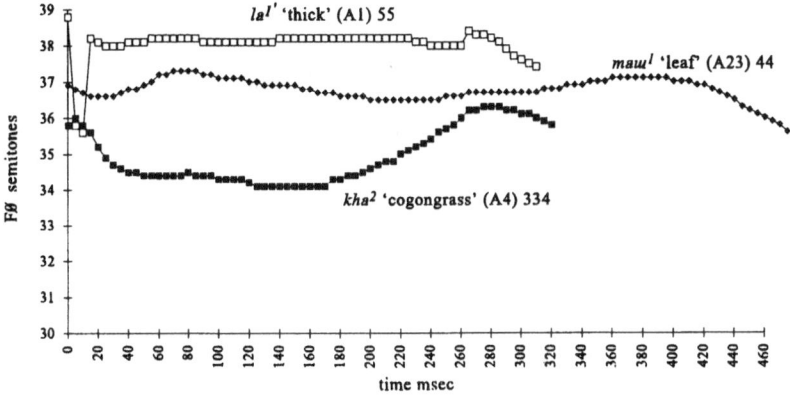

(20) Mu-se tone B pairs

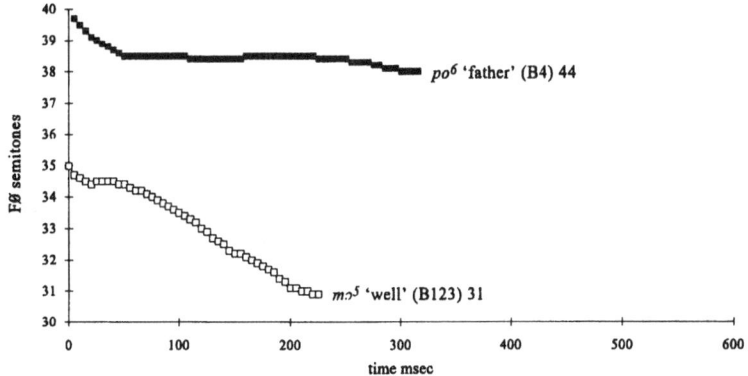

(21) Mu-se tone C pairs

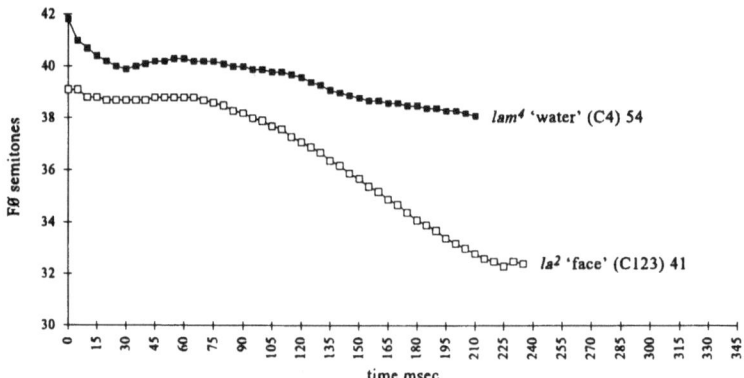

(22) Mu-se tone DL and DS pairs

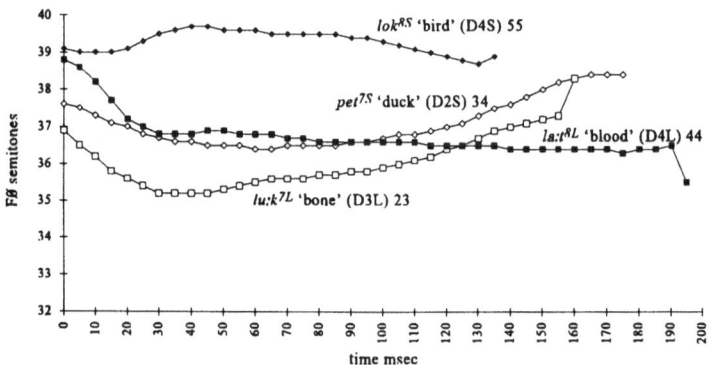

Implications for subgrouping

The various sound changes described here seem to stratify into a north-south sequence. First, in terms of consonants, the northernmost Mangshi is set off from all the rest by its preservation of the ph/f contrast. Mangshi does group with Namhkam and Mu-se in sharing some post-stopped sonorant reflexes of *?d *hn *n *hl *l, forming a northern group in opposition to Pinlon (Panglong) and Mae Hong Son, which do not have this feature.

Mangshi, Mu-se, and our Namhkam data also share the merger of $n=l$ (although the merger is in favor of *l* in some places and *n* in other). This contrast is preserved in Harris Namhkam and to the south in Pinlon (Panglong) and Mae Hong Son.

Mangshi, Mu-se, and our Namhkam (but not Harris' Namhkam) also group together in tone split/merger patterns, sharing the merger A23=B4. To the

Comparative Shan 355

south, Mae Hong Son and Panglong again have in common the approach, if not merger, of B4 = C123 (depending on the status of the final glottalization of the C123 tones).

Our data thus indicate a general distinction between northern and southern characteristics. At the northern end is Mangshi, with preservation of the *ph/f* contrast. At the southern extreme are Pinlon (Panglong) and Mae Hong Son, with the B4 = C123 (near-)merger and preservation of the *n/l* contrast, plus ordinary sonorant reflexes of *glottalized initials. To these southern types may be added (1) Cushing's Shan, with complete merger of B4 with C123, ordinary sonorants from *glottalized initials, and *ph = *f merger; and (2) Dai of Mengding, Yunnan, which Zhou (1983) reports as having the same tonal and consonantal mergers. In between, Namhkam and Mu-se form a transition zone, resembling the southern group in the *ph = *f merger and the northern zone in the *n = l* merger and the post-stopped sonorant reflexes of *ʔb *ʔd. Tonally, our Namhkam goes with the northern group in the relatively unusual A23–B4 merger, which may be taken as an important northern feature.

We recapitulate the tonal developments below in (23) and (24), which summarize the mergers of tones in these two types.

(23) Gedney diagram for Southern group of Shan Panglong, Mae Hong Son, Cushing's Shan (tone values for Panglong)

	A	B	C	DL	DS
1					
2	325	221	332	31	35
3					
4	44	332	41	33	53

(24) Gedney diagram for Northern group (Nɯa) and transition zone: Mangshi, Namhkam, Mu-se (tone values for Mangshi)

	A	B	C	DL	DS
1	25				
2		21	31	31	13
3	33				
4	51	33	52	55	

The transition zone represented in our data by Namhkam and Mu-se includes the area of the Tai Mau speech reported on elsewhere in Harris (1975) and Young (1985). We infer that this area is of some sociolinguistic complexity, with multilingualism and extensive contact among a number of closely-related languages, and probably influence from other Tai languages as well. Young (1985:4) reports that, according to one speaker, Tai Nɯa is the more general category of which Tai Mau is one subcategory, and that her Tai Mau consultants were fluent in Tai Taɯ (Southern Shan?) and often Tai Nɯa also. The possibilities for code-switching, variation, and transfer are obvious.

It also seems quite possible that other parts of this Tai-speaking area will be found to exhibit similar complexity when more detailed data are available.

A similar view to ours of the genetic grouping within Shan is found in Robinson (1994), who has suggested that Tai Nɯa and Khamti share a common history that is distinct from other Southwest Tai languages. These two are set off by five distinctive features from all others: (1) labialized velar stops become velar stops; (2) a tripartite split of the A tone A1–23–4; (3) merger of A23 and B4; (4) the low vowels /ɛ ɔ/ merge with /e o/, respectively; and (5) *ʔb → m. This view questions the unity of the concept Shan altogether by sundering the traditional three-term system into a two-term system:

(25) Tai Nɯa = Shan-Tayok   Burman Shan
      Khamti   Other Southwest Tai

That makes Burman Shan more distantly related to Nɯa-Khamti than in earlier classifications.

Looking farther afield, preliminary investigation indicates that the tripartite division we have suggested extends some distance eastward, as far as the area to the north of Sipsongpanna. We explore this and other questions of subgrouping in Southwestern Tai in Solnit and Edmondson (to appear). In that paper we suggest that the term Shan be reserved for the languages of Burma (perhaps including Khamti, perhaps not) plus a few border communities such as Ruili and Mengding. The languages of our northern zone can be designated as (Tai) Nɯa. Our transitional zone extends eastwards into China, including Gengma and points eastward, and perhaps Menglian. The languages of these areas are perhaps also best called Nɯa, while recognizing that they are transitional in some respects. At present we do not see grounds for distinguishing a 'northern Shan' from Tai Nɯa.

References

Brown, J. Marvin. 1965. From ancient Thai to modern dialects. Reprinted 1985 From ancient Thai to modern dialects and other writings on historical Thai linguistics. Bangkok: White Lotus Press.
Carthew, M. 1952. The history of the Thai in Yunnan. 2205 B.C.–A.D. 1253 Journal of the Siam Society 40(1):1–38.
Chamberlain, James R. 1975. A new look at the history and classification of the Tai languages. In J. Harris and J. Chamberlain (eds.), Studies in Tai linguistics in honor of William J. Gedney, 49–66. Bangkok: Central Institute of English Language.
Chao, Y. R. 1930. Le maître phonétique. Troisieme série 30(2):24–27.
Cihai. 1980. Shanghai: Shanghai Cihai Cishu Chubanshe.
Cushing, Josiah Nelson. 1888a. Elementary handbook of the Shan language. Rangoon. Reprinted in 1971 Farnborough, England: Gregg International Publishers Limited.
——. 1888b. A Shan and English dictionary. Rangoon. Reprinted in 1971 Farnborough, England: Gregg International Publishers Limited.
Diller, Anthony. 1992. Tai languages in Assam: Daughters or ghosts? In C. J. Compton and J. F. Hartmann (eds.), Papers on Tai languages, linguistics, and literatures. Occasional Paper 16, 5–43. DeKalb: Northern Illinois University Center for Southeast Asian Studies.
Egerod, Søren. 1957. Essentials of Shan phonology and script. Academia Sinica. Bulletin of the Institute of History and Philology 29:121–27.
Enriques, Major C. M. 1933. Races of Burma. (Handbooks for the Indian Army.) Delhi: Manager of Publication.
Gedney, William J. 1976. Notes on Tai Nuea. In Thomas W. Gething, Jimmy G. Harris, and Pranee Kalluvanijaya (eds.), Tai linguistics in honor of Fang-Kuei Li, 62–102. Bangkok: Chulalongkorn University Press.
Glick, Irving and Sao Tern Moeng. 1991. Shan for English speakers: Dialogues, readings, and vocabulary. Wheaton: Dunwoody Press.
Grierson, G. A. 1928. Linguistic survey of India 2. Mon-Khmer and Siamese-Chinese families (including Khassi and Tai). Reprint Dehli, Varanasi, and Patna: Motilal Banarsidass.
Hallett, Holt S. 1885. An historical sketch of the Shans. In A. R. Colquhoun, Amongst the Shans. London: Field and Tuer; Simpkin, Marshall and Co.; Hamilton, Adams and Co., and New York: Scribner and Welford.
Harris, Jimmy G. 1975. A comparative word list of three Tai Nuea dialects. In Jimmy G. Harris and James R. Chamberlain (eds.), Studies in Tai linguistics in honor of William J. Gedney. Bangkok: Central Institute of English Language.

———. 1976. Notes on Khamti Shan. In Thomas W. Gething, Jimmy G. Harris, and P. Kullauanijaya (eds.), Tai linguistics in honor of Fang-Kuei Li, Bangkok: Chulalongkorn University Press.

Haudricourt, André-Georges. 1975. Du nouveau sur le tai neua. Asie du sud-est et monde insulindien 6 (4):163–67.

Karlgren, Bernhard. 1929. Philology and ancient China. Instituttet for sammenlignende kulturforskning. Serie A. Oslo: H. A. Scheboug and Co. Reprinted 1989, Cambridge, Mass.: Harvard University Press.

Li Fang-Kuei. 1977. A handbook of comparative Tai. Honolulu: The University Press of Hawaii.

Liamprawat, Suwathana. 1985. Sound correspondences among Tai Mau, Tai Khamti, and Lanna. (in Thai) Journal of Language and Culture 5(2):27–45.

Lowis, C. C. 1919. The tribes of Burma. Ethnographical survey of India, Burma No. 4. Rangoon: Office of the Superintendent, Government Printing, Burma.

Luce, Gordon H. 1985. Phases of pre-Pagan Burma. Oxford: Oxford University Press.

Luo Meizhen. 1984. The changes and developments of vowel length and consonant finals in Dai languages. Minzu Yuwen 6:20–25.

———. 1993. Lun Fangyan: Jiantan Daiyu fangyan de huafen. Dialectology [Preliminary discussions about the divisions among Dai vernaculars]. Minzu Yuwen 3:1–10.

Luo Yongxian. To appear. Dehong Dai-English dictionary. Canberra: Thai Studies Centre, Australian National University.

Min Naing B. A. 1960. တို့ တိုင်းရင်း သား: - ပြည် ထောင်စုသား: Races of Burma. (in Burmese) Rangoon: Ministry of Union Culture.

Mix, Mrs. H. W., ed. 1920. An English and Shan dictionary. Rangoon: American Baptist Mission Press.

Needham, Jack F. 1894. Outline grammar of the (Khâmtî) language. Rangoon: Superintendent Government Printing.

Robinson, Edward. 1994. Features of Proto-Nüa-Khamti. Paper delivered at the Twenty-seventh International Conference on Sino-Tibetan Languages and Linguistics, October 1994, Paris.

Seidenfaden, Erik. 1958. The Thai peoples: The origins and habitats of the Tai peoples with a sketch of their material and spiritual culture. Bangkok: The Siam Society.

Solnit, David, B. and Jerold A. Edmondson. 1992. The northern tier of Southwestern Tai. Paper presented at the Twenty-fifth International Conference on Sino-Tibetan Languages and Linguistics, Bangkok and Chiangmai, Thailand, October 1992.

Terrien de Lacouperie and Albert Etienne Jean Baptiste. 1885. Cradle of the Shan race. In A. R. Colquhoun, Amongst the Shans. London: Field and Tuer; Simpkin, Marshall and Co.; Hamilton, Adams and Co., and New York: Scribner and Welford.

Tint Hswei, Colonel. တင် ဆွေ 1992. National races of the Union of Myanmar ပြည်ထောင်စုမြန်မာနိုင်ငံ၏တိုင်းရင်းသားလူမျိုးများ:. (in Burmese) Yangon: Security Publishing House.

Wang, Jun, ed. 1984. Zhuang-Dong Yuzu yuyan jianzhi. Beijing: Nationalities Publishing House.

Weidert, Alfons. 1971. Tai Khamti phonology. Wiesbaden: Franz Steiner Verlag.

Xing Gongwan. 1987. The introduction to the Tai-yani language on the upper reaches of the Hong He [Red River]. Minzu Yuwen 3:40–46.

Young, Linda W. L. 1985. Shan crestomathy: An introduction to the Dai Mau language and literature. Lanham, Md.: University Press of America.

Yu Cuirong. 1986. Some phenomena of sound change in Daila Dai. Minzu Yuwen 2:29–33.

———. 1990. Phonetic character of Daila vernacular. Minzu Yuwen 1:50–62.

Zhou Yaowen. 1982. Yunnan Dehong Daiwen Gaijin zhong de jige wenti [Questions regarding the reform of the Dehong Dai script of Yunnan]. Paper prepared for the Fifteenth International Conference on Sino-Tibetan Languages and Linguistics, Beijing, 1982.

———. 1983. The phonology and writing system of Mengding Dai. Minzu Yuwen 6:10–15.

Cited Forms

Bouyei

A
above 157, 159
alcoholic beverage 151
appearance 151
arrive, to 149

B
bamboo pole 155, 156
bamboo raft 153
bamboo strip 150, 155
bear 150
bed 149, 153
belly 149
below 146, 147, 148, 152
boat 153, 155
bone 155
book 150, 151
Bouyei 146, 147, 148, 150, 151, 152
bowl 149
break off 149
break off, to 156
burn, to 153
buy, to 152

C
carry on shoulder 147
carry, to 153, 157
carrying pole 8
catch (fish), to 150, 155
charcoal 149
chase away, to 153
chopsticks 150
clean, be 157
cloth 151
clothes 149, 150, 153, 155
cloudy 10
cold 10
collapse 149
come, to 147
copper 157
country 150
cracked rim 149
cross, to 153
cry, to 147, 149, 155
cucumber 149
cut (with scissors), to 158

D
die, to 149
disrobe, to 154
drink, to 149
drive away 148
drum 154
dusk 150

E
each 149, 151
earth 149
eat, to 150, 157
eight 150, 154
evening 154, 156
eye 147, 149

F
far 154
fart 158
fertile 158
fire 156
fish 147, 153
fishing rod 155
five 147, 157, 158
flash (of lightning), to 153
flat 149
flood, to 149
flower 147
folk song 150, 157
follow, to 148, 155
forehead 150

G
give, to 157
glue, to 149
gnaw, to 156

go, to 155, 156
gong 153
good 156
grain drying area 154
grass 148
grass ash 149
grope 147
guard, to 149, 157
guess, to 149
guest 155
Guizhou 146, 150, 151, 152

H

handle 149
handspan 150
hard 157
heart 149
hill 154
hit, to 149
hold in the hands, to 149
horned dragon 155
hot 158
hungry 155

I

inch 154
intestine 155
iron 147

K

kick, to 149
kidney 150
kill, to 155
knife 11

L

ladle out 149, 155, 158
lazy 154, 155
leak, to 156
leg 149, 157
light (lamp), to 149
liver 149, 158
long (face) 148, 153
lungs 150

M

male (chicken) 156
maternal younger brother 10
maternal uncle 150, 157, 158
mother 156
much 151, 156

N

nail 149
name 152
needle 154, 158
neigh, to 149
nine 148, 156

O

older maternal uncle 157
one 147, 149, 154, 157, 158
open (eyes) 147
open, to 148

P

paddy wall 149
paper 146, 147, 155, 157
paternal aunt 147
peel, to 149, 150
person 156
petal 149
plank 149
play, to 152, 158
plough 147
plow 8
pocket 149
politics 147

R

rain 156, 157
raw 149
read, to 151
return, to 156
rice mortar 8
rice plant 8
rice seedling 8, 148
rice straw 8, 150

right 148
river 158
road 11
roof tile 148, 153
rust 153

S

sabre 153
search, to 147
seven 149
shack 149
shell (beans), to 158
shiver, to 155
shop 149
shoulder 147, 153
sink, to 158
slick 147
sliding weight on steelyard 147, 153
snore, to 157
sour plum 156
sparse 154
speak, to 155
spin (yarn), to 157
spinning wheel 147
sprout 148
steal, to 156
stir fry, to 157
straight 155
straw hat 149, 154
strength 154
stupid 148, 153
sun 155, 158
swallow, to 149

T

take off (clothes) 149
ten 149, 155
thin (cloth) 149
thin (not thick) 149
three 146, 147, 151, 152, 153, 157, 158, 159
thunder and lightning 155
tiger 10
toward 154, 156
trample, to 149, 153
turn around, to 149

Index of Cited Forms

U

(unit of area) 150

V

vegetable 149
vomit, to 155

W

wait, to 148, 154, 155
walking stick 150
warn, to 11
wash clothes, to 155
wasp 156
water buffalo 8
wear (hat), to 155
wife 148
wild cat 149
winnowing basket 157
wipe, to 149
write, to 156

Y

yea 158
yellow 156

Dai Tho
(Central Tai language)

A

ant 202
artisan 193
ascend 196
ashes 193, 201, 231
asleep 200

B

back 199, 230
bamboo tube 200
bark (n) 197
bear 198, 227
belly 201, 230
bird 202, 230
black 200, 231
blood 204, 230
body hair 196, 230
bone 200, 230
branch 197, 213, 214, 215
breast 201
buffalo 203, 224, 228
burn 195, 231
buy 193, 203, 211, 224, 231

C

chicken 197
child 204, 229, 231
climb 202
close (eyes) 199
cloud 198, 227, 230
copper 193, 201
cough 201
crossbow 197

D

day 204, 224, 230
descend 204
die 196, 226, 230
dog 198, 227, 230
dream 195, 211
dry field 204
duck 197

E

ear 196, 224, 230
earth 200
eat 198, 224, 230
egg 196, 230
eight 197, 231
emerge 201
evening meal 193
extinguish 200
eye 196, 224, 230

F

fall 197, 230
far 197, 217, 231
fat 193, 201, 230
feces 196
finger 202
fire 193, 203, 231
fire tongs 193
fish 197, 211, 224, 230
five 199, 231
flower 200, 224, 227, 230
fly, to 200
forget 204, 224
four 199, 231
fruit 198, 230

G

grandchild 199
grass 198, 230

H

hand 202, 215, 230
head 196, 224, 230
heart 197, 230
heavy 198, 226, 231
horn 196, 230
horse 202, 229
house 204, 224
hundred 197, 231

I

incubate 193, 203
insect 198
intestines 199
iron 199
itchy 193, 203

J

joint 196

K

kill 196, 231
knee 196, 230

L

laugh 196, 230
leaf 200, 211, 226, 230
leech 197
left 203, 231
let go 197, 224
liquor 199
liver 197, 230
long 204, 211, 231

M

many 199, 231
medicine 200, 224
moon 200, 211, 230
mortar 202
mountain 200, 224, 230
mouth 197, 203, 209, 230
mushroom 200

N

nail 204
name 192, 201, 231
neck 203, 224, 230
needle 196
new 198, 226, 231
night 203, 224, 230
nine 197
nose 200, 211, 227, 230

O

old (age) 196
older sibling 201, 224
one 198, 224, 231
otter 202

P

paddy field 202
pair 193
person 193, 201
pig 198
pull out of the 203

R

rain 195, 230
rat 198
red 200, 214, 231
rice 196, 211
rice, husked 199
ride 196
ripe, cooked 199, 226
river 201, 224, 230
road 204, 224, 231
root 204, 230
round 202, 231

S

saliva 204
salt 197, 231
scrape 198
scratch 197, 225, 230
sell 196, 231
seven 197, 231
sew 202, 231
silver 203, 210
sit 202, 230
six 196
skin 198, 230
sky 203, 230
sleep 202, 228, 230
smell 198, 224, 230, 231
smoke 203, 231
snake 203, 230
soft 201
sour 199
squeeze 201, 230
stand 200, 223, 230
star 200, 230
steal 204
stick 201, 230
stomach 193
stream 196
sugar cane 201
sweat 196
sweet, delicious 199

T

Tai 201
tail 196, 230
tall, high 199
ten 199, 231
thatchgrass 193, 203
thick 198, 231
thin 195, 226, 231
thorn 198
three 199, 231
tie 195, 202, 230
tongue 204, 229, 230
tooth 203, 228, 230
two 231
two (twenty) 202

U

urine 202

V

village 200

W

warm 201, 225
wash 203, 230
wash (clothes) 193, 203
wash (dishes) 204
wash (face) 199
water 202, 223, 229, 230
weave (cloth) 197
weep 199
wind 204, 230
wing 197, 230
wipe 201, 230

Y

yes 193
you 202, 231

Siamese

A

aim, gaze 332
angel 330
ant 313
area 332

B

banyan 103
barbed hook 332
base 332
basket, a kind of 281
be, to 329
bedbug 310
bee 311
bird 7
blood 7

Index of Cited Forms

C

caress 332
carrying pole 8
catfish 103
centipede 306
child 332
cicada 311
civilized 103
cloth, clothing 37
cloud 332
cloudy 10
cockroach 308
cold 10
colored glass 332
corner 300
cotton, ball of 329
country 98
cultivated land 332

D

dance, a form of 333
deer 171
deserted land 104
diamond 333
divine knowledge 333
dream 7
duck 332
dwarfed 332

E

Eugenia grata 332
excrement 275

F

false 333
far 268, 269, 283
fear, revere 332
feces 333
fertile 103
field 102, 103, 104
fingernail 332
finished 333
firefly 308
flame 330, 332
flea 320
flow, to 285
flower 102, 103

fly, a 309
forearm shield 332
forest 104
fragment 330

G

gadfly 310
gender, form 332
ghost 332
giant waterbug 310
gold 104
good 104
grandchild 37
grandmother 283
grass, a kind of 102
great grandchild 331
grub 307

H

hair, mane 332
happiness 103
heaven 103
hill 102, 103
hornet 312

I

imprison, to 281
incline, to 329
intellect 332
intestine 7

K

knife 10

L

leaf 276
left 283
lean, slant 332
lice 332
lotus 102
louse, body 304
louse, chicken 304
louse, head 304
louse, white 331

M

maggot 308
man 330, 332
meat 171
meter 332
millipede 306
mix flour with water 332
monks 333
mosquito 309
mother's younger brother 10
mound 102, 104
mountain 102, 104
mouth 102
mud 331, 332
mushroom 332

N

near 268, 276, 279
needle 332
nine 269
north 103

O

oneself 333
ooze, seep 332

P

perfect 103
pig 7
plaster, mortar 332
plow 8
pluck 328, 332
pound 333
province 98
push 332

R

rain 7
reason 332
reed 333
region 98, 333
remainder 333
revenge 332
rice field 104
rice mortar 8

rice plant 8
rice seedling 8
rice straw 8
right 283
ringworm 274
road 10

S

sandbank 332
scale 332
seed 332
servant 332
seven 330, 332
sheep, Aries 332
short 329, 333
sign, to 330, 333
silkworm 315
small 332
son, child 5
south 103
stink bug 310
stroke, smear 332
swamp 102, 103

T

tall 103
teeth 7
tendon, sinew 332
tense 332
termite 313
three 285
tick 304
tiger 10, 103
tree, a kind of 103
trick 329, 332
trouble 333

U

unity 102

V

village 98

W

warn, to 10

wasp 312
water buffalo 8
water scavenger beetle 308
whole 333
wide 269
wipe 332
wipe, to 331
without cause 333

Z

Zen 333

**Tay
(Central Tai language)**

A

abused, tired 228
adult 228
all of it 231
all of us 231
ant 313
arm 224
ashes 231
ask 224
aunt 223, 224

B

back 230
bamboo 222, 223
bathe 226
bedbug 305, 310
bee 312
belly 230
below 226
belt 224
bent 224
betel 224
bird 230
black 231
blanket 224
blood 230
blow 230
body hair 230
bone 230

break down 228
breathe 230
briefly 225
bright, morning 224
broad 231
buffalo 224
burn 231
butterfly 314
buy 224, 231

C

calabash 225
centipede 306
chair, light pole 225
chest 223, 230
child 229, 231
children 226
chin 224
chop 224, 230
clothing 231
cloud 227, 230
cold 231
comb 224, 230
compensate 225
cook 231
correct 231
count 226, 230
crippled 224
cry 226
curved, bent 224
cut 224, 226, 230

D

dance 231
day 224, 230
deer 224
die 226, 230
different 231
dig 230
dirty 225, 231
dog 227, 230
dragonfly 316
dry 231
dull 231
dust 230

Index of Cited Forms

E

ear 224, 230
earthworm 230
eat 224, 230
egg 230
eight 231
eye 224, 230

F

fading 228
far 231
fat 230
father 230
fear 230
few 231
fight 231
file, to 224
fingernail 230
fire 231
firefly 308
fish 224, 230
five 222, 231
flower 224, 227, 230
foot 226
forget 224
four 221, 231
frog, toad 226
fruit 230
full 226, 231

G

gadfly, horsefly 310
ghost 224
give 230
go 224, 227, 229, 230
go back 225
good 231
grain, stone, seed 228, 230
grass 230
grasshopper 318
green 231
grub 307

H

hail 230
half 224
hand 230
handful 224
hard, not soft 224
harvest 225
hat, cap 226
head 230
head hair 224, 230
hear 230
heart 230
heavy 226, 231
hide 224
hoe 224
hold, pick 226
horn 230
hornet 312
horse 229
hot 225, 231
house 224
housefly 309
huge 231
hundred 231
husband 231

I

insect 306
in(side) 231
insipid 226
intestine 230
investigate 224
invite 228

J

jackfruit 229
jump 226

K

kill 231
knead 224
knife 224
know 230

L

leaf 226, 230
lean on 224
left 231
leg 224, 230
let go 224
level, horizontal 225
link 226
liver 230
location 224
lonesome 224
long 231
look at 230
look for 223
louse, body 304
louse, chicken 304
louse, head 304

M

maggot 308
mantis 308
medicine 224
melon, classifer for 225
millipede 306
monkey 226
moon 230
mosquito 309
mother 230
mountain 224, 230
mouth 230
much 224
mud 230
mustard greens 226

N

name 231
near 231
neck 224, 230
new 226, 231
new year 226
night 224, 230
no 231
nose 230

O

old 231
one 231
owl 224

P

peace 226
peel 226
people 224, 230

pickle 228
pick up with chopsticks 226
pierce 228
play 231
pour 224
pull 230
push 230
put down 224

R

rain 230
rain-drenched 224
red 231
reproduce 224
right 223, 231
ripe, cooked 226
river 224, 230
road 224, 231
root 230
rope 231
round 231

S

salt 231
sand 230
sandfly 309
scold 224
scratch 225, 230
sea 230
search 224
sell 231
separate 226
sesame 224
seven 231
sew 231
shake, shiver 224
sharp 231
shiny 231
shoe 224
short 231
shovel 224
shrimp 320
sibling, older 224
sibling, younger 226
sing 231
sit down 230
skin 230

sky 230
sleep 228, 230
slick 224
small 231
smear 224
smell 224, 230
smell bad 231
smoke 231
smooth, silky 225
snake 230
snow 230
spider 305
spine 230
spit out 230
spread out 231
squeeze 230
stab 230
stable, strong 239
stand 230
star 230
startle 225
stem 224
stick 230
stove 224
straight 231
study 224
stupid 225
suck 230
sun 230
swim 228, 230
swollen 231

T

tail 230
take 226, 230
talk 230
taste, flavor, seasoning 228, 230
teach 231
ten 231
tend to 224
termite 313
that 231
them 231
thick 231
thin, not thick 226, 231
think 230
this 231

three 224, 231
tie 230
toilet 224
tongue 229, 230
tooth 228, 230
top, toy 224
touch 225
tree 224, 226, 229, 230
tree bark 230
tree, kind of 224, 226
trousers 225
twenty 231
twirl 224
two 231

V

vegetable 224

W

walking stick 320
want 226
wash 230
wasp 312, 313
water 223, 229, 230
water barrel 224
waterbug, giant 310
weed 224
wet 231
what 231
white 224, 226, 231
white strip 224
who 222, 231
wide, spacious 225
wife 231
wind 230
window 224
wine 224
wing 230
wipe 230
work 231

Y

year 224, 230
yellow 231
yesterday 224
you 231

Index of Cited Forms

Tay Tac, White, Black, and Red T(h)ai (SW languages)

A

alcoholic beverage 250
amount 253, 259
animals, classifier for 264
answer, to 238
arm 238, 253
ask, to 237
astringent taste 247
aunt 240
axe 248, 249

B

back 236
banana 246, 253
bark, to 257
bathe, to 238, 240, 255
be, to (in a place) 250
beard, moustache 237
bee 263
below, south 253
betel 246
big 247, 250, 252
bird 240, 257
bite, to 248
blood 240
boil, to 240, 254
butterfly 314

C

carry on pole 240
chase, to 248
chest 238, 240
chicken 237, 240, 256
child 240
chisel 247
choose, to 248
cloth 238
clothing 238
clothing, classifier for 263
cloud 247
cold, a 250
come, to 241, 260, 261
cooked, ripe 247, 255

cricket 318, 319
crow, to 241

D

dark 255
day 238, 255
daydream of, to 252
deer 237, 246
dispute over, to 248
dog 238, 241, 250, 260, 261
dove 248
dragonfly 316
dream 263
dry 240, 253

E

ear 238, 240, 279
eat 240
egg 240, 248, 279
eight 237, 255
elbow 247
enter, to 248, 252
eye 237, 240

F

far 238, 270
fat 247, 255, 263, 264
fear, to 238
fever 240, 248
field 240, 241, 245
finger 237
fish basket 248
five 257
flea 240
flower 240, 249
flute 251
fly, to 240
foot 255
forest 237, 240, 246, 263
fragrant 255
frog 240, 246
frog, small 249
fruit 251

G

garden 254

give, to 252
go, to 253
go out, to 246
gold 241, 249, 263
grandfather, paternal 251
grass 238, 250
green 252
gums 237, 240

H

hair (of head) 247
hand 237, 240, 250, 251
head 238, 240, 254
heart 252, 263, 264
heavy shower 249
hoe 255, 257
hole 257
honey 312
horse 240, 241, 261
hot 249
hunt, to 247
hurt, to 246

I

ignorant, stupid 254
imprison, to 248, 279
insect 255
intelligent 241
intestines 247
iron 251, 254, 263

K

katydid 319
kill, to 240, 248
knee 240, 248
knife 240
know, to 256, 257

L

late at night 238, 252, 254
leaf 238, 252, 279
leg 237, 240
(to lie) face down 248
(to lie) face up 249
liver 240, 246, 262
lung 240

M

male (of humans) 237
man, male 246
middle 270
mortar 246
mosquito 250
mother 235, 247, 263
mountain 255, 263

N

near 279
neck 249
new 252, 265, 266
night 249, 255
nine 252, 262

O

old 240
old (persons) 255
older sibling 256, 257, 261
open, to 248
open mouth, to 240
outside 240, 257, 259

P

palm, sole 247
person 246, 249
pestle 238
place for washing, a 241
plant, to 241, 251
plant, tree 255
pleased, happy, to be 238
plow 249
pull, to 238
pull or drag, to 241
put, to 252

R

rain 263
rattan 237
red 240
rice 240, 248
rice field 240, 250
rice seedling 270
right 237
right (hand) 248
ringworm 274
rise, to 241, 261
road, way 246
roof, to 253

S

sand 237, 247
see, to 254
seek, to 237, 238, 253, 255
seven 251
sheath 247
shirt 240, 254
short 241, 255
shoulder 240
side, edge 238
side, ribs 248
silver 235, 263
silver, money 254
sing, to 248
six 252, 254
size 263
sky 247
small, few 253
smile 238
smoke 249
snake 250
soak (rice), to 241, 251, 260, 261
sound 238, 245, 254, 266
spade 237
spider web 250, 253
spill, to 237
spirit 249
split 240
split, to 247
star 240, 252
steal 238, 240, 241, 250
sunshine 240
sweet 238, 250
swell, to 238
sword 237

T

tail 255
take, to 237
tallow 248
ten 241, 251, 255
thick 238
thorn 250
three 238
throw fishnet, to 249
tie, to 247
tiger 237
time 252, 253, 259, 260
tired 253
top (to spin) 248
torn 238, 240, 248
trees, classifier for 263
turbid, dust 248
turn over, to 252

U

use, serve, to 252

V

vegetable 247
vegetables, green 240
visit, to 246, 247

W

wall 237, 247
war, enemy 251
water 240, 241, 253, 255
water buffalo 249
wet 263
wide 270
wife 235, 254
wing 240, 241, 251, 255, 257
work 252

Y

year 240
yellow 238, 254
yesterday 238
yonder 252
young male animal 251
young woman 238

Index of Cited Forms

Zhuang

A

above 47
abuse verbally, to 84
accompany 50
accompany, to 43
admire, to 48
animals, classifier for 83
ant 42, 94
anxious 61
arched 47
arched, to become 48
arm 42, 95
arrive, to 42
arrogant 42
astringent 50
axe 46

B

back bag 39
bad 49
bag 44
bamboo container for grasshoppers 42
banana 72, 81
basket 39, 45
bathe, to 39, 49
bean 43
bear 43
beforehand 71, 72
believe 60
bib 42
bird 94, 133
bitter 42, 46, 48, 49
black 60, 81, 87
block, to 48
blood 9
blow 44
blow, to 42
boat 43, 47, 89, 94
body 46, 90, 94
bone 42, 46, 84
borrow, to 83
bracelet 48
break, to 47, 87
bride 81
bright 47

buffalo 8, 39, 46, 48, 49, 62
burn, to 50
buy 64, 72, 136
buy, to 42, 45, 94, 133, 134, 135

C

calculate, to 81
carry on a pole, to 85
carry on the back, to 81
carry on the shoulder, to 86
carrying 46, 47, 48, 49, 118
carrying pole 8, 46, 47, 48, 80
cat 83
centipede 19
ceramic pot 48
change, to 43
chicken 45, 65, 70, 95, 132, 133, 134
child 5, 75, 116, 127, 130, 133
children 94, 117
chipped rim 83
chop, to 46
chopsticks 45, 109
clamp, to 109
clear 42, 45, 52, 67, 127
cloth 37, 92
cloth for carrying a baby 46
cloud 88, 89
cloudy 10
cold 66, 132
comb 39, 80, 89, 92
come out, to 84, 94
concave 62
corner 49
cotton 45, 116
cover 45, 47, 58, 61
cover, to 58, 61, 133
crack 48, 88, 89
crooked 50, 83
cross 52, 91
curl, to 49

cut, to 45, 49

D

dam 45, 84
deaf 43, 90
declare a fast friendship, to 49
deep 90
deep water 48
demon 47
dense 41, 45, 114
dig, to 82, 136
diligent 48
dishevel, to 49
ditch 48
do, to 20, 42
dog 9, 39, 42, 94, 130
domineering 58, 60
door 42, 45, 81
dream 8
drill 81
dry 46, 136
dry in sun 88, 89
duck 44, 94

E

eat 45, 50, 58, 61, 62, 67, 94, 123, 130, 132, 134, 136
emperor 81
envy 48, 49
even, to 39
evening 46, 47, 48, 132
exchange, to 49
exclamation 42
expand, to 48
expose, to 49
expose to the sun, to 84
extinguish 67
eye 9, 39, 42, 79

F

face 16, 79, 91, 94, 114, 132
faded 68
fall apart, to 50
fall off, to 49

far 82
fat 44, 48, 67, 87, 94, 135
father 39, 42, 44, 127
fight to eat, to 42
finish 64
fire 9, 43, 45, 47, 50, 63, 79, 81, 83, 87, 133
firewood 45, 47, 63
fish 42, 48, 82, 83
five 39, 45, 58, 80, 94, 109
flatter 46
flea 87
flicker 67
flower 9, 39, 92, 93
flush, to 39
fly, to 85, 94
follow 71
foolish 70
force 42
force, strength 43
forget, to 42, 50
four 45, 117
frog 67
fruit 42, 116, 122
fruit pit 39
fungus 116

G

gag 46, 48
gall 46
girl from the mountains 127
girl pickpocket, the 127
give, to 42, 45
give in, to 46
gizzard 42, 45
glare, to 49
grain, classifier for 109
grasp, to 39
groan, to 49
go 43, 46, 49, 50, 62, 64, 65, 66, 71, 74, 75, 109, 117, 122, 123, 124, 130, 134, 135, 136
gong 39, 81, 134

good 46, 64, 65, 66, 67, 75, 79, 81, 82, 83, 87, 118, 125, 134, 135, 136
goose 93
grain 49
green 46
grindstone 40
gulp, to 49

H

hair 44, 83
half 1, 45, 46, 59, 72
hammer 39
hand 11, 18, 36, 42, 47, 66, 68, 90, 110, 116
happy 61
harrow 39
hatch 45
have a speech impediment 42
heaven 92
heavy 47, 87, 94, 120
hold, take 60
horn 45, 92
house 21, 22, 26, 43, 53, 54, 76, 71, 80, 86, 90, 94, 128, 131
hundred 87
husband 43
husk 44, 86, 89

I

increase 72
ink 42, 130
insect 47, 90
inside 42, 46
intestine 45, 94
invade, to 81
iron 19, 39, 109, 128, 131, 132, 136
itch, to 46, 48
itchy 67

J

joint 46, 48
jump, to 81
jump over, to 50

just 64, 65, 135
just now 47, 49, 64

K

kick 88
kill, to 39, 45
kindling 49
knife 11, 85
knives, classifier for 42
know, to 39, 42, 43, 86

L

lack, to 39
ladder 90
lamp 67
large 42
laugh 88, 89
leaf 42, 46, 94
lean, to 81
left 4, 19, 20, 45, 118
lie 46
light 46
light weight 82
liver 41, 42, 45, 79, 87, 114
local fabric 42
long 42
looking 63
louse 42, 43, 44, 80, 88, 89, 90, 92
louse, chicken 43
louse, head 80
love 87
love dearly, to 49
lung 44
lye 46

M

male 42, 44, 123, 132
marriage 46
meat 67, 84, 91, 136
mend clothes, to 45
millet 45
money 72, 73, 126, 127, 130, 131, 133
mosquito 60
mother 84, 91, 114, 127

Index of Cited Forms

mother's 39
mouthful 43
mucus 42
multiply, to 48
must 84

N

narrow 47, 49
nausea 48
near 5, 13, 42, 88
NEG 61, 62, 65, 74, 75
nest 43
new 42, 94
nine 45
nose 81, 85, 94

O

occupy, to 48
old 5, 36, 42, 45
outside 86, 90
overflow, to 81
overweight 42
owe, to 39

P

pair up, to 48
paper 39
patch, to 48
pattern 46
pay, to 114
peel in, to 50
person 46, 47, 49, 58, 60, 63, 71, 117, 123, 131
pick 46
pick up food, to 83
picture 9, 14, 49
pig 9, 42, 79, 94, 128, 132
pillow 45
pinch, to 47
pineapple, a kind of 82
plane 44
plane, to 46
plough 123, 124
plow 8, 94
plum 91

pole 41, 46, 48, 49, 80, 85, 86, 94
pomelo 42, 46
pond 45
pot 39, 49, 86
pound, to 45
praise, to 46
press, to 48, 109
pry, to 39
pull 46
pull out, to 49, 50
pullet 64

Q

quantity 85, 89
quilt 49

R

rain 42, 45, 79, 88, 89
rat 9, 66, 74, 94
raw 87
red 42, 46, 133
reed 91
reed organ 50
reluctant 42
reluctant to go 49
repeat, to 49
report, to 44, 126
rice 8, 39, 46, 48, 78, 89, 91, 94, 116, 117, 130, 133, 136
rice field 10, 16
rice husk 43
rice mortar 8
rice plant 8
rice seedling 8, 82
riddle 81
ride on horseback, to 43
ripe 42
river 44, 46, 52, 87, 91, 116, 135
river bend 49
road 11, 62
roll 35, 65
roof tile 39
room 46
root 47, 84, 116
rotten 42, 46, 63

rub 46
ruined 68

S

saliva 82, 83
salt 43
sand in food 49
scaly dragon 84
scar 40, 49, 81
scare, to 43
scissors 45, 47, 48, 49
scold, to 46, 50, 85
scream, to 48
search 18, 39, 86
search, to 80, 86
seize, to 47
sentence 39, 46, 50
serve, to 42
sesame 90
seven 45
shears 49
shiver 66
shoe 48
short 79, 132, 134, 135
shoulder 47, 84, 86, 89, 94, 114
shut, to 45, 49
side 45, 49
skew, to 50
skin 79, 94
skinny 82, 92
slide down, to 46
slippery 82, 92
sly 39
smoke 46, 48
snow 81, 90
soft shell 88, 89
solidify, to 49
song 45
spear 83
spider 39, 46
splash, to 49
split, to 44
spring 42, 78, 85, 132
sprinkle, to 49
sprout, to 39, 48
squander 49
stack, to 48

star 46, 68
steal, to 46
steelyard 39
step on, to 81
stick, to 83
sticking food 49
stingy 49, 62, 63
stir, to 49
stone 85, 86, 89, 131
stop up 45, 50
strength 42, 44, 47, 86
stretch, to 42
study, to 39
sugarcane 43
sun 79, 84, 88, 89
sunset 49
suppress 39
swallow, to 50
sweat 48, 92
sweep, to 87
sweet 67
swim, to 49

T

table 61, 85, 93, 117, 134
tadpole 90
tail 42, 71, 86
talk 41
tall 79, 94
tangle, to 48
taro 67, 82
tea 86
tear, to 41, 60
tear up, to 45
teeth 8
ten 45, 57, 58
tendon 43, 66
thick 39, 47, 49, 79, 85, 87, 91, 95, 114

thin 41, 45, 46, 79, 83, 85, 87, 94
threaten, to 42
three 45, 87
throat 67
tiger 10
times 84
tired 43
together 49, 65
tooth 46
touch 46
toward 48
tower 114, 116
trample 65, 66
tree 63, 79, 89, 90, 133, 134
tree branch 81
tree root 84
tree stump 47
tuber 42
turn, to 48
two 45
twinkling 68

U

uncultivated 80, 82, 86, 90
undergo 65, 68
unravel 48
unsteady 50
urine 39

V

valley 49
vegetable 42, 61, 88, 94, 136
vehicle 39, 41
vexed 67
village 46, 84, 85, 94

vine 128
vomit, to 84

W

waist 45
wait, to 39
wake up, to 49
walk, to 82
warn, to 11
wash clothes, to 45, 135
water 8, 49, 62, 78, 79, 80, 83, 85, 86, 89, 94, 109, 132, 133, 135
water buffalo 47
wax 109, 114, 116, 130, 132
weave, to 45
weep 75
weigh, to 49
well 42, 46, 65, 85
wet 8, 44, 46, 78, 82, 114
what 42, 43, 48, 69
wheel 65
where 43
where, which 42
whip 45
whitish spot 46
widow 91
wind 46, 47, 79, 85, 86, 89, 114
wine 9, 94
woods 85

Y

year 42, 116, 133
yellow 93, 116

Authors, Languages, and Subjects

A

Abramson, Arthur 191, 208, 209, 215, 219
affiliation 11, 339
African languages 109, 110, 114, 339
Ahom 2, 6, 12, 13, 14, 51, 145, 176, 235, 269, 270, 277, 286, 287, 304, 306, 308, 309–13, 315, 316, 317, 340
Ai-Cham 321, 326
Angkor Wat 6
Anshun 3
Aou 180, 181
Arachnida 293, 304–306
aspiration 9, 10, 18, 36, 37, 38, 43, 45, 51, 88, 148, 153, 155, 156, 167, 168, 194, 207, 208, 209, 236, 237, 246, 247, 249, 258, 268, 275, 281, 282, 284, 285
Assam 1, 6, 21, 269, 277, 286, 292, 338, 340, 357
Atayal(ic) 168, 169, 175, 180

Austro-Tai 161, 163–69, 171, 172, 173, 175–77, 180–84
Ayudhaya 328, 329, 331, 333

B

Ba Thục 13
Bắc Cạn 322
Bắc Giang 271, 272, 280, 298, 322, 323
Bắc Thái 221, 222
Bahnaric 163
Baise 78, 82, 91
Baisha Hlai 178, 326
   see also White Sands Hlai
Ban Bung 165, 173, 179, 182
Bảo Lạc 322
Baoding 3, 183, 286
Basadung 178
Beauclair, Inez de 12, 21
Benedict, Paul K. 2, 16, 19, 20, 161–87, 265
Biandan 141–45
Biao 2
Bijie 3
Bikol 168
Binyang 82, 93

Black Tai 12, 145, 265, 270, 271, 274, 279, 287, 294, 295, 321, 334
Black Thai
   see Tay Dam
Blust, Robert 164, 180, 181, 182, 184
Bo-ai 10, 11, 37, 39
   see also Po-ai
Bonifacy, August 182, 184
Bouyei 1, 2, 5, 8, 11, 20, 36, 48, 53, 78, 80, 84, 95, 141–44, 145, 147–53, 272, 273, 281, 282, 286
Bradley, David 7, 20, 173, 217, 219
breathy phonation 51, 85, 195, 209
Brown, J. Marvin 6, 12, 14, 20, 22, 36, 53, 170, 207, 208, 215, 261, 265, 269, 286, 295, 300, 307, 322, 324, 339, 357
Bu Sha 191
Bunun 145, 167

Burma 1, 13, 14, 21, 24, 145, 163, 176, 180, 211, 212, 216, 218, 219, 292, 337–42, 356–58
see also Myanmar
Buyang 2, 3, 181, 182, 321, 325

C

Cambodian 103, 105, 335
see also Khmer
canonical reduction on the right/left 19, 168, 169
Cao Bằng 13, 14, 44, 192, 193, 205, 207, 218, 221–31, 271, 274, 275, 280, 284, 298, 322, 324
Cao Binh 312, 317, 318
Cao Lan 25, 312, 314, 315, 316, 318, 319, 323
Cebuano 168
Celebes
see Sulawesi
Central Thai 4
Chabant 239, 265
Cham 145
Chamberlain, James R. 3, 5, 11, 13, 18, 20, 191, 193, 213, 214, 215, 216, 217, 219, 265, 270, 274, 278, 286, 291–326, 338, 357
Chamoro 175
Changwat 98, 99
Chen, Matthew 207, 216
Chen Qiguang 179, 181, 182
Chiang Mai (also spelled Chieng Mai) 24, 270, 274, 278
Chieng Kham 270, 274, 278
Chieng Mai
see Chiang Mai
Chieng Rung 270, 274, 278
Chiengrai 24, 270, 278
Chilopoda 293, 306
Chinese
  Amoy 304, 305, 311, 312, 314, 315, 316, 321, 324
  Ancient 22, 55, 144
  Cantonese 57, 79, 99, 105
  Mandarin 57–63, 71–75, 79, 105, 118, 121, 122, 137, 15275, 79, 105, 118, 121, 122, 137, 152
  Middle 5, 7, 16, 17, 57, 59, 60, 144, 152
Chơ Rā 221
Chongzuo 84, 85, 88, 90, 92, 94
Chuang-Chia 192
Chung-Chia 92
cluster 9, 164, 166–72, 177, 273, 275, 276, 281, 282, 283
coda 15, 19, 57, 58, 79, 84, 87, 88, 108, 111, 141, 143, 144, 149, 151, 153, 154, 155, 157, 158, 222, 223, 226, 228, 229, 262
Coedès, Georges 6, 21
Condominas 5, 13, 21, 303
consonant 6, 7, 9, 15, 16, 18, 19, 23, 26, 35, 36, 38, 39, 42–45, 48, 51, 52, 54, 55, 57, 59, 87, 88, 120, 149, 152, 166, 192, 194, 195, 208, 209, 211, 212, 215–19, 223, 224, 226, 229, 236–239, 242–47, 258, 260, 261, 262, 288, 331, 341, 343, 344, 350, 354, 355, 358
Crustacea 293, 299, 303, 320
Cunhua 178
Cushing, Josiah N. 269, 277, 287, 337, 338, 339, 340, 341, 343, 347, 355, 357
customs 13, 14, 24, 78

D

Dabai, Ni 141–46
Dahl, Otto C. 164, 167, 175, 184
Dai 4, 8, 11, 14, 24, 44, 68, 78, 79, 84, 87, 90, 101, 125, 143, 144, 178, 191–95, 204–207, 214, 215, 229, 265, 295, 307, 338, 339, 341, 342, 343, 348, 350, 355, 358, 359
Daxin 85, 92
Dazai 193, 195
Debao 80, 86, 94, 194, 195, 206, 212, 218
Dehong 144, 337, 340–43, 348, 358, 359
Dempwolff, Otto 164, 166, 175, 184
Dhananjayananda, Puttachart 327–46
Điêu, Chính Nhìm 239, 245, 247, 248, 249, 265
Diffloth, G. 191, 210, 216
Diller, Anthony 14, 21, 340, 357
Dingnan 153
Dioi 11, 13, 166, 171, 172, 173, 175, 181, 273, 281, 287, 304–17, 320, 321, 325
Diplopoda 293, 297, 306
Dodd, Wm. Clifton 5, 13, 21
Dogang 178
Donaldson, Jean 20, 235–59, 261, 265, 270, 274, 279, 287, 322, 324
Donglan 80, 99
Du'an 81

Index of Authors, Languages, and Subjects

Duoluo 180, 181
Dushan 153
dyadic 9

E

Eberhard, Wolfram 5, 21, 296, 297, 325
Edmondson, Jerold A. 1–25, 35–55, 57–59, 76, 107, 109, 113, 137, 184, 185, 191, 193, 216, 221, 235–66, 287, 288, 325, 326, 337–59
Egerod, Søren 17, 21, 251, 270, 277, 287, 341, 347, 357
English 6, 7, 20, 21, 25, 98, 103, 105, 106, 215–17, 235, 265, 286, 287, 295, 303, 324, 326, 330, 334, 335, 357, 358
Enping 59
Enriques, C. M. 5, 6, 21, 339, 357
Erickson, Donna 208, 209, 215, 216

F

Fan Honggui 4, 5, 12, 22, 54
Fengshan 83
Ferlus, Michel 22
Fijian 176
Fippinger, Jay and Dorothy 245, 249, 251, 257, 265, 270, 287
Formosan languages 163, 164, 166, 167, 171, 172, 175
Freiberger, Nancy 20, 22, 24

fricatives 6, 14, 15, 18, 36–38, 44, 45, 48, 52, 59, 109, 110, 114, 148, 153, 155–57, 159, 175, 178, 191–95, 207, 239, 240, 247, 249, 258, 266, 268, 275, 281, 292, 343, 349
Fu Maoji 7, 22, 291
Funing 3, 206
Fusui 84, 85, 94
Fuxing 147

G

Gao 180, 181, 182
Gaozhou 59
Gedney diagram 36, 37, 38, 355
Gedney's checklist for tones 216, 239, 240, 266
Gedney's puzzle 9
Gedney, William J. 5, 9, 11, 14–22, 25, 35–38, 43, 44, 54, 163, 165, 172–74, 176, 181, 185, 193, 194, 207, 208, 213–16, 236, 239, 240, 245, 246, 249, 250–54, 256–59, 265, 267–87, 303, 321, 322, 325, 334, 338, 343, 349, 355, 357
Gelao 2–4, 7, 8, 165, 167, 168, 180–83, 292, 321, 325
  see also Kelao
Gengma 337, 342, 356
Geyang 2–4, 8, 9
Goodenough, Ward H. 161, 185
Gordaliza, T. 271, 287
Grierson, George 6, 14, 22, 269, 277, 287, 338, 339, 357

GSR 5, 183, 306, 310, 311, 318, 319, 321
  see also Karlgren, Bernhard
Guangdong Province 1, 57, 59, 78, 107, 296, 337
Guangnan 79, 80, 83, 86, 88
Guangxi-Zhuang Autonomous Region 1, 3, 4, 7, 11–14, 21, 22, 24–26, 35, 39, 53–55, 57, 59, 60, 66, 78, 79, 93, 97, 98, 105–108, 161, 191, 192, 195, 267, 268, 271–74, 280, 281, 283, 287, 296
Guangzhou 63–70
Guinan 59
Guiping 80
Guixian 60, 80–82
Guiyang 153, 287
Guizhou Province 1, 3, 11, 36, 78, 80, 107, 147, 151–53, 272, 287, 296

H

Hà Giang 221, 222, 271, 275, 284, 322, 323
Haas, Mary 16
Hagei 180
Hainan Province 3, 4, 164, 167, 194, 292, 293, 298, 326
Han 25, 39, 42, 43, 55, 57–60, 75, 78, 79, 81, 84, 86, 91, 108, 114, 144, 148, 149, 152, 153, 205
Han Dynasty 7, 23, 78
Hansell, Mark 2

Haudricourt, André 10, 11, 14, 18, 22, 25, 36, 44, 52, 54, 162, 164, 165, 172, 174, 175, 181, 185, 192, 193, 207, 208, 217, 251, 266, 273, 274, 276, 282, 287, 326, 358
Hechi 78, 80
Heitu 178, 183, 286
Henderson, Eugenie 208, 217, 288
Hengxian 82
Hepu 60
Hiligaynon 168
Hlai 2–4, 7, 8, 144, 164, 165, 167, 168, 172–73, 175–83, 183, 184, 194, 276, 282, 286, 288, 291, 292, 295, 296, 297, 304, 306, 308–16, 320, 321
Hmong(ic) 16, 114
Hoàng Văn Ma 161, 186, 221–30
Hou Hanshu 23
Hsipaw 338, 347
Huang Yuanwei 57–76
Huanjiang 80, 89, 90, 93
Hudak, Thomas 21, 22, 53, 54, 76, 216, 251, 266, 325
Huffman, Franklin 192, 217
Hui 39, 145
Hunan Province 78, 296
Huon Gulf 168

I

Ilocano 174
India 1, 14, 22, 145, 287, 292, 337, 340, 357, 358
Indonesian 145, 162, 164, 183

initial 9, 14–19, 23, 24, 26, 35–39, 43, 44, 48, 50–53, 55, 59, 60, 80–90, 108, 115, 120, 129, 144, 145, 148, 149, 152–57, 159, 162, 164, 167, 168, 170–73, 175–82, 193–95, 207–12, 216, 218, 222–24, 227, 229, 236, 237, 239, 241, 242, 244–47, 249, 250, 257, 260–62, 266, 268–77, 279–86, 288, 299, 326, 331, 341–44, 350, 351, 355
Inscription I 328, 329, 333
Insecta 293, 306, 307
Itbayaten 168

J

Jiamao 178–80, 182
Jianshan 80
Jingxi 86, 89, 90
Jinxiu 161
Jinzhou 84, 94

K

Kadai 2, 3, 7, 19–21, 23, 25, 35, 53, 54, 60, 70, 71, 108, 110, 113, 114, 120, 137, 143, 145, 160, 161, 163–71, 176, 177, 179, 181–87, 262, 285, 287, 292, 295, 297, 305, 310, 311, 313–15, 317, 320, 325, 326
Kadazan 164
Kaiping 59
Kaiyuan 194
Kam 2, 3, 7, 9, 78, 113, 143–45, 165, 276, 282

Kam-Sui 2–4, 8–10, 19, 21, 23, 25, 54, 137, 144, 145, 161, 163–65, 169–71, 173, 176, 180, 285, 288, 295, 297, 304–15, 317, 319, 320, 322
Kam-Tai 2, 4, 147, 207, 216
Kanakanabu 168, 175
Karen 76, 162, 163, 216
Karlgren, Bernhard 5, 25, 60, 76, 306, 311, 321, 325, 360, 368
Ke-hsi 347
Kelao 313
 see also Gelao
Khamti 1, 14, 269, 277, 338–40, 356, 358, 359
Khmer 6, 13, 22, 103, 163, 173, 176, 210, 212, 218, 287, 334, 341, 357
 see also Cambodian
Khün 270, 274, 275, 277, 287
King Rama III Records 334
Ko Samuy 274
ku 306
Kullavanijaya, Pranee 20, 97–106, 206, 207, 217, 218, 334

L

L-Thongkum, Theraphan 14, 18, 51, 191–219, 229, 335
Lachi 2, 3, 23, 165, 167, 168, 177, 180–82, 292, 305, 320, 321, 325
Ladefoged, Peter 194, 209, 215, 218, 263, 266
Laha 2, 161, 164, 165, 168, 173, 174, 177, 179–84
Lai Châu 235, 236, 245, 259, 323

Index of Authors, Languages, and Subjects 379

Laibin 81, 88, 90–94
Lakkia 161, 164–68, 172, 176, 178, 180, 182, 183, 291, 292, 310, 313
  see also Lakkja
Lakkja 2, 8, 9, 207, 210, 218
  see also Lakkia
Lang Chanh 266
Lạng Sơn 206, 222, 236, 287, 322, 323
Longzhou (also known as Lungchow) 10, 11, 23, 25, 37, 54, 59, 77, 80, 85, 86, 88–92, 94, 95, 97, 99, 169, 170, 175, 207, 227, 272, 274, 280, 283, 284, 288, 325
Lou Yongxian 35
Lu Tianquiao 107–38
Lungchow
  see Longzhou

M

Maekhong (also known as Mekhong) 104
Maguan 3, 192, 194, 195, 205, 206
Mak 2, 165, 167, 170, 171, 175, 276, 282, 288, 305, 307, 309, 314, 315, 321, 325
Makazayazaya 176
Malagasy 164
Malay 164
Malay Peninsula 1
Malipo 3, 87, 194
Mangshi 42, 343, 348–51, 354–356
Manipuri 338
Manomaivibool, Prapin 191
Manzhu 39
Maonan 2, 8, 39, 78, 144, 145, 286, 288
Mashan 81

Maspero, Henri 13, 24, 212, 218, 271, 274, 288
Matisoff, James A. 162, 163, 164, 178, 185, 207, 208, 217, 218, 286, 288, 321, 326
Matisoff's Rule 162
Mazaudon, Martine 208, 218
Mekhong
  see Maekhong
Mène 300, 304–308
Mengding 337, 341, 355, 356, 359
Menglian 337, 342, 356
Mengshan 9, 60
merger 45, 46
Miao 3, 4, 35, 39, 78, 164, 167, 170, 171, 177, 210, 212, 297
Mien(ic) 16, 24, 114, 210, 211
Ministry of Education 321, 325, 334
Minot, Georges 239, 266, 270, 274, 279, 288
modifier 7
Moeng Nai 269
Moeng Yong 270, 274, 278
Moji 3, 7
Mon 13, 22, 163, 211, 212, 218, 312, 335, 341, 357
Mon Kay 23, 171, 193, 217
Mong Tung 338, 347
Morev, Lev 24
MSC (Modern Standard Chinese) 57, 70–75
Mu-se 343, 350, 351, 353–56
Mubian 86
Mulam 2, 8, 39, 78, 143–45, 286, 313
Munda 163
Myanmar 1, 6, 261, 337–40, 342, 343, 359
  see also Burma

Myitkyina 338

N

Na Rì 221
Nakhon Pathom 102
  see also Nakhorn Pathom
Nakhorn Phanom 99, 101, 272
  see also Nakhon Phanom
Nam Hu 347
Namhkam 340, 342, 343, 350–52, 354–56
Nanchao 338
  see also Nanzhao
Nandan 80
Nanning 22, 26, 54, 62, 67, 70, 71, 74, 75, 78, 80, 105, 108, 287
Nanzhao 5, 338
  see also Nanchao
Napo 86, 99
nasal 238, 250, 253
Ngân Sơn 221
Ngaja-Dayak 164, 168
Nguyễn Văn Huyên 193, 218
Nhắng 311, 314, 317–19, 323
Ni Dabai 20, 141, 158
Nong
  see Nung
Nong Khai (also spelled Nongkhaai) 99, 101, 102, 270, 274, 278
Nong Zhigao 5
Nongkhaai
  see Nong Khai
Noong Lay 173
Nora 14, 269, 277, 340
Nung (also spelled Nong) 2, 5, 14, 24, 169, 170, 176, 182, 191, 206, 207, 221, 226, 271, 272, 274, 279, 280
Nyah Kur 211, 212

O

Obligatory Contour Principle 111

P

Pagan 6, 358
Paiwan(ic) 166–69, 171–77, 179–82
Pak Seng 270, 274, 278
Pali 102, 103, 105, 334
Pallegoix, Jean Baptiste 334
Panglong, 342–45, 350, 354, 355
see also Pinlon
Pingguo 82, 108, 116–18, 137
Pinlon 343–45, 350, 354, 355
see also Panglong
Po Muc 271, 272, 280
Po-ai, 23, 37, 55, 171, 174, 273, 281, 285, 322
see also Bo-ai
(pre-)glottalized 9, 18, 23, 35, 36, 43, 46, 52, 54, 55, 63, 81, 82, 87, 90, 148, 159, 162, 168, 179, 194, 195, 218, 241, 262, 267, 343, 350, 355
(Proto-)Austronesian 145, 163–65, 167–69, 171, 173–75, 177, 179–83
Pu Yang 191
Pubiao (also known as Qabiao) 2, 3, 164, 165, 167, 173, 179–83, 310, 321, 326
Pupeo (also known as Qabiao) 164, 173
Puyuma 181
Pyo 276, 282

Q

Qabiao
see Pubiao
see Pupeo
Qiandui 178, 286
Qin Dynasty 78
Qinzhou 60
Qiubei 84, 93, 192
Qixinguo 192, 195
Quốc Ngữ 13, 15, 16

R

Red Tai (also known as Red Thai) 12, 251, 259, 265, 270, 271, 274, 276, 279, 281, 287
Red Thai
see Red Tai
rhyme 19, 40, 42, 43, 59, 60, 81, 83, 84, 86, 87, 108, 141–45, 148, 149, 153, 154, 222, 223, 226, 236, 262, 264, 282, 351
Robert, R. 236, 245, 252, 254, 256, 266
Rong'an 80
Rongjiang 3, 276, 282, 326
Rongshui 25, 35, 39, 55, 80
Ross, Pete 45
Royal Institute Dictionary 328, 334
Ruili 337, 341, 343, 356
Rukai 164, 167, 171

S

Saek 2, 14, 145, 161–87, 272–76, 281, 282, 314, 316, 320, 322
Saisiyat 168, 180
Sakon Nakhon 270, 278
Salween River 338
Sam Neua 236
Samar-Leyte 168
Sanchong 3, 7

sandhi 107, 109
Sanfang 10, 25, 35, 39–45, 48, 50–53, 55, 264
Sanskrit 102, 103, 105, 330
Sao Tern Moeng 339, 357
Sarawit, Mary 18, 24, 266, 327, 330, 335
Saul, Janice 20, 24, 25
Savina, F. M. 24, 176, 178, 180, 182, 185, 193, 219, 271, 274, 276, 280, 282, 287, 321, 322, 326
Sedik 168
Shafer, Robert 171, 185
Shan 1, 2, 5–7, 12–14, 25, 78, 145, 173, 218, 235, 254, 264, 269, 270, 275, 277, 279, 284, 286, 287, 320, 337–59
Shang Dynasty 6, 7, 58
Shanghai 5, 23, 26, 55, 288, 325, 357
Shangse 85, 88
Shilong 81, 90, 91
Shorto, Harry 163, 176, 186, 335
Shuangqiao 108, 129
Siamese, 4, 5, 9–13, 15–18, 37, 51, 165, 171–74, 216, 235, 245, 249, 251, 252, 256, 258, 264, 267–71, 273–76, 279, 281, 283–85, 288, 304, 306–13, 315, 318, 320, 322, 338, 339, 341
see also Thai
Sichuan Province 137, 147, 153, 265, 292, 342
Sino-Tibetan 12, 19, 54, 58, 78, 161, 163, 216, 217, 235, 267, 324, 358, 359

Index of Authors, Languages, and Subjects

Sipsong Panna (also known as Xishuang Banna) 3, 4, 144, 341, 342
Snyder, Wil C. 107–38
Solnit, David B. 1–25, 35, 54, 137, 184, 185, 287, 288, 325, 326, 337–59
Solntseva, Nina 25, 161, 186
Sơn La 161, 323, 324
Songkhla 270, 286, 334
Spring and Autumn Period 78
Sui 2, 8, 25, 39, 53, 55, 78, 143–45, 165, 167, 173, 175, 180, 182, 276, 282, 286, 288, 291, 292, 294, 326
Sukhothai 208, 216, 328, 329, 333
Sulawesi (also known as Celebes) 175, 292
Surat 270, 274, 278
Swatow 251
syllabic curtain 19
Sz Lok 14, 267, 272, 280

T

Tagalog 164, 168, 171, 172, 176
Tai 1–6, 8–10, 12–26, 36, 37, 40, 42–44, 51–55, 58, 70, 71, 76–78, 95, 98, 107, 137, 141, 144, 145, 147, 160, 163–78, 180–87, 191–95, 201, 204, 206, 207, 212, 213, 215–18, 221, 229, 235, 237, 251, 259, 261, 265–72, 274–79, 281–88, 292, 294–99, 301–303, 322, 325, 327, 328, 330, 333–35, 337–43, 351, 356–59
Tai Dam
  see Tay Dam
Tai-Kadai 2, 3, 191, 192, 194, 210, 212, 217, 291–96, 298, 302, 303
Taishan 59
Tak 270, 274, 278
Tamang 162
taxa 291, 295, 296, 298, 300–303
Tày (formerly known as Thổ) 21, 205, 221–24, 226, 227, 229, 230, 235, 236, 238–41, 245, 249, 251–57, 259–62, 264, 285, 322
Tay Dam (also known as Tai Dam, Thai Dam, or Black Thai) 236, 245, 255, 257, 259
Tay Don (also known as White Tay or White Thai) 236, 261
Tay Tac 235, 236, 238–41, 245, 251, 255–57, 259–62, 264
teleo-reconstruction 162–64
Terrien de Lacouperie, Etienne 25, 359
Thai 1, 2, 4, 7–10, 12–14, 16, 20–22, 24, 25, 53, 78, 79, 97–99, 101–106, 145, 165, 171, 192, 207, 208, 215–18, 235, 264, 265, 270, 276, 278, 286, 287, 300, 312, 327, 328, 330, 333, 334, 338, 339, 341, 357, 358
  see also Siamese
Thai Dam
  see Tay Dam
Thailand 1, 4, 6, 7, 12–14, 21, 24, 25, 97–99, 101, 102, 106, 165, 174, 191, 261, 265, 270, 272, 275, 276, 278, 293, 298, 327, 337, 342, 358
Thakhek 272
Than-Uyên 173, 179, 182
Thao 172, 175
Tho (also known as Thổ) 18, 182, 191–95, 204–207, 209, 212, 214, 215, 229
Three Seals Law 334
Thu 179, 191, 192, 194
Thu Lao 191
Thurgood, Graham 9, 18, 25, 164, 186, 217, 286, 294, 312, 321, 322, 326
Tianbao 18, 206, 212, 285
Tiandeng 80, 85, 86
Tiandong 82, 92, 93, 207
Tian'e 80
Tianlin 83
Tianyang 63, 66, 69, 82, 88, 89, 90
Tibetan 163, 167, 172, 176
tone 21, 41, 54, 107, 114, 137, 151, 152, 205, 206, 210, 211, 215, 217, 219, 222, 223, 227–30, 239, 262
tone splits 4, 9, 11, 12, 16–18, 20, 36, 45, 51–53, 77, 79, 85, 120, 135, 177, 204, 205, 207–209, 212, 215, 217, 240, 247, 256, 258, 265, 338, 343, 349–51, 353, 354, 356
Tong 22
Tongan 168
Tsouic 168, 176
Tsuchida, Shigeru 168, 186
Tujia 39
Tuyên Quang 221

U

Udornthani 99, 101
Ulawa 171

V

Vallibhotama, Srisakra 12, 13, 25
Vickery, M. 213, 219
Viet 305, 307, 309, 310, 312, 315, 318
Vietnam 1, 13, 14, 20–22, 44, 54, 80, 98, 107, 145, 161, 164, 191–93, 216, 217, 221, 222, 230, 235, 236, 245, 261, 268, 271, 272, 275, 276, 283, 292, 293, 298, 342
vocabulary 3, 4, 7–10, 12, 22, 35–37, 42, 44, 50, 51, 80, 85, 87, 91, 92, 94, 95, 155, 156, 212, 213, 259, 265, 287, 288, 293, 324, 343, 350, 357
voiced 9, 14, 15, 17, 18, 35–37, 43–46, 48, 51–53, 82, 85–87, 148, 152, 157, 159, 162, 167, 175, 191–95, 205, 207–12, 214–216, 227, 229, 236, 237, 239, 241, 242, 246, 249, 258, 260–62, 343, 344, 349, 350
voiced-low principle 9, 236, 261
voiceless 6, 9, 18, 36–38, 43–45, 48, 51–53, 59, 87, 88, 148, 152, 155–57, 159, 175, 194, 207–12, 215, 223, 237, 239, 240, 246, 249, 251, 260–62, 338, 343, 344, 349
vowels 335

W

Wang Wei 147–60
Wangmo 141–44, 147–49, 151–53
Wat Pamok Inscription 333
Wat Srichum Inscription 333
Wei Feng 35–56
Wei Xingyun 77–95
White Sands Hlai 165, 168, 172, 178–81, 183
 see also Baisha Hlai
White, Tay
 see Tay Don
White Thai
 see Tay Don
Wulff, K. 14, 25, 273, 274
Wuming 3, 4, 39, 44, 57–75, 77, 79, 81, 82, 85, 86, 88–95, 97, 107–12, 115–22, 127, 136, 166, 169, 170, 273, 275, 281, 282, 288, 300

X

Xia Dynasty 6
Xieng Khouang 270, 274, 276, 278
Xifang 178
Xijiang 13
Xincheng 81
Xinhui 59
Xinhuilong 192, 195
Xishuang Banna
 see Sipsong Panna

Y

Yabem 168
Yang, Quan 19, 21, 54, 109, 113, 137, 321, 326
Yangchun 59
Yangjiang 59
Yangshuo 81
Yangtze 5, 292, 293, 296
Yanshan 86, 87, 194
Yao 3, 16, 24, 39, 78, 177, 210, 218, 297
Yay 2, 14, 22, 36, 54, 175, 272, 273, 274, 281, 294, 300, 304–15, 317, 318, 320, 322, 325
Yerong 2
Yip, Moira 109, 110, 137
Yishan 81, 89
Yongfu 80
Yongjiang 79
Yongning 19, 80, 82, 84, 88
Youjiang 82, 83, 91, 93
Yuanmen 178, 182
Yuanyang 194
Yue 4, 5, 57, 59, 60, 62–75, 79
Yunjing 59

Z

Zhang Jungru 182
Zhang, Junru 25, 55, 87, 95
Zhang Yuansheng 77–95, 108, 117, 120, 126, 127, 137
Zhenning 142
Zhongsha 178, 179, 183
Zhou Yaowen 341, 342, 355, 359
Zhuang 1–5, 7, 8, 11, 13, 14, 16, 19, 21, 22, 24–26, 35, 39, 40, 44, 45, 48, 50–53, 55, 57–95, 97–102, 104, 105, 107, 108, 110, 111, 114–17, 119–22, 125–27, 129, 136, 137, 143, 144, 147, 167, 191–94, 207, 216, 219, 264, 273, 274, 281, 287
Zuojiang 77, 78, 79, 85, 93

www.ingramcontent.com/pod-product-compliance
Lightning Source LLC
Chambersburg PA
CBHW070749020526
44115CB00032B/1449